MW00720886

La Salle and the Discovery of the Great West France and England in North America

by Parkman, Francis, 1823-1893

ISBN: 9781318037094

HardPress
8345 NW 66TH ST #2561
MIAMI FL 33166-2626
USA
Email: info@hardpress.net

Ordering Information:

Quantity sales. Special discounts are available on quantity purchases by corporations, associations, and others. For details, contact the publisher by email at the address above.

Printed in the United States of America, United Kingdom and Australia

Francis Parkman's Works.

NEW LIBRARY EDITION.

Vol. III.

FRANCIS PARKMAN'S WORKS.

New Library Edition.

Pioneers of France in the New World	1 vol.
The Jesuits in North America	1 vol.
La Salle and the Discovery of the Great West	1 vol.
The Old Régime in Canada	1 vol.
Count Frontenac and New France under Louis XIV	1 vol.

A Half Century of Conflict	2 vols.
Montcalm and Wolfe	2 vols.
The Conspiracy of Pontiac and the Indian War after the Conquest of Canada	2 vols.
The Oregon Trail	1 vol.

LA SALLE

AND THE

DISCOVERY OF THE GREAT WEST. FRANCE AND ENGLAND IN NORTH AMERICA.

PART THIRD.

BY
FRANCIS PARKMAN.

BOSTON:
LITTLE, BROWN, AND COMPANY.
1908

———————————

Printers
S. J. PARKHILL & CO., BOSTON, U. S. A.

TO
THE CLASS OF 1844,
Harvard College,
THIS BOOK IS CORDIALLY DEDICATED
BY ONE OF THEIR NUMBER.

[Pg vii]

PREFACE OF THE ELEVENTH EDITION.

When the earlier editions of this book were published, I was aware of the existence of a collection of documents relating to La Salle, and containing important material to which I had not succeeded in gaining access. This collection was in possession of M. Pierre Margry, director of the Archives of the Marine and Colonies at Paris, and was the result of more than thirty years of research. With rare assiduity and zeal, M. Margry had explored not only the vast depository with which he has been officially connected from youth, and of which he is now the chief, but also the other public archives of France, and many private collections in Paris and the provinces. The object of his search was to throw light on the career and achievements of French explorers, and, above all, of La Salle. A collection of extraordinary richness grew gradually upon his hands. In the course of [Pg viii]my own inquiries, I owed much to his friendly aid; but his collections, as a whole, remained inaccessible, since he naturally wished to be the first to make known the results of his labors. An attempt to induce Congress to furnish him with the means of printing documents so interesting to American history was made in 1870 and 1871, by Henry Harrisse, Esq., aided by the American minister at Paris; but it unfortunately failed.

In the summer and autumn of 1872, I had numerous interviews with M. Margry, and at his desire undertook to try to induce some American bookseller to publish the collection. On returning to the United States, I accordingly made an arrangement with Messrs. Little, Brown & Co., of Boston, by which they agreed to print the papers if a certain number of subscriptions should first be obtained. The condition proved very difficult; and it became clear that the best hope of success lay in another appeal to Congress. This was made in the following winter, in conjunction with Hon. E. B. Washburne; Colonel Charles Whittlesey, of Cleveland; O. H. Marshall, Esq., of Buffalo; and other gentlemen interested in early American history.

The attempt succeeded. Congress made an appropriation [Pg ix] for the purchase of five hundred copies of the work, to be printed at Paris, under direction of M. Margry; and the three volumes devoted to La Salle are at length before the public.

Of the papers contained in them which I had not before examined, the most interesting are the letters of La Salle, found in the original by M. Margry, among the immense accumulations of the Archives of the Marine and Colonies and the Bibliothèque Nationale. The narrative of La Salle's companion, Joutel, far more copious than the abstract printed in 1713, under the title of "Journal Historique," also deserves special mention. These, with other fresh material in these three volumes, while they add new facts and throw new light on the character of La Salle, confirm nearly every statement made in the first edition of the Discovery of the Great West. The only exception of consequence relates to the causes of La Salle's failure to find the mouth of the Mississippi in 1684, and to the conduct, on that occasion, of the naval commander, Beaujeu.

This edition is revised throughout, and in part rewritten with large additions. A map of the country traversed by the explorers is also added. The name of La Salle is placed on the titlepage, [Pg x] as seems to be demanded by his increased prominence in the narrative of which he is the central figure.

BOSTON, 10 December, 1878.

NOTE.—The title of M. Margry's printed collection is Découvertes et Établissements des Français dans l'Ouest et dans le Sud de l'Amérique Septentrionale (1614-1754), Mémoires et Documents originaux." I., II., III. Besides the three volumes relating to La Salle, there will be two others, relating to other explorers. In accordance with the agreement with Congress, an independent edition will appear in France, with an introduction setting forth the circumstances of the publication.

[Pg xi]

PREFACE OF THE FIRST EDITION.

The discovery of the "Great West," or the valleys of the Mississippi and the Lakes, is a portion of our history hitherto very obscure. Those magnificent regions were revealed to the world through a series of daring enterprises, of which the motives and even the incidents have been but partially and superficially known. The chief actor in them wrote much, but printed nothing; and the published writings of his associates stand wofully in need of interpretation from the unpublished documents which exist, but which have not heretofore been used as material for history.

This volume attempts to supply the defect. Of the large amount of wholly new material employed in it, by far the greater part is drawn from the various public archives of France, and the rest from private sources. The discovery of many of these documents is due to the indefatigable research of M. Pierre Margry, assistant [Pg xii] director of the Archives of the Marine and Colonies at Paris, whose labors as an investigator of the maritime and colonial history of France can be appreciated only by those who have seen their results. In the department of American colonial history, these results have been invaluable; for, besides several private collections made by him, he rendered important service in the collection of the French portion of the Brodhead documents, selected and arranged the two great series of colonial papers ordered by the Canadian government, and prepared with vast labor analytical indexes of these and of supplementary documents in the French archives, as well as a copious index of the mass of papers relating to Louisiana. It is to be hoped that the valuable publications on the maritime history of France which have appeared from his pen are an earnest of more extended contributions in future.

The late President Sparks, some time after the publication of his Life of La Salle, caused a collection to be made of documents relating to that explorer, with the intention of incorporating them in a future edition. This intention was never carried into effect, and the documents were never used. With the liberality which always distinguished him, he placed them at my [Pg xiii] disposal, and this privilege has been kindly continued by Mrs. Sparks.

Abbé Faillon, the learned author of "La Colonie Française en Canada," has sent me copies of various documents found by him, including family papers of La Salle. Among others who in various ways have aided my inquiries are Dr. John Paul, of Ottawa, Ill.; Count Adolphe de Circourt, and M. Jules Marcou, of Paris; M. A. Gérin Lajoie, Assistant Librarian of the Canadian Parliament; M. J. M. Le Moine, of Quebec; General Dix, Minister of the United States at the Court of France; O. H. Marshall, of Buffalo; J. G. Shea, of New York; Buckingham Smith, of St. Augustine; and Colonel Thomas Aspinwall, of Boston.

The smaller map contained in the book is a portion of the manuscript map of Franquelin, of which an account will be found in the Appendix.

The next volume of the series will be devoted to the efforts of Monarchy and Feudalism under Louis XIV. to establish a permanent power on this continent, and to the stormy career of Louis de Buade, Count of Frontenac.

BOSTON, 16 September, 1869.

[Pg xv]

CONTENTS

CHAPTER VII.
1678.
PARTY STRIFE.

CHAPTER VIII. [Pg xvii]
1677, 1678.

––––––––––––––––––

LA SALLE

AND THE

DISCOVERY OF THE GREAT WEST.

––––––––––––––––––

LA SALLE

AND THE

DISCOVERY OF THE GREAT WEST.

[Pg 3]

INTRODUCTION

The Spaniards discovered the Mississippi. De Soto was buried beneath its waters; and it was down its muddy current that his followers fled from the Eldorado of their dreams, transformed to a wilderness of misery and death. The discovery was never used, and was well-nigh forgotten. On early Spanish maps, the Mississippi is often indistinguishable from other affluents of the Gulf. A century passed after De Soto's journeyings in the South, before a French explorer reached a northern tributary of the great river.

This was Jean Nicollet, interpreter at Three Rivers on the St. Lawrence. He had been some twenty years in Canada, had lived among the savage Algonquins of Allumette Island, and spent eight or nine years among the Nipissings, on the lake which bears their name. Here he became an Indian in all [Pg 4] his habits, but remained, nevertheless, a zealous Catholic, and returned to civilization at last because he could not live without the sacraments. Strange stories were current among the Nipissings of a people without hair or beard, who came from the West to trade with a tribe beyond the Great Lakes. Who could doubt that these strangers were Chinese or Japanese? Such tales may well have excited Nicollet's curiosity; and when, in 1635, or possibly in 1638, he was sent as an ambassador to the tribe in question, he would not have been surprised if on arriving he had found a party of mandarins among them. Perhaps it was with a view to such a contingency that he provided himself, as a dress of ceremony, with a robe of Chinese damask embroidered with birds and flowers. The tribe to which he was sent was that of the Winnebagoes, living near the head of the Green Bay of Lake Michigan. They had come to blows with the Hurons, allies of the French; and Nicollet was charged to negotiate a peace. When he approached the Winnebago town, he sent one of his Indian attendants to announce his coming, put on his robe of damask, and advanced to meet the expectant crowd with a pistol in each hand. The squaws and children fled, screaming that it was a manito, or spirit, armed with thunder and lightning; but the chiefs and warriors regaled him with so bountiful a hospitality that a hundred and twenty beavers were devoured at a single feast. From the Winnebagoes, he passed westward, ascended Fox [Pg 5] River, crossed to the Wisconsin, and descended it so far that, as he reported on his return, in three days more he would have reached the sea. The truth seems to be that he mistook the meaning of his Indian guides, and that the "great water" to which he was so near was not the sea, but the Mississippi.

It has been affirmed that one Colonel Wood, of Virginia, reached a branch of the Mississippi as early as the year 1654, and that about 1670 a certain Captain Bolton penetrated to the river itself. Neither statement is sustained by sufficient evidence. It is further affirmed that, in 1678, a party from New England crossed the Mississippi, reached New Mexico, and, returning, reported their discoveries to the authorities of Boston,—a story without proof or probability. Meanwhile, French Jesuits and fur-traders pushed deeper and deeper into the wilderness of the northern lakes. In 1641, Jogues and Raymbault preached the Faith to a concourse of Indians at the outlet of Lake Superior. Then came the havoc and desolation of the Iroquois war, and for years farther exploration was arrested. In 1658-59 Pierre Esprit Radisson, a Frenchman of St. Malo, and his brother-in-law, Médard Chouart des Groseilliers, penetrated the regions beyond Lake Superior, and roamed westward till, as Radisson declares, they reached what was called the Forked River, "because it has two branches, the one towards the west, the other towards the south, which, we believe, runs towards Mexico,"— which seems to point to the [Pg 6] Mississippi and its great confluent the Missouri. Two years later, the aged Jesuit Ménard attempted to plant a mission on the southern shore of Lake Superior, but perished in the forest by famine or the tomahawk. Allouez succeeded him, explored a part of Lake Superior, and heard, in his turn, of the Sioux and their great river the "Messipi." More and more, the thoughts of the Jesuits—and not of the Jesuits alone—dwelt on this mysterious stream. Through what regions did it flow; and whither would it lead them,—to the South Sea or the "Sea of Virginia;" to Mexico, Japan, or China? The problem was soon to be solved, and the mystery revealed.

[Pg 7]

CHAPTER I

1643-1669.

CAVELIER DE LA SALLE.

THE YOUTH OF LA SALLE: HIS CONNECTION WITH THE JESUITS; HE GOES TO CANADA; HIS CHARACTER; HIS SCHEMES; HIS SEIGNIORY AT LA CHINE; HIS EXPEDITION IN SEARCH OF A WESTERN PASSAGE TO INDIA.

AMONG the burghers of Rouen was the old and rich family of the Caveliers. Though citizens and not nobles, some of their connections held high diplomatic posts and honorable employments at Court. They were destined to find a better claim to distinction. In 1643 was born at Rouen Robert Cavelier, better known by the designation of La Salle.[1] His father Jean and his uncle Henri were wealthy merchants, [Pg 8] living more like nobles than like burghers; and the boy received an education answering to the marked traits of intellect and character which he soon began to display. He showed an inclination for the exact sciences, and especially for the mathematics, in which he made great proficiency. At an early age, it is said, he became connected with the Jesuits; and, though doubt has been expressed of the statement, it is probably true.[2]

LA SALLE AND THE JESUITS.

La Salle was always an earnest Catholic; and yet, judging by the qualities which his after-life evinced, he was not very liable to religious enthusiasm. It is nevertheless clear that the Society of Jesus may have had a powerful attraction for his youthful imagination. This great organization, so complicated yet so harmonious, a mighty machine moved from the centre by a single hand, was an image of regulated power, full of fascination for a mind like his. But if it was likely that he would be drawn into it, it was no less likely that he would soon wish to escape. To find [Pg 9] himself not at the centre of power, but at the circumference; not the mover, but the moved;

the passive instrument of another's will, taught to walk in prescribed paths, to renounce his individuality and become a component atom of a vast whole,—would have been intolerable to him. Nature had shaped him for other uses than to teach a class of boys on the benches of a Jesuit school. Nor, on his part, was he likely to please his directors; for, self-controlled and self-contained as he was, he was far too intractable a subject to serve their turn. A youth whose calm exterior hid an inexhaustible fund of pride; whose inflexible purposes, nursed in secret, the confessional and the "manifestation of conscience" could hardly drag to the light; whose strong personality would not yield to the shaping hand; and who, by a necessity of his nature, could obey no initiative but his own,—was not after the model that Loyola had commended to his followers.

La Salle left the Jesuits, parting with them, it is said, on good terms, and with a reputation of excellent acquirements and unimpeachable morals. This last is very credible. The cravings of a deep ambition, the hunger of an insatiable intellect, the intense longing for action and achievement, subdued in him all other passions; and in his faults the love of pleasure had no part. He had an elder brother in Canada, the Abbé Jean Cavelier, a priest of St. Sulpice. Apparently, it was this that shaped his destinies. His connection with the Jesuits had deprived him, [Pg 10] under the French law, of the inheritance of his father, who had died not long before. An allowance was made to him of three or (as is elsewhere stated) four hundred livres a year, the capital of which was paid over to him; and with this pittance he sailed for Canada, to seek his fortune, in the spring of 1666.[3]

LA SALLE AT MONTREAL.

Next, we find him at Montreal. In another volume, we have seen how an association of enthusiastic devotees had made a settlement at this place.[4] Having in some measure accomplished its work, it was now dissolved; and the corporation of priests, styled the Seminary of St. Sulpice, which had taken a prominent part in the enterprise, and, indeed, had been created with a view to it, was now the proprietor and the feudal lord of Montreal. It was destined to retain its seignorial rights until the abolition of the feudal tenures of Canada in our own day, and it still holds vast possessions in the city and island. These worthy ecclesiastics, models of a discreet and sober conservatism, were holding a post with which a band of veteran soldiers or warlike frontiersmen would have been better matched. Montreal was perhaps the most dangerous place in Canada. In time [Pg 11] of war, which might have been called the normal condition of the colony, it was exposed by its position to incessant inroads of the Iroquois, or Five Nations, of New York; and no man could venture into the forests or the fields without bearing his life in his hand. The savage confederates had just received a sharp chastisement at the hands of Courcelle, the governor; and the result was a treaty of peace which might at any moment be broken, but which was an inexpressible relief while it lasted.

The priests of St. Sulpice were granting out their lands, on very easy terms, to settlers. They wished to extend a thin line of settlements along the front of their island, to form a sort of outpost, from which an alarm could be given on any descent of the Iroquois. La Salle was the man for such a purpose. Had the priests understood him,—which they evidently did not, for some of them suspected him of levity, the last foible with which he could be charged,—had they understood him, they would have seen in him a young man in whom the fire of youth glowed not the less ardently for the veil of reserve that covered it; who would shrink from no danger, but would not court it in bravado; and who would cling with an invincible tenacity of gripe to any purpose which he might espouse. There is good reason to think that he had come to Canada with purposes already conceived, and that he was ready to avail himself of any stepping-stone which might help to realize them. Queylus, Superior of the Seminary, made him a [Pg 12] generous offer; and he accepted it. This was the gratuitous grant of a large tract of land at the place now called La Chine, above the great rapids of the same name, and eight or nine miles from Montreal. On one hand, the place was greatly exposed to attack; and, on the other, it was favorably situated for the fur-trade. La Salle and his successors became its feudal proprietors, on the sole condition of delivering to the Seminary, on every change of ownership, a medal of fine silver, weighing one mark.[5] He entered on the improvement of his new domain with what means he could command, and began to grant out his land to such settlers as would join him.

Approaching the shore where the city of Montreal now stands, one would have seen a row of small compact dwellings, extending along a narrow street, parallel to the river, and then, as now, called St. Paul Street. On a hill at the right stood the windmill of the seigniors, built of stone, and pierced with loopholes to serve, in time of need, as a place of defence. On the left, in an angle formed by the junction of a rivulet with the St. Lawrence, was a square bastioned fort of stone. Here lived the military governor, appointed by the Seminary, and commanding a few soldiers of the regiment of Carignan. In front, on the line of the street, were the enclosure and buildings of the Seminary, and, [Pg 13] nearly adjoining them, those of the Hôtel-Dieu, or Hospital, both provided for defence in case of an Indian attack. In the hospital enclosure was a small church, opening on the street, and, in the absence of any other, serving for the whole settlement.[6]

Landing, passing the fort, and walking southward along the shore, one would soon have left the rough clearings, and entered the primeval forest. Here, mile after mile, he would have journeyed on in solitude, when the hoarse roar of the rapids, foaming in fury on his left, would have reached his listening ear; and at length, after a walk of some three hours, he would have found the rude beginnings of a settlement. It was where the St. Lawrence widens into the broad expanse called the Lake of St. Louis. Here, La Salle had traced out the circuit of a palisaded village, and assigned to each settler half an arpent, or about the third of an acre, within the enclosure, for which he was to render to the young seignior a yearly acknowledgment of three capons, besides six deniers—that is, half a sou—in money. To each was assigned, moreover, sixty arpents of land beyond the limits of the village, with the perpetual rent of half a sou for each arpent.

He also set apart a common, two hundred arpents in extent, for the use of the settlers, on condition of the payment [Pg 14] by each of five sous a year. He reserved four hundred and twenty arpents for his own personal domain, and on this he began to clear the ground and erect buildings. Similar to this were the beginnings of all the Canadian seigniories formed at this troubled period.[7]

LA CHINE.

That La Salle came to Canada with objects distinctly in view, is probable from the fact that he at once began to study the Indian languages,—and with such success that he is said, within two or three years, to have mastered the Iroquois and seven or eight other languages and dialects.[8] From the shore of his seigniory, he could gaze westward over the broad breast of the Lake of St. Louis, bounded by the dim forests of Chateauguay and Beauharnois; but his thoughts flew far beyond, across the wild and lonely world that stretched towards the sunset. Like Champlain, and all the early explorers, he dreamed of a passage to the South Sea, and a new road for commerce to the riches of China and Japan. Indians often came to his secluded settlement; and, on one occasion, he was visited by a band of the Seneca Iroquois, not long before the scourge of the colony, but now, in virtue of the treaty, wearing the semblance [Pg 15] of friendship. The visitors spent the winter with him, and told him of a river called the Ohio, rising in their country, and flowing into the sea, but at such a distance that its mouth could only be reached after a journey of eight or nine months. Evidently, the Ohio and the Mississippi are here merged into one.[9] In accordance with geographical views then prevalent, he conceived that this great river must needs flow into the "Vermilion Sea;" that is, the Gulf of California. If so, it would give him what he sought, a western passage to China; while, in any case, the populous Indian tribes said to inhabit its banks might be made a source of great commercial profit.

SCHEMES OF DISCOVERY.

La Salle's imagination took fire. His resolution was soon formed; and he descended the St. Lawrence to Quebec, to gain the countenance of the governor for his intended exploration. Few men were more skilled than he in the art of clear and plausible statement. Both the governor Courcelle and the intendant Talon were readily won over to his plan; for which, however, they seem to have given him no more substantial aid than that of the governor's letters patent authorizing the enterprise.[10] The cost was to be his own; and he had no money, having spent it all on his seigniory. He therefore proposed that the Seminary, [Pg 16] which had given it to him, should buy it back again, with such improvements as he had made. Queylus, the Superior, being favorably disposed towards him, consented, and bought of him the greater part; while La Salle sold the remainder, including the clearings, to one Jean Milot, an iron-monger, for twenty-eight hundred livres.[11] With this he bought four canoes, with the necessary supplies, and hired fourteen men.

Meanwhile, the Seminary itself was preparing a similar enterprise. The Jesuits at this time not only held an ascendency over the other ecclesiastics in Canada, but exercised an inordinate influence on the civil government. The Seminary priests of Montreal were jealous of these powerful rivals, and eager to emulate their zeal in the saving of souls and the conquering of new domains for the Faith. Under this impulse, they had, three years before, established a mission at Quinté, on the north shore of Lake Ontario, in charge of two of their number, one of whom was the Abbé Fénelon, elder brother of the celebrated Archbishop of Cambray. Another of them, Dollier de Casson, had spent the winter in a hunting-camp of the Nipissings, where an Indian prisoner, captured in the Northwest, told him of populous tribes of that quarter living in heathenish darkness. On this, the Seminary priests resolved to essay their conversion; and an expedition, to be directed by Dollier, was fitted out to this end. [Pg 17]

DEPARTURE.

He was not ill suited to the purpose. He had been a soldier in his youth, and had fought valiantly as an officer of cavalry under Turenne. He was a man of great courage; of a tall, commanding person; and of uncommon bodily strength, which he had notably proved in the campaign of Courcelle against the Iroquois, three years before.[12] On going to Quebec to procure the necessary outfit, he was urged by Courcelle to modify his plans so far as to act in concert with La Salle in exploring the mystery of the great unknown river of the West. Dollier and his brother priests consented. One of them, Galinée, was joined with him as a colleague, because he was skilled in surveying, and could make a map of their route. Three canoes were procured, and seven hired men completed the party. It was determined that La Salle's expedition and that of the Seminary should be combined in one,—an arrangement ill suited to the character of the young explorer, who was unfit for any enterprise of which he was not the undisputed chief.

Midsummer was near, and there was no time to lose. Yet the moment was most unpropitious, for a Seneca chief had lately been murdered by three scoundrel soldiers of the fort of Montreal; and, while they were undergoing their trial, it became known [Pg 18] that three other Frenchmen had treacherously put to death several Iroquois of the Oneida tribe, in order to get possession of their furs. The whole colony trembled in expectation of a new outbreak of the war. Happily, the event proved otherwise. The authors of the last murder escaped; but the three soldiers were shot at Montreal, in presence of a considerable number of the Iroquois, who declared themselves satisfied with the atonement; and on this same day, the sixth of July, the adventurers began their voyage.

FOOTNOTES:

[1] The following is the *acte de naissance*, discovered by Margry in the *registres de l'état civil*, Paroisse St. Herbland, Rouen: "Le vingt-deuxième

jour de novembre, 1643, a été baptisé Robert Cavelier, fils de honorable homme Jean Cavelier et de Catherine Geest; ses parrain et marraine honorables personnes Nicolas Geest et Marguerite Morice."

La Salle's name in full was René-Robert Cavelier, Sieur de la Salle. La Salle was the name of an estate near Rouen, belonging to the Caveliers. The wealthy French burghers often distinguished the various members of their families by designations borrowed from landed estates. Thus, François Marie Arouet, son of an ex-notary, received the name of Voltaire, which he made famous.

[2] Margry, after investigations at Rouen, is satisfied of its truth (*Journal Général de l'Instruction Publique*, xxxi. 571.) Family papers of the Caveliers, examined by the Abbé Faillon, and copies of some of which he has sent to me, lead to the same conclusion. We shall find several allusions hereafter to La Salle's having in his youth taught in a school, which, in his position, could only have been in connection with some religious community. The doubts alluded to have proceeded from the failure of Father Felix Martin, S. J., to find the name of La Salle on the list of novices. If he had looked for the name of Robert Cavelier, he would probably have found it. The companion of La Salle, Hennepin, is very explicit with regard to this connection with the Jesuits, a point on which he had no motive for falsehood.

[3] It does not appear what vows La Salle had taken. By a recent ordinance (1666), persons entering religious orders could not take the final vows before the age of twenty-five. By the family papers above mentioned, it appears, however, that he had brought himself under the operation of the law, which debarred those who, having entered religious orders, afterwards withdrew, from claiming the inheritance of relatives who had died after their entrance.

[4] The Jesuits in North America, chap. xv.

[5] *Transport de la Seigneurie de St. Sulpice*, cited by Faillon. La Salle called his new domain as above. Two or three years later, it received the name of La Chine, for a reason which will appear.

[6] A detailed plan of Montreal at this time is preserved in the Archives de l'Empire, and has been reproduced by Faillon. There is another, a few years later, and still more minute, of which a fac-simile will be found in the Library of the Canadian Parliament.

[7] The above particulars have been unearthed by the indefatigable Abbé Faillon. Some of La Salle's grants are still preserved in the ancient records of Montreal.

[8] *Papiers de Famille.* He is said to have made several journeys into the forests, towards the North, in the years 1667 and 1668, and to have satisfied himself that little could be hoped from explorations in that direction.

[9] According to Dollier de Casson, who had good opportunities of knowing, the Iroquois always called the Mississippi the Ohio, while the Algonquins gave it its present name.

[10] *Patoulet à Colbert, 11 Nov., 1669.*

[11] *Cession de la Seigneurie; Contrat de Vente* (Margry, i. 103, 104).

[12] He was the author of the very curious and valuable *Histoire de Montréal,* preserved in the Bibliothèque Mazarine, of which a copy is in my possession. The Historical Society of Montreal has recently resolved to print it.

[Pg 19]

CHAPTER II.

1669-1671.

LA SALLE AND THE SULPITIANS.

THE FRENCH IN WESTERN NEW YORK. — LOUIS JOLIET. — THE SULPITIANS ON LAKE ERIE; AT DETROIT; AT SAUT STE. MARIE. — THE MYSTERY OF LA SALLE: HE DISCOVERS THE OHIO; HE DESCENDS THE ILLINOIS; DID HE REACH THE MISSISSIPPI?

LA CHINE was the starting-point; and the combined parties, in all twenty-four men with seven canoes, embarked on the Lake of St. Louis. With them were two other canoes, bearing the party of Senecas who had wintered at La Salle's settlement, and who were now to act as guides. Father Galinée recounts the journey. He was no woodsman: the river, the forests, the rapids, were all new to him, and he dilates on them with the minuteness of a novice. Above all, he admired the Indian birch canoes. "If God," he says, "grants me the grace of returning to France, I shall try to carry one with me." Then he describes the bivouac: "Your lodging is as extraordinary as your vessels; for, after paddling or carrying the canoes all day, you find mother earth ready to receive your wearied body. If the weather is fair, you make a fire and lie down [Pg 20] to sleep without further trouble; but if it rains, you must peel bark from the trees, and make a shed by laying it on a frame of sticks. As for your food, it is enough to make you burn all the cookery books that ever were written; for in the woods of Canada one finds means to live well without bread, wine, salt, pepper, or spice. The ordinary food is Indian corn, or Turkey wheat as they call it in France, which is crushed between two stones and boiled, seasoning it with meat or fish, when you can get them. This sort of life seemed so strange to us that we all felt the effects of it; and before we were a hundred leagues from Montreal, not one of us was free from some malady or other. At last, after all our misery, on the second of August, we discovered Lake Ontario, like a great sea with no land beyond it."

Thirty-five days after leaving La Chine, they reached Irondequoit Bay, on the south side of the lake. Here they were met by a number of Seneca Indians, who professed friendship and invited them to their villages, fifteen or twenty miles distant. As this was on their way to the upper waters of the Ohio, and as they hoped to find guides at the villages to conduct them, they accepted the invitation. Dollier, with most of the men, remained to guard the canoes; while La Salle, with Galinée and eight other Frenchmen, accompanied by a troop of Indians, set out on the morning of the twelfth, and reached the principal village before evening. It stood on a [Pg 21] hill, in the midst of a clearing nearly two leagues in compass.[13] A rude stockade surrounded it; and as the visitors drew near they saw a band of old men seated on the grass, waiting to receive them. One of these veterans, so feeble with age that he could hardly stand, made them an harangue, in which he declared that the Senecas were their brothers, and invited them to enter the village. They did so, surrounded by a crowd of savages, and presently found themselves in the midst of a disorderly cluster of large but filthy abodes of bark, about a hundred and fifty in number, the most capacious of which was assigned to their use. Here they made their quarters, and were soon overwhelmed by Seneca hospitality. Children brought them pumpkins and berries from the woods; and boy messengers came to summon them to endless feasts, where they were regaled with the flesh of dogs and with boiled maize seasoned with oil pressed from nuts and the seed of sunflowers.

La Salle had flattered himself that he knew enough Iroquois to hold communication with the Senecas; but he failed completely in the attempt. The priests had a Dutch interpreter, who spoke Iroquois fluently, but knew so little French, and was withal so obstinate, that he proved useless; so that it was necessary to employ a man in the service of the Jesuit Fremin, whose mission was at this village. What the party needed was a guide to conduct them to the Ohio; and [Pg 22] soon after their arrival a party of warriors appeared, with a young prisoner belonging to one of the tribes of that region. Galinée wanted to beg or buy him from his captors; but the Senecas had other intentions. "I saw," writes the priest, "the most miserable spectacle I ever beheld in my life." It was the prisoner tied to a stake and tortured for six hours with diabolical ingenuity, while the crowd danced and yelled with delight, and the chiefs and elders sat in a row smoking their pipes and watching the contortions of the victim with an air of serene enjoyment. The body was at last cut up and eaten, and in the evening the whole population occupied themselves in scaring away the angry ghost by beating with sticks against the bark sides of the lodges.

La Salle and his companions began to fear for their own safety. Some of their hosts wished to kill them in revenge for the chief murdered near Montreal; and as these and others were at times in a frenzy of drunkenness, the position of the French became critical. They suspected that means had been used to prejudice the Senecas against them. Not only could they get no guides, but they were told that if they went to the Ohio the tribes of those parts would infallibly kill them. Their Dutch interpreter became disheartened and unmanageable, and, after staying a month at the village, the hope of getting farther on their way seemed less than ever. Their plan, it was clear, must be changed; and an Indian from Otinawatawa, a kind of Iroquois colony at the head [Pg 23] of Lake Ontario, offered to guide them to his village and show them a better way to the Ohio. They left the Senecas, coasted the south shore of the lake, passed the mouth of the Niagara, where they heard the distant roar of the cataract, and on the twenty-fourth of September reached Otinawatawa, which was a few miles north of the present town of Hamilton. The inhabitants proved friendly, and La Salle received the welcome present of a Shawanoe prisoner, who told them that the Ohio could be reached in six weeks, and that he would guide them to it. Delighted at this good fortune, they were about to set out; when they heard, to their astonishment, of the arrival of two other Frenchmen at a neighboring village.

LOUIS JOLIET.

One of the strangers was destined to hold a conspicuous place in the history of western discovery. This was Louis Joliet, a young man of about the age of La Salle. Like him, he had studied for the priesthood; but the world and the wilderness had conquered his early inclinations, and changed him to an active and adventurous fur-trader. Talon had sent him to discover and explore the copper-mines of Lake Superior. He had failed in the attempt, and was now returning. His Indian guide, afraid of passing the Niagara portage lest he should meet enemies, had led him from Lake Erie, by way of Grand River, towards the head of Lake Ontario; and thus it was that he met La Salle and the Sulpitians.

[Pg 24]

This meeting caused a change of plan. Joliet showed the priests a map which he had made of such parts of the Upper Lakes as he had visited, and gave them a copy of it; telling them, at the same time, of the Pottawattamies and other tribes of that region in grievous need of spiritual succor. The result was a determination on their part to follow the route which he suggested, notwithstanding the remonstrances of La Salle, who in vain reminded them that the Jesuits had preoccupied the field, and would regard them as intruders. They resolved that the Pottawattamies should no longer sit in darkness; while, as for the Mississippi, it could be reached, as they conceived, with less risk by this northern route than by that of the south.

La Salle was of a different mind. His goal was the Ohio, and not the northern lakes. A few days before, while hunting, he had been attacked by a fever, sarcastically ascribed by Galinée to his having seen three large rattle-snakes crawling up a rock. He now told his two colleagues that he was in no condition to go forward, and should be forced to part with them. The staple of La Salle's character, as his life will attest, was an invincible determination of purpose, which set at naught all risks and all sufferings. He had cast himself with all his resources into this enterprise; and, while his faculties remained, he was not a man to recoil from it. On the other hand, the masculine fibre of which he was made did not always withhold him from the practice of the arts of address, [Pg 25] and the use of what Dollier de Casson styles *belles paroles*. He respected the priesthood, with the exception, it seems, of the Jesuits; and he was under obligations to the Sulpitians of Montreal. Hence there can be no doubt that he used his illness as a pretext for escaping from their company without ungraciousness, and following his own path in his own way.

SEPARATION.

On the last day of September, the priests made an altar, supported by the paddles of the canoes laid on forked sticks. Dollier said mass; La Salle and his followers received the sacrament, as did also those of his late colleagues; and thus they parted, the Sulpitians and their party descending the Grand River towards Lake Erie, while La Salle, as they supposed, began his return to Montreal. What course he actually took we shall soon inquire; and meanwhile, for a few moments, we will follow the priests. When they reached Lake Erie, they saw it tossing like an angry ocean. They had no mind to tempt the dangerous and unknown navigation, and encamped for the winter in the forest near the peninsula called the Long Point. Here they gathered a good store of chestnuts, hickory-nuts, plums, and grapes, and built themselves a log cabin, with a recess at the end for an altar. They passed the winter unmolested, shooting game in abundance, and saying mass three times a week. Early in spring, they planted a large cross, attached to it the arms of France, and took formal possession of the country in [Pg 26] the name of Louis XIV. This done, they resumed their voyage, and, after many troubles, landed one evening in a state of exhaustion on or near Point Pelée, towards the western extremity of Lake Erie. A storm rose as they lay asleep, and swept off a great part of their baggage, which, in their fatigue, they had left at the edge of the water. Their altar-service was lost with the rest,—a misfortune which they ascribed to the jealousy and malice of the Devil. Debarred henceforth from saying mass, they resolved to return to Montreal and leave the Pottawattamies uninstructed. They presently entered the strait by which Lake Huron joins Lake Erie, and landing near where Detroit now stands, found a large stone, somewhat suggestive of the human figure, which the Indians had bedaubed with paint, and which they worshipped as a manito. In view of their late misfortune, this device of the arch-enemy excited their utmost resentment. "After the loss of our altar-service," writes Galinée, "and the hunger we had suffered, there was not a man of us who was not filled with hatred against this false deity. I devoted one of my axes to breaking him in pieces; and then, having fastened our canoes side by side, we carried the largest piece to the middle of the river, and threw it, with all the rest, into the water, that he might never be heard of again. God rewarded us immediately for this good action, for we killed a deer and a bear that same day."

AT STE. MARIE DU SAUT.

This is the first recorded passage of white men [Pg 27] through the Strait of Detroit; though Joliet had, no doubt, passed this way on his return from the Upper Lakes.[14] The two missionaries took this course, with the intention of proceeding to the Saut Ste. Marie, and there joining the Ottawas, and other tribes of that region, in their yearly descent to Montreal. They issued upon Lake Huron; followed its eastern shores till they reached the Georgian Bay, near the head of which the Jesuits had established their great mission of the Hurons, destroyed, twenty years before, by the Iroquois;[15] and, ignoring or slighting the labors of the rival missionaries, held their way northward along the rocky archipelago that edged those lonely coasts. They passed the Manitoulins, and, ascending the strait by which Lake Superior discharges its waters, arrived on the twenty-fifth of May at Ste. Marie du Saut. Here they found the two Jesuits, Dablon and Marquette, in a square fort of cedar pickets, built by their men within the past year, and enclosing a chapel and a house. Near by, they had cleared a large tract of land, and sown it with wheat, Indian corn, peas, and other crops. The new-comers were graciously received, and invited to vespers in the chapel; but they very soon found La Salle's prediction made good, and saw that the Jesuit fathers wanted no help from St. Sulpice. Galinée, [Pg 28] on his part, takes occasion to remark, that, though the Jesuits had baptized a few Indians at the Saut, not one of them was a good enough Christian to receive the Eucharist; and he intimates that the case, by their own showing, was still worse at their mission of St. Esprit. The two Sulpitians did not care to prolong their stay; and, three days after their arrival, they left the Saut,—not, as they expected, with the Indians, but with a French guide, furnished by the Jesuits. Ascending French River to Lake Nipissing, they crossed to the waters of the Ottawa, and descended to Montreal, which they reached on the eighteenth of June. They had made no discoveries and no converts; but Galinée, after his arrival, made the earliest map of the Upper Lakes known to exist.[16]

LA SALLE'S DISCOVERIES.

We return now to La Salle, only to find ourselves involved in mist and obscurity. What did he do after he left the two priests? Unfortunately, a definite answer is not possible; and the next two years of his life remain in some measure an enigma. That he was busied in active exploration, and that he made important discoveries, is certain; but the extent and character of these discoveries remain wrapped in doubt. He is known to have kept journals and made maps; and these were in existence, and in possession of his niece, Madeleine Cavelier, then in advanced [Pg 29] age, as late as the year 1756; beyond which time the most diligent inquiry has failed to trace them. Abbé Faillon affirms that some of La Salle's men, refusing to follow him, returned to La Chine, and that the place then received its name, in derision of the young adventurer's dream of a westward passage to China.[17] As for himself, the only distinct record of his movements is that contained in a paper, entitled "Histoire de Monsieur de la Salle." It is an account of his explorations, and of the state of parties in Canada previous to the year 1678,—taken from the lips of La Salle himself, by a person whose name does not appear, but who declares that he had ten or twelve conversations with him at Paris, whither he had come with a petition to the Court. The writer himself had never been in America, and was ignorant of its geography; hence blunders on his part might reasonably be expected. His statements, however, are in some measure intelligible; and the following is the substance of them.

After leaving the priests, La Salle went to Onondaga, where we are left to infer that he succeeded better in getting a guide than he had before done among the Senecas. Thence he made his way to a point six or seven leagues distant from Lake Erie, where he reached a branch of the Ohio, and, descending it, followed the river as far as the rapids at Louisville,—or, as has been maintained, beyond [Pg 30] its confluence with the Mississippi. His men now refused to go farther, and abandoned him, escaping to the English and the Dutch; whereupon he retraced his steps alone.[18] This must have been in the winter of 1669-70, or in the following spring; unless there is an error of date in the statement of Nicolas Perrot, the famous *voyageur*, who says that he met him in the summer of 1670, hunting on the Ottawa with a party of Iroquois.[19]

THE RIVER ILLINOIS.

But how was La Salle employed in the following year? The same memoir has its solution to the [Pg 31] problem. By this it appears that the indefatigable explorer embarked on Lake Erie, ascended the Detroit to Lake Huron, coasted the unknown shores of Michigan, passed the Straits of Michilimackinac, and, leaving Green Bay behind him, entered what is described as an incomparably larger bay, but which was evidently the southern portion of Lake Michigan. Thence he crossed to a river flowing westward,— evidently the Illinois,—and followed it until it was joined by another river flowing from the northwest to the southeast. By this, the Mississippi only can be meant; and he is reported to have said that he descended it to the thirty-sixth degree of latitude; where he stopped, assured that it discharged itself not into the Gulf of

California, but into the Gulf of Mexico, and resolved to follow it thither at a future day, when better provided with men and supplies.[20]

THE MISSISSIPPI.

The first of these statements,—that relating to the [Pg 32] Ohio,— confused, vague, and in great part incorrect, as it certainly is, is nevertheless well sustained as regards one essential point. La Salle himself, in a memorial addressed to Count Frontenac in 1677, affirms that he discovered the Ohio, and descended it as far as to a fall which obstructed it.[21] Again, his rival, Louis Joliet, whose testimony on this point cannot be suspected, made two maps of the region of the Mississippi and the Great Lakes. The Ohio is laid down on both of them, with an inscription to the effect that it had been explored by La Salle.[22] That [Pg 33] he discovered the Ohio may then be regarded as established. That he descended it to the Mississippi, he himself does not pretend; nor is there reason to believe that he did so.

With regard to his alleged voyage down the Illinois, the case is different. Here, he is reported to have made a statement which admits but one interpretation,—that of the discovery by him of the Mississippi prior to its discovery by Joliet and Marquette. This statement is attributed to a man not prone to vaunt his own exploits, who never proclaimed them in print, and whose testimony, even in his own case, must therefore have weight. But it comes to us through the medium of a person strongly biassed in favor of La Salle, and against Marquette and the Jesuits.

LA SALLE'S DISCOVERIES.

Seven years had passed since the alleged discovery, and La Salle had not before laid claim to it; although it was matter of notoriety that during five years it had been claimed by Joliet, and that his claim was generally admitted. The correspondence of the governor and the intendant is silent as to La Salle's having penetrated to the Mississippi, though the attempt was made under the auspices of the latter, as his own letters declare; while both had the discovery of the great river earnestly at heart. The governor, Frontenac, La Salle's ardent supporter and [Pg 34] ally, believed in 1672, as his letters show, that the Mississippi flowed into the Gulf of California; and, two years later, he announces to the minister Colbert its discovery by Joliet.[23] After La Salle's death, his brother, his nephew, and his niece addressed a memorial to the king, petitioning for certain grants in consideration of the discoveries of their relative, which they specify at some length; but they do not pretend that he reached the Mississippi before his expeditions of 1679 to 1682.[24] This silence is the more significant, as it is this very niece who had possession of the papers in which La Salle recounts the journeys of which the issues are in question.[25] [Pg 35] Had they led him to the Mississippi, it is reasonably certain that she would have made it known in her memorial. La Salle discovered the Ohio, and in all probability the Illinois also; but that he discovered the Mississippi has not been proved, nor, in the light of the evidence we have, is it likely.

FOOTNOTES:

[13] This village seems to have been that attacked by Denonville in 1687. It stood on Boughton Hill, near the present town of Victor.

[14] The Jesuits and fur-traders, on their way to the Upper Lakes, had followed the route of the Ottawa, or, more recently, that of Toronto and the Georgian Bay. Iroquois hostility had long closed the Niagara portage and Lake Erie against them.

[15] The Jesuits in North America.

[16] See Appendix. The above narrative is from *Récit de ce qui s'est passé de plus remarquable dans le Voyage de MM. Dollier et Galinée.* (Bibliothèque Nationale.)

[17] Dollier de Casson alludes to this as "cette transmigration célèbre qui se fit de la Chine dans ces quartiers."

[18] The following is the passage relating to this journey in the remarkable paper above mentioned. After recounting La Salle's visit with the

Sulpitians to the Seneca village, and stating that the intrigues of the Jesuit missionary prevented them from obtaining a guide, it speaks of the separation of the travellers and the journey of Galinée and his party to the Saut Ste. Marie, where "les Jésuites les congédièrent." It then proceeds as follows: "Cependant M{r.} de la Salle continua son chemin par une rivière qui va de l'est à l'ouest; et passe à Onontaqué [*Onondaga*], puis à six ou sept lieues au-dessous du Lac Erié; et estant parvenu jusqu'au 280me ou 83me degré de longitude, et jusqu'au 41me degré de latitude, trouva un sault qui tombe vers l'ouest dans un pays bas, marescageux, tout couvert de vielles souches, dont il y en a quelques-unes qui sont encore sur pied. Il fut donc contraint de prendre terre, et suivant une hauteur qui le pouvoit mener loin, il trouva quelques sauvages qui luy dirent que fort loin de là le mesme fleuve qui se perdoit dans cette terre basse et vaste se réunnissoit en un lit. Il continua donc son chemin, mais comme la fatigue estoit grande, 23 ou 24 hommes qu'il avoit menez jusques là le quittèrent tous en une nuit, regagnèrent le fleuve, et se sauvèrent, les uns à la Nouvelle Hollande et les autres à la Nouvelle Angleterre. Il se vit donc seul à 400 lieues de chez luy, où il ne laisse pas de revenir, remontant la rivière et vivant de chasse, d'herbes, et de ce que luy donnèrent les sauvages qu'il rencontra en son chemin."

[19] Perrot, *Mémoires*, 119, 120.

[20] The memoir—after stating, as above, that he entered Lake Huron, doubled the peninsula of Michigan, and passed La Baye des Puants (*Green Bay*)—says: "Il reconnut une baye incomparablement plus large; au fond de laquelle vers l'ouest il trouva un très-beau havre et au fond de ce havre un fleuve qui va de l'est à l'ouest. Il suivit ce fleuve, et estant parvenu jusqu'environ le 280me degré de longitude et le 39me de latitude, il trouva un autre fleuve qui se joignant au premier coulait du nordouest au sudest, et il suivit ce fleuve jusqu'au 36me degré de latitude."

The "très-beau havre" may have been the entrance of the river Chicago, whence, by an easy portage, he might have reached the Des Plaines branch of the Illinois. We shall see that he took this course in his famous exploration of 1682.

The intendant Talon announces, in his despatches of this year that he had sent La Salle southward and westward to explore.

[21] The following are his words (he speaks of himself in the third person): "L'année 1667, et les suivantes, il fit divers voyages avec beaucoup de

62| Page

dépenses, dans lesquels il découvrit le premier beaucoup de pays au sud des grands lacs, et *entre autres la grande rivière d'Ohio*; il la suivit jusqu'à un endroit où elle tombe de fort haut dans de vastes marais, à la hauteur de 37 degrés, après avoir été grossie par une autre rivière fort large qui vient du nord; et toutes ces eaux se déchargent selon toutes les apparences dans le Golfe du Mexique."

This "autre rivière," which, it seems, was above the fall, may have been the Miami or the Scioto. There is but one fall on the river, that of Louisville, which is not so high as to deserve to be described as "fort haut," being only a strong rapid. The latitude, as will be seen, is different in the two accounts, and incorrect in both.

[22] One of these maps is entitled *Carte de la découverte du Sieur Joliet*, 1674. Over the lines representing the Ohio are the words, "Route du sieur de la Salle pour aller dans le Mexique." The other map of Joliet bears, also written over the Ohio, the words, "Rivière par où descendit le sieur de la Salle au sortir du lac Erié pour aller dans le Mexique." I have also another manuscript map, made before the voyage of Joliet and Marquette, and apparently in the year 1673, on which the Ohio is represented as far as to a point a little below Louisville, and over it is written, "Rivière Ohio, ainsy appellée par les Iroquois à cause de sa beauté, par où le sieur de la Salle est descendu." The Mississippi is not represented on this map; but—and this is very significant, as indicating the extent of La Salle's exploration of the following year—a small part of the upper Illinois is laid down.

[23] *Lettre de Frontenac au Ministre, 14 Nov., 1674.* He here speaks of "la grande rivière qu'il [*Joliet*] a trouvée, qui va du nord au sud, et qui est aussi large que celle du Saint-Laurent vis-à-vis de Québec." Four years later, Frontenac speaks slightingly of Joliet, but neither denies his discovery of the Mississippi, nor claims it for La Salle, in whose interest he writes.

[24] *Papiers de Famille; Mémoire présenté au Roi.* The following is an extract: "Il parvient ... jusqu'à la rivière des Illinois. Il y construisit un fort situé à 350 lieues au-delà du fort de Frontenac, et suivant ensuite le cours de cette rivière, il trouva qu'elle se jettoit dans un grand fleuve appellé par ceux du pays Mississippi, c'est à dire *grande eau*, environ cent lieues au-dessous du fort qu'il venoit de construire." This fort was Fort Crèvecœur, built in 1680, near the site of Peoria. The memoir goes on to relate the descent of La Salle to the Gulf, which concluded this expedition of 1679-82.

[25] The following is an extract, given by Margry, from a letter of the aged Madeleine Cavelier, dated 21 Février, 1756, and addressed to her nephew, M. Le Baillif, who had applied for the papers in behalf of the minister, Silhouette: "J'ay cherché une occasion sûre pour vous anvoyé les papiers de M. de la Salle. Il y a des cartes que j'ay jointe à ces papiers, qui doivent prouver que, en 1675, M. de Lasalle avet déja fet deux voyages en ces decouverte, puisqu'il y avet une carte, que je vous envoye, par laquelle il est fait mention de l'androit auquel M. de Lasalle aborda près le fleuve de Mississipi; un autre androit qu'il nomme le fleuve Colbert; en un autre il prans possession de ce pais au nom du roy et fait planter une crois."

The words of the aged and illiterate writer are obscure, but her expression "aborda près" seems to indicate that La Salle had not reached the Mississippi prior to 1675, but only approached it. Finally, a memorial presented to Seignelay, along with the official narrative of 1679-81, by a friend of La Salle, whose object was to place the discoverer and his achievements in the most favorable light, contains the following: "Il [*La Salle*] a esté le premier à former le dessein de ces descouvertes, qu'il communiqua, il y a plus de quinze ans, à M. de Courcelles, gouverneur, et à M. Talon, intendant du Canada, qui l'approuvèrent. Il a fait ensuite plusieurs voyages de ce costé-là, et un entr'autres en 1669 avec MM. Dolier et Galinée, prestres du Séminaire de St. Sulpice. *Il est vray que le sieur Jolliet, pour le prévenir, fit un voyage in 1673, à la rivière Colbert*; mais ce fut uniquement pour y faire commerce." See Margry, ii. 285. This passage is a virtual admission that Joliet reached the Mississippi (*Colbert*) before La Salle.

Margry, in a series of papers in the *Journal Général de l'Instruction Publique* for 1862, first took the position that La Salle reached the Mississippi in 1670 and 1671, and has brought forward in defence of it all the documents which his unwearied research enabled him to discover. Father Tailhan, S.J., has replied at length, in the copious notes to his edition of Nicolas Perrot, but without having seen the principal document cited by Margry, and of which extracts have been given in the notes to this chapter.

[Pg 36]

CHAPTER III.

1670-1672.

THE JESUITS ON THE LAKES.

WHAT were the Jesuits doing? Since the ruin of their great mission of the Hurons, a perceptible change had taken place in them. They had put forth exertions almost superhuman, set at naught famine, disease, and death, lived with the self-abnegation of saints and died with the devotion of martyrs; and the result of all had been a disastrous failure. From no short-coming on their part, but from the force of events beyond the sphere of their influence, a very demon of havoc had crushed their incipient churches, slaughtered their converts, uprooted the populous communities on which their hopes had rested, and scattered them in bands of wretched fugitives far and wide through the wilderness.[26] They had devoted themselves in the fulness of faith to the building up [Pg 37] of a Christian and Jesuit empire on the conversion of the great stationary tribes of the lakes; and of these none remained but the Iroquois, the destroyers of the rest,—among whom, indeed, was a field which might stimulate their zeal by an abundant promise of sufferings and martyrdoms, but which, from its geographical position, was too much exposed to Dutch and English influence to promise great and decisive results. Their best hopes were now in the North and the West; and thither, in great part, they had turned their energies.

REPORTS OF THE JESUITS.

We find them on Lake Huron, Lake Superior, and Lake Michigan, laboring vigorously as of old, but in a spirit not quite the same. Now, as before, two objects inspired their zeal,—the "greater glory of

God," and the influence and credit of the Order of Jesus. If the one motive had somewhat lost in power, the other had gained. The epoch of the saints and martyrs was passing away; and henceforth we find the Canadian Jesuit less and less an apostle, more and more an explorer, a man of science, and a politician. The yearly reports of the missions are still, for the edification of the pious reader, filled with intolerably tedious stories of baptisms, conversions, and the exemplary deportment of neophytes,—for these have become a part of the formula; but they are relieved abundantly by more mundane topics. One finds observations on the winds, currents, and tides of the Great Lakes; speculations on a subterranean outlet of Lake Superior; accounts of [Pg 38] its copper-mines, and how we, the Jesuit fathers, are laboring to explore them for the profit of the colony; surmises touching the North Sea, the South Sea, the Sea of China, which we hope ere long to discover; and reports of that great mysterious river of which the Indians tell us,—flowing southward, perhaps to the Gulf of Mexico, perhaps to the Vermilion Sea,—and the secrets whereof, with the help of the Virgin, we will soon reveal to the world.

The Jesuit was as often a fanatic for his Order as for his faith; and oftener yet the two fanaticisms mingled in him inextricably. Ardently as he burned for the saving of souls, he would have none saved on the Upper Lakes except by his brethren and himself. He claimed a monopoly of conversion, with its attendant monopoly of toil, hardship, and martyrdom. Often disinterested for himself, he was inordinately ambitious for the great corporate power in which he had merged his own personality; and here lies one cause, among many, of the seeming contradictions which abound in the annals of the Order.

Prefixed to the *Relation* of 1671 is that monument of Jesuit hardihood and enterprise, the map of Lake Superior,—a work of which, however, the exactness has been exaggerated, as compared with other Canadian maps of the day. While making surveys, the priests were diligently looking for copper. Father Dablon reports that they had found it in greatest abundance on Isle Minong, now

Isle Royale. "A day's journey from the head of the lake, on the [Pg 39] south side, there is," he says, "a rock of copper weighing from six hundred to eight hundred pounds, lying on the shore where any who pass may see it;" and he further speaks of great copper boulders in the bed of the river Ontonagan. [27]

STE. MARIE DU SAUT.

There were two principal missions on the Upper Lakes, which were, in a certain sense, the parents of the rest. One of these was Ste. Marie du Saut,—the same visited by Dollier and Galinée,—at the outlet of Lake Superior. This was a noted fishing-place; for the rapids were full of white-fish, and Indians came thither in crowds. The permanent residents were an Ojibwa band, whom the French called Sauteurs, and whose bark lodges were clustered [Pg 40] at the foot of the rapids, near the fort of the Jesuits. Besides these, a host of Algonquins, of various tribes, resorted thither in the spring and summer,—living in abundance on the fishery, and dispersing in winter to wander and starve in scattered hunting-parties far and wide through the forests.

The other chief mission was that of St. Esprit, at La Pointe, near the western extremity of Lake Superior. Here were the Hurons, fugitives twenty years before from the slaughter of their countrymen; and the Ottawas, who, like them, had sought an asylum from the rage of the Iroquois. Many other tribes—Illinois, Pottawattamies, Foxes, Menomonies, Sioux, Assiniboins, Knisteneaux, and a multitude besides—came hither yearly to trade with the French. Here was a young Jesuit, Jacques Marquette, lately arrived from the Saut Ste. Marie. His savage flock disheartened him by its backslidings; and the best that he could report of the Hurons, after all the toil and all the blood lavished in their conversion, was, that they "still retain a little Christianity;" while the Ottawas are "far removed from the kingdom of God, and addicted beyond all other tribes to foulness, incantations, and sacrifices to evil spirits."[28]

MARQUETTE AND ANDRÉ.

Marquette heard from the Illinois—yearly visitors at La Pointe—of the great river which they had crossed on their way,[29] and which, as he conjectured, flowed [Pg 41] into the Gulf of California. He heard marvels of it also from the Sioux, who lived on its banks; and a strong desire possessed him to explore the mystery of its course. A sudden calamity dashed his hopes. The Sioux—the Iroquois of the West, as the Jesuits call them—had hitherto kept the peace with the expatriated tribes of La Pointe; but now, from some cause not worth inquiry, they broke into open war, and so terrified the Hurons and Ottawas that they abandoned their settlements and fled. Marquette followed his panic-stricken flock, who, passing the Saut Ste. Marie, and descending to Lake Huron, stopped at length,—the Hurons at Michilimackinac, and the Ottawas at the Great Manitoulin Island. Two missions were now necessary to minister to the divided bands. That of Michilimackinac was assigned to Marquette, and that of the Manitoulin Island to Louis André. The former took post at Point St. Ignace, on the north shore of the Straits of Michilimackinac, while the latter began the mission of St. Simon at the new abode of the Ottawas. When winter came, scattering his flock to their hunting-grounds, André made a missionary tour among the Nipissings and other neighboring tribes. The shores of Lake Huron had long been an utter [Pg 42] solitude, swept of their denizens by the terror of the all-conquering Iroquois; but now that these tigers had felt the power of the French, and learned for a time to leave their Indian allies in peace, the fugitive hordes were returning to their ancient abodes. André's experience among them was of the roughest. The staple of his diet was acorns and *tripe de roche*,—a species of lichen, which, being boiled, resolved itself into a black glue, nauseous, but not void of nourishment. At times, he was reduced to moss, the bark of trees, or moccasins and old moose-skins cut into strips and boiled. His hosts treated him very ill, and the worst of their fare was always his portion. When spring came to his relief, he returned to his post of St. Simon, with impaired digestion and unabated zeal.

THE GREEN BAY MISSION.

Besides the Saut Ste. Marie and Michilimackinac, both noted fishing-places, there was another spot, no less famous for game and fish, and therefore a favorite resort of Indians. This was the head of the Green Bay of Lake Michigan.[30] Here and in adjacent districts several distinct tribes had made their abode. The Menomonies were on the river which bears their name; the Pottawattamies and Winnebagoes were [Pg 43] near the borders of the bay; the Sacs, on Fox River; the Mascoutins, Miamis, and Kickapoos, on the same river, above Lake Winnebago; and the Outagamies, or Foxes, on a tributary of it flowing from the north. Green Bay was manifestly suited for a mission; and, as early as the autumn of 1669, Father Claude Allouez was sent thither to found one. After nearly perishing by the way, he set out to explore the destined field of his labors, and went as far as the town of the Mascoutins. Early in the autumn of 1670, having been joined by Dablon, Superior of the missions on the Upper Lakes, he made another journey, but not until the two fathers had held a council with the congregated tribes at St. François Xavier; for so they named their mission of Green Bay. Here, as they harangued their naked audience, their gravity was put to the proof; for a band of warriors, anxious to do them honor, walked incessantly up and down, aping the movements of the soldiers on guard before the governor's tent at Montreal. "We could hardly keep from laughing," writes Dablon, "though, we were discoursing on very important subjects; namely, the mysteries of our religion, and the things necessary to escaping from eternal fire."[31]

The fathers were delighted with the country, which Dablon calls an earthly paradise; but he adds that the way to it is as hard as the path to heaven. He alludes especially to the rapids of Fox River, which gave the two travellers great trouble. Having [Pg 44] safely passed them, they saw an Indian idol on the bank, similar to that which Dollier and Galinée found at Detroit,—being merely a rock, bearing some resemblance to a man, and hideously painted. With the help of their attendants, they threw it into the river. Dablon expatiates on the buffalo, which he describes apparently on the report of others, as his description is not very accurate. Crossing Winnebago Lake, the two priests followed the river leading to the town of the Mascoutins and Miamis, which they reached on the fifteenth of September.[32] These two tribes lived together within the compass of the same enclosure of palisades,—to the number, it is said, of more than three thousand souls. The missionaries, who had brought a highly colored picture of the Last Judgment, called the Indians to council and displayed it before them; while Allouez, who spoke Algonquin, harangued them on hell, demons, and eternal flames. They listened with open ears, beset him night and day with questions, and invited him and his companion to unceasing feasts. They were welcomed in every lodge, and followed everywhere with eyes of curiosity, wonder, and awe. Dablon overflows with praises of the Miami chief, who was honored by his subjects like a king, and [Pg 45] whose demeanor towards his guests had no savor of the savage.

Their hosts told them of the great river Mississippi, rising far in the north and flowing southward,—they knew not whither,—and of many tribes that dwelt along its banks. When at length they took their departure, they left behind them a reputation as medicine-men of transcendent power.

THE CROSS AMONG THE FOXES.

In the winter following, Allouez visited the Foxes, whom he found in extreme ill-humor. They were incensed against the French by the ill-usage which some of their tribe had lately met when on a trading visit to Montreal; and they received the Faith with shouts of derision. The priest was horror-stricken at what he saw. Their lodges, each containing from five to ten families, seemed in his eyes like seraglios; for some of the chiefs had eight wives. He armed himself with patience, and at length gained a hearing. Nay, he succeeded so well, that when he showed them his crucifix they would throw tobacco on it as an offering; and, on another visit which he made them soon after, he taught the whole village to make the sign of the cross. A war-party was going out against their enemies, and he bethought him of telling them the story of the Cross and the Emperor Constantine. This so wrought upon them that they all daubed the figure of a cross on their shields of bull-hide, set out for the war, and came back victorious, extolling the sacred symbol as a great war-medicine. [Pg 46]

"Thus it is," writes Dablon, who chronicles the incident, "that our holy faith is established among these people; and we have good hope that we shall soon carry it to the famous river called the Mississippi, and perhaps even to the South Sea."[33] Most things human have their phases of the ludicrous; and the heroism of these untiring priests is no exception to the rule.

TRADING WITH INDIANS.

The various missionary stations were much alike. They consisted of a chapel (commonly of logs) and one or more houses, with perhaps a store-house and a workshop; the whole fenced with palisades, and forming, in fact, a stockade fort, surrounded with clearings and cultivated fields. It is evident that the priests had need of other hands than their own and those of the few lay brothers attached to the mission. They required men inured to labor, accustomed to the forest life, able to guide canoes and handle tools and weapons. In the earlier epoch of the missions, when enthusiasm was at its height, they were served in great measure by volunteers, who joined them through devotion or penitence, and who were known as *donnés* or "given men." Of late, the number of these had much diminished; and they now relied chiefly on hired men, or *engagés*. These were employed in building, hunting, fishing, clearing, and tilling the ground, guiding canoes, and (if faith is to be placed in reports current throughout the colony) in trading with the Indians for the profit [Pg 47] of the missions. This charge of trading—which, if the results were applied exclusively to the support of the missions, does not of necessity involve much censure—is vehemently reiterated in many quarters, including the official despatches of the governor of

Canada; while, so far as I can discover, the Jesuits never distinctly denied it, and on several occasions they partially admitted its truth.[34]

FOOTNOTES:

[26] See "The Jesuits in North America."

[27] He complains that the Indians were very averse to giving information on the subject, so that the Jesuits had not as yet discovered the metal *in situ*, though they hoped soon to do so. The Indians told him that the copper had first been found by four hunters, who had landed on a certain island, near the north shore of the lake. Wishing to boil their food in a vessel of bark, they gathered stones on the shore, heated them red hot, and threw them in, but presently discovered them to be pure copper. Their repast over, they hastened to re-embark, being afraid of the lynxes and the hares, which, on this island, were as large as dogs, and which would have devoured their provisions, and perhaps their canoe. They took with them some of the wonderful stones; but scarcely had they left the island, when a deep voice, like thunder, sounded in their ears, "Who are these thieves who steal the toys of my children?" It was the God of the Waters, or some other powerful manito. The four adventurers retreated in great terror; but three of them soon died, and the fourth survived only long enough to reach his village, and tell the story. The island has no foundation, but floats with the movement of the wind; and no Indian dares land on its shores, dreading the wrath of the manito. Dablon, *Relation*, 1670, 84.

[28] *Lettre du Père Jacques Marquette au R. P. Supérieur des Missions;* in *Relation*, 1670, 87.

[29] The Illinois lived at this time beyond the Mississippi, thirty days' journey from La Pointe; whither they had been driven by the Iroquois, from their former abode near Lake Michigan. Dablon (*Relation*, 1671, 24, 25) says that they lived seven days' journey beyond the Mississippi, in eight villages. A few years later, most of them returned to the east side, and made their abode on the river Illinois.

[30] The Baye des Puants of the early writers; or, more correctly, La Baye des Eaux Puantes. The Winnebago Indians, living near it, were called Les Puans, apparently for no other reason than because some portion of the bay was said to have an odor like the sea.

Lake Michigan, the "Lac des Illinois" of the French, was, according to a letter of Father Allouez, called "Machihiganing" by the Indians. Dablon writes the name "Mitchiganon."

[31] *Relation*, 1671, 43.
[32] This town was on the Neenah or Fox River, above Lake Winnebago. The Mascoutins, Fire Nation, or Nation of the Prairie, are extinct or merged in other tribes. See "The Jesuits in North America." The Miamis soon removed to the banks of the river St. Joseph, near Lake Michigan.
[33] *Relation*, 1672, 42.
[34] This charge was made from the first establishment of the missions. For remarks on it, see "The Jesuits in North America" and "The Old Régime in Canada."

[Pg 48]

CHAPTER IV.

1667-1672.

FRANCE TAKES POSSESSION OF THE WEST.

TALON.—SAINT-LUSSON.—PERROT.—THE CEREMONY AT SAUT STE. MARIE.—THE
SPEECH OF ALLOUEZ.—COUNT FRONTENAC.

JEAN TALON, intendant of Canada, was full of projects for the good
of the colony. On the one hand, he set himself to the development
of its industries, and, on the other, to the extension of its domain. He
meant to occupy the interior of the continent, control the rivers,
which were its only highways, and hold it for France against every
other nation. On the east, England was to be hemmed within a
narrow strip of seaboard; while, on the south, Talon aimed at
securing a port on the Gulf of Mexico, to keep the Spaniards in
check, and dispute with them the possession of the vast regions
which they claimed as their own. But the interior of the continent
was still an unknown world. It behooved him to explore it; and to
that end he availed himself of Jesuits, officers, fur-traders, and
enterprising schemers like La Salle. His efforts at discovery seem to
have been conducted with a singular economy [Pg 49] of the King's
purse. La Salle paid all the expenses of his first expedition made
under Talon's auspices; and apparently of the second also, though
the intendant announces it in his despatches as an expedition sent
out by himself.[35] When, in 1670, he ordered Daumont de Saint-
Lusson to search for copper mines on Lake Superior, and at the same
time to take formal possession of the whole interior for the King, it
was arranged that he should pay the costs of the journey by trading
with the Indians.[36]

SAINT-LUSSON AND PERROT.

Saint-Lusson set out with a small party of men, and Nicolas Perrot
as his interpreter. Among Canadian *voyageurs*, few names are so

conspicuous as that of Perrot; not because there were not others who matched him in achievement, but because he could write, and left behind him a tolerable account of what he had seen.[37] He was at this time twenty-six years old, and had formerly been an *engagé* of the Jesuits. He was a man of enterprise, courage, and [Pg 50] address,—the last being especially shown in his dealings with Indians, over whom he had great influence. He spoke Algonquin fluently, and was favorably known to many tribes of that family.

Saint-Lusson wintered at the Manitoulin Islands; while Perrot, having first sent messages to the tribes of the north, inviting them to meet the deputy of the governor at the Saut Ste. Marie in the following spring, proceeded to Green Bay, to urge the same invitation upon the tribes of that quarter. They knew him well, and greeted him with clamors of welcome. The Miamis, it is said, received him with a sham battle, which was designed to do him honor, but by which nerves more susceptible would have been severely shaken.[38] They entertained him also with a grand game of *la crosse*, the Indian ball-play. Perrot gives a marvellous account of the authority and state of the Miami chief, who, he says, was attended day and night by a guard of warriors,—an assertion which would be incredible, were it not sustained by the account of the same chief given by the Jesuit Dablon. Of the tribes of the Bay, the greater part promised to send delegates to the Saut; but the Pottawattamies dissuaded the Miami potentate from attempting so long a journey, lest the fatigue incident to it might injure his health; and he [Pg 51] therefore deputed them to represent him and his tribesmen at the great meeting. Their principal chiefs, with those of the Sacs, Winnebagoes, and Menomonies, embarked, and paddled for the place of rendezvous, where they and Perrot arrived on the fifth of May.[39]

Saint-Lusson was here with his men, fifteen in number, among whom was Louis Joliet;[40] and Indians were fast thronging in from their wintering grounds, attracted, as usual, by the fishery of the rapids or moved by the messages sent by Perrot,—Crees, Monsonis, Amikoués, Nipissings, and many more. When fourteen tribes, or their representatives, had arrived, Saint-Lusson prepared to execute the commission with which he was charged.

At the foot of the rapids was the village of the Sauteurs, above the village was a hill, and hard by stood the fort of the Jesuits. On the morning of the fourteenth of June, Saint-Lusson led his followers to the top of the hill, all fully equipped and under arms. Here, too, in the vestments of their priestly office, were four Jesuits,—Claude Dablon, Superior of the Missions of the lakes, Gabriel Druilletes, Claude Allouez, and Louis André.[41] All around the great throng of Indians stood, or crouched, or reclined at length, with eyes and ears intent. A [Pg 52] large cross of wood had been made ready. Dablon, in solemn form, pronounced his blessing on it; and then it was reared and planted in the ground, while the Frenchmen, uncovered, sang the *Vexilla Regis*. Then a post of cedar was planted beside it, with a metal plate attached, engraven with the royal arms; while Saint-Lusson's followers sang the *Exaudiat*, and one of the Jesuits uttered a prayer for the King. Saint-Lusson now advanced, and, holding his sword in one hand, and raising with the other a sod of earth, proclaimed in a loud voice,—

"In the name of the Most High, Mighty, and Redoubted Monarch, Louis, Fourteenth of that name, Most Christian King of France and of Navarre, I take possession of this place, Sainte Marie du Saut, as also of Lakes Huron and Superior, the Island of Manitoulin, and all countries, rivers, lakes, and streams contiguous and adjacent thereunto,—both those which have been discovered and those which may be discovered hereafter, in all their length and breadth, bounded on the one side by the seas of the North and of the West, and on the other by the South Sea: declaring to the nations thereof that from this time forth they are vassals of his Majesty, bound to obey his laws and follow his customs; promising them on his part all succor and protection against the incursions and invasions of their enemies: declaring to all other potentates, princes, sovereigns, states, and republics,—to them and to their subjects,—that they cannot and are not to seize or settle upon any [Pg 53] parts of the aforesaid countries, save only under the good pleasure of His Most Christian Majesty, and of him who will govern in his behalf; and this on pain of incurring his resentment and the efforts of his arms. *Vive le Roi.*"[42]

The Frenchmen fired their guns and shouted "Vive le Roi," and the yelps of the astonished Indians mingled with the din.

What now remains of the sovereignty thus pompously proclaimed? Now and then the accents of France on the lips of some straggling boatman or vagabond half-breed,—this, and nothing more.

ALLOUEZ'S HARANGUE.

When the uproar was over, Father Allouez addressed the Indians in a solemn harangue; and these were his words: "It is a good work, my brothers, an important work, a great work, that brings us together in council to-day. Look up at the cross which rises so high above your heads. It was there that Jesus Christ, the Son of God, after making himself a man for the love of men, was nailed and died, to satisfy his Eternal Father for our sins. He is the master of our lives; the ruler of Heaven, Earth, and Hell. It is he of whom I am continually speaking to you, and whose name and word I have borne through all your country. But look at this post to which are fixed the arms of the great chief of France, whom we call King. He lives across the sea. He is the chief of the greatest chiefs, and has no equal on earth. All the chiefs whom you have ever seen are but children [Pg 54] beside him. He is like a great tree, and they are but the little herbs that one walks over and tramples under foot. You know Onontio,[43] that famous chief at Quebec; you know and you have seen that he is the terror of the Iroquois, and that his very name makes them tremble, since he has laid their country waste and burned their towns with fire. Across the sea there are ten thousand Onontios like him, who are but the warriors of our great King, of whom I have told you. When he says, 'I am going to war,' everybody obeys his orders; and each of these ten thousand chiefs raises a troop of a hundred warriors, some on sea and some on land. Some embark in great ships, such as you have seen at Quebec. Your canoes carry only four or five men, or, at the most, ten or twelve; but our ships carry four or five hundred, and sometimes a thousand. Others go to war by land, and in such numbers that if they stood in a double file they would reach from here to Mississaquenk, which is more than twenty leagues off. When our King attacks his enemies, he is more terrible than the thunder: the earth trembles; the air and the sea are all on fire with the blaze of his cannon: he is seen in the midst of his warriors, covered over with the blood of his enemies, whom he kills in such numbers that he does not reckon them by the scalps, but by the streams of blood which he causes to flow. He takes so many prisoners that he holds them in no account, but lets them go where they will, to show [Pg 55] that he is not afraid of them. But now nobody dares make war on him. All the nations beyond the sea have submitted to him and begged humbly for peace. Men come from every quarter of the earth to listen to him and admire him. All that is done in the world is decided by him alone.

"But what shall I say of his riches? You think yourselves rich when you have ten or twelve sacks of corn, a few hatchets, beads, kettles, and other things of that sort. He has cities of his own, more than there are of men in all this country for five hundred leagues around. In each city there are store-houses where there are hatchets enough to cut down all your forests, kettles enough to cook all your moose, and beads enough to fill all your lodges. His house is longer than from here to the top of the Saut,—that is to say, more than half a league,—and higher than your tallest trees; and it holds more families than the largest of your towns."[44] The father added more in a similar strain; but the peroration of his harangue is not on record.

Whatever impression this curious effort of Jesuit rhetoric may have produced upon the hearers, it did not prevent them from stripping the royal arms from the post to which they were nailed, as soon as Saint-Lusson and his men had left the Saut; probably, not because they understood the import of the symbol, but because they feared it as a charm. Saint-Lusson [Pg 56] proceeded to Lake Superior, where, however, he accomplished nothing, except, perhaps, a traffic with the Indians on his own account; and he soon after returned to Quebec. Talon was resolved to find the Mississippi, the most interesting object of search, and seemingly the most attainable, in the wild and vague domain which he had just claimed for the King. The Indians had described it; the Jesuits were eager to discover it; and La Salle, if he had not reached it, had explored two several avenues by which it might be approached. Talon looked about him for a fit agent of the enterprise, and made choice of Louis Joliet, who had returned from Lake Superior.[45] But the intendant was not to see the fulfilment of his design. His busy and useful career in Canada was drawing to an end. A misunderstanding had arisen between him and the governor, Courcelle. Both were faithful servants of the King; but the relations between the two chiefs of the colony were of a nature necessarily so critical, that a conflict of authority was scarcely to be avoided. Each thought his functions encroached upon, and both asked for recall. Another governor succeeded; one who was to stamp his mark, broad, bold, and ineffaceable, on the most memorable page of French-American History,—Louis de Buade, Count of Palluau and Frontenac.

FOOTNOTES:

[35] At least, La Salle was in great need of money, about the time of his second journey. On the sixth of August, 1671, he had received on credit, "dans son grand besoin et nécessité," from Branssac, fiscal attorney of the Seminary, merchandise to the amount of four hundred and fifty livres; and on the eighteenth of December of the following year he gave his promise to pay the same sum, in money or furs, in the August following. Faillon found the papers in the ancient records of Montreal.

[36] In his despatch of 2d Nov., 1671, Talon writes to the King that "Saint-Lusson's expedition will cost nothing, as he has received beaver enough from the Indians to pay him."

[37] *Mœurs, Coustumes, et Relligion des Sauvages de l'Amérique Septentrionale.* This work of Perrot, hitherto unpublished, appeared in

1864, under the editorship of Father Tailhan, S.J. A great part of it is incorporated in La Potherie.

[38] See La Potherie, ii. 125. Perrot himself does not mention it. Charlevoix erroneously places this interview at Chicago. Perrot's narrative shows that he did not go farther than the tribes of Green Bay; and the Miamis were then, as we have seen, on the upper part of Fox River.

[39] Perrot, *Mémoires*, 127.

[40] *Procès Verbal de la Prise de Possession, etc., 14 Juin, 1671.* The names are attached to this instrument.

[41] Marquette is said to have been present; but the official act just cited, proves the contrary. He was still at St. Esprit.

[42] *Procès Verbal de la Prise de Possession.*

[43] The Indian name of the governor of Canada.

[44] A close translation of Dablon's report of the speech. See *Relation*, 1671, 27.

[45] *Lettre de Frontenac au Ministre, 2 Nov., 1672.* In the Brodhead Collection, by a copyist's error, the name of the Chevalier de Grandfontaine is substituted for that of Talon.

[Pg 57]

CHAPTER V.

1672-1675.

THE DISCOVERY OF THE MISSISSIPPI.

JOLIET SENT TO FIND THE MISSISSIPPI. MARQUETTE. —DEPARTURE. —GREEN BAY. —
THE WISCONSIN. —THE MISSISSIPPI. —INDIANS. —MANITOUS. —THE ARKANSAS. —
THE ILLINOIS. —JOLIET'S MISFORTUNE. —MARQUETTE AT CHICAGO: HIS ILLNESS; HIS
DEATH.

IF Talon had remained in the colony, Frontenac would infallibly
have quarrelled with him; but he was too clear-sighted not to
approve his plans for the discovery and occupation of the interior.
Before sailing for France, Talon recommended Joliet as a suitable
agent for the discovery of the Mississippi, and the governor accepted
his counsel.[46]

Louis Joliet was the son of a wagon-maker in the service of the
Company of the Hundred Associates,[47] then owners of Canada. He
was born at Quebec in 1645, and was educated by the Jesuits. When
still very young, he resolved to be a priest. He received the tonsure
and the minor orders at the age of seventeen. [Pg 58] Four years after,
he is mentioned with especial honor for the part he bore in the
disputes in philosophy, at which the dignitaries of the colony were
present, and in which the intendant himself took part.[48] Not long
after, he renounced his clerical vocation, and turned fur-trader.
Talon sent him, with one Péré, to explore the copper-mines of Lake
Superior; and it was on his return from this expedition that he met
La Salle and the Sulpitians near the head of Lake Ontario.[49]

In what we know of Joliet, there is nothing that reveals any salient
or distinctive trait of character, any especial breadth of view or
boldness of design. He appears to have been simply a merchant,
intelligent, well educated, courageous, hardy, and enterprising.
Though he had renounced the priesthood, he retained his partiality
for the Jesuits; and it is more than probable that their influence had

aided not a little to determine Talon's choice. One of their [Pg 59] number, Jacques Marquette, was chosen to accompany him.

MARQUETTE.

He passed up the lakes to Michilimackinac, and found his destined companion at Point St. Ignace, on the north side of the strait, where, in his palisaded mission-house and chapel, he had labored for two years past to instruct the Huron refugees from St. Esprit, and a band of Ottawas who had joined them. Marquette was born in 1637, of an old and honorable family at Laon, in the north of France, and was now thirty-five years of age. When about seventeen, he had joined the Jesuits, evidently from motives purely religious; and in 1666 he was sent to the missions of Canada. At first, he was destined to the station of Tadoussac; and to prepare himself for it, he studied the Montagnais language under Gabriel Druilletes. But his destination was changed, and he was sent to the Upper Lakes in 1668, where he had since remained. His talents as a linguist must have been great; for within a few years he learned to speak with ease six Indian languages. The traits of his character are unmistakable. He was of the brotherhood of the early Canadian missionaries, and the true counterpart of Garnier or Jogues. He was a devout votary of the Virgin Mary, who, imaged to his mind in shapes of the most transcendent loveliness with which the pencil of human genius has ever informed the canvas, was to him the object of an adoration not unmingled with a sentiment of chivalrous devotion. The longings of a sensitive heart, [Pg 60] divorced from earth, sought solace in the skies. A subtile element of romance was blended with the fervor of his worship, and hung like an illumined cloud over the harsh and hard realities of his daily lot. Kindled by the smile of his celestial mistress, his gentle and noble nature knew no fear. For her he burned to dare and to suffer, discover new lands and conquer new realms to her sway.

He begins the journal of his voyage thus: "The day of the Immaculate Conception of the Holy Virgin; whom I had continually invoked since I came to this country of the Ottawas to obtain from God the favor of being enabled to visit the nations on the river Mississippi,—this very day was precisely that on which M. Joliet arrived with orders from Count Frontenac, our governor, and from M. Talon, our intendant, to go with me on this discovery. I was all the more delighted at this good news, because I saw my plans about to be accomplished, and found myself in the happy necessity of exposing my life for the salvation of all these tribes,—and especially of the Illinois, who, when I was at Point St. Esprit, had begged me very earnestly to bring the word of God among them."

DEPARTURE.

The outfit of the travellers was very simple. They provided themselves with two birch canoes, and a supply of smoked meat and Indian corn; embarked with five men, and began their voyage on the seventeenth of May. They had obtained all possible information from the Indians, and had made, by means [Pg 61] of it, a species of map of their intended route. "Above all," writes Marquette, "I placed our voyage under the protection of the Holy Virgin Immaculate, promising that if she granted us the favor of discovering the great river, I would give it the name of the Conception."[50] Their course was westward; and, plying their paddles, they passed the Straits of Michilimackinac, and coasted the northern shores of Lake Michigan, landing at evening to build their camp-fire at the edge of the forest, and draw up their canoes on the strand. They soon reached the river Menomonie, and ascended it to the village of the Menomonies, or Wild-rice Indians.[51] When they told them the object of their voyage, they were filled with astonishment, and used their best ingenuity to dissuade them. The banks of the Mississippi, they said, were inhabited by ferocious tribes, who put every stranger to death, tomahawking all new-comers without cause or provocation. They added that there was a demon in a certain part of the river, whose roar could be heard at a great distance, and who would engulf them in the abyss where he dwelt; that its waters were full of frightful monsters, who would devour them and their canoe;

and, finally, that the [Pg 62] heat was so great that they would perish inevitably. Marquette set their counsel at naught, gave them a few words of instruction in the mysteries of the Faith, taught them a prayer, and bade them farewell.

The travellers next reached the mission at the head of Green Bay; entered Fox River; with difficulty and labor dragged their canoes up the long and tumultuous rapids; crossed Lake Winnebago; and followed the quiet windings of the river beyond, where they glided through an endless growth of wild rice, and scared the innumerable birds that fed upon it. On either hand rolled the prairie, dotted with groves and trees, browsing elk and deer.[52] On the seventh of June, they reached the Mascoutins and Miamis, who, since the visit of Dablon and Allouez, had been joined by the Kickapoos. Marquette, who had an eye for natural beauty, was delighted with the situation of the town, which he describes as standing on the crown of a hill; while, all around, the prairie stretched beyond the sight, interspersed with groves and belts of tall forest. But he was still more delighted when he saw a cross planted in the midst of the place. The Indians had decorated it with a number of dressed deer-skins, red girdles, and bows and arrows, which they had hung upon it as an offering to the Great Manitou of the French; a sight by which Marquette says he was "extremely consoled."

[Pg 63]

THE WISCONSIN RIVER.

The travellers had no sooner reached the town than they called the chiefs and elders to a council. Joliet told them that the governor of Canada had sent him to discover new countries, and that God had sent his companion to teach the true faith to the inhabitants; and he prayed for guides to show them the way to the waters of the Wisconsin. The council readily consented; and on the tenth of June the Frenchmen embarked again, with two Indians to conduct them. All the town came down to the shore to see their departure. Here were the Miamis, with long locks of hair dangling over each ear, after a fashion which Marquette thought very becoming; and here, too, the Mascoutins and the Kickapoos, whom he describes as mere boors in comparison with their Miami townsmen. All stared alike at the seven adventurers, marvelling that men could be found to risk an enterprise so hazardous.

The river twisted among lakes and marshes choked with wild rice; and, but for their guides, they could scarcely have followed the perplexed and narrow channel. It brought them at last to the portage, where, after carrying their canoes a mile and a half over the prairie and through the marsh, they launched them on the Wisconsin, bade farewell to the waters that flowed to the St. Lawrence, and committed themselves to the current that was to bear them they knew not whither,—perhaps to the Gulf of Mexico, perhaps to the South Sea or the Gulf of California. They glided calmly down the tranquil stream, by [Pg 64] islands choked with trees and matted with entangling grape-vines; by forests, groves, and prairies, the parks and pleasure-grounds of a prodigal Nature; by thickets and marshes and broad bare sand-bars; under the shadowing trees, between whose tops looked down from afar the bold brow of some woody bluff. At night, the bivouac,—the canoes inverted on the bank, the flickering fire, the meal of bison-flesh or venison, the evening pipes, and slumber beneath the stars; and when in the morning they embarked again, the mist hung on the river like a bridal veil, then melted before the sun, till the glassy water and the languid woods basked breathless in the sultry glare.[53]

THE MISSISSIPPI.

On the seventeenth of June they saw on their right the broad meadows, bounded in the distance by rugged hills, where now stand the town and fort of Prairie du Chien. Before them a wide and rapid current coursed athwart their way, by the foot of lofty heights wrapped thick in forests. They had found what they sought, and "with a joy," writes Marquette, "which I cannot express," they steered forth their canoes on the eddies of the Mississippi.

Turning southward, they paddled down the stream, through a solitude unrelieved by the faintest trace of man. A large fish, apparently one of the huge cat-fish of the Mississippi, blundered against Marquette's canoe, with a force which seems to have startled him; and once, as they drew in their net, they caught [Pg 65] a "spade-fish," whose eccentric appearance greatly astonished them. At length the buffalo began to appear, grazing in herds on the great prairies which then bordered the river; and Marquette describes the fierce and stupid look of the old bulls, as they stared at the intruders through the tangled mane which nearly blinded them.

THE ILLINOIS INDIANS.

They advanced with extreme caution, landed at night, and made a fire to cook their evening meal; then extinguished it, embarked again, paddled some way farther, and anchored in the stream, keeping a man on the watch till morning. They had journeyed more than a fortnight without meeting a human being, when, on the twenty-fifth, they discovered footprints of men in the mud of the western bank, and a well-trodden path that led to the adjacent prairie. Joliet and Marquette resolved to follow it; and leaving the canoes in charge of their men, they set out on their hazardous adventure. The day was fair, and they walked two leagues in silence, following the path through the forest and across the sunny prairie, till they discovered an Indian village on the banks of a river, and two others on a hill half a league distant.[54] Now, with beating hearts, they invoked the aid of Heaven, and, again advancing, came so near, without being seen, that they could [Pg 66] hear the voices of the Indians among the wigwams. Then they stood forth in full view, and shouted to attract attention. There was great commotion in the village. The inmates swarmed out of their huts, and four of their chief men presently came forward to meet the strangers, advancing very deliberately, and holding up toward the sun two calumets, or peace-pipes, decorated with feathers. They stopped abruptly before the two Frenchmen, and stood gazing at them without speaking a word. Marquette was much relieved on seeing that they wore French cloth, whence he judged that they must be friends and allies. He broke the silence, and asked them who they were; whereupon they answered that they were Illinois, and offered the pipe; which having been duly smoked, they all went together to the village. Here the chief received the travellers after a singular fashion, meant to do them honor. He stood stark naked at the door of a large wigwam, holding up both hands as if to shield his eyes. "Frenchmen, how bright the sun shines when you come to visit us! All our village awaits you; and you shall enter our wigwams in peace." So saying, he led them into his own, which was crowded to suffocation with savages, staring at their guests in silence. Having smoked with the chiefs and old men, they were invited to visit the great chief of all the Illinois, at one of the villages they had seen in the distance; and thither they proceeded, followed by a throng of warriors, squaws, and children. On [Pg 67] arriving, they were forced to smoke again, and listen to a speech of welcome from the great chief, who delivered it standing between two old men, naked like himself. His lodge was crowded with the dignitaries of the tribe, whom Marquette addressed in Algonquin, announcing himself as a messenger sent by the God who had made them, and whom it behooves them to recognize and obey. He added a few words touching the power and glory of Count Frontenac, and concluded by asking information concerning the Mississippi, and the tribes along its banks, whom he was on his way to visit. The chief replied with a speech of compliment; assuring his guests that their presence added flavor to his tobacco, made the river more calm, the sky more serene, and the earth more beautiful. In conclusion, he gave them a young slave and a calumet, begging them at the same time to abandon their purpose of descending the Mississippi.

A feast of four courses now followed. First, a wooden bowl full of a porridge of Indian meal boiled with grease was set before the guests; and the master of ceremonies fed them in turn, like infants, with a large spoon. Then appeared a platter of fish; and the same functionary, carefully removing the bones with his fingers, and blowing on the morsels to cool them, placed them in the mouths of the two Frenchmen. A large dog, killed and cooked for the occasion, was next placed before them; but, failing to tempt their fastidious appetites, was supplanted by a [Pg 68] dish of fat buffalo-meat, which concluded the entertainment. The crowd having dispersed, buffalo-robes were spread on the ground, and Marquette and Joliet spent the night on the scene of the late festivity. In the morning, the chief, with some six hundred of his tribesmen, escorted them to their canoes, and bade them, after their stolid fashion, a friendly farewell.

A REAL DANGER.

Again they were on their way, slowly drifting down the great river. They passed the mouth of the Illinois, and glided beneath that line of rocks on the eastern side, cut into fantastic forms by the elements, and marked as "The Ruined Castles" on some of the early French maps. Presently they beheld a sight which reminded them that the Devil was still lord paramount of this wilderness. On the flat face of a high rock were painted, in red, black, and green, a pair of monsters, each "as large as a calf, with horns like a deer, red eyes, a beard like a tiger, and a frightful expression of countenance. The face is something like that of a man, the body covered with scales; and the tail so long that it passes entirely round the body, over the head and between the legs, ending like that of a fish." Such is the account which the worthy Jesuit gives of these manitous, or Indian gods.[55] He confesses that at first they frightened [Pg 69] him; and his imagination and that of his credulous companions was so wrought upon by these unhallowed efforts of Indian art, that they continued for a long time to talk of them as they plied their paddles. They were thus engaged, when they were suddenly aroused by a real danger. A torrent of yellow mud rushed furiously athwart the calm blue current of the Mississippi, boiling and surging, and sweeping in its course logs, branches, and uprooted trees. They had reached the mouth of the Missouri, where that savage river, descending from its mad career through a vast unknown of barbarism, poured its turbid floods into the bosom of its gentler sister. Their light canoes whirled on the miry vortex like dry leaves on an angry brook. "I never," writes Marquette, "saw anything more terrific;" but they escaped with their fright, and held their way down the turbulent and swollen current of the now united rivers.[56] They passed the lonely forest that covered [Pg 70] the site of the destined city of St. Louis, and, a few days later, saw on their left the mouth of the stream to which the Iroquois had given the well-merited name of Ohio, or the "Beautiful River."[57] Soon they began to see the marshy shores buried in a dense growth of the cane, with its tall straight stems and feathery light-green foliage. The sun glowed through the hazy air with a languid stifling heat, and by day and night mosquitoes in myriads left them no peace. They floated slowly down the current, crouched in the shade of the sails which they had spread as awnings, when suddenly they saw Indians on the east bank. The surprise was mutual, and each party was as much frightened as the other. Marquette hastened to display the calumet which the Illinois had given him by way of passport; and the Indians, recognizing the pacific symbol, replied with an invitation to land. Evidently, they were in communication with Europeans, for they were armed with guns, knives, and hatchets, wore garments of cloth, and carried their gunpowder in small bottles of thick glass. They feasted the Frenchmen with buffalo-meat, bear's oil, and white plums; and gave them a variety of doubtful information, [Pg 71] including the agreeable but delusive assurance that they would reach the mouth of the river in ten days. It was, in fact, more than a thousand miles distant.

THE LOWER MISSISSIPPI.

They resumed their course, and again floated down the interminable monotony of river, marsh, and forest. Day after day passed on in solitude, and they had paddled some three hundred miles since their meeting with the Indians, when, as they neared the mouth of the Arkansas, they saw a cluster of wigwams on the west bank. Their inmates were all astir, yelling the war-whoop, snatching their weapons, and running to the shore to meet the strangers, who, on their part, called for succor to the Virgin. In truth, they had need of her aid; for several large wooden canoes, filled with savages, were putting out from the shore, above and below them, to cut off their retreat, while a swarm of headlong young warriors waded into the water to attack them. The current proved too strong; and, failing to reach the canoes of the Frenchmen, one of them threw his war-club, which flew over the heads of the startled travellers. Meanwhile, Marquette had not ceased to hold up his calumet, to which the excited crowd gave no heed, but strung their bows and notched their arrows for immediate action; when at length the elders of the village arrived, saw the peace-pipe, restrained the ardor of the youth, and urged the Frenchmen to come ashore. Marquette and his companions complied, trembling, and found a better reception than [Pg 72] they had reason to expect. One of the Indians spoke a little Illinois, and served as interpreter; a friendly conference was followed by a feast of sagamite and fish; and the travellers, not without sore misgivings, spent the night in the lodges of their entertainers.[58]

THE ARKANSAS.

Early in the morning, they embarked again, and proceeded to a village of the Arkansas tribe, about eight leagues below. Notice of their coming was sent before them by their late hosts; and as they drew near they were met by a canoe, in the prow of which stood a naked personage, holding a calumet, singing, and making gestures of friendship. On reaching the village, which was on the east side,[59] opposite the mouth of the river Arkansas, they were conducted to a sort of scaffold, before the lodge of the war-chief. The space beneath had been prepared for their reception, the ground being neatly covered with rush mats. On these they were seated; the warriors sat around them in a semi-circle; then the elders of the tribe; and then the promiscuous crowd of villagers, standing, and staring over the heads of the more dignified members of the assembly. All the men were naked; but, to compensate for the lack of clothing, they wore strings of beads in their noses and ears. The women were clothed in shabby skins, and wore their hair clumped in a mass behind each [Pg 73] ear. By good luck, there was a young Indian in the village, who had an excellent knowledge of Illinois; and through him Marquette endeavored to explain the mysteries of Christianity, and to gain information concerning the river below. To this end he gave his auditors the presents indispensable on such occasions, but received very little in return. They told him that the Mississippi was infested by hostile Indians, armed with guns procured from white men; and that they, the Arkansas, stood in such fear of them that they dared not hunt the buffalo, but were forced to live on Indian corn, of which they raised three crops a year.

During the speeches on either side, food was brought in without ceasing,—sometimes a platter of sagamite or mush; sometimes of corn boiled whole; sometimes a roasted dog. The villagers had large earthen pots and platters, made by themselves with tolerable skill, as well as hatchets, knives, and beads, gained by traffic with the Illinois and other tribes in contact with the French or Spaniards. All day there was feasting without respite, after the merciless practice of Indian hospitality; but at night some of their entertainers proposed to kill and plunder them,—a scheme which was defeated by the vigilance of the chief, who visited their quarters, and danced the calumet dance to reassure his guests.

The travellers now held counsel as to what course they should take. They had gone far enough, as they thought, to establish one important point,—that [Pg 74] the Mississippi discharged its waters, not into the Atlantic or sea of Virginia, nor into the Gulf of California or Vermilion Sea, but into the Gulf of Mexico. They thought themselves nearer to its mouth than they actually were, the distance being still about seven hundred miles; and they feared that if they went farther they might be killed by Indians or captured by Spaniards, whereby the results of their discovery would be lost. Therefore they resolved to return to Canada, and report what they had seen.

They left the Arkansas village, and began their homeward voyage on the seventeenth of July. It was no easy task to urge their way upward, in the heat of midsummer, against the current of the dark and gloomy stream, toiling all day under the parching sun, and sleeping at night in the exhalations of the unwholesome shore, or in the narrow confines of their birchen vessels, anchored on the river. Marquette was attacked with dysentery. Languid and well-nigh spent, he invoked his celestial mistress, as day after day, and week after week, they won their slow way northward. At length, they reached the Illinois, and, entering its mouth, followed its course, charmed, as they went, with its placid waters, its shady forests, and its rich plains, grazed by the bison and the deer. They stopped at a spot soon to be made famous in the annals of western discovery. This was a village of the Illinois, then called "Kaskaskia;" a name afterwards transferred to [Pg 75] another locality.[60] A chief, with a band of young warriors, offered to guide them to the Lake of the Illinois; that is to say, Lake Michigan. Thither they repaired; and, coasting its shores, reached Green Bay at the end of September, after an absence of about four months, during which they had paddled their canoes somewhat more than two thousand five hundred miles.[61]

RETURN TO CANADA.

Marquette remained to recruit his exhausted strength; but Joliet descended to Quebec, to bear the report of his discovery to Count Frontenac. Fortune had wonderfully favored him on his long and perilous journey; but now she abandoned him on the very threshold of home. At the foot of the rapids of La Chine, and immediately above Montreal, [Pg 76] his canoe was overset, two of his men and an Indian boy were drowned, all his papers were lost, and he himself narrowly escaped.[62] In a letter to Frontenac, he speaks of the accident as follows: "I had escaped every peril from the Indians; I had passed forty-two rapids; and was on the point of disembarking, full of joy at the success of so long and difficult an enterprise, when my canoe capsized, after all the danger seemed over. I lost two men and my box of papers, within sight of the first French settlements, which I had left almost two years before. Nothing remains to me but my life, and the ardent desire to employ it on any service which you may please to direct."[63]

[Pg 77]

MARQUETTE'S MISSION.

Marquette spent the winter and the following summer at the mission of Green Bay, still suffering from his malady. In the autumn, however, it abated; and he was permitted by his Superior to attempt the execution of a plan to which he was devotedly attached,—the founding, at the principal town of the Illinois, of a mission to be called the "Immaculate Conception," a name which he had already given to the river Mississippi. He set out on this errand on the twenty-fifth of October, accompanied by two men, named Pierre and Jacques, one of whom had been with him on his great journey of discovery. A band of Pottawattamies and another band of Illinois also joined him. The united parties—ten canoes in all—followed the east shore of Green Bay as far as the inlet then called "Sturgeon Cove," from the head of which they crossed by a difficult portage through the forest to the shore of Lake Michigan. November had come. The bright hues of the autumn foliage were changed to rusty brown. The shore was desolate, and the lake was stormy. They were more [Pg 78] than a month in coasting its western border, when at length they reached the river Chicago, entered it, and ascended about two leagues. Marquette's disease had lately returned, and hemorrhage now ensued. He told his two companions that this journey would be his last. In the condition in which he was, it was impossible to go farther. The two men built a log hut by the river, and here they prepared to spend the winter; while Marquette, feeble as he was, began the spiritual exercises of Saint Ignatius, and confessed his two companions twice a week.

Meadow, marsh, and forest were sheeted with snow, but game was abundant. Pierre and Jacques killed buffalo and deer, and shot wild turkeys close to their hut. There was an encampment of Illinois within two days' journey; and other Indians, passing by this well-known thoroughfare, occasionally visited them, treating the exiles kindly, and sometimes bringing them game and Indian corn. Eighteen leagues distant was the camp of two adventurous French traders,—one of them, a noted *coureur de bois*, nicknamed La Taupine;[64] and the other, a self-styled surgeon. They also visited Marquette, and befriended him to the best of their power.

THE MISSION AT KASKASKIA.

Urged by a burning desire to lay, before he died, the foundation of his new mission of the Immaculate Conception, Marquette begged his two followers to [Pg 79] join him in a *novena*, or nine days' devotion to the Virgin. In consequence of this, as he believed, his disease relented; he began to regain strength, and in March was able to resume the journey. On the thirtieth of the month, they left their hut, which had been inundated by a sudden rise of the river, and carried their canoe through mud and water over the portage which led to the Des Plaines. Marquette knew the way, for he had passed by this route on his return from the Mississippi. Amid the rains of opening spring, they floated down the swollen current of the Des Plaines, by naked woods and spongy, saturated prairies, till they reached its junction with the main stream of the Illinois, which they descended to their destination, the Indian town which Marquette calls "Kaskaskia." Here, as we are told, he was received "like an angel from Heaven." He passed from wigwam to wigwam, telling the listening crowds of God and the Virgin, Paradise and Hell, angels and demons; and, when he thought their minds prepared, he summoned them all to a grand council.

It took place near the town, on the great meadow which lies between the river and the modern village of Utica. Here five hundred chiefs and old men were seated in a ring; behind stood fifteen hundred youths and warriors, and behind these again all the women and children of the village. Marquette, standing in the midst, displayed four large pictures of the Virgin; harangued the assembly on the mysteries of the Faith, and exhorted them to adopt it. [Pg 80] The temper of his auditory met his utmost wishes. They begged him to stay among them and continue his instructions; but his life was fast ebbing away, and it behooved him to depart.

BURIAL OF MARQUETTE.

A few days after Easter he left the village, escorted by a crowd of Indians, who followed him as far as Lake Michigan. Here he embarked with his two companions. Their destination was Michilimackinac, and their course lay along the eastern borders of the lake. As, in the freshness of advancing spring, Pierre and Jacques urged their canoe along that lonely and savage shore, the priest lay with dimmed sight and prostrated strength, communing with the Virgin and the angels. On the nineteenth of May, he felt that his hour was near; and, as they passed the mouth of a small river, he requested his companions to land. They complied, built a shed of bark on a rising ground near the bank, and carried thither the dying Jesuit. With perfect cheerfulness and composure, he gave directions for his burial, asked their forgiveness for the trouble he had caused them, administered to them the sacrament of penitence, and thanked God that he was permitted to die in the wilderness, a missionary of the Faith and a member of the Jesuit brotherhood. At night, seeing that they were fatigued, he told them to take rest, saying that he would call them when he felt his time approaching. Two or three hours after, they heard a feeble voice, and, hastening to his side, found him at the point of death. He expired calmly, murmuring [Pg 81] the names of Jesus and Mary, with his eyes fixed on the crucifix which one of his followers held before him. They dug a grave beside the hut, and here they buried him according to the directions which he had given them; then, re-embarking, they made their way to Michilimackinac, to bear the tidings to the priests at the mission of St. Ignace.[65]

In the winter of 1676, a party of Kiskakon Ottawas were hunting on Lake Michigan; and when, in the following spring, they prepared to return home, they bethought them, in accordance with an Indian custom, of taking with them the bones of Marquette, who had been their instructor at the mission of St. Esprit. They repaired to the spot, found the grave, opened it, washed and dried the bones and placed them carefully in a box of birch-bark. Then, in a procession of thirty canoes, they bore it, singing their funeral songs, to St. Ignace of Michilimackinac. As they approached, priests, Indians, and traders all thronged to the shore. The relics of Marquette were received with solemn ceremony, and buried beneath the floor of the little chapel of the mission.[66]

[Pg 82]

FOOTNOTES:

[46] *Lettre de Frontenac au Ministre, 2 Nov., 1672; Ibid., 14 Nov., 1674.*

[47] See "The Jesuits in North America."

[48] "Le 2 Juillet (1666) les premières disputes de philosophie se font dans la congrégation avec succès. Toutes les puissances s'y trouvent; M. l'Intendant entr'autres y a argumenté très-bien. M. Jolliet et Pierre Francheville y ont très-bien répondu de toute la logique."—*Journal des Jésuites.*

[49] Nothing was known of Joliet till Shea investigated his history. Ferland, in his *Notes sur les Registres de Notre-Dame de Québec*; Faillon, in his *Colonie Française en Canada*; and Margry, in a series of papers in the *Journal Général de l'Instruction Publique*,—have thrown much new light on his life. From journals of a voyage made by him at a later period to the coast of Labrador, given in substance by Margry, he seems to have been a man of close and intelligent observation. His mathematical acquirements appear to have been very considerable.

[50] The doctrine of the Immaculate Conception, sanctioned in our own time by the Pope, was always a favorite tenet of the Jesuits; and Marquette was especially devoted to it.

[51] The Malhoumines, Malouminek, Oumalouminek, or Nation des Folles-Avoines, of early French writers. The *folle-avoine*, wild oats or

"wild rice" (*Zizania aquatica*), was their ordinary food, as also of o[...]
tribes of this region.

[52] Dablon, on his journey with Allouez in 1670, was delighted with the
aspect of the country and the abundance of game along this river. Carver,
a century later, speaks to the same effect, saying that the birds rose up in
clouds from the wild-rice marshes.

[53] The above traits of the scenery of the Wisconsin are taken from
personal observation of the river during midsummer.

[54] The Indian villages, under the names of Peouaria (*Peoria*) and
Moingouena, are represented in Marquette's map upon a river
corresponding in position with the Des Moines; though the distance from
the Wisconsin, as given by him, would indicate a river farther north.

[55] The rock where these figures were painted is immediately above the
city of Alton. The tradition of their existence remains, though they are
entirely effaced by time. In 1867, when I passed the place, a part of the
rock had been quarried away, and, instead of Marquette's monsters, it bore
a huge advertisement of "Plantation Bitters." Some years ago, certain
persons, with more zeal than knowledge, proposed to restore the figures,
after conceptions of their own; but the idea was abandoned.

Marquette made a drawing of the two monsters, but it is lost. I have,
however, a fac-simile of a map made a few years later, by order of
the Intendant Duchesneau, which is decorated with the portrait of
one of them, answering to Marquette's description, and probably
copied from his drawing. St. Cosme, who saw them in 1699, says
that they were even then almost effaced. Douay and Joutel also
speak of them,—the former, bitterly hostile to his Jesuit
contemporaries, charging Marquette with exaggeration in his
account of them. Joutel could see nothing terrifying in their
appearance; but he says that his Indians made sacrifices to them as
they passed.

[56] The Missouri is called "Pekitanouï" by Marquette. It also bears, on
early French maps, the names of "Rivière des Osages," and "Rivière des
Emissourites," or "Oumessourits." On Marquette's map, a tribe of this
name is placed near its banks, just above the Osages. Judging by the course
of the Mississippi that it discharged into the Gulf of Mexico, he conceived
the hope of one day reaching the South Sea by way of the Missouri.

ette's map, "Ouabouskiaou." On some of the earliest
bache" (Wabash).
lled "Mitchigamea," is represented on several

, the Arkansas were all on the west side.

[60] Marquette says that it consisted at this time of seventy-four lodges. These, like the Huron and Iroquois lodges, contained each several fires and several families. This village was about seven miles below the site of the present town of Ottawa.

[61] The journal of Marquette, first published in an imperfect form by Thevenot, in 1681, has been reprinted by Mr. Lenox, under the direction of Mr. Shea, from the manuscript preserved in the archives of the Canadian Jesuits. It will also be found in Shea's *Discovery and Exploration of the Mississippi Valley*, and the *Relations Inédites* of Martin. The true map of Marquette accompanies all these publications. The map published by Thevenot and reproduced by Bancroft is not Marquette's. The original of this, of which I have a fac-simile, bears the title *Carte de la Nouvelle Découverte que les Pères Jésuites ont faite en l'année 1672, et continuée par le Père Jacques Marquette, etc.* The return route of the expedition is incorrectly laid down on it. A manuscript map of the Jesuit Raffeix, preserved in the Bibliothèque Impériale, is more accurate in this particular. I have also another contemporary manuscript map, indicating the various Jesuit stations in the West at this time, and representing the Mississippi, as discovered by Marquette. For these and other maps, see Appendix.

[62] *Lettre de Frontenac au Ministre, Québec, 14 Nov., 1674.*

[63] This letter is appended to Joliet's smaller map of his discoveries. See Appendix. Compare *Détails sur le Voyage de Louis Joliet* and *Relation de la Descouverte de plusieurs Pays situez au midi de la Nouvelle France, faite en 1673* (Margry, i. 259). These are oral accounts given by Joliet after the loss of his papers. Also, *Lettre de Joliet, Oct. 10, 1674* (Harrisse). On the seventh of October, 1675, Joliet married Claire Bissot, daughter of a wealthy Canadian merchant, engaged in trade with the northern Indians. This drew Joliet's attention to Hudson's Bay; and he made a journey thither in 1679, by way of the Saguenay. He found three English forts on the bay, occupied by about sixty men, who had also an armed vessel of twelve guns and several small trading-craft. The English held out great inducements to Joliet to join them; but he declined, and returned to Quebec, where he reported that unless these formidable rivals were dispossessed, the trade of Canada would be ruined. In consequence of this report, some of the

principal merchants of the colony formed a company to compete with the English in the trade of Hudson's Bay. In the year of this journey, Joliet received a grant of the islands of Mignan; and in the following year, 1652, he received another grant, of the great island of Anticosti in the lower St. Lawrence. In 1681 he was established here, with his wife and six servants. He was engaged in fisheries; and, being a skilful navigator and surveyor, he made about this time a chart of the St. Lawrence. In 1690, Sir William Phips, on his way with an English fleet to attack Quebec, made a descent on Joliet's establishment, burnt his buildings, and took prisoners his wife and his mother-in-law. In 1694 Joliet explored the coasts of Labrador, under the auspices of a company formed for the whale and seal fishery. On his return, Frontenac made him royal pilot for the St. Lawrence; and at about the same time he received the appointment of hydrographer at Quebec. He died, apparently poor, in 1699 or 1700, and was buried on one of the islands of Mignan. The discovery of the above facts is due in great part to the researches of Margry.

[64] Pierre Moreau, *alias* La Taupine, was afterwards bitterly complained of by the Intendant Duchesneau, for acting as the governor's agent in illicit trade with the Indians.

[65] The contemporary *Relation* tells us that a miracle took place at the burial of Marquette. One of the two Frenchmen, overcome with grief and colic, bethought him of applying a little earth from the grave to the seat of pain. This at once restored him to health and cheerfulness.

[66] For Marquette's death, see the contemporary *Relation*, published by Shea, Lenox, and Martin, with the accompanying *Lettre et Journal*. The river where he died is a small stream in the west of Michigan, some distance south of the promontory called the "Sleeping Bear." It long bore his name, which is now borne by a larger neighboring stream, Charlevoix's account of Marquette's death is derived from tradition, and is not supported by the contemporary narrative. In 1877, human bones, with fragments of birch-bark, were found buried on the supposed site of the Jesuit chapel at Point St. Ignace.

In 1847, the missionary of the Algonquins at the Lake of Two Mountains, above Montreal, wrote down a tradition of the death of Marquette, from the lips of an old Indian woman, born in 1777, at Michilimackinac. Her ancestress had been baptized by the subject of the story. The tradition has a resemblance to that related as fact by Charlevoix. The old squaw said that the Jesuit was returning, very ill, to Michilimackinac, when a storm forced him and his two men to land near a little river. Here he told them that he should die, and directed them to ring a bell over his grave and plant a cross. They all remained four days at the spot; and, though without food, the men felt no hunger. On the night of the fourth day he died, and the men buried him as he had directed. On waking in the morning, they saw a sack of Indian corn, a quantity of bacon, and some biscuit, miraculously sent to them, in accordance with the promise of Marquette, who had told them that they should have food enough for their journey to Michilimackinac. At the same instant, the stream began to rise, and in a few moments encircled the grave of the Jesuit, which formed, thenceforth, an islet in the waters. The tradition adds, that an Indian battle afterwards took place on the banks of this stream, between Christians and infidels; and that the former gained the victory, in consequence of invoking the name of Marquette. This story bears the attestation of the priest of the Two Mountains that it is a literal translation of the tradition, as recounted by the old woman.

It has been asserted that the Illinois country was visited by two priests, some time before the visit of Marquette. This assertion was first made by M. Noiseux, late Grand Vicar of Quebec, who gives no authority for it. Not the slightest indication of any such visit appears in any contemporary document or map, thus far discovered. The contemporary writers, down to the time of Marquette and La Salle, all speak of the Illinois as an unknown country. The entire groundlessness of Noiseux's assertion is shown by Shea, in a paper in the "Weekly Herald," of New York, April 21, 1855.

CHAPTER VI.

1673-1678.

LA SALLE AND FRONTENAC.

OBJECTS OF LA SALLE. — FRONTENAC FAVORS HIM. — PROJECTS OF FRONTENAC. — CATARAQUI. — FRONTENAC ON LAKE ONTARIO. — FORT FRONTENAC. — LA SALLE AND FÉNELON. — SUCCESS OF LA SALLE: HIS ENEMIES.

WE turn from the humble Marquette, thanking God with his last breath that he died for his Order and his Faith; and by our side stands the masculine form of Cavelier de la Salle. Prodigious was the contrast between the two discoverers: the one, with clasped hands and upturned eyes, seems a figure evoked from some dim legend of mediæval saintship; the other, with feet firm planted on the hard earth, breathes the self-relying energies of modern practical enterprise. Nevertheless, La Salle's enemies called him a visionary. His projects perplexed and startled them. At first, they ridiculed him; and then, as step by step he advanced towards his purpose, they denounced and maligned him. What was this purpose? It was not of sudden growth, but developed as years went on. La Salle at La Chine dreamed of a western passage to China, and nursed vague [Pg 84] schemes of western discovery. Then, when his earlier journeyings revealed to him the valley of the Ohio and the fertile plains of Illinois, his imagination took wing over the boundless prairies and forests drained by the great river of the West. His ambition had found its field. He would leave barren and frozen Canada behind, and lead France and civilization into the valley of the Mississippi. Neither the English nor the Jesuits should conquer that rich domain: the one must rest content with the country east of the Alleghanies, and the other with the forests, savages, and beaver-skins of the northern lakes. It was for him to call into light the latent riches of the great West. But the way to his land of promise was rough and long: it lay through Canada, filled with hostile traders and hostile priests, and barred by ice for half the year. The difficulty was soon solved. La Salle became convinced that the Mississippi flowed, not into the Pacific or the Gulf of California, but into the Gulf of Mexico. By a fortified post at its mouth, he could guard it against both English and Spaniards, and secure for the trade of the interior an access and an outlet under his own control, and open at every season. Of this trade, the hides of the buffalo would at first form the staple, and along with furs would reward the enterprise till other resources should be developed.

Such were the vast projects that unfolded themselves in the mind of La Salle. Canada must needs be, at the outset, his base of action, and without the [Pg 85] support of its authorities he could do nothing. This support he found. From the moment when Count Frontenac assumed the government of the colony, he seems to have looked with favor on the young discoverer. There were points of likeness between the two men. Both were ardent, bold, and enterprising. The irascible and fiery pride of the noble found its match in the reserved and seemingly cold pride of the ambitious burgher. Each could comprehend the other; and they had, moreover, strong prejudices and dislikes in common. An understanding, not to say an alliance, soon grew up between them.

PROJECTS OF FRONTENAC.

Frontenac had come to Canada a ruined man. He was ostentatious, lavish, and in no way disposed to let slip an opportunity of mending his fortune. He presently thought that he had found a plan by which he could serve both the colony and himself. His predecessor, Courcelle, had urged upon the King the expediency of building a fort on Lake Ontario, in order to hold the Iroquois in check and intercept the trade which the tribes of the Upper Lakes had begun to carry on with the Dutch and English of New York. Thus a stream of wealth would be turned into Canada, which would otherwise enrich her enemies. Here, to all appearance, was a great public good, and from the military point of view it was so in fact; but it was clear that the trade thus secured might be made to profit, not the colony at large, but those alone who had control of the fort, which would then become the instrument of a monopoly. This [Pg 86] the governor understood; and, without doubt, he meant that the projected establishment should pay him tribute. How far he and La Salle were acting in concurrence at this time, it is not easy to say; but Frontenac often took counsel of the explorer, who, on his part, saw in the design a possible first step towards the accomplishment of his own far-reaching schemes.

EXPEDITION OF FRONTENAC

Such of the Canadian merchants as were not in the governor's confidence looked on his plan with extreme distrust. Frontenac, therefore, thought it expedient "to make use," as he expresses it, "of address." He gave out merely that he intended to make a tour through the upper parts of the colony with an armed force, in order to inspire the Indians with respect, and secure a solid peace. He had neither troops, money, munitions, nor means of transportation; yet there was no time to lose, for, should he delay the execution of his plan, it might be countermanded by the King. His only resource, therefore, was in a prompt and hardy exertion of the royal authority; and he issued an order requiring the inhabitants of Quebec, Montreal, Three Rivers, and other settlements to furnish him, at their own cost, as soon as the spring sowing should be over, with a certain number of armed men, besides the requisite canoes. At the same time, he invited the officers settled in the country to join the expedition,—an invitation which, anxious as they were to gain his good graces, few of them cared to decline. Regardless of murmurs and discontent, he pushed his preparation [Pg 87] vigorously, and on the third of June left Quebec with his guard, his staff, a part of the garrison of the Castle of St. Louis, and a number of volunteers. He had already sent to La Salle, who was then at Montreal, directing him to repair to Onondaga, the political centre of the Iroquois, and invite their sachems to meet the governor in council at the Bay of Quinté on the north of Lake Ontario. La Salle had set out on his mission, but first sent Frontenac a map, which convinced him that the best site for his proposed fort was the mouth of the Cataraqui, where Kingston now stands. Another messenger was accordingly despatched, to change the rendezvous to this point.

Meanwhile, the governor proceeded at his leisure towards Montreal, stopping by the way to visit the officers settled along the bank, who, eager to pay their homage to the newly risen sun, received him with a hospitality which under the roof of a log hut was sometimes graced by the polished courtesies of the salon and the boudoir. Reaching Montreal, which he had never before seen, he gazed, we may suppose, with some interest at the long row of humble dwellings which lined the bank, the massive buildings of the Seminary, and the spire of the church predominant over all. It was a rude scene, but the greeting that awaited him savored nothing of the rough simplicity of the wilderness. Perrot, the local governor, was on the shore with his soldiers and the inhabitants, drawn up under arms and firing [Pg 88] a salute to welcome the representative of the King. Frontenac was compelled to listen to a long harangue from the judge of the place, followed by another from the syndic. Then there was a solemn procession to the church, where he was forced to undergo a third effort of oratory from one of the priests. *Te Deum* followed, in thanks for his arrival; and then he took refuge in the fort. Here he remained thirteen days, busied with his preparations, organizing the militia, soothing their mutual jealousies, and settling knotty questions of rank and precedence. During this time, every means, as he declares, was used to prevent him from proceeding; and among other devices a rumor was set on foot that a Dutch fleet, having just captured Boston, was on its way to attack Quebec.[67]

FRONTENAC'S JOURNEY

Having sent men, canoes, and baggage, by land, to La Salle's old settlement of La Chine, Frontenac himself followed on the twenty-eighth of June. Including Indians from the missions, he now had with him about four hundred men and a hundred and twenty canoes, besides two large flat-boats, which he caused to be painted in red and blue, with strange devices, intended to dazzle the Iroquois by a display of unwonted splendor. Now their hard task began. Shouldering canoes through the forest, dragging the flat-boats along the shore, working like beavers,—sometimes [Pg 89] in water to the knees, sometimes to the armpits, their feet cut by the sharp stones, and they themselves well-nigh swept down by the furious current,— they fought their way upward against the chain of mighty rapids that break the navigation of the St. Lawrence. The Indians were of the greatest service. Frontenac, like La Salle, showed from the first a special faculty of managing them; for his keen, incisive spirit was exactly to their liking, and they worked for him as they would have worked for no man else. As they approached the Long Saut, rain fell in torrents; and the governor, without his cloak, and drenched to the skin, directed in person the amphibious toil of his followers. Once, it is said, he lay awake all night, in his anxiety lest the biscuit should be wet, which would have ruined the expedition. No such mischance took place, and at length the last rapid was passed, and smooth water awaited them to their journey's end. Soon they reached the Thousand Islands, and their light flotilla glided in long file among those watery labyrinths, by rocky islets, where some lonely pine towered like a mast against the sky; by sun-scorched crags, where the brown lichens crisped in the parching glare; by deep dells, shady and cool, rich in rank ferns, and spongy, dark-green mosses; by still coves, where the water-lilies lay like snow-flakes on their broad, flat leaves,—till at length they neared their goal, and the glistening bosom of Lake Ontario opened on their sight.

[Pg 90]

Frontenac, to impose respect on the Iroquois, now set his canoes in order of battle. Four divisions formed the first line, then came the two flat-boats; he himself, with his guards, his staff, and the gentlemen volunteers, followed, with the canoes of Three Rivers on his right, and those of the Indians on his left, while two remaining divisions formed a rear line. Thus, with measured paddles, they advanced over the still lake, till they saw a canoe approaching to meet them. It bore several Iroquois chiefs, who told them that the dignitaries of their nation awaited them at Cataraqui, and offered to guide them to the spot. They entered the wide mouth of the river, and passed along the shore, now covered by the quiet little city of Kingston, till they reached the point at present occupied by the barracks, at the western end of Cataraqui bridge. Here they stranded their canoes and disembarked. Baggage was landed, fires lighted, tents pitched, and guards set. Close at hand, under the lee of the forest, were the camping sheds of the Iroquois, who had come to the rendezvous in considerable numbers.

> FRONTENAC AT CATARAQUI

At daybreak of the next morning, the thirteenth of July, the drums beat, and the whole party were drawn up under arms. A double line of men extended from the front of Frontenac's tent to the Indian camp; and, through the lane thus formed, the savage deputies, sixty in number, advanced to the place of council. They could not hide their admiration at the martial array of the French, many of whom were old [Pg 91] soldiers of the regiment of Carignan; and when they reached the tent they ejaculated their astonishment at the uniforms of the governor's guard who surrounded it. Here the ground had been carpeted with the sails of the flat-boats, on which the deputies squatted themselves in a ring and smoked their pipes for a time with their usual air of deliberate gravity; while Frontenac, who sat surrounded by his officers, had full leisure to contemplate the formidable adversaries whose mettle was hereafter to put his own to so severe a test. A chief named Garakontié, a noted friend of the French, at length opened the council, in behalf of all the five Iroquois nations, with expressions of great respect and deference towards "Onontio;" that is to say, the governor of Canada. Whereupon Frontenac, whose native arrogance where Indians were concerned always took a form which imposed respect without exciting anger, replied in the following strain:—

"Children! Mohawks, Oneidas, Onondagas, Cayugas, and Senecas. I am glad to see you here, where I have had a fire lighted for you to smoke by, and for me to talk to you. You have done well, my children, to obey the command of your Father. Take courage: you will hear his word, which is full of peace and tenderness. For do not think that I have come for war. My mind is full of peace, and she walks by my side. Courage, then, children, and take rest."

With that, he gave them six fathoms of tobacco, [Pg 92] reiterated his assurances of friendship, promised that he would be a kind father so long as they should be obedient children, regretted that he was forced to speak through an interpreter, and ended with a gift of guns to the men, and prunes and raisins to their wives and children. Here closed this preliminary meeting, the great council being postponed to another day.

During the meeting, Raudin, Frontenac's engineer, was tracing out the lines of a fort, after a predetermined plan; and the whole party, under the direction of their officers, now set themselves to construct it. Some cut down trees, some dug the trenches, some hewed the palisades; and with such order and alacrity was the work urged on, that the Indians were lost in astonishment. Meanwhile, Frontenac spared no pains to make friends of the chiefs, some of whom he had constantly at his table. He fondled the Iroquois children, and gave them bread and sweetmeats, and in the evening feasted the squaws to make them dance. The Indians were delighted with these attentions, and conceived a high opinion of the new Onontio.

FRONTENAC AND THE INDIANS.

On the seventeenth, when the construction of the fort was well advanced, Frontenac called the chiefs to a grand council, which was held with all possible state and ceremony. His dealing with the Indians on this and other occasions was truly admirable. Unacquainted as he was with them, he seems to have had an instinctive perception of the treatment they required. His predecessors had never ventured to [Pg 93] address the Iroquois as "Children," but had always styled them "Brothers;" and yet the assumption of paternal authority on the part of Frontenac was not only taken in good part, but was received with apparent gratitude. The martial nature of the man, his clear, decisive speech, and his frank and downright manner, backed as they were by a display of force which in their eyes was formidable, struck them with admiration, and gave tenfold effect to his words of kindness. They thanked him for that which from another they would not have endured.

Frontenac began by again expressing his satisfaction that they had obeyed the commands of their Father, and come to Cataraqui to hear what he had to say. Then he exhorted them to embrace Christianity; and on this theme he dwelt at length, in words excellently adapted to produce the desired effect,—words which it would be most superfluous to tax as insincere, though doubtless they lost nothing in emphasis because in this instance conscience and policy aimed alike. Then, changing his tone, he pointed to his officers, his guard, the long files of the militia, and the two flat-boats, mounted with cannon, which lay in the river near by. "If," he said, "your Father can come so far, with so great a force, through such dangerous rapids, merely to make you a visit of pleasure and friendship, what would he do, if you should awaken his anger, and make it necessary for him to punish his disobedient children? He is the arbiter of peace and war. [Pg 94] Beware how you offend him!" And he warned them not to molest the Indian allies of the French, telling them, sharply, that he would chastise them for the least infraction of the peace.

From threats he passed to blandishments, and urged them to confide in his paternal kindness, saying that, in proof of his affection, he was building a store-house at Cataraqui, where they could be supplied with all the goods they needed, without the necessity of a long and dangerous journey. He warned them against listening to bad men, who might seek to delude them by misrepresentations and falsehoods; and he urged them to give heed to none but "men of character, like the Sieur de la Salle." He expressed a hope that they would suffer their children to learn French from the missionaries, in order that they and his nephews—meaning the French colonists—

might become one people; and he concluded by requesting them to give him a number of their children to be educated in the French manner, at Quebec.

TREATY WITH THE INDIANS.

This speech, every clause of which was reinforced by abundant presents, was extremely well received; though one speaker reminded him that he had forgotten one important point, inasmuch as he had not told them at what prices they could obtain goods at Cataraqui. Frontenac evaded a precise answer, but promised them that the goods should be as cheap as possible, in view of the great difficulty of transportation. As to the request concerning their children, they said that they could not accede to it till they [Pg 95] had talked the matter over in their villages; but it is a striking proof of the influence which Frontenac had gained over them, that, in the following year, they actually sent several of their children to Quebec to be educated,—the girls among the Ursulines, and the boys in the household of the governor.

Three days after the council, the Iroquois set out on their return; and as the palisades of the fort were now finished, and the barracks nearly so, Frontenac began to send his party homeward by detachments. He himself was detained for a time by the arrival of another band of Iroquois, from the villages on the north side of Lake Ontario. He repeated to them the speech he had made to the others; and, this final meeting over, he embarked with his guard, leaving a sufficient number to hold the fort, which was to be provisioned for a year by means of a convoy then on its way up the river. Passing the rapids safely, he reached Montreal on the first of August.

His enterprise had been a complete success. He had gained every point, and, in spite of the dangerous navigation, had not lost a single canoe. Thanks to the enforced and gratuitous assistance of the inhabitants, the whole had cost the King only about ten thousand francs, which Frontenac had advanced on his own credit. Though in a commercial point of view the new establishment was of very questionable benefit to the colony at large, the governor had, nevertheless, conferred an inestimable blessing on all Canada by the assurance he had gained of a long [Pg 96] respite from the fearful scourge of Iroquois hostility. "Assuredly," he writes, "I may boast of having impressed them at once with respect, fear, and good-will."[68] He adds that the fort at Cataraqui, with the aid of a vessel now building, will command Lake Ontario, keep the peace with the Iroquois, and cut off the trade with the English; and he proceeds to say that by another fort at the mouth of the Niagara, and another vessel on Lake Erie, we, the French, can command all the Upper Lakes. This plan was an essential link in the schemes of La Salle; and we shall soon find him employed in executing it.

A curious incident occurred soon after the building of the fort on Lake Ontario. Frontenac, on his way back, quarrelled with Perrot, the governor of Montreal, whom, in view of his speculations in the fur-trade, he seems to have regarded as a rival in business; but who, by his folly and arrogance, would have justified any reasonable measure of severity. Frontenac, however, was not reasonable. He arrested Perrot, threw him into prison, and set up a man of his own as governor in his place; and as the judge of Montreal was not in his interest, he removed him, and substituted another on whom he could rely. Thus for a time he had Montreal well in hand.

The priests of the Seminary, seigniors of the island, regarded these arbitrary proceedings with extreme uneasiness. They claimed the right of nominating their own governor; and Perrot, though he held a [Pg 97] commission from the King, owed his place to their appointment. True, he had set them at nought, and proved a veritable King Stork; yet nevertheless they regarded his removal as an infringement of their rights.

During the quarrel with Perrot, La Salle chanced to be at Montreal, lodged in the house of Jacques Le Ber, who, though one of the principal merchants and most influential inhabitants of the settlement, was accustomed to sell goods across his counter in person to white men and Indians, his wife taking his place when he was absent. Such were the primitive manners of the secluded little colony. Le Ber, at this time, was in the interest of Frontenac and La Salle; though he afterwards became one of their most determined opponents. Amid the excitement and discussion occasioned by Perrot's arrest, La Salle declared himself an adherent of the governor, and warned all persons against speaking ill of him in his hearing.

ABBÉ FÉNELON.

The Abbé Fénelon, already mentioned as half-brother to the famous Archbishop, had attempted to mediate between Frontenac and Perrot, and to this end had made a journey to Quebec on the ice, in midwinter. Being of an ardent temperament, and more courageous than prudent, he had spoken somewhat indiscreetly, and had been very roughly treated by the stormy and imperious Count. He returned to Montreal greatly excited, and not without cause. It fell to his lot to preach the Easter sermon. The [Pg 98] service was held in the little church of the Hôtel-Dieu, which was crowded to the porch, all the chief persons of the settlement being present. The curé of the parish, whose name also was Perrot, said High Mass, assisted by La Salle's brother, Cavelier, and two other priests. Then Fénelon mounted the pulpit. Certain passages of his sermon were obviously levelled against Frontenac. Speaking of the duties of those clothed with temporal authority, he said that the magistrate, inspired with the spirit of Christ, was as ready to pardon offences against himself as to punish those against his prince; that he was full of respect for the ministers of the altar, and never maltreated them when they attempted to reconcile enemies and restore peace; that he never made favorites of those who flattered him, nor under specious pretexts oppressed other persons in authority who opposed his enterprises; that he used his power to serve his king, and not to his own advantage; that he remained content with his salary, without disturbing the commerce of the country, or abusing those who refused him a share in their profits; and that he never troubled the people by inordinate and unjust levies of men and material, using the name of his prince as a cover to his own designs.[69]

[Pg 99]

LA SALLE AND FÉNELON.

La Salle sat near the door; but as the preacher proceeded he suddenly rose to his feet in such a manner as to attract the notice of the congregation. As they turned their heads, he signed to the principal persons among them, and by his angry looks and gesticulation called their attention to the words of Fénelon. Then meeting the eye of the curé, who sat beside the altar, he made the same signs to him, to which the curé replied by a deprecating shrug of the shoulders. Fénelon changed color, but continued his sermon.[70]

This indecent proceeding of La Salle, and the zeal with which throughout the quarrel he took the part of the governor, did not go unrewarded. Henceforth, Frontenac was more than ever his friend; and this plainly appeared in the disposition made, through his influence, of the new fort on Lake Ontario. Attempts had been made to induce the king to have it demolished; but it was resolved at last that, being built, it should be allowed to stand; and, after long delay, a final arrangement was made for its maintenance, in the manner following: In the autumn of 1674, La Salle went to France, with letters of strong recommendation from Frontenac.[71] He was well [Pg 100] received at Court; and he made two petitions to the King,—the one for a patent of nobility, in consideration of his services as an explorer; and the other for a grant in seigniory of Fort Frontenac, for so he called the new post, in honor of his patron. On his part, he offered to pay back the ten thousand francs which the fort had cost the King; to maintain it at his own charge, with a garrison equal to that of Montreal, besides fifteen or twenty laborers; to form a French colony around it; to build a church, whenever the number of inhabitants should reach one hundred; and, meanwhile, to support one or more Récollet friars; and, finally, to form a settlement of domesticated Indians in the neighborhood. His offers were accepted. He was raised to the rank of the untitled nobles; received a grant of the fort and lands adjacent, to the extent of four leagues in front and half a league in depth, besides the neighboring islands; and was invested with the government of the fort and settlement, subject to the orders of the governor-general.[72]

[Pg 101]

La Salle returned to Canada, proprietor of a seigniory which, all things considered, was one of the most valuable in the colony. His friends and his family, rejoicing in his good fortune and not unwilling to share it, made him large advances of money, enabling him to pay the stipulated sum to the King, to rebuild the fort in stone, maintain soldiers and laborers, and procure in part, at least, the necessary outfit. Had La Salle been a mere merchant, he was in a fair way to make a fortune, for he was in a position to control the better part of the Canadian fur-trade. But he was not a mere merchant; and no commercial profit could content his ambition.

Those may believe, who will, that Frontenac did not expect a share in the profits of the new post. That he did expect it, there is positive evidence; for a deposition is extant, taken at the instance of his enemy the Intendant Duchesneau, in which three witnesses attest that the governor, La Salle, his lieutenant La Forest, and one Boisseau, had formed a partnership to carry on the trade of Fort Frontenac.

ENEMIES OF LA SALLE.

No sooner was La Salle installed in his new post than the merchants of Canada joined hands to oppose him. Le Ber, once his friend, became his bitter enemy; for he himself had hoped to share the monopoly of Fort Frontenac, of which he and one Bazire had at first been placed provisionally in control, [Pg 102] and from which he now saw himself ejected. La Chesnaye, Le Moyne, and others of more or less influence took part in the league, which, in fact, embraced all the traders in the colony except the few joined with Frontenac and La Salle. Duchesneau, intendant of the colony, aided the malcontents. As time went on, their bitterness grew more bitter; and when at last it was seen that, not satisfied with the monopoly of Fort Frontenac, La Salle aimed at the control of the valleys of the Ohio and the Mississippi, and the usufruct of half a continent, the ire of his opponents redoubled, and Canada became for him a nest of hornets, buzzing in wrath and watching the moment to sting. But there was another element of opposition, less noisy, but not less formidable; and this arose from the Jesuits. Frontenac hated them; and they, under befitting forms of duty and courtesy, paid him back in the same coin. Having no love for the governor, they would naturally have little for his partisan and *protégé*; but their opposition had another and a deeper root, for the plans of the daring young schemer jarred with their own.

PURPOSES OF THE JESUITS.

We have seen the Canadian Jesuits in the early apostolic days of their mission, when the flame of their zeal, fed by an ardent hope, burned bright and high. This hope was doomed to disappointment. Their avowed purpose of building another Paraguay on the borders of the Great Lakes[73] was never accomplished, [Pg 103] and their missions and their converts were swept away in an avalanche of ruin. Still, they would not despair. From the lakes they turned their eyes to the Valley of the Mississippi, in the hope to see it one day the seat of their new empire of the Faith. But what did this new Paraguay mean? It meant a little nation of converted and domesticated savages, docile as children, under the paternal and absolute rule of Jesuit fathers, and trained by them in industrial pursuits, the results of which were to inure, not to the profit of the producers, but to the building of churches, the founding of colleges, the establishment of warehouses and magazines, and the construction of works of defence,—all controlled by Jesuits, and forming a part of the vast possessions of the Order. Such was the old

Paraguay;[74] and such, we may suppose, would have been the new, had the plans of those who designed it been realized.

I have said that since the middle of the century the religious exaltation of the early missions had sensibly declined. In the nature of things, that grand enthusiasm was too intense and fervent to be long sustained. But the vital force of Jesuitism had suffered no diminution. That marvellous *esprit de corps*, that extinction of self and absorption of the individual in the Order which has marked the Jesuits from their first existence as a body, was no whit changed or lessened,—a principle, which, though [Pg 104] different, was no less strong than the self-devoted patriotism of Sparta or the early Roman Republic.

The Jesuits were no longer supreme in Canada; or, in other words, Canada was no longer simply a mission. It had become a colony. Temporal interests and the civil power were constantly gaining ground; and the disciples of Loyola felt that relatively, if not absolutely, they were losing it. They struggled vigorously to maintain the ascendency of their Order, or, as they would have expressed it, the ascendency of religion; but in the older and more settled parts of the colony it was clear that the day of their undivided rule was past. Therefore, they looked with redoubled solicitude to their missions in the West. They had been among its first explorers; and they hoped that here the Catholic Faith, as represented by Jesuits, might reign with undisputed sway. In Paraguay, it was their constant aim to exclude white men from their missions. It was the same in North America. They dreaded fur-traders, partly because they interfered with their teachings and perverted their converts, and partly for other reasons. But La Salle was a fur-trader, and far worse than a fur-trader: he aimed at occupation, fortification, and settlement. The scope and vigor of his enterprises, and the powerful influence that aided them, made him a stumbling-block in their path. He was their most dangerous rival for the control of the West, and from first to last they set themselves against him.

[Pg 105]

SPIRIT OF LA SALLE.

What manner of man was he who could conceive designs so vast and defy enmities so many and so powerful? And in what spirit did he embrace these designs? We will look hereafter for an answer.

FOOTNOTES:

[67] *Lettre de Frontenac à Colbert, 13 Nov., 1673.* This rumor, it appears, originated with the Jesuit Dablon. *Journal du Voyage du Comte de Frontenac au lac Ontario.* The Jesuits were greatly opposed to the establishment of forts and trading-posts in the upper country, for reasons that will appear hereafter.

[68] *Lettre de Frontenac au Ministre, 13 Nov., 1673.*

[69] Faillon, *Colonie Française*, iii. 497, and manuscript authorities there cited. I have examined the principal of these. Faillon himself is a priest of St. Sulpice. Compare H. Verreau, *Les Deux Abbés de Fénelon*, chap. vii.

[70] *Information faicte par nous, Charles le Tardieu, Sieur de Tilly, et Nicolas Dupont, etc., etc., contre le Sr Abbé de Fénelon.* Tilly and Dupont were sent by Frontenac to inquire into the affair. Among the deponents is La Salle himself.

[71] In his despatch to the minister Colbert, of the fourteenth of November, 1674, Frontenac speaks of La Salle as follows: "I cannot help, Monseigneur, recommending to you the Sieur de la Salle, who is about to go to France, and who is a man of intelligence and ability, more capable than anybody else I know here to accomplish every kind of enterprise and discovery which may be intrusted to him, as he has the most perfect knowledge of the state of the country, as you will see, if you are disposed to give him a few moments of audience."

[72] *Mémoire pour l'entretien du Fort Frontenac, par le Sr de la Salle, 1674. Petition du Sr de la Salle au Roi. Lettres patentes de concession, du Fort de Frontenac et terres adjacentes au profit du Sr de la Salle; données à Compiègne le 13 Mai, 1675. Arrêt qui accepte les offres faites par Robert Cavelier Sr de la Salle; à Compiègne le 13 Mai, 1675. Lettres de noblesse pour le Sr Cavelier de la Salle; données à Compiègne le 13 Mai, 1675. Papiers de Famille. Mémoire au Roi.*

[73] This purpose is several times indicated in the *Relations*. For an instance, see "The Jesuits in North America," 245.

[74] Compare Charlevoix, *Histoire de Paraguay*, with Robertson, *Letters on Paraguay*.

[Pg 106]

CHAPTER VII.

1678.

PARTY STRIFE.

LA SALLE'S MEMOIR.

ONE of the most curious monuments of La Salle's time is a long memoir, written by a person who made his acquaintance at Paris in the summer of 1678, when, as we shall soon see, he had returned to France in prosecution of his plans. The writer knew the Sulpitian Galinée,[75] who, as he says, had a very high opinion of La Salle; and he was also in close relations with the discoverer's patron, the Prince de Conti.[76] He says that he had ten or twelve interviews with La Salle; and, becoming interested in him and in that which he communicated, he wrote down the substance of his conversation. The paper is divided into two [Pg 107] parts: the first, called "Mémoire sur Mr. de la Salle," is devoted to the state of affairs in Canada, and chiefly to the Jesuits; the second, entitled "Histoire de Mr. de la Salle," is an account of the discoverer's life, or as much of it as the writer had learned from him.[77] Both parts bear throughout the internal evidence of being what they profess to be; but they embody the statements of a man of intense partisan feeling, transmitted through the mind of another person in sympathy with him, and evidently sharing his prepossessions. In one respect, however, the paper is of unquestionable historical value; for it gives us a vivid and not an exaggerated picture of the bitter strife of parties which then raged in Canada, and which was destined to tax to the utmost the vast energy and fortitude of La Salle. At times, the memoir is fully sustained by contemporary evidence; but often, again, it rests on its own unsupported authority. I give an abstract of its statements as I find them.

The following is the writer's account of La Salle: "All those among my friends who have seen him find him a man of great intelligence and sense. He rarely speaks of any subject except when questioned about it, and his words are very few and very precise. He distinguishes perfectly between that which he knows with certainly and that which he knows with some mingling of doubt. When he does not know, he does [Pg 108] not hesitate to avow it; and though I have heard him say the same thing more than five or six times, when persons were present who had not heard it before, he always said it in the same manner. In short, I never heard anybody speak whose words carried with them more marks of truth."[78]

JESUIT ASCENDENCY.

After mentioning that he is thirty-three or thirty-four years old, and that he has been twelve years in America, the memoir declares that he made the following statements: that the Jesuits are masters at Quebec; that the bishop is their creature, and does nothing but in concert with them;[79] that he is not well inclined towards the Récollets,[80] who have little [Pg 109] credit, but who are protected by Frontenac; that in Canada the Jesuits think everybody an enemy to religion who is an enemy to them; that, though they refused absolution to all who sold brandy to the Indians, they sold it themselves, and that he, La Salle, had himself detected them in it;[81] that the bishop laughs at the orders of the King when they do not agree with the wishes of the Jesuits; that the Jesuits dismissed one of their servants named Robert, because he told of their trade in brandy; that Albanel,[82] in particular, carried on a great fur-trade, and that the Jesuits have built their college in part from the profits of this kind of traffic; that they [Pg 110] admitted that they carried on a trade, but denied that they gained so much by it as was commonly supposed.[83]

FEMALE INQUISITORS.

The memoir proceeds to affirm that they trade largely with the Sioux at Ste. Marie, and with other tribes at Michilimackinac, and that they are masters of the trade of that region, where the forts are in their possession.[84] An Indian said, in full council, at Quebec, that he had prayed and been a Christian as long as the Jesuits would stay and teach him, but since no more beaver were left in his country, the missionaries were gone also. The Jesuits, pursues the memoir, will have no priests but themselves in their missions, and call them all Jansenists, not excepting the priests of St. Sulpice.

The bishop is next accused of harshness and intolerance, as well as of growing rich by tithes, and even by trade, in which it is affirmed he has a covert interest.[85] It is added that there exists in Quebec, under the auspices of the Jesuits, an association [Pg 111] called the Sainte Famille, of which Madame Bourdon[86] is superior. They meet in the cathedral every Thursday, with closed doors, where they relate to each other—as they are bound by a vow to do—all they have learned, whether good or evil, concerning other people, during the week. It is a sort of female inquisition, for the benefit of the Jesuits, the secrets of whose friends, it is said, are kept, while no such discretion is observed with regard to persons not of their party.[87]

[Pg 112]

Here follow a series of statements which it is needless to repeat, as they do not concern La Salle. They relate to abuse of the confessional, hostility to other priests, hostility to civil authorities, and over-hasty baptisms, in regard to which La Salle is reported to have made a comparison, unfavorable to the Jesuits, between them and the Récollets and Sulpitians.

PLOTS AGAINST LA SALLE.

We now come to the second part of the memoir, entitled "History of Monsieur de la Salle." After stating that he left France at the age of twenty-one or twenty-two, with the purpose of attempting some new discovery, it makes the statements repeated in a former chapter, concerning his discovery of the Ohio, the Illinois, and possibly the Mississippi. It then mentions the building of Fort Frontenac, and says that one object of it was to prevent the Jesuits from becoming undisputed masters of the fur-trade.[88] Three years ago, it pursues, La Salle came to France, and obtained a grant of the fort; and it proceeds to give examples of the means used by the party opposed to him to injure his good name and bring him within reach of the law. Once, when he was at Quebec, the farmer of the King's revenue, one of the richest [Pg 113] men in the place, was extremely urgent in his proffers of hospitality, and at length, though he knew La Salle but slightly, persuaded him to lodge in his house. He had been here but a few days when his host's wife began to enact the part of the wife of Potiphar, and this with so much vivacity that on one occasion La Salle was forced to take an abrupt leave, in order to avoid an infringement of the laws of hospitality. As he opened the door, he found the husband on the watch, and saw that it was a plot to entrap him.[89]

Another attack, of a different character, though in the same direction, was soon after made. The remittances which La Salle received from the various members and connections of his family were sent through the hands of his brother, Abbé Cavelier, from whom his enemies were, therefore, very eager to alienate him. To this end, a report was made to reach the priest's ears that La Salle had seduced a young woman, with whom he was living in an open and scandalous manner at Fort Frontenac. The effect of this device exceeded the wishes of its contrivers; for the priest, aghast at what he had heard, set out for the fort, to administer his fraternal rebuke, but on arriving, in place of the expected abomination, found his brother, assisted by two Récollet friars, ruling with edifying propriety over a most exemplary household.

[Pg 114]

Thus far the memoir. From passages in some of La Salle's letters, it may be gathered that Abbé Cavelier gave him at times no little annoyance. In his double character of priest and elder brother, he seems to have constituted himself the counsellor, monitor, and guide of a man who, though many years his junior, was in all respects incomparably superior to him, as the sequel will show. This must have been almost insufferable to a nature like that of La Salle, who, nevertheless, was forced to arm himself with patience, since his brother held the purse-strings. On one occasion his forbearance was put to a severe proof, when, wishing to marry a damsel of good connections in the colony, Abbé Cavelier saw fit for some reason to interfere, and prevented the alliance.[90]

INTRIGUES OF THE JESUITS.

To resume the memoir. It declares that the Jesuits procured an ordinance from the Supreme Council prohibiting traders from going into the Indian country, in order that they, the Jesuits, being already established there in their missions, might carry on trade without competition. But La Salle induced a good number of the Iroquois to settle around his fort; thus bringing the trade to his own door, without breaking the ordinance. These Iroquois, he is further reported to have said, were very fond of him, and aided him in rebuilding the fort with cut stone. The Jesuits told the Iroquois on the south side of the lake, where they were established [Pg 115] as missionaries, that La Salle was strengthening his defences with the view of making war on them. They and the intendant, who was their creature, endeavored to embroil the Iroquois with the French in order to ruin La Salle; writing to him at the same time that he was the bulwark of the country, and that he ought to be always on his guard. They also tried to persuade Frontenac that it was necessary to raise men and prepare for war. La Salle suspected them; and seeing that the Iroquois, in consequence of their intrigues, were in an excited state, he induced the governor to come to Fort Frontenac to pacify them. He accordingly did so; and a council was held, which ended in a complete restoration of confidence on the part of the

Iroquois.[91] At this council they accused the two Jesuits, Bruyas and Pierron,[92] of spreading reports that the French were preparing to attack them. La Salle thought that the [Pg 116] object of the intrigue was to make the Iroquois jealous of him, and engage Frontenac in expenses which would offend the King. After La Salle and the governor had lost credit by the rupture, the Jesuits would come forward as pacificators, in the full assurance that they could restore quiet, and appear in the attitude of saviors of the colony.

La Salle, pursues his reporter, went on to say that about this time a quantity of hemlock and verdigris was given him in a salad; and that the guilty person was a man in his employ named Nicolas Perrot, otherwise called Jolycœur, who confessed the crime.[93] The memoir adds that La Salle, who recovered from the effects of the poison, wholly exculpates the Jesuits.

This attempt, which was not, as we shall see, the only one of the kind made against La Salle, is alluded to by him in a letter to a friend at Paris, [Pg 117] written in Canada when he was on the point of departure on his great expedition to descend the Mississippi. The following is an extract from it:

LA SALLE EXCULPATES THE JESUITS.

"I hope to give myself the honor of sending you a more particular account of this enterprise when it shall have had the success which I hope for it; but I have need of a strong protection for its support. It traverses the commercial operations of certain persons, who will find it hard to endure it. They intended to make a new Paraguay in these parts, and the route which I close against them gave them facilities for an advantageous correspondence with Mexico. This check will infallibly be a mortification to them; and you know how they deal with whatever opposes them. *Nevertheless, I am bound to render them the justice to say that the poison which was given me was not at all of their instigation.* The person who was conscious of the guilt, believing that I was their enemy because he saw that our sentiments were opposed, thought to exculpate himself by accusing them, and I confess that at the time I was not sorry to have this indication of their ill-will; but having afterwards carefully examined the affair, I clearly discovered the falsity of the accusation which this rascal had made against them. I nevertheless pardoned him, in order not to give notoriety to the affair; as the mere suspicion might sully their reputation, to which I should scrupulously avoid doing the slightest injury unless I thought it necessary to the good of the public, and unless the fact were fully proved. Therefore, [Pg 118] Monsieur, if anybody shared the suspicion which I felt, oblige me by undeceiving him."[94]

This letter, so honorable to La Salle, explains the statement made in the memoir, that, notwithstanding his grounds of complaint against the Jesuits, he continued to live on terms of courtesy with them, entertained them at his fort, and occasionally corresponded with them. The writer asserts, however, that they intrigued with his men to induce them to desert,—employing for this purpose a young man named Deslauriers, whom they sent to him with letters of recommendation. La Salle took him into his service; but he soon after escaped, with several other men, and took refuge in the Jesuit missions.[95] The object of the intrigue is said to have been the reduction of La Salle's garrison to a number less than that which he was bound to maintain, thus exposing him to a forfeiture of his title of possession.

RENEWED INTRIGUES.

He is also stated to have declared that Louis Joliet was an impostor,[96] and a *donné* of the Jesuits,—that [Pg 119] is, a man who worked for them without pay; and, further, that when he, La Salle, came to court to ask for privileges enabling him to pursue his discoveries, the Jesuits represented in advance to the minister Colbert that his head was turned, and that he was fit for nothing but a mad-house. It was only by the aid of influential friends that he was at length enabled to gain an audience.

Here ends this remarkable memoir, which, criticise it as we may, does not exaggerate the jealousies and enmities that beset the path of the discoverer.

FOOTNOTES:

[75] *Ante*, p. 17.

[76] Louis-Armand de Bourbon, second Prince de Conti. The author of the memoir seems to have been Abbé Renaudot, a learned churchman.

[77] Extracts from this have already been given in connection with La Salle's supposed discovery of the Mississippi. *Ante*, p. 29.

[78] "Tous ceux de mes amis qui l'ont vu luy trouve beaucoup d'esprit et un très-grand sens; il ne parle guère que des choses sur lesquelles on l'interroge; il les dit en très-peu de mots et très-bien circonstanciées; il distingue parfaitement ce qu'il scait avec certitude, de ce qu'il scait avec quelque mélange de doute. Il avoue sans aucune façon ne pas savoir ce qu'il ne scait pas, et quoyque je luy aye ouy dire plus de cinq ou six fois les mesme choses à l'occasion de quelques personnes qui ne les avaient point encore entendues, je les luy ay toujours ouy dire de la mesme manière. En un mot je n'ay jamais ouy parler personne dont les paroles portassent plus de marques de vérité."

[79]] "Il y a une autre chose qui me déplait, qui est l'entière dépendence dans laquelle les Prêtres du Séminaire de Québec et le Grand Vicaire de l'Evêque sont pour les Pères Jésuites, car il ne fait pas la moindre chose sans leur ordre; ce qui fait qu'indirectement ils sont les maîtres de ce qui regarde le spirituel, qui, comme vous savez, est une grande machine pour remuer tout le reste."—*Lettre de Frontenac à Colbert, 2 Nov., 1672.*

[80] "Ces réligieux [*les Récollets*] sont fort protégés partout par le comte de Frontenac, gouverneur du pays, et à cause de cela assez maltraités par l'évesque, parceque la doctrine de l'évesque et des Jésuites est que les affaires de la Réligion chrestienne n'iront point bien dans ce pays-là que quand le gouverneur sera créature des Jésuites, ou que l'évesque sera gouverneur."—*Mémoire sur Mr de la Salle.*

[81] "Ils [*les Jésuites*] refusent l'absolution à ceux qui ne veulent pas promettre de n'en plus vendre [*de l'eau-de-vie*], et s'ils meurent en cet état, ils les privent de la sépulture ecclésiastique; au contraire ils se permettent à eux-mêmes sans aucune difficulté ce mesme trafic quoique toute sorte de trafic soit interdite à tous les ecclésiastiques par les ordonnances du Roy, et par une bulle expresse du Pape. La Bulle et les ordonnances sont

notoires, et quoyqu'ils cachent le trafic qu'ils font d'eau-de-vie, M. de la Salle prétend qu'il ne l'est pas moins; qu'outre la notoriété il en a des preuves certaines, et qu'il les a surpris dans ce trafic, et qu'ils luy ont tendu des pièges pour l'y surprendre.... Ils ont chassé leur valet Robert à cause qu'il révéla qu'ils en traitaient jour et nuit."—*Ibid.* The writer says that he makes this last statement, not on the authority of La Salle, but on that of a memoir made at the time when the intendant, Talon, with whom he elsewhere says that he was well acquainted, returned to France. A great number of particulars are added respecting the Jesuit trade in furs.

[82] Albanel was prominent among the Jesuit explorers at this time. He is best known by his journey up the Saguenay to Hudson's Bay in 1672.

[83] "Pour vous parler franchement, ils [*les Jésuites*] songent autant à la conversion du Castor qu'à celle des âmes."—*Lettre de Frontenac à Colbert, 2 Nov., 1672.*

In his despatch of the next year, he says that the Jesuits ought to content themselves with instructing the Indians in their old missions, instead of neglecting them to make new ones in countries where there are "more beaver-skins to gain than souls to save."

[84] These forts were built by them, and were necessary to the security of their missions.

[85] François Xavier de Laval-Montmorency, first bishop of Quebec, was a prelate of austere character. His memory is cherished in Canada by adherents of the Jesuits and all ultramontane Catholics.

[86] This Madame Bourdon was the widow of Bourdon, the engineer (see "The Jesuits in North America," 297). If we may credit the letters of Marie de l'Incarnation, she had married him from a religious motive, in order to charge herself with the care of his motherless children; stipulating in advance that he should live with her, not as a husband, but as a brother. As may be imagined, she was regarded as a most devout and saint-like person.

[87] "Il y a dans Québec une congrégation de femmes et de filles qu'ils [*les Jésuites*] appellent la sainte famille, dans laquelle on fait vœu sur les Saints Evangiles de dire tout ce qu'on sait de bien et de mal des personnes qu'on connoist. La Supérieure de cette compagnie s'appelle Madame Bourdon; une M$^{de.}$ d'Ailleboust est, je crois, l'assistante et une M$^{de.}$ Charron, la Trésorière. La Compagnie s'assemble tous les Jeudis dans la Cathédrale, à porte fermée, et là elles se disent les unes aux autres tout ce qu'elles ont appris. C'est une espèce d'Inquisition contre toutes les personnes qui ne sont pas unies avec les Jésuites. Ces personnes sont accusées de tenir secret

ce qu'elles apprennent de mal des personnes de leur party et de n'avoir pas la mesme discretion pour les autres."—*Mémoire sur M^r. de la Salle.*

The Madame d'Ailleboust mentioned above was a devotee like Madame Bourdon, and, in one respect, her history was similar. See "The Jesuits in North America," 360.

The association of the Sainte Famille was founded by the Jesuit Chaumonot at Montreal in 1663. Laval, Bishop of Quebec, afterwards encouraged its establishment at that place; and, as Chaumonot himself writes, caused it to be attached to the cathedral. *Vie de Chaumonot,* 83. For its establishment at Montreal, see Faillon, *Vie de Mlle. Mance,* i. 233.

"Ils [*les Jésuites*] ont tous une si grande envie de savoir tout ce qui se fait dans les familles qu'ils ont des Inspecteurs à gages dans la Ville, qui leur rapportent tout ce qui se fait dans les maisons," etc., etc.—*Lettre de Frontenac au Ministre, 13 Nov., 1673.*

[88] Mention has been made (p. 88, *note*) of the report set on foot by the Jesuit Dablon, to prevent the building of the fort.
[89] This story is told at considerable length, and the advances of the lady particularly described.
[90] Letter of La Salle, in possession of M. Margry.
[91] Louis XIV. alludes to this visit, in a letter to Frontenac, dated 28 April, 1677. "I cannot but approve," he writes, "of what you have done, in your voyage to Fort Frontenac, to reconcile the minds of the Five Iroquois Nations, and to clear yourself from the suspicions they had entertained, and from the motives that might induce them to make war." Frontenac's despatches of this year, as well as of the preceding and following years, are missing from the archives.

In a memoir written in November, 1680, La Salle alludes to "le désir que l'on avoit que Monseigneur le Comte de Frontenac fît la guerre aux Iroquois." See Thomassy, *Géologie Pratique de la Louisiane,* 203.

[92] Bruyas was about this time stationed among the Onondagas. Pierron was among the Senecas. He had lately removed to them from the Mohawk

country. *Relation des Jésuites, 1673-79,* 140 (Shea). Bruyas was also for a long time among the Mohawks.

[93] This puts the character of Perrot in a new light; for it is not likely that any other can be meant than the famous *voyageur*. I have found no mention elsewhere of the synonyme of Jolycœur. Poisoning was the current crime of the day, and persons of the highest rank had repeatedly been charged with it. The following is the passage:—

"Quoiqu'il en soit, M^r. de la Salle se sentit quelque temps après empoisonné d'une salade dans laquelle on avoit meslé du ciguë, qui est poison en ce pays là, et du verd de gris. Il en fut malade à l'extrémité, vomissant presque continuellement 40 ou 50 jours après, et il ne réchappa que par la force extrême de sa constitution. Celuy qui luy donna le poison fut un nommé Nicolas Perrot, autrement Jolycœur, l'un de ses domestiques.... Il pouvait faire mourir cet homme, qui a confessé son crime, mais il s'est contenté de l'enfermer les fers aux pieds."—*Histoire de M^r. de la Salle.*

[94] The following words are underlined in the original: *"Je suis pourtant obligé de leur rendre une justice, que le poison qu'on m'avoit donné n'éstoit point de leur instigation."*—*Lettre de La Salle au Prince de Conti, 31 Oct., 1678.*

[95] In a letter to the King, Frontenac mentions that several men who had been induced to desert from La Salle had gone to Albany, where the English had received them well. *Lettre de Frontenac au Roy, 6 Nov., 1679.* The Jesuits had a mission in the neighboring tribe of the Mohawks and elsewhere in New York.

[96] This agrees with expressions used by La Salle in a memoir addressed by him to Frontenac in November, 1680. In this, he intimates his belief that Joliet went but little below the mouth of the Illinois, thus doing flagrant injustice to that brave explorer.

CHAPTER VIII.

1677, 1678.

THE GRAND ENTERPRISE.

LA SALLE AT FORT FRONTENAC.—LA SALLE AT COURT: HIS MEMORIAL.—APPROVAL OF THE KING.—MONEY AND MEANS.—HENRI DE TONTY.—RETURN TO CANADA.

"IF," writes a friend of La Salle," he had preferred gain to glory, he had only to stay at his fort, where he was making more than twenty-five thousand livres a year."[97] He loved solitude and he loved power; and at Fort Frontenac he had both, so far as each consisted with the other. The nearest settlement was a week's journey distant, and he was master of all around him. He had spared no pains to fulfil the conditions on which his wilderness seigniory had been granted, and within two years he had demolished the original wooden fort, replacing it by another much larger, enclosed on the land side by ramparts and bastions of stone, and on the water side by palisades. It contained a range of barracks of squared timber, a guard-house, a lodging for officers, a forge, a well, [Pg 121] a mill, and a bakery. Nine small cannon were mounted on the walls. Two officers and a surgeon, with ten or twelve soldiers, made up the garrison; and three or four times that number of masons, laborers, and canoe-men were at one time maintained at the place.

LA SALLE AT FORT FRONTENAC.

Along the shore south of the fort was a small village of French families, to whom La Salle had granted farms, and, farther on, a village of Iroquois, whom he had persuaded to settle here. Near these villages were the house and chapel of two Récollet friars, Luc Buisset and Louis Hennepin. More than a hundred French acres of land had been cleared of wood, and planted in part with crops; while cattle, fowls, and swine had been brought up from Montreal. Four vessels, of from twenty-five to forty tons, had been built for the lake and the river; but canoes served best for ordinary uses, and La Salle's followers became so skilled in managing them that they were reputed the best canoe-men in America. Feudal lord of the forests around him, commander of a garrison raised and paid by himself, founder of the mission, and patron of the church, he reigned the autocrat of his lonely little empire.[98]

[Pg 122]

LA SALLE'S MEMORIAL.

It was not solely or chiefly for commercial gain that La Salle had established Fort Frontenac. He regarded it as a first step towards greater things; and now, at length, his plans were ripe and his time was come. In the autumn of 1677 he left the fort in charge of his lieutenant, descended the St. Lawrence to Quebec, and sailed for France. He had the patronage of Frontenac and the help of strong friends in Paris. It is said, as we have seen already, that his enemies denounced him, in advance, as a madman; but a memorial of his, which his friends laid before the minister Colbert, found a favorable hearing. In it he set forth his plans, or a portion of them. He first recounted briefly the discoveries he had made, and then described the country he had seen south and west of the great lakes. "It is nearly all so beautiful and so fertile; so free from forests, and so full of meadows, brooks, and rivers; so abounding in fish, game, and venison, that one can find there in plenty, and with little trouble, all that is needful for the support of flourishing colonies. The soil will produce everything that is raised in France. Flocks and herds can be left out at pasture all winter; and there are even native wild cattle, which, instead of hair, have a fine wool that may answer for making cloth and hats. Their hides are better than those of France, as appears [Pg 123] by the sample which the Sieur de la Salle has brought with him. Hemp and cotton grow here naturally, and may be manufactured with good results; so there can be no doubt that colonies planted here would become very prosperous. They would be increased by a great number of western Indians, who are in the main of a tractable and social disposition; and as they have the use neither of our weapons nor of our goods, and are not in intercourse with other Europeans, they will readily adapt themselves to us and imitate our way of life as soon as they taste the advantages of our friendship and of the commodities we bring them, insomuch that these countries will infallibly furnish, within a few years, a great many new subjects to the Church and the King.

"It was the knowledge of these things, joined to the poverty of Canada, its dense forests, its barren soil, its harsh climate, and the snow that covers the ground for half the year, that led the Sieur de la Salle to undertake the planting of colonies in these beautiful countries of the West."

Then he recounts the difficulties of the attempt,—the vast distances, the rapids and cataracts that obstruct the way; the cost of men, provisions, and munitions; the danger from the Iroquois, and the rivalry of the English, who covet the western country, and would gladly seize it for themselves. "But this last reason," says the memorial, "only animates the Sieur de la Salle the more, and impels [Pg 124] him to anticipate them by the promptness of his action."

He declares that it was for this that he had asked for the grant of Fort Frontenac; and he describes what he had done at that post, in order to make it a secure basis for his enterprise. He says that he has now overcome the chief difficulties in his way, and that he is ready to plant a new colony at the outlet of Lake Erie, of which the English, if not prevented, might easily take possession. Towards the accomplishment of his plans, he asks the confirmation of his title to Fort Frontenac, and the permission to establish at his own cost two other posts, with seigniorial rights over all lands which he may discover and colonize within twenty years, and the government of all the country in question. On his part, he proposes to renounce all share in the trade carried on between the tribes of the Upper Lakes and the people of Canada.

La Salle seems to have had an interview with the minister, in which the proposals of his memorial were somewhat modified. He soon received in reply the following patent from the King:—

THE KING'S APPROVAL.

"Louis, by the grace of God King of France and Navarre, to our dear and well-beloved Robert Cavelier, Sieur de la Salle, greeting. We have received with favor the very humble petition made us in your name, to permit you to labor at the discovery of the western parts of New France; and we have the more willingly entertained this proposal, [Pg 125] since we have nothing more at heart than the exploration of this country, through which, to all appearance, a way may be found to Mexico.... For this and other causes thereunto moving us, we permit you by these presents, signed with our hand, to labor at the discovery of the western parts of our aforesaid country of New France; and, for the execution of this enterprise, to build forts at such places as you may think necessary, and enjoy possession thereof under the same clauses and conditions as of Fort Frontenac, conformably to our letters patent of May thirteenth, 1675, which, so far as needful, we confirm by these presents. And it is our will that they be executed according to their form and tenor: on condition, nevertheless, that you finish this enterprise within five years, failing which, these presents shall be void, and of no effect; that you carry on no trade with the savages called Ottawas, or with other tribes who bring their peltries to Montreal; and that you do the whole at your own cost and that of your associates, to whom we have granted the sole right of trade in buffalo-hides. And we direct the Sieur Count Frontenac, our governor and lieutenant-general, and also Duchesneau, intendant of justice, police, and finance, and the officers of the supreme council of the aforesaid country, to see to the execution of these presents; for such is our pleasure.

"Given at St. Germain en Laye, this 12th day of May, 1678, and of our reign the 35th year."

This patent grants both more and less than the [Pg 126] memorial had asked. It authorizes La Salle to build and own, not two forts only, but as many as he may see fit, provided that he do so within five years; and it gives him, besides, the monopoly of buffalo-hides, for which at first he had not petitioned. Nothing is said of colonies. To discover the country, secure it by forts, and find, if possible, a way to Mexico, are the only object set forth; for Louis XIV. always discountenanced settlement in the West, partly as tending to deplete Canada, and partly as removing his subjects too far from his paternal control. It was but the year before that he refused to Louis Joliet the permission to plant a trading station in the Valley of the Mississippi.[99] La Salle, however, still held to his plan of a commercial and industrial colony, and in connection with it to another purpose, of which his memorial had made no mention. This was the building of a vessel on some branch of the Mississippi, in order to sail down that river to its mouth, and open a route to commerce through the Gulf of Mexico. It is evident that this design was already formed; for he had no sooner received his patent, than he engaged ship-carpenters, and procured iron, cordage, and anchors, not for one vessel, but for two.

MONEY AND MEANS.

What he now most needed was money; and having none of his own, he set himself to raising it from others. A notary named Simonnet lent him four thousand livres; an advocate named Raoul, twenty-four [Pg 127] thousand; and one Dumont, six thousand. His cousin François Plet, a merchant of Rue St. Martin, lent him about eleven thousand, at the interest of forty per cent; and when he returned to Canada, Frontenac found means to procure him another loan of about fourteen thousand, secured by the mortgage of Fort Frontenac. But his chief helpers were his family, who became sharers in his undertaking. "His brothers and relations," says a memorial afterwards addressed by them to the King, "spared nothing to enable him to respond worthily to the royal goodness;" and the document adds, that, before his allotted five years were ended, his discoveries had cost them more than five hundred thousand livres (francs).[100] La Salle himself believed, and made others believe, that there was more profit than risk in his schemes.

Lodged rather obscurely in Rue de la Truanderie, and of a nature reserved and shy, he nevertheless found countenance and support from personages no less exalted than Colbert, Seignelay, and the Prince de Conti. Others, too, in stations less conspicuous, warmly espoused his cause, and none more so than the learned Abbé Renaudot, who helped him with tongue and pen, and seems to have been instrumental in introducing to him a man who afterwards proved invaluable. This was Henri de Tonty, an Italian [Pg 128] officer, a *protégé* of the Prince de Conti, who sent him to La Salle as a person suited to his purposes, Tonty had but one hand, the other having been blown off by a grenade in the Sicilian wars.[101] His father, who had been governor of Gaeta, but who had come to France in consequence of political disturbances in Naples, had earned no small reputation as a financier, and had invented the form of life insurance still called the Tontine. La Salle learned to know his new lieutenant on the voyage across the Atlantic; and, soon after reaching Canada, he wrote of him to his patron in the following terms: "His honorable character and his amiable disposition were well known to you; but perhaps you would not have thought him capable of doing things for which a strong constitution, an acquaintance with the country, and the use of both hands seemed absolutely necessary. Nevertheless, his energy and address make him equal to anything; and now, at a season when everybody is in fear of the ice, he is setting out to begin a new fort, two hundred leagues from this place, and to which I have taken the liberty to give the name of Fort Conti. It is situated near that great cataract, more than a hundred and twenty *toises* in height, by which the lakes of higher elevation precipitate themselves into Lake Frontenac [Ontario]. From there one goes by water, five hundred leagues, to the place where Fort Dauphin is to be begun; from which it only remains to descend the great [Pg 129] river of the Bay of St. Esprit, to reach the Gulf of Mexico."[102]

Besides Tonty, La Salle found in France another ally, La Motte de Lussière, to whom he offered a share in the enterprise, and who joined him at Rochelle, the place of embarkation. Here vexatious delays occurred. Bellinzani, director of trade, who had formerly taken lessons in rascality in the service of Cardinal Mazarin, abused his official position to throw obstacles in the way of La Salle, in order to extort money from him; and he extorted, in fact, a considerable sum, which his victim afterwards reclaimed. It was not till the fourteenth of July that La Salle, with Tonty, La Motte, and thirty men, set sail for Canada, and two months more elapsed before he reached Quebec. Here, to increase his resources and strengthen his position, he seems to have made a league with several Canadian merchants, [Pg 130] some of whom had before been his enemies, and were to be so again. Here, too, he found Father Louis Hennepin, who had come down from Fort Frontenac to meet him.[103]

FOOTNOTES:

[97] *Mémoire pour Monseigneur le Marquis de Seignelay sur les Descouvertes du Sieur de la Salle*, 1682.

[98] *État de la dépense faite par M*ʳ *de la Salle, Gouverneur du Fort Frontenac. Récit de Nicolas de la Salle. Revue faite au Fort de Frontenac, 1677; Mémoire sur le Projet du Sieur de la Salle* (Margry, i. 329). Plan of Fort Frontenac, published by Faillon, from the original sent to France by Denonville in 1685. *Relation des Découvertes du Sieur de la Salle*. When Frontenac was at the fort in September, 1677, he found only four *habitants*. It appears, by the *Relation des Découvertes du Sieur de la Salle*, that, three or four years later, there were thirteen or fourteen families. La Salle spent 34,426 francs on the fort. *Mémoire au Roy, Papiers de Famille*.

[99] *Colbert à Duchesneau, 28 Avril, 1677.*

[100] *Mémoire au Roy, présenté sous la Régence; Obligation du Sieur de la Salle envers le Sieur Plet; Autres Emprunts de Cavelier de la Salle* (Margry, i. 423-432).

[101] Tonty, *Mémoire*, in Margry, *Relations et Mémoires inédits*, 5.

[102] *Lettre de La Salle, 31 Oct., 1678.* Fort Conti was to have been built on the site of the present Fort Niagara. The name of Lac de Conti was given by La Salle to Lake Erie. The fort mentioned as Fort Dauphin was built, as we shall see, on the Illinois, though under another name. La Salle, deceived by Spanish maps, thought that the Mississippi discharged itself into the Bay of St. Esprit (Mobile Bay).

Henri de Tonty signed his name in the Gallicized, and not in the original Italian form *Tonti.* He wore a hand of iron or some other metal, which was usually covered with a glove. La Potherie says that he once or twice used it to good purpose when the Indians became disorderly, in breaking the heads of the most contumacious or knocking out their teeth. Not knowing at the time the secret of the unusual efficacy of his blows, they regarded him as a "medicine" of the first order. La Potherie erroneously ascribes the loss of his hand to a sabre-cut received in a *sortie* at Messina.

[103] *La Motte de Lussière à ——, sans date; Mémoire de la Salle sur les Extorsions commises par Bellinzani; Société formée par La Salle; Relation de Henri de Tonty,* 1684 (Margry, i. 338, 573; ii. 2, 25).

[Pg 131]

CHAPTER IX.

1678-1679.

LA SALLE AT NIAGARA.

FATHER LOUIS HENNEPIN: HIS PAST LIFE; HIS CHARACTER.—EMBARKATION.—
NIAGARA FALLS.—INDIAN JEALOUSY.—LA MOTTE AND THE SENECAS.—A
DISASTER.—LA SALLE AND HIS FOLLOWERS.

HENNEPIN was all eagerness to join in the adventure; and, to his great satisfaction, La Salle gave him a letter from his Provincial, Father Le Fèvre, containing the coveted permission. Whereupon, to prepare himself, he went into retreat at the Récollet convent of Quebec, where he remained for a time in such prayer and meditation as his nature, the reverse of spiritual, would permit. Frontenac, always partial to his Order, then invited him to dine at the château; and having visited the bishop and asked his blessing, he went down to the Lower Town and embarked. His vessel was a small birch canoe, paddled by two men. With sandalled feet, a coarse gray capote, and peaked hood, the cord of St. Francis about his waist, and a rosary and crucifix hanging at his side, the father set forth on his memorable journey. He [Pg 132] carried with him the furniture of a portable altar, which in time of need he could strap on his back like a knapsack.

He slowly made his way up the St. Lawrence, stopping here and there, where a clearing and a few log houses marked the feeble beginning of a parish and a seigniory. The settlers, though good Catholics, were too few and too poor to support a priest, and hailed the arrival of the friar with delight. He said mass, exhorted a little, as was his custom, and on one occasion baptized a child. At length he reached Montreal, where the enemies of the enterprise enticed away his two canoe-men. He succeeded in finding two others, with whom he continued his voyage, passed the rapids of the upper St. Lawrence, and reached Fort Frontenac at eleven o'clock at night of the second of November, where his brethren of the mission,

Ribourde and Buisset, received him with open arms.[104] La Motte, with most of the men, appeared on the eighth; but La Salle and Tonty did not arrive till more than a month later. Meanwhile, in pursuance of his orders, fifteen men set out in canoes for Lake Michigan and the Illinois, to trade with the Indians and collect provisions, while La Motte embarked in a small vessel for Niagara, accompanied by Hennepin.[105]

Father Hennepin Celebrating Mass.
Drawn by Howard Pyle.

[Pg 133]

HENNEPIN

This bold, hardy, and adventurous friar, the historian of the expedition, and a conspicuous actor in it, has unwittingly painted his own portrait with tolerable distinctness. "I always," he says, "felt a strong inclination to fly from the world and live according to the rules of a pure and severe virtue; and it was with this view that I entered the Order of St. Francis."[106] He then speaks of his zeal for the saving of souls, but admits that a passion for travel and a burning desire to visit strange lands had no small part in his inclination for the missions.[107] Being in a convent in Artois, his Superior sent him to Calais, at the season of the herring-fishery, to beg alms, after the practice of the Franciscans. Here and at Dunkirk he made friends of the sailors, and was never tired of their stories. So insatiable, indeed, was his appetite for them, that "often," he says, "I hid myself behind tavern doors while the sailors were telling of their voyages. The tobacco smoke made me very sick at the stomach; but, notwithstanding, I listened attentively to all they said about their adventures at sea and their travels in distant countries. I could have passed whole days and nights in this way without eating."[108]

He presently set out on a roving mission through [Pg 134] Holland; and he recounts various mishaps which befell him, "in consequence of my zeal in laboring for the saving of souls," "I was at the bloody fight of Seneff," he pursues, "where so many perished by fire and sword, and where I had abundance of work in comforting and consoling the poor wounded soldiers. After undergoing great fatigues, and running extreme danger in the sieges of towns, in the trenches, and in battles, where I exposed myself freely for the salvation of others while the soldiers were breathing nothing but blood and carnage, I found myself at last in a way of satisfying my old inclination for travel."[109]

He got leave from his superiors to go to Canada, the most adventurous of all the missions, and accordingly sailed in 1675, in the ship which carried La Salle, who had just obtained the grant of Fort Frontenac. In the course of the voyage, he took it upon him to reprove a party of girls who were amusing themselves and a circle of officers and other passengers by dancing on deck. La Salle, who was among the spectators, was annoyed at Hennepin's interference, and told him that he was behaving like a pedagogue. The friar retorted, by alluding— unconsciously, as he says—to the circumstance that La Salle was once a pedagogue himself, having, according to Hennepin, been for ten or twelve years teacher of a class in a Jesuit school. La Salle, he adds, turned pale with rage, and never forgave him [Pg 135] to his dying day, but always maligned and persecuted him.[110]

On arriving in Canada, he was sent up to Fort Frontenac, as a missionary. That wild and remote post was greatly to his liking. He planted a gigantic cross, superintended the building of a chapel for himself and his colleague Buisset, and instructed the Iroquois colonists of the place. He visited, too, the neighboring Indian settlements, —paddling his canoe in summer, when the lake was open, and journeying in winter on snow-shoes, with a blanket slung at his back. His most noteworthy journey was one which he made in the winter,—apparently of 1677,—with a soldier of the fort. They crossed the eastern extremity of Lake Ontario on snow-shoes, and pushed southward through the forests, towards Onondaga,— stopping at evening to dig away the snow, which was several feet deep, and collect wood for their fire, which they were forced to replenish repeatedly during the night, to keep themselves from freezing. At length, they reached the great Onondaga town, where the Indians were much amazed at their hardihood. Thence they proceeded eastward to the Oneidas, and afterwards to the Mohawks, who regaled them with small frogs, pounded up with a porridge of Indian corn. Here Hennepin found the Jesuit Bruyas, who permitted him to copy a dictionary [Pg 136] of the Mohawk language[111] which he had compiled; and here he presently met three Dutchmen, who urged him to visit the neighboring settlement of Orange, or Albany,—an invitation which he seems to have declined.[112]

They were pleased with him, he says, because he spoke Dutch. Bidding them farewell, he tied on his snow-shoes again, and returned with his companion to Fort Frontenac. Thus he inured himself to the hardships of the woods, and prepared for the execution of the grand plan of discovery which he calls his own,— "an enterprise," to borrow his own words, "capable of terrifying anybody but me."[113] When the later editions of his book appeared, doubts had been expressed of his veracity. "I here protest to you, before God," he writes, addressing the reader, "that my narrative is faithful and sincere, and that you may believe everything related in it."[114] And yet, as we shall see, this reverend father was the most impudent of liars; and the narrative of which he speaks is a rare monument of brazen mendacity. Hennepin, however, had seen and dared much; for [Pg 137] among his many failings fear had no part, and where his vanity or his spite was not involved, he often told the truth. His books have their value, with all their enormous fabrications.[115]

La Motte and Hennepin, with sixteen men, went on board the little vessel of ten tons, which lay at Fort Frontenac. The friar's two brethren, Buisset and Ribourde, threw their arms about his neck as they bade him farewell; while his Indian proselytes, learning whither he was bound, stood with their hands pressed upon their mouths, in amazement at the perils which awaited their ghostly instructor. La Salle, with the rest of the party, was to follow as soon as he could finish his preparations. It was a boisterous and gusty day, the eighteenth of November. The sails were spread; the shore receded,—the stone walls of the fort, the huge cross that the friar had reared, the wigwams, the settlers' cabins, the group of staring Indians on the strand. The lake was rough; and the men, crowded in so small a craft, grew nervous and uneasy. They hugged the northern shore, to escape the fury of the wind, which blew savagely from the northeast; while the long gray sweep of naked forests on their right betokened that winter was fast closing in. On the twenty-sixth, they reached the neighborhood of the Indian town of [Pg 138] Taiaiagon,[116] not far from Toronto, and ran their vessel, for safety, into the mouth of a river,—probably the Humber,—where the ice closed about her, and they were forced to cut her out with axes. On the fifth of December, they attempted to cross to the mouth of the Niagara; but darkness overtook them, and they spent a comfortless night, tossing on the troubled lake, five or six miles from shore. In the morning, they entered the mouth of the Niagara, and landed on the point at its eastern side, where now stand the historic ramparts of Fort Niagara. Here they found a small village of Senecas, attracted hither by the fisheries, who gazed with curious eyes at the vessel, and listened in wonder as the voyagers sang *Te Deum* in gratitude for their safe arrival.

NIAGARA FALLS.

Hennepin, with several others, now ascended the river in a canoe to the foot of the mountain ridge of Lewiston, which, stretching on the right hand and on the left, forms the acclivity of a vast plateau, rent with the mighty chasm, along which, from this point to the cataract, seven miles above, rush, with the fury of an Alpine torrent, the gathered waters of four inland oceans. To urge the canoe farther was impossible. He landed, with his companions, on the west bank, near the foot of that part of the ridge now called Queenstown Heights, climbed the steep ascent, and pushed through the wintry forest on a [Pg 139] tour of exploration. On his left sank the cliffs, the furious river raging below; till at length, in primeval solitudes unprofaned as yet by the pettiness of man, the imperial cataract burst upon his sight.[117]

The explorers passed three miles beyond it, and encamped for the night on the banks of Chippewa Creek, scraping away the snow, which was a foot deep, in order to kindle a fire. In the morning they retraced their steps, startling a number of deer and wild turkeys on their way, and rejoined their companions at the mouth of the river.

[Pg 140]

LA MOTTE AND THE SENECAS.

La Motte now began the building of a fortified house, some two leagues above the mouth of the Niagara.[118] Hot water was used to soften the frozen ground; but frost was not the only obstacle. The Senecas of the neighboring village betrayed a sullen jealousy at a design which, indeed, boded them no good. Niagara was the key to the four great lakes above; and whoever held possession of it could, in no small measure, control the fur-trade of the interior. Occupied by the French, it would in time of peace intercept the trade which the Iroquois carried on between the western Indians and the Dutch and English at Albany, and in time of war threaten them with serious danger. La Motte saw the necessity of conciliating these formidable neighbors, and, if possible, cajoling them to give their consent to the plan. La Salle, indeed, had instructed him to that effect. He resolved on a journey to the great village of the Senecas, and called on Hennepin, who was busied in building a bark chapel for himself, to accompany him. They accordingly set out with several men well armed and equipped, and bearing at their backs presents of very considerable value. The village was beyond the Genesee, southeast of the site of Rochester.[119] After a march of five days, they reached it on the last day of December. They were conducted [Pg 141] to the lodge of the great chief, where they were beset by a staring crowd of women and children. Two Jesuits, Raffeix and Julien Garnier, were in the village; and their presence boded no good for the embassy. La Motte, who seems to have had little love for priests of any kind, was greatly annoyed at seeing them; and when the chiefs assembled to hear what he had to say, he insisted that the two fathers should leave the council-house. At this, Hennepin, out of respect for his cloth, thought it befitting that he should retire also. The chiefs, forty-two in number, squatted on the ground, arrayed in ceremonial robes of beaver, wolf, or black-squirrel skin. "The senators of Venice," writes Hennepin, "do not look more grave or speak more deliberately than the counsellors of the Iroquois." La Motte's interpreter harangued the attentive conclave, placed gift after gift at their feet,—coats, scarlet cloth, hatchets, knives, and beads,—and used all his eloquence to persuade them that the building of a fort on the banks of the Niagara, and a vessel on Lake Erie, were measures vital to their interest. They gladly took the gifts, but answered the interpreter's speech with evasive generalities; and having been entertained with the burning of an Indian prisoner, the discomfited embassy returned, half-famished, to Niagara.

Meanwhile, La Salle and Tonty were on their way from Fort Frontenac, with men and supplies, to join La Motte and his advance party. They were [Pg 142] in a small vessel, with a pilot either unskilful or treacherous. On Christmas eve, he was near wrecking them off the Bay of Quinté. On the next day they crossed to the mouth of the Genesee; and La Salle, after some delay, proceeded to the neighboring town of the Senecas, where he appears to have arrived just after the departure of La Motte and Hennepin. He, too, called them to a council, and tried to soothe the extreme jealousy with which they regarded his proceedings. "I told them my plan," he says, "and gave the best pretexts I could, and I succeeded in my attempt."[120] More fortunate than La Motte, he persuaded them to consent to his carrying arms and ammunition by the Niagara portage, building a vessel above the cataract, and establishing a fortified warehouse at the mouth of the river.

JEALOUSIES.

This success was followed by a calamity. La Salle had gone up the Niagara to find a suitable place for a ship-yard, when he learned that the pilot in charge of the vessel he had left had disobeyed his orders, and ended by wrecking it on the coast. Little was saved except the anchors and cables destined for the new vessel to be built above the cataract. This loss threw him into extreme perplexity, and, as

Hennepin says, "would have made anybody but him give up the enterprise."[121] The whole party were now gathered [Pg 143] at the palisaded house which La Motte had built, a little below the mountain ridge of Lewiston. They were a motley crew of French, Flemings, and Italians, all mutually jealous. La Salle's enemies had tampered with some of the men; and none of them seemed to have had much heart for the enterprise. The fidelity even of La Motte was doubtful. "He served me very ill," says La Salle; "and Messieurs de Tonty and de la Forest knew that he did his best to debauch all my men."[122] His health soon failed under the hardships of these winter journeyings, and he returned to Fort Frontenac, half-blinded by an inflammation of the eyes.[123] La Salle, seldom happy in the choice of subordinates, had, perhaps, in all his company but one man whom he could fully trust; and this was Tonty. He and Hennepin were on indifferent terms. Men thrown together in a rugged enterprise like this quickly learn to know each other; and the vain and assuming friar was not likely to commend himself to La Salle's brave and loyal lieutenant. Hennepin says that it was La Salle's policy to govern through the dissensions of his followers; and, from whatever cause, it is certain that those beneath him were rarely in perfect harmony.

FOOTNOTES:

[104] Hennepin, *Description de la Louisiane* (1683), 19; Ibid., *Voyage Curieux* (1704), 66. Ribourde had lately arrived.

[105] *Lettre de La Motte de la Lussière, sans date; Relation de Henri de Tonty écrite de Québec, le 14 Novembre, 1684* (Margry, i. 573). This paper, apparently addressed to Abbé Renaudot, is entirely distinct from Tonty's memoir of 1693, addressed to the minister Ponchartrain.

[106] Hennepin, *Nouvelle Découverte* (1697), 8.

[107] Ibid., *Avant Propos*, 5.

[108] Ibid., *Voyage Curieux* (1704), 12.

[109] Hennepin, *Voyage Curieux* (1704), 18.

[110] Ibid. *Avis au Lecteur*. He elsewhere represents himself as on excellent terms with La Salle; with whom, he says, he used to read histories of travels at Fort Frontenac, after which they discussed together their plans of discovery.

[111] This was the *Racines Agnières* of Bruyas. It was published by Mr. Shea in 1862. Hennepin seems to have studied it carefully; for on several occasions he makes use of words evidently borrowed from it, putting them into the mouths of Indians speaking a dialect different from that of the Agniers, or Mohawks.

[112] Compare Brodhead in *Hist. Mag.*, x. 268.

[113] "Une enterprise capable d'épouvanter tout autre que moi."— Hennepin, *Voyage Curieux, Avant Propos* (1704).

[114] "Je vous proteste ici devant Dieu, que ma Relation est fidèle et sincère," etc.—Ibid., *Avis au Lecteur*.

[115] The nature of these fabrications will be shown hereafter. They occur, not in the early editions of Hennepin's narrative, which are comparatively truthful, but in the edition of 1697 and those which followed. La Salle was dead at the time of their publication.

[116] This place is laid down on a manuscript map sent to France by the Intendant Duchesneau, and now preserved in the Archives de la Marine, and also on several other contemporary maps.

[117] Hennepin's account of the falls and river of Niagara—especially his second account, on his return from the West—is very minute, and on the whole very accurate. He indulges in gross exaggeration as to the height of the cataract, which, in the edition of 1683, he states at five hundred feet, and raises to six hundred in that of 1697. He also says that there was room for four carriages to pass abreast under the American Fall without being wet. This is, of course, an exaggeration at the best; but it is extremely probable that a great change has taken place since his time. He speaks of a small lateral fall at the west side of the Horse Shoe Fall which does not now exist. Table Rock, now destroyed, is distinctly figured in his picture. He says that he descended the cliffs on the west side to the foot of the cataract, but that no human being can get down on the east side.

The name of Niagara, written *Onguiaahra* by Lalemant in 1641, and *Ongiara* by Sanson, on his map of 1657, is used by Hennepin in its present form. His description of the falls is the earliest known to exist. They are clearly indicated on the map of Champlain, 1632. For early references to them, see "The Jesuits in North America," 235, *note*. A brief but curious notice of them is given by Gendron, *Quelques Particularitez du Pays des Hurons*, 1659. The indefatigable Dr. O'Callaghan has discovered thirty-nine distinct forms of the name Niagara. *Index to Colonial Documents of New*

York, 465. It is of Iroquois origin, and in the Mohawk dialect is pronounced Nyàgarah.

[118] Tonty, *Relation*, 1684 (Margry, i. 573).
[119] Near the town of Victor. It is laid down on the map of Galinée, and other unpublished maps. Compare Marshall, *Historical Sketches of the Niagara Frontier*, 14.
[120] *Lettre de La Salle à un de ses associés* (Margry, ii. 32).
[121] *Description de la Louisiane* (1683), 41. It is characteristic of Hennepin that, in the editions of his book published after La Salle's death, he substitutes, for "anybody but him," "anybody but those who had formed so generous a design,"—meaning to include himself, though he lost nothing by the disaster, and had not formed the design.

On these incidents, compare the two narratives of Tonty, of 1684 and 1693. The book bearing Tonty's name is a compilation full of errors. He disowned its authorship.

[122] *Lettre de La Salle, 22 Août, 1682* (Margry, ii. 212).
[123] *Lettre de La Motte, sans date.*

[Pg 144]

CHAPTER X.

1679.

THE LAUNCH OF THE "GRIFFIN."

THE NIAGARA PORTAGE.—A VESSEL ON THE STOCKS.—SUFFERING AND
DISCONTENT.—LA SALLE'S WINTER JOURNEY.—THE VESSEL LAUNCHED.—FRESH
DISASTERS.

THE NIAGARA PORTAGE.

A MORE important work than that of the warehouse at the mouth of
the river was now to be begun. This was the building of a vessel
above the cataract. The small craft which had brought La Motte and
Hennepin with their advance party had been hauled to the foot of the
rapids at Lewiston, and drawn ashore with a capstan, to save her
from the drifting ice. Her lading was taken out, and must now be
carried beyond the cataract to the calm water above. The distance to
the destined point was at least twelve miles, and the steep heights
above Lewiston must first be climbed. This heavy task was
accomplished on the twenty-second of January. The level of the
plateau was reached, and the file of burdened men, some thirty in
number, toiled slowly on its way over the snowy plains and through
the gloomy forests of spruce and naked oak-trees; while Hennepin
plodded through the drifts with his portable altar [Pg 145] lashed fast
to his back. They came at last to the mouth of a stream which entered
the Niagara two leagues above the cataract, and which was
undoubtedly that now called Cayuga Creek.[124]

[Pg 146]

Trees were felled, the place cleared, and the master-carpenter set his
ship-builders at work. Meanwhile, two Mohegan hunters, attached
to the party, made bark wigwams to lodge the men. Hennepin had
his chapel, apparently of the same material, where he placed his

altar, and on Sundays and saints' days said mass, preached, and exhorted; while some of the men, who knew the Gregorian chant, lent their aid at the service. When the carpenters were ready to lay the keel of the vessel, La Salle asked the friar to drive the first bolt; "but the modesty of my religious profession," he says, "compelled me to decline this honor."

Fortunately, it was the hunting-season of the Iroquois, and most of the Seneca warriors were in the forests south of Lake Erie; yet enough remained to cause serious uneasiness. They loitered sullenly about the place, expressing their displeasure at the proceedings of the French. One of them, pretending [Pg 147] to be drunk, attacked the blacksmith and tried to kill him; but the Frenchman, brandishing a red-hot bar of iron, held him at bay till Hennepin ran to the rescue, when, as he declares, the severity of his rebuke caused the savage to desist.[125] The work of the ship-builders advanced rapidly; and when the Indian visitors beheld the vast ribs of the wooden monster, their jealousy was redoubled. A squaw told the French that they meant to burn the vessel on the stocks. All now stood anxiously on the watch. Cold, hunger, and discontent found imperfect antidotes in Tonty's energy and Hennepin's sermons.

SUFFERING AND DISCONTENT.

La Salle was absent, and his lieutenant commanded in his place. Hennepin says that Tonty was jealous because he, the friar, kept a journal, and that he was forced to use all manner of just precautions to prevent the Italian from seizing it. The men, being half-starved, in consequence of the loss of their provisions on Lake Ontario, were restless and moody; and their discontent was fomented by one of their number, who had very probably been tampered with by La Salle's enemies.[126] The Senecas refused to [Pg 148] supply them with corn, and the frequent exhortations of the Récollet father proved an insufficient substitute. In this extremity, the two Mohegans did excellent service,—bringing deer and other game, which relieved the most pressing wants of the party, and went far to restore their cheerfulness.

La Salle, meanwhile, had gone down to the mouth of the river, with a sergeant and a number of men; and here, on the high point of land where Fort Niagara now stands, he marked out the foundations of two blockhouses.[127] Then, leaving his men to build them, he set out on foot for Fort Frontenac, where the condition of his affairs demanded his presence, and where he hoped to procure supplies to replace those lost in the wreck of his vessel. It was February, and the distance was some two hundred and fifty miles, through the snow-encumbered forests of the Iroquois and over the ice of Lake Ontario. Two men attended him, and a dog dragged his baggage on a sledge. For food, they had only a bag of parched corn, which failed them two days before they reached the fort; and they made the rest of the journey fasting.

THE SHIP FINISHED.

During his absence, Tonty finished the vessel, which was of about forty-five tons' burden.[128] As [Pg 149] spring opened, she was ready for launching. The friar pronounced his blessing on her; the assembled company sang *Te Deum*; cannon were fired; and French and Indians, warmed alike by a generous gift of brandy, shouted and yelped in chorus as she glided into the Niagara. Her builders towed her out and anchored her in the stream, safe at last from incendiary hands; and then, swinging their hammocks under her deck, slept in peace, beyond reach of the tomahawk. The Indians gazed on her with amazement. Five small cannon looked out from her portholes; and on her prow was carved a portentous monster, the Griffin, whose name she bore, in honor of the armorial bearings of Frontenac. La Salle had often been heard to say that he would make the griffin fly above the crows, or, in other words, make Frontenac triumph over the Jesuits.

They now took her up the river, and made her fast below the swift current at Black Rock. Here they finished her equipment, and waited for La Salle's return; but the absent commander did not appear. The spring and more than half of the summer had passed before they saw him again. At length, early in August, he arrived at the mouth of the Niagara, bringing three more friars; for, though no friend of the Jesuits, he was zealous for the Faith, and was rarely without a missionary in his journeyings. Like Hennepin, the three friars were all Flemings. One [Pg 150] of them, Melithon Watteau, was to remain at Niagara; the others, Zenobe Membré and Gabriel Ribourde, were to preach the Faith among the tribes of the West. Ribourde was a hale and cheerful old man of sixty-four. He went four times up and down the Lewiston heights, while the men were climbing the steep pathway with their loads. It required four of them, well stimulated with brandy, to carry up the principal anchor destined for the "Griffin."

La Salle brought a tale of disaster. His enemies, bent on ruining the enterprise, had given out that he was embarked on a harebrained venture, from which he would never return. His creditors, excited by rumors set afloat to that end, had seized on all his property in the settled parts of Canada, though his seigniory of Fort Frontenac alone would have more than sufficed to pay all his debts. There was no remedy. To defer the enterprise would have been to give his adversaries the triumph that they sought; and he hardened himself against the blow with his usual stoicism.[129]

FOOTNOTES:

[124] It has been a matter of debate on which side of the Niagara the first vessel on the Upper Lakes was built. A close study of Hennepin, and a careful examination of the localities, have convinced me that the spot was that indicated above. Hennepin repeatedly alludes to a large detached rock, rising out of the water at the foot of the rapids above Lewiston, on the west side of the river. This rock may still be seen immediately under the western end of the Lewiston suspension-bridge. Persons living in the neighborhood remember that a ferry-boat used to pass between it and the cliffs of the

western shore; but it has since been undermined by the current and has inclined in that direction, so that a considerable part of it is submerged, while the gravel and earth thrown down from the cliff during the building of the bridge has filled the intervening channel. Opposite to this rock, and on the east side of the river, says Hennepin, are three mountains, about two leagues below the cataract. (*Nouveau Voyage* (1704), 462, 466.) To these "three mountains," as well as to the rock, he frequently alludes. They are also spoken of by La Hontan, who clearly indicates their position. They consist in the three successive grades of the acclivity: first, that which rises from the level of the water, forming the steep and lofty river-bank; next, an intermediate ascent, crowned by a sort of terrace, where the tired men could find a second resting-place and lay down their burdens, whence a third effort carried them with difficulty to the level top of the plateau. That this was the actual "portage," or carrying place of the travellers, is shown by Hennepin (1704), 114, who describes the carrying of anchors and other heavy articles up these heights in August, 1679. La Hontan also passed the Falls by way of the "three mountains" eight years later. La Hontan (1703), 106. It is clear, then, that the portage was on the east side, whence it would be safe to conclude that the vessel was built on the same side. Hennepin says that she was built at the mouth of a stream (*rivière*) entering the Niagara two leagues above the Falls. Excepting one or two small brooks, there is no stream on the west side but Chippewa Creek, which Hennepin had visited and correctly placed at about a league from the cataract. His distances on the Niagara are usually correct. On the east side there is a stream which perfectly answers the conditions. This is Cayuga Creek, two leagues above the Falls. Immediately in front of it is an island about a mile long, separated from the shore by a narrow and deep arm of the Niagara, into which Cayuga Creek discharges itself. The place is so obviously suited to building and launching a vessel, that, in the early part of this century, the government of the United States chose it for the construction of a schooner to carry supplies to the garrisons of the Upper Lakes. The neighboring village now bears the name of La Salle.

In examining this and other localities on the Niagara, I have been greatly aided by my friend O. H. Marshall, Esq., of Buffalo, who is unrivalled in his knowledge of the history and traditions of the Niagara frontier.

[125] Hennepin (1704), 97. On a paper drawn up at the instance of the Intendant Duchesneau, the names of the greater number of La Salle's men

are preserved. These agree with those given by Hennepin: thus, the master-carpenter, whom he calls Maître Moyse, appears as Moïse Hillaret; and the blacksmith, whom he calls La Forge, is mentioned as—(illegible) dit la Forge.

[126] "This bad man," says Hennepin, "would infallibly have debauched our workmen, if I had not reassured them by the exhortations which I made them on fête-days and Sundays, after divine service." (1704), 98.

[127] *Lettre de La Salle, 22 Août, 1682* (Margry, ii. 197); *Relation de Tonty*, 1684 (Ibid., i. 577). He called this new post Fort Conti. It was burned some months after, by the carelessness of the sergeant in command, and was the first of a succession of forts on this historic spot.

[128] Hennepin (1683), 46. In the edition of 1697, he says that it was of sixty tons. I prefer to follow the earlier and more trustworthy narrative.

[129] La Salle's embarrassment at this time was so great that he purposed to send Tonty up the lakes in the "Griffin," while he went back to the colony to look after his affairs; but suspecting that the pilot, who had already wrecked one of his vessels, was in the pay of his enemies, he resolved at last to take charge of the expedition himself, to prevent a second disaster. (*Lettre de La Salle, 22 Août, 1682*; Margry, ii. 214.) Among the creditors who bore hard upon him were Migeon, Charon, Giton, and Peloquin, of Montreal, in whose name his furs at Fort Frontenac had been seized. The intendant also placed under seal all his furs at Quebec, among which is set down the not very precious item of two hundred and eighty-four skins of *enfants du diable*, or skunks.

[Pg 151]

CHAPTER XI.

1679.

LA SALLE ON THE UPPER LAKES.

THE VOYAGE OF THE "GRIFFIN."—DETROIT.—A STORM.—ST. IGNACE OF MICHILIMACKINAC.—RIVALS AND ENEMIES.—LAKE MICHIGAN.—HARDSHIPS.—A THREATENED FIGHT.—FORT MIAMI.—TONTY'S MISFORTUNES.—FOREBODINGS.

THE "Griffin" had lain moored by the shore, so near that Hennepin could preach on Sundays from the deck to the men encamped along the bank. She was now forced up against the current with tow-ropes and sails, till she reached the calm entrance of Lake Erie. On the seventh of August, La Salle and his followers embarked, sang *Te Deum*, and fired their cannon. A fresh breeze sprang up; and with swelling canvas the "Griffin" ploughed the virgin waves of Lake Erie, where sail was never seen before. For three days they held their course over these unknown waters, and on the fourth turned northward into the Strait of Detroit. Here, on the right hand and on the left, lay verdant prairies, dotted with groves and bordered with lofty forests. They saw walnut, chestnut, and wild plum trees, and oaks festooned with grape-vines; herds of deer, [Pg 152] and flocks of swans and wild turkeys. The bulwarks of the "Griffin" were plentifully hung with game which the men killed on shore, and among the rest with a number of bears, much commended by Hennepin for their want of ferocity and the excellence of their flesh. "Those," he says, "who will one day have the happiness to possess this fertile and pleasant strait, will be very much obliged to those who have shown them the way." They crossed Lake St. Clair,[130] and still sailed northward against the current, till now, sparkling in the sun, Lake Huron spread before them like a sea.

ST. IGNACE.

For a time they bore on prosperously. Then the wind died to a calm, then freshened to a gale, then rose to a furious tempest; and the vessel tossed wildly among the short, steep, perilous waves of the raging lake. Even La Salle called on his followers to commend themselves to Heaven. All fell to their prayers but the godless pilot, who was loud in complaint against his commander for having brought him, after the honor he had won on the ocean, to drown at last ignominiously in fresh water. The rest clamored to the saints. St. Anthony of Padua was promised a chapel to be built in his honor, if he would but save them from their jeopardy; while in the same breath La Salle and the friars declared him patron of their great enterprise.[131] The saint heard their prayers. [Pg 153]The obedient winds were tamed; and the "Griffin" plunged on her way through foaming surges that still grew calmer as she advanced. Now the sun shone forth on woody islands, Bois Blanc and Mackinaw and the distant Manitoulins,—on the forest wastes of Michigan and the vast blue bosom of the angry lake; and now her port was won, and she found her rest behind the point of St. Ignace of Michilimackinac, floating in that tranquil cove where crystal waters cover but cannot hide the pebbly depths beneath. Before her rose the house and chapel of the Jesuits, enclosed with palisades; on the right, the Huron village, with its bark cabins and its fence of tall pickets; on the left, the square compact houses of the French traders; and, not far off, the clustered wigwams of an Ottawa village.[132] Here was a centre of the Jesuit missions, and a centre of the Indian trade; and here, under the shadow of the cross, was much sharp practice in the service of Mammon. Keen traders, with or without a license, and lawless *coureurs de bois*, whom a few years of forest life had weaned from civilization, made St. Ignace their resort; and here there were many of them when the "Griffin" came. They and their employers hated and feared La Salle, who, sustained as he was by the governor, might set at nought the prohibition of the King, debarring him from traffic with these tribes. Yet, while plotting [Pg 154] against him, they took pains to allay his distrust by a show of welcome.

The "Griffin" fired her cannon, and the Indians yelped in wonder and amazement. The adventurers landed in state, and marched under arms to the bark chapel of the Ottawa village, where they heard mass. La Salle knelt before the altar, in a mantle of scarlet bordered with gold. Soldiers, sailors, and artisans knelt around him,—black Jesuits, gray Récollets, swarthy *voyageurs*, and painted savages; a devout but motley concourse.

As they left the chapel, the Ottawa chiefs came to bid them welcome, and the Hurons saluted them with a volley of musketry. They saw the "Griffin" at her anchorage, surrounded by more than a hundred bark canoes, like a Triton among minnows. Yet it was with more wonder than good-will that the Indians of the mission gazed on the "floating fort," for so they called the vessel. A deep jealousy of La Salle's designs had been infused into them. His own followers, too, had been tampered with. In the autumn before, it may be remembered, he had sent fifteen men up the lakes to trade for him, with orders to go thence to the Illinois and make preparation against his coming. Early in the summer, Tonty had been despatched in a canoe from Niagara to look after them.[133] It was high time. Most of the men had been seduced from their duty, and had disobeyed [Pg 155] their orders, squandered the goods intrusted to them, or used them in trading on their own account. La Salle found four of them at Michilimackinac. These he arrested, and sent Tonty to the Falls of Ste. Marie, where two others were captured, with their plunder. The rest were in the woods, and it was useless to pursue them.

RIVALS AND ENEMIES.

Anxious and troubled as to the condition of his affairs in Canada. La Salle had meant, after seeing his party safe at Michilimackinac, to leave Tonty to conduct it to the Illinois, while he himself returned to the colony. But Tonty was still at Ste. Marie, and he had none to trust but himself. Therefore, he resolved at all risks to remain with his men; "for," he says, "I judged my presence absolutely necessary to retain such of them as were left me, and prevent them from being enticed away during the winter." Moreover, he thought that he had detected an intrigue of his enemies to hound on the Iroquois against the Illinois, in order to defeat his plan by involving him in the war.

Early in September he set sail again, and passing westward into Lake Michigan,[134] cast anchor near one of the islands at the entrance of Green Bay. Here, for once, he found a friend in the person of a Pottawattamie chief, who had been so wrought upon [Pg 156] by the politic kindness of Frontenac that he declared himself ready to die for the children of Onontio.[135] Here, too, he found several of his advance party, who had remained faithful and collected a large store of furs. It would have been better had they proved false, like the rest. La Salle, who asked counsel of no man, resolved, in spite of his followers, to send back the "Griffin" laden with these furs, and others collected on the way, to satisfy his creditors.[136] It was a rash resolution, for it involved trusting her to the pilot, who had already proved either incompetent or treacherous. She fired a parting shot, and on the eighteenth of September set sail for Niagara, with orders to return to the head of Lake Michigan as soon as she had discharged her cargo. La Salle, with the fourteen men who remained, in four canoes deeply laden with a forge, tools, merchandise, and arms, put out from the island and resumed his voyage.

POTTAWATTAMIES.

The parting was not auspicious. The lake, glassy and calm in the afternoon, was convulsed at night with a sudden storm, when the canoes were midway between the island and the main shore. It was with difficulty that they could keep together, the men [Pg 157] shouting to each other through the darkness. Hennepin, who was in the smallest canoe with a heavy load, and a carpenter for a companion who was awkward at the paddle, found himself in jeopardy which demanded all his nerve. The voyagers thought themselves happy when they gained at last the shelter of a little sandy cove, where they dragged up their canoes, and made their cheerless bivouac in the drenched and dripping forest. Here they spent five days, living on pumpkins and Indian corn, the gift of their Pottawattamie friends, and on a Canada porcupine brought in by La Salle's Mohegan hunter. The gale raged meanwhile with relentless fury. They trembled when they thought of the "Griffin." When at length the tempest lulled, they re-embarked, and steered southward along the shore of Wisconsin; but again the storm fell upon them, and drove them for safety to a bare, rocky islet. Here they made a fire of drift-wood, crouched around it, drew their blankets over their heads, and in this miserable plight, pelted with sleet and rain, remained for two days.

At length they were afloat again; but their prosperity was brief. On the twenty-eighth, a fierce squall drove them to a point of rocks covered with bushes, where they consumed the little that remained of their provisions. On the first of October they paddled about thirty miles, without food, when they came to a village of Pottawattamies, who ran down to the shore to help them to land; but La Salle, fearing [Pg 158] that some of his men would steal the merchandise and desert to the Indians, insisted on going three leagues farther, to the great indignation of his followers. The lake, swept by an easterly gale, was rolling its waves against the beach, like the ocean in a storm. In the attempt to land, La Salle's canoe was nearly swamped. He and his three canoe-men leaped into the water, and in spite of the surf, which nearly drowned them, dragged their vessel ashore with all its load. He then went to the rescue of Hennepin, who with his awkward companion was in woful need of succor. Father Gabriel, with his sixty-four years, was no match for the surf and the violent undertow. Hennepin, finding himself safe, waded to his relief, and carried him ashore on his sturdy shoulders; while the old friar, though drenched to the skin, laughed gayly under his cowl as his brother missionary staggered with him up the beach.[137]

When all were safe ashore, La Salle, who distrusted the Indians they had passed, took post on a hill, and ordered his followers to prepare their guns for action. Nevertheless, as they were starving, an effort must be risked to gain a supply of food; and he sent three men back to the village to purchase it. Well armed, but faint with toil and famine, they made their way through the stormy forest bearing a pipe of peace, but on arriving saw that the scared inhabitants had fled. They found, however, a stock of corn, of [Pg 159] which they took a portion, leaving goods in exchange, and then set out on their return.

Meanwhile, about twenty of the warriors, armed with bows and arrows, approached the camp of the French to reconnoitre. La Salle went to meet them with some of his men, opened a parley with them, and kept them seated at the foot of the hill till his three messengers returned, when on seeing the peace-pipe the warriors set up a cry of joy. In the morning they brought more corn to the camp, with a supply of fresh venison, not a little cheering to the exhausted Frenchmen, who, in dread of treachery, had stood under arms all night.

HARDSHIPS.

This was no journey of pleasure. The lake was ruffled with almost ceaseless storms; clouds big with rain above, a turmoil of gray and gloomy waves beneath. Every night the canoes must be shouldered through the breakers and dragged up the steep banks, which, as they neared the site of Milwaukee, became almost insurmountable. The men paddled all day, with no other food than a handful of Indian corn. They were spent with toil, sick with the haws and wild berries which they ravenously devoured, and dejected at the prospect before them. Father Gabriel's good spirits began to fail. He fainted several times from famine and fatigue, but was revived by a certain "confection of Hyacinth" administered by Hennepin, who had a small box of this precious specific.

At length they descried at a distance, on the stormy shore, two or three eagles among a busy [Pg 160] congregation of crows or turkey buzzards. They paddled in all haste to the spot. The feasters took flight; and the starved travellers found the mangled body of a deer, lately killed by the wolves. This good luck proved the inauguration of plenty. As they approached the head of the lake, game grew abundant; and, with the aid of the Mohegan, there was no lack of bear's meat and venison. They found wild grapes, too, in the woods, and gathered them by cutting down the trees to which the vines clung.

ENCOUNTER WITH INDIANS.

While thus employed, they were startled by a sight often so fearful in the waste and the wilderness,—the print of a human foot. It was clear that Indians were not far off. A strict watch was kept, not, as it proved, without cause; for that night, while the sentry thought of little but screening himself and his gun from the floods of rain, a party of Outagamies crept under the bank, where they lurked for some time before he discovered them. Being challenged, they came forward, professing great friendship, and pretending to have mistaken the French for Iroquois. In the morning, however, there was an outcry from La Salle's servant, who declared that the visitors had stolen his coat from under the inverted canoe where he had placed it; while some of the carpenters also complained of being robbed. La Salle well knew that if the theft were left unpunished, worse would come of it. First, he posted his men at the woody point of a peninsula, whose sandy neck was interposed between them and [Pg 161] the main forest. Then he went forth, pistol in hand, met a young Outagami, seized him, and led him prisoner to his camp. This done, he again set out, and soon found an Outagami chief,—for the wigwams were not far distant,—to whom he told what he had done, adding that unless the stolen goods were restored, the prisoner should be killed. The Indians were in perplexity, for they had cut the coat to pieces and divided it. In this dilemma they resolved, being strong in numbers, to rescue their comrade by force. Accordingly, they came down to the edge of the forest, or posted themselves behind fallen trees on the banks, while La Salle's men in their stronghold braced their nerves for the fight. Here three Flemish friars with their rosaries, and eleven Frenchmen with their guns, confronted a hundred and twenty screeching Outagamies. Hennepin, who had seen service, and who had always an exhortation at his tongue's end, busied himself to inspire the rest with a courage equal to his own. Neither party, however, had an appetite for the fray. A parley ensued: full compensation was made for the stolen goods, and the aggrieved Frenchmen were farther propitiated with a gift of beaver-skins.

Their late enemies, now become friends, spent the next day in dances, feasts, and speeches. They entreated La Salle not to advance farther, since the Illinois, through whose country he must pass, would be sure to kill him; for, added these friendly counsellors, they hated the French because they had been [Pg 162] instigating the Iroquois to invade their country, Here was another subject of anxiety. La Salle was confirmed in his belief that his busy and unscrupulous enemies were intriguing for his destruction.

He pushed on, however, circling around the southern shore of Lake Michigan, till he reached the mouth of the St. Joseph, called by him the Miamis. Here Tonty was to have rejoined him with twenty men, making his way from Michilimackinac along the eastern shore of the lake; but the rendezvous was a solitude,—Tonty was nowhere to be seen. It was the first of November; winter was at hand, and the streams would soon be frozen. The men clamored to go forward, urging that they should starve if they could not reach the villages of the Illinois before the tribe scattered for the winter hunt. La Salle was inexorable. If they should all desert, he said, he, with his Mohegan hunter and the three friars, would still remain and wait for Tonty. The men grumbled, but obeyed; and, to divert their thoughts, he set them at building a fort of timber on a rising ground at the mouth of the river.

They had spent twenty days at this task, and their work was well advanced, when at length Tonty appeared. He brought with him only half of his men. Provisions had failed; and the rest of his party had been left thirty leagues behind, to sustain themselves by hunting. La Salle told him to return and hasten them forward. He set out with two men. A violent north wind arose. He tried to run [Pg 163] his canoe ashore through the breakers. The two men could not manage their vessel, and he with his one hand could not help them. She swamped, rolling over in the surf. Guns, baggage, and provisions were lost; and the three voyagers returned to the Miamis, subsisting on acorns by the way. Happily, the men left behind, excepting two deserters, succeeded, a few days after, in rejoining the party.[138]

FOREBODINGS.

Thus was one heavy load lifted from the heart of La Salle. But where was the "Griffin"? Time enough, and more than enough, had passed for her voyage to Niagara and back again. He scanned the dreary horizon with an anxious eye. No returning sail gladdened the watery solitude, and a dark foreboding gathered on his heart. Yet further delay was impossible. He sent back two men to Michilimackinac to meet her, if she still existed, and pilot her to his new fort of the Miamis, and then prepared to ascend the river, whose weedy edges were already glassed with thin flakes of ice.[139]

FOOTNOTES:

[130] They named it Sainte Claire, of which the present name is a perversion.

[131] Hennepin (1683), 58.

[132] There is a rude plan of the establishment in La Hontan, though in several editions its value is destroyed by the reversal of the plate.

[133] *Relation de Tonty, 1684; Ibid., 1693.* He was overtaken at the Detroit by the "Griffin."

[134] Then usually known as Lac des Illinois, because it gave access to the country of the tribes so called. Three years before, Allouez gave it the name of Lac St. Joseph, by which it is often designated by the early writers. Membré, Douay, and others, call it Lac Dauphin.

[135] "The Great Mountain," the Iroquois name for the governor of Canada. It was borrowed by other tribes also.

[136] In the license of discovery granted to La Salle, he is expressly prohibited from trading with the Ottawas and others who brought furs to Montreal. This traffic on the lakes was, therefore, illicit. His enemy, the

Intendant Duchesneau, afterwards used this against him. *Lettre de Duchesneau au Ministre, 10 Nov., 1680.*

[137] Hennepin (1683), 79.

[138] Hennepin (1683), 112; *Relation de Tonty*, 1693.

[139] The official account of this journey is given at length in the *Relation des Découvertes et des Voyages du Sieur de la Salle*, 1679-1681. This valuable document, compiled from letters and diaries of La Salle, early in the year 1682, was known to Hennepin, who evidently had a copy of it before him when he wrote his book, in which he incorporated many passages from it.

[Pg 164]

CHAPTER XII.

1679, 1680.

LA SALLE ON THE ILLINOIS.

THE ST. JOSEPH.—ADVENTURE OF LA SALLE.—THE PRAIRIES.—FAMINE.—THE GREAT TOWN OF THE ILLINOIS.—INDIANS.—INTRIGUES.—DIFFICULTIES.—POLICY OF LA SALLE.—DESERTION.—ANOTHER ATTEMPT TO POISON LA SALLE.

LA SALLE'S ADVENTURE.

ON the third of December the party re-embarked, thirty-three in all, in eight canoes,[140] and ascended the chill current of the St. Joseph, bordered with dreary meadows and bare gray forests. When they approached the site of the present village of South Bend, they looked anxiously along the shore on their right to find the portage or path leading to the headquarters of the Illinois. The Mohegan was absent, hunting; and, unaided by his practised eye, they passed the path without seeing it. La Salle landed to search the woods. Hours passed, and he did not return. Hennepin and Tonty grew uneasy, disembarked, bivouacked, ordered guns to be fired, and sent out men to scour the country. Night came, but not their lost leader. Muffled in their blankets and [Pg 165] powdered by the thick-falling snow-flakes, they sat ruefully speculating as to what had befallen him; nor was it till four o'clock of the next afternoon that they saw him approaching along the margin of the river. His face and hands were besmirched with charcoal; and he was further decorated with two opossums which hung from his belt, and which he had killed with a stick as they were swinging head downwards from the bough of a tree, after the fashion of that singular beast. He had missed his way in the forest, and had been forced to make a wide circuit around the edge of a swamp; while the snow, of which the air was full, added to his perplexities. Thus he pushed on through the rest of the day and the greater part of the night, till, about two o'clock in the morning, he reached the river again, and fired his gun as a signal to his party. Hearing no answering shot, he pursued his way along the bank, when he presently saw the gleam of a fire among the dense thickets close at hand. Not doubting that he had found the bivouac of his party, he hastened to the spot. To his surprise, no human being was to be seen. Under a tree beside the fire was a heap of dry grass impressed with the form of a man who must have fled but a moment before, for his couch was still warm. It was no doubt an Indian, ambushed on the bank, watching to kill some passing enemy. La Salle called out in several Indian languages; but there was dead silence all around. He then, with admirable coolness, took possession of the quarters he had found, shouting to [Pg 166] their invisible proprietor that he was about to sleep in his bed; piled a barricade of bushes around the spot, rekindled the dying fire, warmed his benumbed hands, stretched himself on the dried grass, and slept undisturbed till morning.

The Mohegan had rejoined the party before La Salle's return, and with his aid the portage was soon found. Here the party encamped. La Salle, who was excessively fatigued, occupied, together with Hennepin, a wigwam covered in the Indian manner with mats of reeds. The cold forced them to kindle a fire, which before daybreak set the mats in a blaze; and the two sleepers narrowly escaped being burned along with their hut.

THE KANKAKEE.

In the morning, the party shouldered their canoes and baggage and began their march for the sources of the river Illinois, some five miles distant. Around them stretched a desolate plain, half-covered with snow and strewn with the skulls and bones of buffalo; while, on its farthest verge, they could see the lodges of the Miami Indians, who had made this place their abode. As they filed on their way, a man named Duplessis, bearing a grudge against La Salle, who walked just before him, raised his gun to shoot him through the back, but was prevented by one of his comrades. They soon reached a spot where the oozy, saturated soil quaked beneath their tread. All around were clumps of alder-bushes, tufts of rank grass, and pools of glistening water. In the midst a dark and lazy current, which a tall man might [Pg 167] bestride, crept twisting like a snake among the weeds and rushes. Here were the sources of the Kankakee, one of the heads of the Illinois.[141] They set their canoes on this thread of water, embarked their baggage and themselves, and pushed down the sluggish streamlet, looking, at a little distance, like men who sailed on land. Fed by an unceasing tribute of the spongy soil, it quickly widened to a river; and they floated on their way through a voiceless, lifeless solitude of dreary oak barrens, or boundless marshes overgrown with reeds. At night, they built their fire on ground made firm by frost, and bivouacked among the rushes. A few days brought them to a more favored region. On the right hand and on the [Pg 168] left stretched the boundless prairie, dotted with leafless groves and bordered by gray wintry forests, scorched by the fires kindled in the dried grass by Indian hunters, and strewn with the carcasses and the bleached skulls of innumerable buffalo. The plains were scored with their pathways, and the muddy edges of the river were full of their hoof-prints. Yet not one was to be seen. At night, the horizon glowed with distant fires; and by day the savage hunters could be descried at times roaming on the verge of the prairie. The men, discontented and half-starved, would have deserted to them had they dared. La Salle's Mohegan could kill no game except two lean deer, with a few wild geese and swans. At length, in their straits, they made a happy discovery. It was a buffalo bull, fast mired in a slough. They killed him, lashed a cable about him, and then twelve men dragged out the shaggy monster, whose ponderous carcass demanded their utmost efforts.

The scene changed again as they descended. On either hand ran ranges of woody hills, following the course of the river; and when they mounted to their tops, they saw beyond them a rolling sea of dull green prairie, a boundless pasture of the buffalo and the deer, in our own day strangely transformed,—yellow in harvest-time with ripened wheat, and dotted with the roofs of a hardy and valiant yeomanry.[142]

[Pg 169]

THE ILLINOIS TOWN.

They passed the site of the future town of Ottawa, and saw on their right the high plateau of Buffalo Rock, long a favorite dwelling-place of Indians. A league below, the river glided among islands bordered with stately woods. Close on their left towered a lofty cliff,[143] crested with trees that overhung the rippling current; while before them spread the valley of the Illinois, in broad low meadows, bordered on the right by the graceful hills at whose foot now lies the village of Utica. A population far more numerous then tenanted the valley. Along the right bank of the river were clustered the lodges of a great Indian town. Hennepin counted four hundred and sixty of them.[144] In shape, they were somewhat like the [Pg 170] arched top of a baggage-wagon. They were built of a framework of poles, covered with mats of rushes closely interwoven; and each contained three or four fires, of which the greater part served for two families.

HUNGER RELIEVED.

Here, then, was the town; but where were the inhabitants? All was silent as the desert. The lodges were empty, the fires dead, and the ashes cold. La Salle had expected this; for he knew that in the autumn the Illinois always left their towns for their winter hunting, and that the time of their return had not yet come. Yet he was not the less [Pg 171] embarrassed, for he would fain have bought a supply of food to relieve his famished followers. Some of them, searching the deserted town, presently found the *caches*, or covered pits, in which the Indians hid their stock of corn. This was precious beyond measure in their eyes, and to touch it would be a deep offence. La Salle shrank from provoking their anger, which might prove the ruin of his plans; but his necessity overcame his prudence, and he took thirty *minots* of corn, hoping to appease the owners by presents.

Thus provided, the party embarked again, and resumed their downward voyage.

On New Year's Day, 1680, they landed and heard mass. Then Hennepin wished a happy new year to La Salle first, and afterwards to all the men, making them a speech, which, as he tells us, was "most touching."[145] He and his two brethren next embraced the whole company in turn, "in a manner," writes the father, "most tender and affectionate," exhorting them, at the same time, to patience, faith, and constancy. Four days after these solemnities, they reached the long expansion of the river then called Pimitoui, and now known as Peoria Lake, and leisurely made their way downward to the site of the city of Peoria.[146] Here, as evening drew near, they [Pg 172] saw a faint spire of smoke curling above the gray forest, betokening that Indians were at hand. La Salle, as we have seen, had been warned that these tribes had been taught to regard him as their enemy; and when, in the morning, he resumed his course, he was prepared alike for peace or war.

The shores now approached each other; and the Illinois was once more a river, bordered on either hand with overhanging woods.[147]

At nine o'clock, doubling a point, he saw about eighty Illinois wigwams, on both sides of the river. He instantly ordered the eight canoes to be ranged in line, abreast, across the stream,—Tonty on the right, and he himself on the left. The men laid down their paddles and seized their weapons; while, in this warlike guise, the current bore them swiftly into the midst of the surprised and astounded savages. The camps were in a panic. Warriors whooped and howled; squaws and children screeched in chorus. Some snatched their bows and war-clubs; some ran in terror; and, in the midst of the hubbub, La Salle leaped ashore, followed by his men. None knew better how to deal with Indians; and he made no sign of friendship, knowing that it might be construed as a token of fear. His little knot of Frenchmen stood, gun in hand, passive, yet prepared for battle. [Pg 173] The Indians, on their part, rallying a little from their fright, made all haste to proffer peace. Two of their chiefs came forward, holding out the calumet; while another began a loud harangue, to check the young warriors who were aiming their arrows from the farther bank. La Salle, responding to these friendly overtures, displayed another calumet; while Hennepin caught several scared children and soothed them with winning blandishments.[148] The uproar was quelled; and the strangers were presently seated in the midst of the camp, beset by a throng of wild and swarthy figures.

ILLINOIS HOSPITALITY.

Food was placed before them; and, as the Illinois code of courtesy enjoined, their entertainers conveyed the morsels with their own hands to the lips of these unenviable victims of their hospitality, while others rubbed their feet with bear's grease. La Salle, on his part, made them a gift of tobacco and hatchets; and when he had escaped from their caresses, rose and harangued them. He told them that he had been forced to take corn from their granaries, lest his men should die of hunger; but he prayed them not to be offended, promising full restitution or ample payment. He had come, he said, to protect them against their enemies, and teach them to pray to the true God. As for the Iroquois, they were subjects of the Great King, and therefore brethren of the French; yet, nevertheless, should they begin a war and invade the country of the Illinois, he would [Pg 174] stand by them, give them guns, and fight in their defence, if they would permit him to build a fort among them for the security of his men. It was also, he added, his purpose to build a great wooden canoe, in which to descend the Mississippi to the sea, and then return, bringing them the goods of which they stood in need; but if they would not consent to his plans and sell provisions to his men, he would pass on to the Osages, who would then reap all the benefits of intercourse with the French, while they were left destitute, at the mercy of the Iroquois.[149]

This threat had its effect, for it touched their deep-rooted jealousy of the Osages. They were lavish of promises, and feasts and dances consumed the day. Yet La Salle soon learned that the intrigues of his enemies were still pursuing him. That evening, unknown to him, a stranger appeared in the Illinois camp. He was a Mascoutin chief, named Monso, attended by five or six Miamis, and bringing a gift of knives, hatchets, and kettles to the Illinois.[150] The chiefs assembled in a secret nocturnal session, where, smoking their pipes, they listened with open ears to the harangue of the envoys. Monso told them that he had come in behalf of certain Frenchmen, whom he named, to warn his hearers against the designs of La Salle, whom he denounced [Pg 175] as a partisan and spy of the Iroquois, affirming that he was now on his way to stir up the tribes beyond the Mississippi to join in a war against the Illinois, who, thus assailed from the east and from the west, would be utterly destroyed. There was no hope for them, he added, but in checking the farther progress of La Salle, or, at least, retarding it, thus causing his men to desert him. Having thrown his fire-brand, Monso and his party left the camp in haste, dreading to be confronted with the object of their aspersions.[151]

FRESH INTRIGUES.

In the morning, La Salle saw a change in the behavior of his hosts. They looked on him askance, cold, sullen, and suspicious. There was one Omawha, a chief, whose favor he had won the day before by the politic gift of two hatchets and three knives, and who now came to him in secret to tell him what had taken place at the nocturnal council. La Salle at once saw in it a device of his enemies; and this belief was confirmed, when, in the afternoon, Nicanopé, brother of the head chief, sent to invite the Frenchmen to a feast. They repaired to his lodge; but before dinner was served,—that is to say, while the guests, white and red, were seated on [Pg 176] mats, each with his hunting-knife in his hand, and the wooden bowl before him which was to receive his share of the bear's or buffalo's meat, or the corn boiled in fat, with which he was to be regaled,—while such was the posture of the company, their host arose and began a long speech. He told the Frenchmen that he had invited them to his lodge less to refresh their bodies with good cheer than to cure their minds of the dangerous purpose which possessed them, of descending the Mississippi. Its shores, he said, were beset by savage tribes, against whose numbers and ferocity their valor would avail nothing; its waters were infested by serpents, alligators, and unnatural monsters; while the river itself, after raging among rocks and whirlpools, plunged headlong at last into a fathomless gulf, which would swallow them and their vessel forever.

LA SALLE AND THE INDIANS.

La Salle's men were for the most part raw hands, knowing nothing of the wilderness, and easily alarmed at its dangers; but there were two among them, old *coureurs de bois*, who unfortunately knew too much; for they understood the Indian orator, and explained his speech to the rest. As La Salle looked around on the circle of his followers, he read an augury of fresh trouble in their disturbed and rueful visages. He waited patiently, however, till the speaker had ended, and then answered him, through his interpreter, with great composure. First, he thanked him for the friendly warning which his affection had impelled him to utter; but, he continued, [Pg 177] the greater the danger, the greater the honor; and even if the danger were real, Frenchmen would never flinch from it. But were not the Illinois jealous? Had they not been deluded by lies? "We were not asleep, my brother, when Monso came to tell you, under cover of night, that we were spies of the Iroquois. The presents he gave you, that you might believe his falsehoods, are at this moment buried in the earth under this lodge. If he told the truth, why did he skulk away in the dark? Why did he not show himself by day? Do you not see that when we first came among you, and your camp was all in confusion, we could have killed you without needing help from the Iroquois? And now, while I am speaking, could we not put your old men to death, while your young warriors are all gone away to hunt? If we meant to make war on you, we should need no help from the Iroquois, who have so often felt the force of our arms. Look at what we have brought you. It is not weapons to destroy you, but merchandise and tools for your good. If you still harbor evil thoughts of us, be frank as we are, and speak them boldly. Go after this impostor Monso, and bring him back, that we may answer him face to face; for he never saw either us or the Iroquois, and what can he know of the plots that he pretends to reveal?"[152] Nicanopé had nothing to [Pg 178] reply, and, grunting assent in the depths of his throat, made a sign that the feast should proceed.

The French were lodged in huts, near the Indian camp; and, fearing treachery, La Salle placed a guard at night. On the morning after the feast, he came out into the frosty air and looked about him for the sentinels. Not one of them was to be seen. Vexed and alarmed, he entered hut after hut and roused his drowsy followers. Six of the number, including two of the best carpenters, were nowhere to be found. Discontented and mutinous from the first, and now terrified by the fictions of Nicanopé, they had deserted, preferring the hardships of the midwinter forest to the mysterious terrors of the Mississippi. La Salle mustered the rest before him, and inveighed sternly against the cowardice and baseness of those who had thus abandoned him, regardless of his many favors. If any here, he added, are afraid, let them but wait till the spring, and they shall have free leave to return to Canada, safely and without dishonor.[153]

LA SALLE AGAIN POISONED.

This desertion cut him to the heart. It showed him that he was leaning on a broken reed; and he felt that, on an enterprise full of doubt and peril, there were scarcely four men in his party whom he could trust. Nor was desertion the worst he had to fear; for here, as at Fort Frontenac, an attempt was made to kill him. Tonty tells us that poison was [Pg 179] placed in the pot in which their food was cooked, and that La Salle was saved by an antidote which some of his friends had given him before he left France. This, it will be remembered, was an epoch of poisoners. It was in the following month that the notorious La Voisin was burned alive, at Paris, for practices to which many of the highest nobility were charged with being privy, not excepting some in whose veins ran the blood of the gorgeous spendthrift who ruled the destinies of France.[154]

In these early French enterprises in the West, it was to the last degree difficult to hold men to their duty. Once fairly in the wilderness, completely freed from the sharp restraints of authority in which they had passed their lives, a spirit of lawlessness broke out among them with a violence proportioned to the pressure which had hitherto controlled it. Discipline had no resources and no guarantee; while those outlaws of the forest, the *coureurs de bois*, were always before their eyes, a standing example of unbridled license. La Salle, eminently skilful in his dealings with Indians, was rarely so happy with his own countrymen; and yet the desertions from which he was continually suffering were due far more to the inevitable difficulty of his position than to any want of conduct on his part.

FOOTNOTES:

[140] *Lettre de Duchesneau à ——, 10 Nov., 1680.*

[141] The Kankakee was called at this time the Theakiki, or Haukiki (Marest); a name which, as Charlevoix says, was afterwards corrupted by the French to Kiakiki whence, probably, its present form. In La Salle's time, the name "Theakiki" was given to the river Illinois through all its course. It was also called the Rivière Seignelay, the Rivière des Macopins, and the Rivière Divine, or Rivière de la Divine. The latter name, when Charlevoix visited the country in 1721, was confined to the northern branch. He gives an interesting and somewhat graphic account of the portage and the sources of the Kankakee, in his letter dated *De la Source du Theakiki, ce dix-sept Septembre*, 1721.

Why the Illinois should ever have been called the "Divine," it is not easy to see. The Memoirs of St. Simon suggest an explanation. Madame de Frontenac and her friend Mademoiselle d'Outrelaise, he tells us, lived together in apartments at the Arsenal, where they held their *salon* and exercised a great power in society. They were called at court *les Divines*. (St. Simon, v. 335: Cheruel.) In compliment to Frontenac, the river may have been named after his wife or her friend. The suggestion is due to M. Margry. I have seen a map by Raudin, Frontenac's engineer, on which the river is called "Rivière de la Divine ou l'Outrelaise."

[142] The change is very recent. Within the memory of men not yet old, wolves and deer, besides wild swans, wild turkeys, cranes, and pelicans, abounded in this region. In 1840, a friend of mine shot a deer from the window of a farmhouse, near the present town of La Salle. Running wolves on horseback was his favorite amusement in this part of the country. The buffalo long ago disappeared; but the early settlers found frequent remains of them. Mr. James Clark, of Utica, Ill., told me that he once found a large quantity of their bones and skulls in one place, as if a herd had perished in the snowdrifts.

[143] "Starved Rock." It will hold, hereafter, a conspicuous place in the narrative.

[144] *La Louisiane*, 137. Allouez (*Relation*, 1673-79) found three hundred and fifty-one lodges. This was in 1677. The population of this town, which embraced five or six distinct tribes of the Illinois, was continually changing. In 1675, Marquette addressed here an auditory composed of five hundred chiefs and old men, and fifteen hundred young men, besides women and children. He estimates the number of fires at five or six hundred. (*Voyages du Père Marquette*, 98: Lenox.) Membré, who was here in 1680, says that it then contained seven or eight thousand souls. (Membré in Le Clerc, *Premier Établissement de la Foy*, ii. 173.) On the remarkable manuscript map of Franquelin, 1684, it is set down at twelve hundred warriors, or about six thousand souls. This was after the destructive inroad of the Iroquois. Some years later, Rasle reported upwards of twenty-four hundred families. (*Lettre à son Frère, in Lettres Édifiantes.*)

At times, nearly the whole Illinois population was gathered here. At other times, the several tribes that composed it separated, some dwelling apart from the rest; so that at one period the Illinois formed eleven villages, while at others they were gathered into two, of which this was much the larger. The meadows around it were extensively cultivated, yielding large crops, chiefly of Indian corn. The lodges were built along the river-bank for a distance of a mile, and sometimes far more. In their shape, though not in their material, they resembled those of the Hurons. There were no palisades or embankments.

This neighborhood abounds in Indian relics. The village graveyard appears to have been on a rising ground, near the river immediately in front of the town of Utica. This is the only part of the river bottom, from this point to the Mississippi, not liable to inundation in the spring floods. It now forms part of a farm occupied by a tenant of Mr. James Clark. Both Mr. Clark and his tenant informed me that every year great quantities of human bones and teeth were turned up here by the plough. Many implements of stone are also found, together with beads and other ornaments of Indian and European fabric.

[145] "Les paroles les plus touchantes."—*Hennepin* (1683), 139. The later editions add the modest qualification, "que je pus."

[146] Peoria was the name of one of the tribes of the Illinois. Hennepin's dates here do not exactly agree with those of La Salle (*Lettre du 29 Sept., 1680*), who says that they were at the Illinois village on the first of January, and at Peoria Lake on the fifth.

[147] At least, it is so now at this place. Perhaps, in La Salle's time, it was not wholly so; for there is evidence, in various parts of the West, that the forest has made considerable encroachments on the open country.

[148] Hennepin (1683), 142.

[149] Hennepin (1683), 144-149. The later editions omit a part of the above.

[150] "Un sauvage, nommé Monso, qui veut dire Chevreuil."—*La Salle*. Probably Monso is a misprint for Mouso, as *mousoa* is Illinois for *chevreuil*, or deer.

[151] Hennepin (1683), 151, (1704), 205; Le Clerc, ii. 157; *Mémoire du Voyage de M. de la Salle*. This is a paper appended to Frontenac's Letter to the Minister, 9 Nov., 1680. Hennepin prints a translation of it in the English edition of his later work. It charges the Jesuit Allouez with being at the bottom of the intrigue. Compare *Lettre de La Salle, 29 Sept., 1680* (Margry, ii. 41), and *Mémoire de La Salle*, in Thomassy, *Géologie Pratique de la Louisiane*, 203.

The account of the affair of Monso, in the spurious work bearing Tonty's name, is mere romance.

[152] The above is a paraphrase, with some condensation, from Hennepin, whose account is substantially identical with that of La Salle.

[153] Hennepin (1683), 162. *Déclaration faite par Moyse Hillaret, charpentier de barque, cy devant au service du Sr de la Salle.*

[154] The equally noted Brinvilliers was burned four years before. An account of both will be found in the Letters of Madame de Sévigné. The memoirs of the time abound in evidence of the frightful prevalence of these practices, and the commotion which they excited in all ranks of society.

[Pg 180]

CHAPTER XIII.

1680.

FORT CRÈVECŒUR.

BUILDING OF THE FORT.

LA SALLE now resolved to leave the Indian camp, and fortify himself for the winter in a strong position, where his men would be less exposed to dangerous influence, and where he could hold his ground against an outbreak of the Illinois or an Iroquois invasion. At the middle of January, a thaw broke up the ice which had closed the river; and he set out in a canoe, with Hennepin, to visit the site he had chosen for his projected fort. It was half a league below the camp, on a low hill or knoll, two hundred yards from the southern bank. On either side was a deep ravine, and in front a marshy tract, overflowed at high water. Thither, then, the party was removed. They dug a ditch behind the hill, connecting the two ravines, and thus completely isolating it. The hill was nearly square in form. An embankment of earth was thrown up on every side: its declivities [Pg 181] were sloped steeply down to the bottom of the ravines and the ditch, and further guarded by *chevaux-de-frise*; while a palisade, twenty-five feet high, was planted around the whole. The lodgings of the men, built of musket-proof timber, were at two of the angles; the house of the friars at the third; the forge and magazine at the fourth; and the tents of La Salle and Tonty in the area within.

Hennepin laments the failure of wine, which prevented him from saying mass; but every morning and evening he summoned the men to his cabin to listen to prayers and preaching, and on Sundays and fête-days they chanted vespers. Father Zenobe usually spent the day in the Indian camp, striving, with very indifferent success, to win them to the Faith, and to overcome the disgust with which their manners and habits inspired him.

Such was the first civilized occupation of the region which now forms the State of Illinois. La Salle christened his new fort Fort Crèvecœur. The name tells of disaster and suffering, but does no justice to the iron-hearted constancy of the sufferer. Up to this time he had clung to the hope that his vessel, the "Griffin," might still be safe. Her safety was vital to his enterprise. She had on board articles of the last necessity to him, including the rigging and anchors of another vessel which he was to build at Fort Crèvecœur, in order to descend the Mississippi and sail thence to the West Indies. But now his last hope had well-nigh vanished. Past all reasonable [Pg 182] doubt, the "Griffin" was lost; and in her loss he and all his plans seemed ruined alike.

Nothing, indeed, was ever heard of her. Indians, fur-traders, and even Jesuits, have been charged with contriving her destruction. Some say that the Ottawas boarded and burned her, after murdering those on board; others accuse the Pottawattamies; others affirm that her own crew scuttled and sunk her; others, again, that she foundered in a storm.[155] As for La Salle, the belief grew in him to a settled conviction that she had been treacherously sunk by the pilot and the sailors to whom he had intrusted her; and he thought he had found evidence that the authors of the crime, laden with the merchandise they had taken from her, had reached the Mississippi and ascended it, hoping to join Du Lhut, a famous chief of *coureurs de bois*, and enrich themselves by traffic with the northern tribes.[156]

[Pg 183]

LA SALLE'S ANXIETIES.

But whether her lading was swallowed in the depths of the lake, or lost in the clutches of traitors, the evil was alike past remedy. She was gone, it mattered little how. The main-stay of the enterprise was broken; yet its inflexible chief lost neither heart nor hope. One path, beset with hardships and terrors, still lay open to him. He might return on foot to Fort Frontenac, and bring thence the needful succors.

La Salle felt deeply the dangers of such a step. His men were uneasy, discontented, and terrified by the stories with which the jealous Illinois still constantly filled their ears, of the whirlpools and the monsters of the Mississippi. He dreaded lest, in his absence, they should follow the example of their comrades, and desert. In the midst of his anxieties, a lucky accident gave him the means of disabusing them. He was hunting, one day, near the fort, when he met a young Illinois on his way home, half-starved, from a distant war excursion. He had been absent so long that he knew nothing of what had passed between his countrymen and the French. La Salle gave him a turkey he had shot, invited him to the fort, fed him, and made him presents. Having thus warmed his heart, he questioned him, with apparent carelessness, as to the countries he had visited, and especially as to the Mississippi,—on which the young warrior, seeing no reason to disguise the truth, gave him all the information he required. La Salle now made him the present of a hatchet, to [Pg 184] engage him to say nothing of what had passed, and, leaving him in excellent humor, repaired, with some of his followers, to the Illinois camp. Here he found the chiefs seated at a feast of bear's meat, and he took his place among them on a mat of rushes. After a pause, he charged them with having deceived him in regard to the Mississippi; adding that he knew the river perfectly, having been instructed concerning it by the Master of Life. He then described it to them with so much accuracy that his astonished hearers, conceiving that he owed his knowledge to "medicine," or sorcery, clapped their hands to their mouths in sign of wonder, and confessed that all they had said was but an artifice, inspired by their earnest desire that he should remain among them.[157] On this, La Salle's men took heart again; and their courage rose still more when, soon after, a band of Chickasa, Arkansas, and Osage warriors, from the Mississippi, came to the camp on a friendly visit, and assured the

French not only that the river was navigable to the sea, but that the tribes along its banks would give them a warm welcome.

ANOTHER VESSEL.

La Salle had now good reason to hope that his followers would neither mutiny nor desert in his absence. One chief purpose of his intended journey was to procure the anchors, cables, and rigging of [Pg 185] the vessel which he meant to build at Fort Crèvecœur, and he resolved to see her on the stocks before he set out. This was no easy matter, for the pit-sawyers had deserted. "Seeing," he writes, "that I should lose a year if I waited to get others from Montreal, I said one day, before my people, that I was so vexed to find that the absence of two sawyers would defeat my plans and make all my trouble useless, that I was resolved to try to saw the planks myself, if I could find a single man who would help me with a will." Hereupon, two men stepped forward and promised to do their best. They were tolerably successful, and, the rest being roused to emulation, the work went on with such vigor that within six weeks the hull of the vessel was half finished. She was of forty tons' burden, and was built with high bulwarks, to protect those on board from Indian arrows.

La Salle now bethought him that, in his absence, he might get from Hennepin service of more value than his sermons; and he requested him to descend the Illinois, and explore it to its mouth. The friar, though hardy and daring, would fain have excused himself, alleging a troublesome bodily infirmity; but his venerable colleague Ribourde, himself too old for the journey, urged him to go, telling him that if he died by the way, his apostolic labors would redound to the glory of God. Membré had been living for some time in the Indian camp, and was thoroughly out of humor with the objects of his missionary [Pg 186] efforts, of whose obduracy and filth he bitterly complained. Hennepin proposed to take his place, while he should assume the Mississippi adventure; but this Membré declined, preferring to remain where he was. Hennepin now reluctantly accepted the proposed task. "Anybody but me," he says, with his usual modesty, "would have been very much frightened at the dangers of such a journey; and, in fact, if I had not placed all my trust in God, I should not have been the dupe of the Sieur de la Salle, who exposed my life rashly."[158]

On the last day of February, Hennepin's canoe lay at the water's edge; and the party gathered on the bank to bid him farewell. He had two companions,—Michel Accau, and a man known as the Picard du Gay,[159] though his real name was Antoine Auguel. The canoe was well laden with gifts for the Indians,—tobacco, knives, beads, awls, and other goods, to a very considerable value, supplied at La Salle's cost; "and, in fact," observes Hennepin, "he is liberal enough towards his friends."[160]

[Pg 187]

DEPARTURE OF HENNEPIN.

The friar bade farewell to La Salle, and embraced all the rest in turn. Father Ribourde gave him his benediction. "Be of good courage and let your heart be comforted," said the excellent old missionary, as he spread his hands in benediction over the shaven crown of the reverend traveller. Du Gay and Accau plied their paddles; the canoe receded, and vanished at length behind the forest. We will follow Hennepin hereafter on his adventures, imaginary and real. Meanwhile, we will trace the footsteps of his chief, urging his way, in the storms of winter, through those vast and gloomy wilds,— those realms of famine, treachery, and death,—that lay betwixt him and his far-distant goal of Fort Frontenac.

On the first of March,[161] before the frost was yet out of the ground, when the forest was still leafless, and the oozy prairies still patched with snow, a band of discontented men were again gathered on the shore for another leave-taking. Hard by, the unfinished ship lay on the stocks, white and fresh from the saw and axe, ceaselessly reminding them of the hardship and peril that was in store. Here you would have seen the calm, impenetrable face of La Salle, and with him the Mohegan hunter, who seems to have felt towards him that admiring attachment which he could always inspire in his Indian retainers. Besides the Mohegan, four Frenchmen were to accompany him,—Hunaut, La Violette, Collin, and Dautray.[162] [Pg 188] His parting with Tonty was an anxious one, for each well knew the risks that environed both. Embarking with his followers in two canoes, he made his way upward amid the drifting ice; while the faithful Italian, with two or three honest men and twelve or thirteen knaves, remained to hold Fort Crèvecœur in his absence.

FOOTNOTES:

[155] Charlevoix, i. 459; La Potherie, ii. 140; La Hontan, *Memoir on the Fur-Trade of Canada*. I am indebted for a copy of this paper to Winthrop Sargent, Esq., who purchased the original at the sale of the library of the poet Southey. Like Hennepin, La Hontan went over to the English; and this memoir is written in their interest.

[156] *Lettre de La Salle à La Barre, Chicagou, 4 Juin, 1683.* This is a long letter, addressed to the successor of Frontenac in the government of Canada. La Salle says that a young Indian belonging to him told him that three years before he saw a white man, answering the description of the pilot, a prisoner among a tribe beyond the Mississippi. He had been captured with four others on that river, while making his way with canoes, laden with goods, towards the Sioux. His companions had been killed. Other circumstances, which La Salle details at great length, convinced him that the white prisoner was no other than the pilot of the "Griffin." The evidence, however, is not conclusive.

[157] *Relation des Découvertes et des Voyages du Sr de la Salle, Seigneur et Gouverneur du Fort de Frontenac, au delà des grands Lacs de la Nouvelle France, faits par ordre de Monseigneur Colbert*, 1679, 80 et 81. Hennepin gives a story which is not essentially different, except that he makes himself a conspicuous actor in it.

[158] All the above is from Hennepin; and it seems to be marked by his characteristic egotism. It appears, from La Salle's letters, that Accau was the real chief of the party; that their orders were to explore not only the Illinois, but also a part of the Mississippi; and that Hennepin volunteered

to go with the others. Accau was chosen because he spoke several Indian languages.

[159] An eminent writer has mistaken "Picard" for a personal name. Du Gay was called "Le Picard," because he came from the province of Picardy.

[160] (1683), 188. This commendation is suppressed in the later editions.

[161] Tonty erroneously places their departure on the twenty-second.

[162] *Déclaration faite par Moyse Hillaret, charpentier de barque.*

[Pg 189]

CHAPTER XIV.

1680.

HARDIHOOD OF LA SALLE.

The Winter Journey. — The Deserted Town. — Starved Rock. — Lake Michigan. — The Wilderness. — War Parties. — La Salle's Men Give Out. — Ill Tidings. — Mutiny. — Chastisement of the Mutineers.

LA SALLE well knew what was before him, and nothing but necessity spurred him to this desperate journey. He says that he could trust nobody else to go in his stead, and that unless the articles lost in the "Griffin" were replaced without delay, the expedition would be retarded a full year, and he and his associates consumed by its expenses. "Therefore," he writes to one of them, "though the thaws of approaching spring greatly increased the difficulty of the way, interrupted as it was everywhere by marshes and rivers, to say nothing of the length of the journey, which is about five hundred leagues in a direct line, and the danger of meeting Indians of four or five different nations through whose country we were to pass, as well as an Iroquois army which we knew was coming that way; though we must suffer all the [Pg 190] time from hunger; sleep on the open ground, and often without food; watch by night and march by day, loaded with baggage, such as blanket, clothing, kettle, hatchet, gun, powder, lead, and skins to make moccasins; sometimes pushing through thickets, sometimes climbing rocks covered with ice and snow, sometimes wading whole days through marshes where the water was waist-deep or even more, at a season when the snow was not entirely melted, — though I knew all this, it did not prevent me from resolving to go on foot to Fort Frontenac, to learn for myself what had become of my vessel, and bring back the things we needed."[163]

The winter had been a severe one; and when, an hour after leaving the fort, he and his companions reached the still water of Peoria Lake, they found it sheeted with ice from shore to shore. They carried their canoes up the bank, made two rude sledges, placed the light vessels upon them, and dragged them to the upper end of the lake, where they encamped. In the morning they found the river still covered with ice, too weak to bear them and too strong to permit them to break a way for the canoes. They spent the whole day in carrying them through the woods, toiling knee-deep in saturated snow. Rain fell in floods, and they took shelter at night in a deserted Indian hut.

In the morning, the third of March, they dragged [Pg 191] their canoes half a league farther; then launched them, and, breaking the ice with clubs and hatchets, forced their way slowly up the stream. Again their progress was barred, and again they took to the woods, toiling onward till a tempest of moist, half-liquid snow forced them to bivouac for the night. A sharp frost followed, and in the morning the white waste around them was glazed with a dazzling crust. Now, for the first time, they could use their snow-shoes. Bending to their work, dragging their canoes, which glided smoothly over the polished surface, they journeyed on hour after hour and league after league, till they reached at length the great town of the Illinois, still void of its inhabitants.[164]

> THE DESERTED TOWN.

It was a desolate and lonely scene,—the river gliding dark and cold between its banks of rushes; the empty lodges, covered with crusted snow; the vast white meadows; the distant cliffs, bearded with shining icicles; and the hills wrapped in forests, which glittered from afar with the icy incrustations that cased each frozen twig. Yet there was life in the savage landscape. The men saw buffalo wading in the snow, and they killed one of them. More than this: they discovered the tracks of moccasins. They cut rushes by the edge of the river, piled them on the bank, and set them on fire, that the smoke might attract the eyes of savages roaming near.

[Pg 192]

On the following day, while the hunters were smoking the meat of the buffalo, La Salle went out to reconnoitre, and presently met three Indians, one of whom proved to be Chassagoac, the principal chief of the Illinois.[165] La Salle brought them to his bivouac, feasted them, gave them a red blanket, a kettle, and some knives and hatchets, made friends with them, promised to restrain the Iroquois from attacking them, told them that he was on his way to the settlements to bring arms and ammunition to defend them against their enemies, and, as the result of these advances, gained from the chief a promise that he would send provisions to Tonty's party at Fort Crèvecœur.

After several days spent at the deserted town, La Salle prepared to resume his journey. Before his departure, his attention was attracted to the remarkable cliff of yellow sandstone, now called Starved Rock, a mile or more above the village,—a natural fortress, which a score of resolute white men might make good against a host of savages; and he soon afterwards sent Tonty an order to examine it, and make it his stronghold in case of need.[166]

On the fifteenth the party set out again, carried [Pg 193] their canoes along the bank of the river as far as the rapids above Ottawa, then launched them and pushed their way upward, battling with the floating ice, which, loosened by a warm rain, drove down the swollen current in sheets. On the eighteenth they reached a point some miles below the site of Joliet, and here found the river once more completely closed. Despairing of farther progress by water, they hid their canoes on an island, and struck across the country for Lake Michigan.

LA SALLE'S JOURNEY.

It was the worst of all seasons for such a journey. The nights were cold, but the sun was warm at noon, and the half-thawed prairie was one vast tract of mud, water, and discolored, half-liquid snow. On the twenty-second they crossed marshes and inundated meadows, wading to the knee, till at noon they were stopped by a river, perhaps the Calumet. They made a raft of hard-wood timber, for there was no other, and shoved themselves across. On the next day they could see Lake Michigan dimly glimmering beyond the waste of woods; and, after crossing three swollen streams, they reached it at evening. On the twenty-fourth they followed its shore, till, at nightfall, they arrived at the fort which they had built in the autumn at the mouth of the St. Joseph. Here La Salle found Chapelle and Leblanc, the two men whom he had sent from hence to Michilimackinac, in search of the "Griffin."[167] They reported that they had made the circuit of the lake, and had neither [Pg 194] seen her nor heard tidings of her. Assured of her fate, he ordered them to rejoin Tonty at Fort Crèvecœur; while he pushed onward with his party through the unknown wild of Southern Michigan.

"The rain," says La Salle, "which lasted all day, and the raft we were obliged to make to cross the river, stopped us till noon of the twenty-fifth, when we continued our march through the woods, which was so interlaced with thorns and brambles that in two days and a half our clothes were all torn, and our faces so covered with blood that we hardly knew each other. On the twenty-eighth we found the woods more open, and began to fare better, meeting a good deal of game, which after this rarely failed us; so that we no longer carried provisions with us, but made a meal of roast meat wherever we happened to kill a deer, bear, or turkey. These are the choicest feasts on a journey like this; and till now we had generally gone without them, so that we had often walked all day without breakfast.

INDIAN ALARMS.

"The Indians do not hunt in this region, which is debatable ground between five or six nations who are at war, and, being afraid of each other, do not venture into these parts except to surprise each other, and always with the greatest precaution and all possible secrecy. The reports of our guns and the carcasses of the animals we killed soon led some of them to find our trail. In fact, on the evening of the twenty-eighth, having made our fire by the edge of a prairie, we were surrounded by them; but as the [Pg 195] man on guard waked us, and we posted ourselves behind trees with our guns, these savages, who are called Wapoos, took us for Iroquois, and thinking that there must be a great many of us because we did not travel secretly, as they do when in small bands, they ran off without shooting their arrows, and gave the alarm to their comrades, so that we were two days without meeting anybody."

La Salle guessed the cause of their fright; and, in order to confirm their delusion, he drew with charcoal, on the trunks of trees from which he had stripped the bark, the usual marks of an Iroquois war-party, with signs for prisoners and for scalps, after the custom of those dreaded warriors. This ingenious artifice, as will soon appear, was near proving the destruction of the whole party. He also set fire to the dry grass of the prairies over which he and his men had just passed, thus destroying the traces of their passage. "We practised this device every night, and it answered very well so long as we were passing over an open country; but on the thirtieth we got into great marshes, flooded by the thaws, and were obliged to cross them in mud or water up to the waist; so that our tracks betrayed us to a band of Mascoutins who were out after Iroquois. They followed us through these marshes during the three days we were crossing them; but we made no fire at night, contenting ourselves with taking off our wet clothes and wrapping ourselves in our blankets on some dry knoll, where we slept till morning. At [Pg 196] last, on the night of the second of April, there came a hard frost, and our clothes, which were drenched when we took them off, froze stiff as sticks, so that we could not put them on in the morning without making a fire to thaw them. The fire betrayed us to the Indians, who were encamped across the marsh; and they ran towards us with loud cries, till they were stopped halfway by a stream so deep that they could not get over, the ice which had formed in the night not being strong enough to bear them. We went to meet them, within gun-shot; and whether our fire-arms frightened them, or whether they thought us more numerous than we were, or whether they really meant us no harm, they called out, in the Illinois language, that they had taken us for

Iroquois, but now saw that we were friends and brothers; whereupon, they went off as they came, and we kept on our way till the fourth, when two of my men fell ill and could not walk."

In this emergency, La Salle went in search of some watercourse by which they might reach Lake Erie, and soon came upon a small river, which was probably the Huron. Here, while the sick men rested, their companions made a canoe. There were no birch-trees; and they were forced to use elm-bark, which at that early season would not slip freely from the wood until they loosened it with hot water. Their canoe being made, they embarked in it, and for a time floated prosperously down the stream, when at length the way was barred by a matted [Pg 197] barricade of trees fallen across the water. The sick men could now walk again, and, pushing eastward through the forest, the party soon reached the banks of the Detroit.

THE JOURNEY'S END.

La Salle directed two of the men to make a canoe, and go to Michilimackinac, the nearest harborage. With the remaining two, he crossed the Detroit on a raft, and, striking a direct line across the country, reached Lake Erie not far from Point Pelée. Snow, sleet, and rain pelted them with little intermission: and when, after a walk of about thirty miles, they gained the lake, the Mohegan and one of the Frenchmen were attacked with fever and spitting of blood. Only one man now remained in health. With his aid, La Salle made another canoe, and, embarking the invalids, pushed for Niagara. It was Easter Monday when they landed at a cabin of logs above the cataract, probably on the spot where the "Griffin" was built. Here several of La Salle's men had been left the year before, and here they still remained. They told him woful news. Not only had he lost the "Griffin," and her lading of ten thousand crowns in value, but a ship from France, freighted with his goods, valued at more than twenty-two thousand livres, had been totally wrecked at the mouth of the St. Lawrence; and of twenty hired men on their way from Europe to join him, some had been detained by his enemy, the Intendant

Duchesneau, while all but four of the remainder, being told that he was dead, had found means to return home.

[Pg 198]

His three followers were all unfit for travel: he alone retained his strength and spirit. Taking with him three fresh men at Niagara, he resumed his journey, and on the sixth of May descried, looming through floods of rain, the familiar shores of his seigniory and the bastioned walls of Fort Frontenac. During sixty-five days he had toiled almost incessantly, travelling, by the course he took, about a thousand miles through a country beset with every form of peril and obstruction,—"the most arduous journey," says the chronicler, "ever made by Frenchmen in America."

Such was Cavelier de la Salle. In him, an unconquerable mind held at its service a frame of iron, and tasked it to the utmost of its endurance. The pioneer of western pioneers was no rude son of toil, but a man of thought, trained amid arts and letters.[168] He had reached his goal; but for him there was neither rest nor peace. Man and Nature seemed in arms against him. His agents had plundered him; his creditors had seized his property; and several of his canoes, richly laden, had been lost in the rapids of the St. Lawrence.[169] He hastened to Montreal, where [Pg 199] his sudden advent caused great astonishment; and where, despite his crippled resources and damaged credit, he succeeded, within a week, in gaining the supplies which he required and the needful succors for the forlorn band on the Illinois. He had returned to Fort Frontenac, and was on the point of embarking for their relief, when a blow fell upon him more disheartening than any that had preceded.

THE MUTINEERS.

On the twenty-second of July, two *voyageurs*, Messier and Laurent, came to him with a letter from Tonty, who wrote that soon after La Salle's departure nearly all the men had deserted, after destroying Fort Crèvecœur, plundering the magazine, and throwing into the river all the arms, goods, and stores which they could not carry off. The messengers who brought this letter were speedily followed by two of the *habitants* of Fort Frontenac, who had been trading on the lakes, and who, with a fidelity which the unhappy La Salle rarely knew how to inspire, had travelled day and night to bring him their tidings. They reported that they had met the deserters, and that, having been reinforced by recruits gained at Michilimackinac and Niagara, they now numbered twenty men.[170] They had destroyed the fort on the [Pg 200] St. Joseph, seized a quantity of furs belonging to La Salle at Michilimackinac, and plundered the magazine at Niagara. Here they had separated, eight of them coasting the south side of Lake Ontario to find harborage at Albany, a common refuge at that time of this class of scoundrels; while the remaining twelve, in three canoes, made for Fort Frontenac along the north shore, intending to kill La Salle as the surest means of escaping punishment.

CHASTISEMENT.

He lost no time in lamentation. Of the few men at his command he chose nine of the trustiest, embarked with them in canoes, and went to meet the marauders. After passing the Bay of Quinté, he took his station with five of his party at a point of land suited to his purpose, and detached the remaining four to keep watch. In the morning, two canoes were discovered approaching without suspicion, one of them far in advance of the other. As the foremost drew near, La Salle's canoe darted out from under the leafy shore,—two of the men handling the paddles, while he, with the remaining two, levelled their guns at the deserters, and called on them to surrender. Astonished and dismayed, they yielded at once; while two more, who were in the second canoe, hastened to follow their example. La Salle now returned to the fort with his prisoners, placed [Pg 201] them in custody, and again set forth. He met the third canoe upon the lake at about six o'clock in the evening. His men vainly plied their paddles in pursuit. The mutineers reached the shore, took post among rocks and trees, levelled their guns, and showed fight. Four of La Salle's men made a circuit to gain their rear and dislodge them, on which they stole back to their canoe and tried to escape in the darkness. They were pursued, and summoned to yield; but they replied by aiming their guns at their pursuers, who instantly gave them a volley, killed two of them, and captured the remaining three. Like their companions, they were placed in custody at the fort, to await the arrival of Count Frontenac.[171]

FOOTNOTES:

[163] *Lettre de La Salle à un de ses associés* (Thouret?), *29 Sept., 1680* (Margry, ii. 50).

[164] Membré says that he was in the town at the time; but this could hardly have been the case. He was, in all probability, among the Illinois, in their camp near Fort Crèvecœur.

[165] The same whom Hennepin calls Chassagouasse. He was brother of the chief, Nicanopé, who, in his absence, had feasted the French on the day after the nocturnal council with Monso. Chassagoac was afterwards baptized by Membré or Ribourde, but soon relapsed into the superstitions of his people, and died, as the former tells us, "doubly a child of perdition." See Le Clerc, ii. 181.

[166] Tonty, *Mémoire.* The order was sent by two Frenchmen, whom La Salle met on Lake Michigan.

[167] *Déclaration de Moyse Hillaret; Relation des Découvertes.*

[168] A Rocky Mountain trapper, being complimented on the hardihood of himself and his companions, once said to the writer, "That's so; but a gentleman of the right sort will stand hardship better than anybody else." The history of Arctic and African travel and the military records of all time are a standing evidence that a trained and developed mind is not the enemy, but the active and powerful ally, of constitutional hardihood. The culture that enervates instead of strengthening is always a false or a partial one.

[169] Zenobe Membré in Le Clerc, ii. 202.

[170] When La Salle was at Niagara, in April, he had ordered Dautray, the best of the men who had accompanied him from the Illinois, to return thither as soon as he was able. Four men from Niagara were to go with him and he was to rejoin Tonty with such supplies as that post could furnish. Dautray set out accordingly, but was met on the lakes by the

deserters, who told him that Tonty was dead, and seduced his men. (*Relation des Découvertes.*) Dautray himself seems to have remained true; at least, he was in La Salle's service immediately after, and was one of his most trusted followers. He was of good birth, being the son of Jean Bourdon, a conspicuous personage in the early period of the colony; and his name appears on official records as Jean Bourdon, Sieur d'Autray.

[171] La Salle's long letter, written apparently to his associate Thouret, and dated 29 Sept., 1680, is the chief authority for the above. The greater part of this letter is incorporated, almost verbatim, in the official narrative called *Relation des Découvertes*. Hennepin, Membré, and Tonty also speak of the journey from Fort Crèvecœur. The death of the two mutineers was used by La Salle's enemies as the basis of a charge of murder.

[Pg 202]

CHAPTER XV.

1680.

INDIAN CONQUERORS.

THE ENTERPRISE RENEWED.—ATTEMPT TO RESCUE TONTY.—BUFFALO.—A
FRIGHTFUL DISCOVERY.—IROQUOIS FURY.—THE RUINED TOWN.—A NIGHT OF
HORROR.—TRACES OF THE INVADERS.—NO NEWS OF TONTY.

> ANOTHER EFFORT.

AND now La Salle's work must be begun afresh. He had staked all, and all had seemingly been lost. In stern, relentless effort he had touched the limits of human endurance; and the harvest of his toil was disappointment, disaster, and impending ruin. The shattered fabric of his enterprise was prostrate in the dust. His friends desponded; his foes were blatant and exultant. Did he bend before the storm? No human eye could pierce the depths of his reserved and haughty nature; but the surface was calm, and no sign betrayed a shaken resolve or an altered purpose. Where weaker men would have abandoned all in despairing apathy, he turned anew to his work with the same vigor and the same apparent confidence as if borne on the full tide of success.

His best hope was in Tonty. Could that brave and true-hearted officer and the three or four faithful [Pg 203] men who had remained with him make good their foothold on the Illinois, and save from destruction the vessel on the stocks and the forge and tools so laboriously carried thither, then a basis was left on which the ruined enterprise might be built up once more. There was no time to lose. Tonty must be succored soon, or succor would come too late. La Salle had already provided the necessary material, and a few days sufficed to complete his preparations. On the tenth of August he embarked again for the Illinois. With him went his lieutenant La Forest, who held of him in fief an island, then called Belle Isle, opposite Fort Frontenac.[172] A surgeon, ship-carpenters, joiners, masons, soldiers, *voyageurs* and laborers completed his company, twenty-five men in all, with everything needful for the outfit of the vessel.

His route, though difficult, was not so long as that which he had followed the year before. He ascended the river Humber; crossed to Lake Simcoe, and thence descended the Severn to the Georgian Bay of Lake Huron; followed its eastern shore, coasted the Manitoulin Islands, and at length reached Michilimackinac. Here, as usual, all was hostile; and he had great difficulty in inducing the Indians, who had been excited against him, to sell him provisions. Anxious to reach his destination, he pushed forward with twelve men, leaving La Forest to bring on the [Pg 204] rest. On the fourth of November[173] he reached the ruined fort at the mouth of the St. Joseph, and left five of his party, with the heavy stores, to wait till La Forest should come up, while he himself hastened forward with six Frenchmen and an Indian. A deep anxiety possessed him. The rumor, current for months past, that the Iroquois, bent on destroying the Illinois, were on the point of invading their country had constantly gained strength. Here was a new disaster, which, if realized, might involve him and his enterprise in irretrievable wreck.

He ascended the St. Joseph, crossed the portage to the Kankakee, and followed its course downward till it joined the northern branch of the Illinois. He had heard nothing of Tonty on the way, and neither here nor elsewhere could he discover the smallest sign of the passage of white men. His friend, therefore, if alive, was probably still at his post; and he pursued his course with a mind lightened, in some small measure, of its load of anxiety.

BUFFALO.

When last he had passed here, all was solitude; but now the scene was changed. The boundless waste was thronged with life. He beheld that wondrous spectacle, still to be seen at times on the plains of the remotest West, and the memory of which can quicken the pulse and stir the blood after [Pg 205] the lapse of years: far and near, the prairie was alive with buffalo; now like black specks dotting the distant swells; now trampling by in ponderous columns, or filing in long lines, morning, noon, and night, to drink at the river,—wading, plunging, and snorting in the water; climbing the muddy shores, and staring with wild eyes at the passing canoes. It was an opportunity not to be lost. The party landed, and encamped for a hunt. Sometimes they hid under the shelving bank, and shot them as they came to drink; sometimes, flat on their faces, they dragged themselves through the long dead grass, till the savage bulls, guardians of the herd, ceased their grazing, raised their huge heads, and glared through tangled hair at the dangerous intruders. The hunt was successful. In three days the hunters killed twelve buffalo, besides deer, geese, and swans. They cut the meat into thin flakes, and dried it in the sun or in the smoke of their fires. The men were in high spirits,—delighting in the sport, and rejoicing in the prospect of relieving Tonty and his hungry followers with a plentiful supply.

They embarked again, and soon approached the great town of the Illinois. The buffalo were far behind; and once more the canoes glided on their way through a voiceless solitude. No hunters were seen; no saluting whoop greeted their ears. They passed the cliff afterwards called the Rock of St. Louis, where La Salle had ordered Tonty to build his stronghold; but as he scanned its lofty top he [Pg 206] saw no palisades, no cabins, no sign of human hand, and still its primeval crest of forests overhung the gliding river. Now the meadow opened before them where the great town had stood. They gazed, astonished and confounded: all was desolation. The town had vanished, and the meadow was black with fire. They plied their paddles, hastened to the spot, landed; and as they looked around their cheeks grew white, and the blood was frozen in their veins.

A NIGHT OF HORROR.

Before them lay a plain once swarming with wild human life and covered with Indian dwellings, now a waste of devastation and death, strewn with heaps of ashes, and bristling with the charred poles and stakes which had formed the framework of the lodges. At the points of most of them were stuck human skulls, half picked by birds of prey.[174] Near at hand was the burial-ground of the village. The travellers sickened with horror as they entered its revolting precincts. Wolves in multitudes fled at their approach; while clouds of crows or buzzards, rising from the hideous repast, wheeled above their heads, or settled on the naked branches of the neighboring forest. Every grave had been rifled, and the bodies flung down from the scaffolds where, after the Illinois custom, many of them had been placed. The field was strewn with broken bones and torn and [Pg 207] mangled corpses. A hyena warfare had been waged against the dead. La Salle knew the handiwork of the Iroquois. The threatened blow had fallen, and the wolfish hordes of the five cantons had fleshed their rabid fangs in a new victim.[175]

Not far distant, the conquerors had made a rude fort of trunks, boughs, and roots of trees laid together to form a circular enclosure; and this, too, was garnished with skulls, stuck on the broken branches and protruding sticks. The *caches*, or subterranean store-houses of the villagers, had been broken open and the contents scattered. The cornfields were laid waste, and much of the corn thrown into heaps and half burned. As La Salle surveyed this scene of havoc, one thought engrossed him: where were Tonty and his men? He searched the Iroquois fort: there were abundant traces of its savage occupants, and, among them, a few fragments of French clothing. [Pg 208] He examined the skulls; but the hair, portions of which clung to nearly all of them, was in every case that of an Indian. Evening came on before he had finished the search. The sun set, and the wilderness sank to its savage rest. Night and silence brooded over the waste, where, far as the raven could wing his flight, stretched the dark domain of solitude and horror.

Yet there was no silence at the spot where La Salle and his companions made their bivouac. The howling of the wolves filled the air with fierce and dreary dissonance. More dangerous foes were not far off, for before nightfall they had seen fresh Indian tracks; "but, as it was very cold," says La Salle, "this did not prevent us from making a fire and lying down by it, each of us keeping watch in turn. I spent the night in a distress which you can imagine better than I can write it; and I did not sleep a moment with trying to make up my mind as to what I ought to do. My ignorance as to the position of those I was looking after, and my uncertainty as to what would become of the men who were to follow me with La Forest if they arrived at the ruined village and did not find me there, made me apprehend every sort of trouble and disaster. At last, I decided to keep on my way down the river, leaving some of my men behind in charge of the goods, which it was not only useless but dangerous to carry with me, because we should be forced to abandon them when the winter fairly set in, which would be very soon."

[Pg 209]

FEARS FOR TONTY.

This resolution was due to a discovery he had made the evening before, which offered, as he thought, a possible clew to the fate of Tonty and the men with him. He thus describes it: "Near the garden of the Indians, which was on the meadows, a league from the village and not far from the river, I found six pointed stakes set in the ground and painted red. On each of them was the figure of a man with bandaged eyes, drawn in black. As the savages often set stakes of this sort where they have killed people, I thought, by their number and position, that when the Iroquois came, the Illinois, finding our men alone in the hut near their garden, had either killed them or made them prisoners. And I was confirmed in this, because, seeing no signs of a battle, I supposed that on hearing of the approach of the Iroquois, the old men and other non-combatants had fled, and that the young warriors had remained behind to cover their flight, and afterwards followed, taking the French with them; while the

Iroquois, finding nobody to kill, had vented their fury on the corpses in the graveyard."

Uncertain as was the basis of this conjecture, and feeble as was the hope it afforded, it determined him to push forward, in order to learn more. When daylight returned, he told his purpose to his followers, and directed three of them to await his return near the ruined village. They were to hide themselves on an island, conceal their fire at night, make no smoke by day, fire no guns, and keep a close [Pg 210] watch. Should the rest of the party arrive, they, too, were to wait with similar precautions. The baggage was placed in a hollow of the rocks, at a place difficult of access; and, these arrangements made, La Salle set out on his perilous journey with the four remaining men, Dautray, Hunaut, You, and the Indian. Each was armed with two guns, a pistol, and a sword; and a number of hatchets and other goods were placed in the canoe, as presents for Indians whom they might meet.

Several leagues below the village they found, on their right hand close to the river, a sort of island, made inaccessible by the marshes and water which surrounded it. Here the flying Illinois had sought refuge with their women and children, and the place was full of their deserted huts. On the left bank, exactly opposite, was an abandoned camp of the Iroquois. On the level meadow stood a hundred and thirteen huts, and on the forest trees which covered the hills behind were carved the totems, or insignia, of the chiefs, together with marks to show the number of followers which each had led to the war. La Salle counted five hundred and eighty-two warriors. He found marks, too, for the Illinois killed or captured, but none to indicate that any of the Frenchmen had shared their fate.

SEARCH FOR TONTY.

As they descended the river, they passed, on the same day, six abandoned camps of the Illinois; and opposite to each was a camp of the invaders. The former, it was clear, had retreated in a body;

while [Pg 211] the Iroquois had followed their march, day by day, along the other bank. La Salle and his men pushed rapidly onward, passed Peoria Lake, and soon reached Fort Crèvecœur, which they found, as they expected, demolished by the deserters. The vessel on the stocks was still left entire, though the Iroquois had found means to draw out the iron nails and spikes. On one of the planks were written the words: "*Nous sommes tous sauvages: ce 15, 1680,*"—the work, no doubt, of the knaves who had pillaged and destroyed the fort.

La Salle and his companions hastened on, and during the following day passed four opposing camps of the savage armies. The silence of death now reigned along the deserted river, whose lonely borders, wrapped deep in forests, seemed lifeless as the grave. As they drew near the mouth of the stream they saw a meadow on their right, and on its farthest verge several human figures, erect, yet motionless. They landed, and cautiously examined the place. The long grass was trampled down, and all around were strewn the relics of the hideous orgies which formed the ordinary sequel of an Iroquois victory. The figures they had seen were the half-consumed bodies of women, still bound to the stakes where they had been tortured. Other sights there were, too revolting for record.[176] All the remains were those [Pg 212] of women and children. The men, it seemed, had fled, and left them to their fate.

Here, again, La Salle sought long and anxiously, without finding the smallest sign that could indicate the presence of Frenchmen. Once more descending the river, they soon reached its mouth. Before them, a broad eddying current rolled swiftly on its way; and La Salle beheld the Mississippi,—the object of his day-dreams, the destined avenue of his ambition and his hopes. It was no time for reflections. The moment was too engrossing, too heavily charged with anxieties and cares. From a rock on the shore, he saw a tree stretched forward above the stream; and stripping off its bark to make it more conspicuous, he hung upon it a board on which he had drawn the figures of himself and his men, seated in their canoe, and bearing a pipe of peace. To this he tied a letter for Tonty, informing him that he had returned up the river to the ruined village.

His four men had behaved admirably throughout, and they now offered to continue the journey if he saw fit, and follow him to the sea; but he thought it useless to go farther, and was unwilling to abandon the three men whom he had ordered to await his return. Accordingly, they retraced their course, and, paddling at times both day and night, urged their canoe so swiftly that they reached the village in the incredibly short space of four days.[177]

[Pg 213]

THE COMET.

The sky was clear, and as night came on the travellers saw a prodigious comet blazing above this scene of desolation. On that night, it was chilling with a superstitious awe the hamlets of New England and the gilded chambers of Versailles; but it is characteristic of La Salle, that, beset as he was with perils and surrounded with ghastly images of death, he coolly notes down the phenomenon, not as a portentous messenger of war and woe, but rather as an object of scientific curiosity.[178]

He found his three men safely ensconced upon their island, where they were anxiously looking for his return. After collecting a store of half-burnt corn from the ravaged granaries of the Illinois, the whole party began to ascend the river, and on the sixth of January reached the junction of the Kankakee with the northern branch. On their way downward they had descended the former stream; they now chose the latter, and soon discovered, by the margin [Pg 214] of the water, a rude cabin of bark. La Salle landed and examined the spot, when an object met his eye which cheered him with a bright gleam of hope. It was but a piece of wood; but the wood had been cut with a saw. Tonty and his party, then, had passed this way, escaping from the carnage behind them. Unhappily, they had left no token of their passage at the fork of the two streams; and thus La

Salle, on his voyage downward, had believed them to be still on the river below.

With rekindled hope, the travellers pursued their journey, leaving their canoes, and making their way overland towards the fort on the St. Joseph.

"Snow fell in extraordinary quantities all day," writes La Salle, "and it kept on falling for nineteen days in succession, with cold so severe that I never knew so hard a winter, even in Canada. We were obliged to cross forty leagues of open country, where we could hardly find wood to warm ourselves at evening, and could get no bark whatever to make a hut, so that we had to spend the night exposed to the furious winds which blow over these plains. I never suffered so much from cold, or had more trouble in getting forward; for the snow was so light, resting suspended as it were among the tall grass, that we could not use snow-shoes. Sometimes it was waist deep; and as I walked before my men, as usual, to encourage them by breaking the path, I often had much ado, though I am rather tall, to lift my legs above the [Pg 215] drifts, through which I pushed by the weight of my body."

FORT MIAMI.

At length they reached their goal, and found shelter and safety within the walls of Fort Miami. Here was the party left in charge of La Forest; but, to his surprise and grief, La Salle heard no tidings of Tonty. He found some amends for the disappointment in the fidelity and zeal of La Forest's men, who had restored the fort, cleared ground for planting, and even sawed the planks and timber for a new vessel on the lake.

And now, while La Salle rests at Fort Miami, let us trace the adventures which befell Tonty and his followers, after their chief's departure from Fort Crèvecœur.

FOOTNOTES:

[172] *Robert Cavelier, Sr de la Salle, à François Daupin, Sr de la Forest, 10 Juin, 1679.*

[173] This date is from the *Relation*. Membré says the twenty-eighth; but he is wrong, by his own showing, as he says that the party reached the Illinois village on the first of December, which would be an impossibility.

[174] "Il ne restoit que quelques bouts de perches brulées qui montroient quelle avoit été l'étendue du village, et sur la plupart desquelles il y avoit des têtes de morts plantées et mangées des corbeaux."—*Relation des Découvertes du Sr de la Salle.*

[175] "Beaucoup de carcasses à demi rongées par les loups, les sépulchres démolis, les os tirés de leurs fosses et épars par la campagne; ... enfin les loups et les corbeaux augmentoient encore par leurs hurlemens et par leurs cris l'horreur de ce spectacle."—*Relation des Découvertes du Sr de la Salle.*

The above may seem exaggerated; but it accords perfectly with what is well established concerning the ferocious character of the Iroquois and the nature of their warfare. Many other tribes have frequently made war upon the dead. I have myself known an instance in which five corpses of Sioux Indians placed in trees, after the practice of the Western bands of that people, were thrown down and kicked into fragments by a war party of the Crows, who then held the muzzles of their guns against the skulls, and blew them to pieces. This happened near the head of the Platte, in the summer of 1846. Yet the Crows are much less ferocious than were the Iroquois in La Salle's time.

[176] "On ne sçauroit exprimer la rage de ces furieux ni les tourmens qu'ils avoient fait souffrir aux misérables Tamaroa [*a tribe of the Illinois*]. Il y en avoit encore dans des chaudières qu'ils avoient laissées pleines sur les feux, qui depuis s'étoient éteints," etc., etc.—*Relation des Découvertes.*

[177] The distance is about two hundred and fifty miles. The letters of La Salle, as well as the official narrative compiled from them, say that they left the village on the second of December, and returned to it on the eleventh, having left the mouth of the river on the seventh.

[178] This was the "Great Comet of 1680." Dr. B. A. Gould writes me: "It appeared in December, 1680, and was visible until the latter part of

February, 1681, being especially brilliant in January." It was said to be the largest ever seen. By observations upon it, Newton demonstrated the regular revolutions of comets around the sun. "No comet," it is said, "has threatened the earth with a nearer approach than that of 1680." (*Winthrop on Comets, Lecture II*. p. 44.) Increase Mather, in his *Discourse concerning Comets*, printed at Boston in 1683, says of this one: "Its appearance was very terrible; the Blaze ascended above 60 Degrees almost to its Zenith." Mather thought it fraught with terrific portent to the nations of the earth.

[Pg 216]

CHAPTER XVI.

1680.

TONTY AND THE IROQUOIS.

THE DESERTERS.—THE IROQUOIS WAR.—THE GREAT TOWN OF THE ILLINOIS.—THE ALARM.—ONSET OF THE IROQUOIS.—PERIL OF TONTY.—A TREACHEROUS TRUCE.—INTREPIDITY OF TONTY.—MURDER OF RIBOURDE.—WAR UPON THE DEAD.

WHEN La Salle set out on his rugged journey to Fort Frontenac, he left, as we have seen, fifteen men at Fort Crèvecœur,—smiths, ship-carpenters, house-wrights, and soldiers, besides his servant L'Espérance and the two friars Membré and Ribourde. Most of the men were ripe for mutiny. They had no interest in the enterprise, and no love for its chief. They were disgusted with the present, and terrified at the future. La Salle, too, was for the most part a stern commander, impenetrable and cold; and when he tried to soothe, conciliate, and encourage, his success rarely answered to the excellence of his rhetoric. He could always, however, inspire respect, if not love; but now the restraint of his presence was removed. He had not been long absent, when a fire-brand was thrown into the midst of the discontented and restless crew.

[Pg 217]

It may be remembered that La Salle had met two of his men, La Chapelle and Leblanc, at his fort on the St. Joseph, and ordered them to rejoin Tonty. Unfortunately, they obeyed. On arriving, they told their comrades that the "Griffin" was lost, that Fort Frontenac was seized by the creditors of La Salle, that he was ruined past recovery, and that they, the men, would never receive their pay. Their wages were in arrears for more than two years; and, indeed, it would have been folly to pay them before their return to the settlements, as to do so would have been a temptation to desert. Now, however, the effect on their minds was still worse, believing, as many of them did, that they would never be paid at all.

La Chapelle and his companion had brought a letter from La Salle to Tonty, directing him to examine and fortify the cliff so often mentioned, which overhung the river above the great Illinois village. Tonty, accordingly, set out on his errand with some of the men. In his absence, the malcontents destroyed the fort, stole powder, lead, furs, and provisions, and deserted, after writing on the side of the unfinished vessel the words seen by La Salle, "*Nous sommes tous sauvages.*"[179] The brave [Pg 218] young Sieur de Boisrondet and the servant L'Espérance hastened to carry the news to Tonty, who at once despatched four of those with him, by two different routes, to inform La Salle of the disaster.[180] Besides the two just named, there now remained with him only one hired man and the Récollet friars. With this feeble band, he was left among a horde of treacherous savages, who had been taught to regard him as a secret enemy. Resolved, apparently, to disarm their jealousy by a show of confidence, he took up his abode in the midst of them, making his quarters in the great village, whither, as spring opened, its inhabitants returned, to the number, according to Membré, of seven or eight thousand. Hither he conveyed the forge and such tools as he could recover, and here he hoped to maintain himself till La Salle should reappear. The spring and the summer were past, and he looked anxiously for his coming, unconscious that a storm was gathering in [Pg 219] the east, soon to burst with devastation over the fertile wilderness of the Illinois.

I have recounted the ferocious triumphs of the Iroquois in another volume.[181] Throughout a wide semi-circle around their cantons, they had made the forest a solitude; destroyed the Hurons, exterminated the Neutrals and the Eries, reduced the formidable Andastes to helpless insignificance, swept the borders of the St. Lawrence with fire, spread terror and desolation among the Algonquins of Canada; and now, tired of peace, they were seeking, to borrow their own savage metaphor, new nations to devour. Yet it was not alone their homicidal fury that now impelled them to another war. Strange as it may seem, this war was in no small measure one of commercial advantage. They had long traded with the Dutch and English of New York, who gave them, in exchange for their furs, the guns, ammunition, knives, hatchets, kettles, beads, and brandy which had become indispensable to them. Game was scarce in their country. They must seek their beaver and other skins in the vacant territories of the tribes they had destroyed; but this did not content them. The French of Canada were seeking to secure a monopoly of the furs of the north and west; and, of late, the enterprises of La Salle on the tributaries of the Mississippi had especially roused the jealousy of the Iroquois, fomented, moreover, by Dutch and English traders.[182] These crafty savages would fain [Pg 220] reduce all these regions to subjection, and draw thence an exhaustless supply of furs, to be bartered for English goods with the traders of Albany. They turned their eyes first towards the Illinois, the most important, as well as one of the most accessible, of the western Algonquin tribes; and among La Salle's enemies were some in whom jealousy of a hated rival could so far override all the best interests of the colony that they did not scruple to urge on the Iroquois to an invasion which they hoped would prove his ruin. The chiefs convened, war was decreed, the war-dance was danced, the war-song sung, and five hundred warriors began their march. In their path lay the town of the Miamis, neighbors and kindred of the Illinois. It was always their policy to divide and conquer; and these forest Machiavels had intrigued so well among the Miamis, working craftily on their jealousy, that they induced them to join in the invasion, though there is every reason to believe that they had marked these infatuated allies as their next victims.[183]

THE ILLINOIS TOWN.

Go to the banks of the Illinois where it flows by the village of Utica, and stand on the meadow that borders it on the north. In front glides the river, a musket-shot in width; and from the farther bank rises, with gradual slope, a range of wooded hills [Pg 221] that hide from sight the vast prairie behind them. A mile or more on your left these gentle acclivities end abruptly in the lofty front of the great cliff, called by the French the Rock of St. Louis, looking boldly out from the forests that environ it; and, three miles distant on your right, you discern a gap in the steep bluffs that here bound the valley, marking the mouth of the river Vermilion, called Aramoni by the French.[184] Now stand in fancy on this same spot in the early autumn of the year 1680. You are in the midst of the great town of the Illinois,— hundreds of mat-covered lodges, and thousands of congregated savages. Enter one of their dwellings: they will not think you an intruder. Some friendly squaw will lay a mat for you by the fire; you may seat yourself upon it, smoke your pipe, and study the lodge and its inmates by the light that streams through the holes at the top. Three or four fires smoke and smoulder on the ground down the middle [Pg 222] of the long arched structure; and, as to each fire there are two families, the place is somewhat crowded when all are present. But now there is breathing room, for many are in the fields. A squaw sits weaving a mat of rushes; a warrior, naked except his moccasins, and tattooed with fantastic devices, binds a stone arrow-head to its shaft, with the fresh sinews of a buffalo. Some lie asleep, some sit staring in vacancy, some are eating, some are squatted in lazy chat around a fire. The smoke brings water to your eyes; the fleas annoy you; small unkempt children, naked as young puppies, crawl about your knees and will not be repelled. You have seen enough; you rise and go out again into the sunlight. It is, if not a peaceful, at least a languid scene. A few voices break the stillness, mingled with the joyous chirping of crickets from the grass. Young men lie flat on their faces, basking in the sun; a group of their elders are smoking around a buffalo-skin on which they have just been playing a game of chance with cherry-stones. A lover and his mistress, perhaps, sit together under a shed of bark, without uttering a word. Not far off is the graveyard, where lie the dead of the village, some buried in the earth, some wrapped in skins and laid aloft on scaffolds, above the reach of wolves. In the cornfields around, you see squaws at their labor, and children driving off intruding birds; and your eye ranges over the meadows beyond, spangled with the yellow blossoms of the resin-weed and the Rudbeckia, [Pg 223] or over the bordering hills still green with the foliage of summer.[185]

This, or something like it, one may safely affirm, was the aspect of the Illinois village at noon of the tenth of September.[186] In a hut apart from the rest, you would probably have found the Frenchmen. Among them was a man, not strong in person, and disabled, moreover, by the loss of a hand, yet in this den of barbarism betraying the language and bearing of one formed in the most polished civilization of Europe. This was Henri de Tonty. The others were young Boisrondet, the servant L'Espérance, and a Parisian youth named Étienne Renault. The [Pg 224] friars, Membré and Ribourde, were not in the village, but at a hut a league distant, whither they had gone to make a "retreat" for prayer and meditation. Their missionary labors had not been fruitful; they had made no converts, and were in despair at the intractable character of the objects of their zeal. As for the other Frenchmen, time, doubtless, hung heavy on their hands; for nothing can surpass the vacant monotony of an Indian town when there is neither hunting, nor war, nor feasts, nor dances, nor gambling, to beguile the lagging hours.

THE ALARM.

Suddenly the village was wakened from its lethargy as by the crash of a thunderbolt. A Shawanoe, lately here on a visit, had left his Illinois friends to return home. He now reappeared, crossing the river in hot haste, with the announcement that he had met, on his way, an army of Iroquois approaching to attack them. All was panic and confusion. The lodges disgorged their frightened inmates; women and children screamed, startled warriors snatched their weapons. There were less than five hundred of them, for the greater part of the young men had gone to war. A crowd of excited savages thronged about Tonty and his Frenchmen, already objects of their suspicion, charging them, with furious gesticulation, with having stirred up their enemies to invade them. Tonty defended himself in broken Illinois, but the naked mob were but half convinced. They seized the forge and tools and flung them into the river, with all the goods that had [Pg 225] been saved from the deserters; then, distrusting their power to defend themselves, they manned the wooden canoes which lay in multitudes by the bank, embarked their women and children, and paddled down the stream to that island of dry land in the midst of marshes which La Salle afterwards found filled with their deserted huts. Sixty warriors remained here to guard them, and the rest returned to the village. All night long fires blazed along the shore. The excited warriors greased their bodies, painted their faces, befeathered their heads, sang their war-songs, danced, stamped, yelled, and brandished their hatchets, to work up their courage to face the crisis. The morning came, and with it came the Iroquois.

Young warriors had gone out as scouts, and now they returned. They had seen the enemy in the line of forest that bordered the river Aramoni, or Vermilion, and had stealthily reconnoitred them. They were very numerous,[187] and armed for the most part with guns, pistols, and swords. Some had bucklers of wood or raw-hide, and some wore those corselets of tough twigs interwoven with cordage which their fathers had used when fire-arms were unknown. The scouts added more, for they declared that they had seen a Jesuit among the Iroquois; nay, [Pg 226] that La Salle himself was there, whence it must follow that Tonty and his men were enemies and traitors. The supposed Jesuit was but an Iroquois chief arrayed in a black hat, doublet, and stockings; while another, equipped after a somewhat similar fashion, passed in the distance for La Salle. But the Illinois were furious. Tonty's life hung by a hair. A crowd of savages surrounded him, mad with rage and terror. He had come lately from Europe, and knew little of Indians, but, as the friar Membré says of him, "he was full of intelligence and courage," and when they heard him declare that he and his Frenchmen would go with them to fight the Iroquois, their threats grew less clamorous and their eyes glittered with a less deadly lustre.

TONTY'S MEDIATION.

Whooping and screeching, they ran to their canoes, crossed the river, climbed the woody hill, and swarmed down upon the plain beyond. About a hundred of them had guns; the rest were armed with bows and arrows. They were now face to face with the enemy, who had emerged from the woods of the Vermilion, and were advancing on the open prairie. With unwonted spirit, for their repute as warriors was by no means high, the Illinois began, after their fashion, to charge; that is, they leaped, yelled, and shot off bullets and arrows, advancing as they did so; while the Iroquois replied with gymnastics no less agile and howlings no less terrific, mingled with the rapid clatter of their guns. Tonty saw that it would go hard with his allies. It was of the last [Pg 227] moment to stop the fight, if possible. The Iroquois were, or professed to be, at peace with the French; and, taking counsel of his courage, he resolved on an attempt to mediate, which may well be called a desperate one. He laid aside his gun, took in his hand a wampum belt as a flag of truce, and walked forward to meet the savage multitude, attended by Boisrondet, another Frenchman, and a young Illinois who had the hardihood to accompany him. The guns of the Iroquois still flashed thick and fast. Some of them were aimed at him, on which he sent back the two Frenchmen and the Illinois, and advanced alone, holding out the wampum belt.[188] A moment more, and he was among the infuriated warriors. It was a frightful spectacle,—the contorted forms, bounding, crouching, twisting, to deal or dodge the shot; the small keen eyes that shone like an angry snake's; the parted lips pealing their [Pg 228] fiendish yells; the painted features writhing with fear and fury, and every passion of an Indian fight,—man, wolf, and devil, all in one.[189] With his swarthy complexion and his half-savage dress, they thought he was an Indian, and thronged about him, glaring murder. A young warrior stabbed at his heart with a knife, but the point glanced aside against a rib, inflicting only a deep gash. A chief called out that, as his ears were not pierced, he must be a Frenchman. On this, some of them tried to stop the bleeding, and led him to the rear, where an angry parley ensued, while the yells and firing still resounded in the front. Tonty, breathless, and bleeding at the mouth with the force of the blow he had received, found words to declare that the Illinois were under the protection of the King and the governor of Canada, and to demand that they should be left in peace.[190]

PERIL OF TONTY.

A young Iroquois snatched Tonty's hat, placed it on the end of his gun, and displayed it to the Illinois, who, thereupon thinking he was killed, [Pg 229] renewed the fight; and the firing in front clattered more angrily than before. A warrior ran in, crying out that the Iroquois were giving ground, and that there were Frenchmen among the Illinois, who fired at them. On this, the clamor around Tonty was redoubled. Some wished to kill him at once; others resisted. "I was never," he writes, "in such perplexity; for at that moment there was an Iroquois behind me, with a knife in his hand, lifting my hair as if he were going to scalp me. I thought it was all over with me, and that my best hope was that they would knock me in the head instead of burning me, as I believed they would do." In fact, a Seneca chief demanded that he should be burned; while an Onondaga chief, a friend of La Salle, was for setting him free. The dispute grew fierce and hot. Tonty told them that the Illinois were twelve hundred strong, and that sixty Frenchmen were at the village, ready to back them. This invention, though not fully believed, had no little effect. The friendly Onondaga carried his point; and the Iroquois, having failed to surprise their enemies, as they had hoped, now saw an opportunity to delude them by a truce. They sent back Tonty with a belt of peace: he held it aloft in sight of the Illinois; chiefs and old warriors ran to stop the fight; the yells and the firing ceased; and Tonty, like one waked from a hideous nightmare, dizzy, almost fainting with loss of blood, staggered across the intervening prairie, to rejoin his friends. He was met by the two friars, Ribourde [Pg 230] and Membré, who in their secluded hut, a league from the village, had but lately heard of what was passing, and who now, with benedictions and thanksgiving, ran to embrace him as a man escaped from the jaws of death.

The Illinois now withdrew, re-embarking in their canoes, and crossing again to their lodges; but scarcely had they reached them, when their enemies appeared at the edge of the forest on the opposite bank. Many found means to cross, and, under the pretext of seeking for provisions, began to hover in bands about the skirts of the town, constantly increasing in numbers. Had the Illinois dared to remain, a massacre would doubtless have ensued; but they knew their foe too well, set fire to their lodges, embarked in haste, and paddled down the stream to rejoin their women and children at the sanctuary among the morasses. The whole body of the Iroquois now crossed the river, took possession of the abandoned town, building for themselves a rude redoubt or fort of the trunks of trees and of the posts and poles forming the framework of the lodges which escaped the fire. Here they ensconced themselves, and finished the work of havoc at their leisure.

Tonty and his companions still occupied their hut; but the Iroquois, becoming suspicious of them, forced them to remove to the fort, crowded as it was with the savage crew. On the second day, there was an alarm. The Illinois appeared in numbers on the low hills, half a mile behind the town; and the Iroquois, [Pg 231] who had felt their courage, and who had been told by Tonty that they were twice as numerous as themselves, showed symptoms of no little uneasiness. They proposed that he should act as mediator, to which he gladly assented, and crossed the meadow towards the Illinois, accompanied by Membré, and by an Iroquois who was sent as a hostage. The Illinois hailed the overtures with delight, gave the ambassadors some refreshment, which they sorely needed, and sent back with them a young man of their nation as a hostage on their part. This indiscreet youth nearly proved the ruin of the negotiation; for he was no sooner among the Iroquois than he showed such an eagerness to close the treaty, made such promises, professed such gratitude, and betrayed so rashly the numerical weakness of the Illinois, that he revived all the insolence of the invaders. They turned furiously upon Tonty, and charged him with having robbed them of the glory and the spoils of victory. "Where are all your Illinois warriors, and where are the sixty Frenchmen that you said were among them?" It needed all Tonty's tact and coolness to extricate himself from this new danger.

IROQUOIS TREACHERY.

The treaty was at length concluded; but scarcely was it made, when the Iroquois prepared to break it, and set about constructing canoes of elm-bark, in which to attack the Illinois women and children in their island sanctuary. Tonty warned his allies that the pretended peace was but a snare for their destruction. The Iroquois, on their part, grew hourly more [Pg 232] jealous of him, and would certainly have killed him, had it not been their policy to keep the peace with Frontenac and the French.

Several days after, they summoned him and Membré to a council. Six packs of beaver-skins were brought in; and the savage orator presented them to Tonty in turn, explaining their meaning as he did so. The first two were to declare that the children of Count Frontenac—that is, the Illinois—should not be eaten; the next was a plaster to heal Tonty's wound; the next was oil wherewith to anoint him and Membré, that they might not be fatigued in travelling; the next proclaimed that the sun was bright; and the sixth and last required them to decamp and go home.[191] Tonty thanked them for their gifts, but demanded when they themselves meant to go and leave the Illinois in peace. At this, the conclave grew angry; and, despite their late pledge, some of them said that before they went they would eat Illinois flesh. Tonty instantly kicked away the packs of beaver-skins, the Indian symbol of the scornful rejection of a proposal, telling them that since they meant to eat the governor's children he would have none of their presents. The chiefs, [Pg 233] in a rage, rose and drove him from the lodge. The French withdrew to their hut, where they stood all night on the watch, expecting an attack, and resolved to sell their lives dearly. At daybreak, the chiefs ordered them to begone.

MURDER OF RIBOURDE.

Tonty, with admirable fidelity and courage, had done all in the power of man to protect the allies of Canada against their ferocious assailants; and he thought it unwise to persist further in a course which could lead to no good, and which would probably end in the destruction of the whole party. He embarked in a leaky canoe with Membré, Ribourde, Boisrondet, and the remaining two men, and began to ascend the river. After paddling about five leagues, they landed to dry their baggage and repair their crazy vessel; when Father Ribourde, breviary in hand, strolled across the sunny meadows for an hour of meditation among the neighboring groves. Evening approached, and he did not return. Tonty, with one of the men, went to look for him, and, following his tracks, presently discovered those of a band of Indians, who had apparently seized or murdered him. Still, they did not despair. They fired their guns to guide him, should he still be alive; built a huge fire by the bank, and then, crossing the river, lay watching it from the other side. At midnight, they saw the figure of a man hovering around the blaze; then many more appeared, but Ribourde was not among them. In truth, a band of Kickapoos, enemies of the Iroquois, about whose camp they had [Pg 234] been prowling in quest of scalps, had met and wantonly murdered the inoffensive old man. They carried his scalp to their village, and danced round it in triumph, pretending to have taken it from an enemy. Thus, in his sixty-fifth year, the only heir of a wealthy Burgundian house perished under the war-clubs of the savages for whose salvation he had renounced station, ease, and affluence.[192]

ATTACK OF THE IROQUOIS.

Meanwhile, a hideous scene was enacted at the ruined village of the Illinois. Their savage foes, balked of a living prey, wreaked their fury on the dead. They dug up the graves; they threw down the scaffolds. Some of the bodies they burned; some they threw to the dogs; some, it is affirmed, they ate.[193] Placing the skulls on stakes as trophies, they turned to pursue the Illinois, who, when the French withdrew, had abandoned their asylum and retreated down the river. The Iroquois, still, it seems, in awe of them, followed them along the opposite bank, each night encamping face to face [Pg 235] with them; and thus the adverse bands moved slowly southward, till they were near the mouth of the river. Hitherto, the compact array of the Illinois had held their enemies in check; but now, suffering from hunger, and lulled into security by the assurances of the Iroquois that their object was not to destroy them, but only to drive them from the country, they rashly separated into their several tribes. Some descended the Mississippi; some, more prudent, crossed to the western side. One of their principal tribes, the Tamaroas, more credulous than the rest, had the fatuity to remain near the mouth of the Illinois, where they were speedily assailed by all the force of the Iroquois. The men fled, and very few of them were killed; but the women and children were captured to the number, it is said, of seven hundred.[194] Then followed that scene of torture of which, some two weeks later, La Salle saw the revolting traces.[195] Sated, at length, with horrors, the conquerors withdrew, leading with them a host of captives, and exulting in their triumphs over women, children, and the dead.

After the death of Father Ribourde, Tonty and his companions remained searching for him till noon [Pg 236] of the next day, and then in despair of again seeing him, resumed their journey. They ascended the river, leaving no token of their passage at the junction of its northern and southern branches. For food, they gathered acorns and dug roots in the meadows. Their canoe proved utterly worthless; and, feeble as they were, they set out on foot for Lake Michigan. Boisrondet wandered off, and was lost. He had dropped the flint of his gun, and he had no bullets; but he cut a pewter porringer into slugs, with which he shot wild turkeys by discharging his piece with a fire-brand, and after several days he had the good fortune to rejoin the party. Their object was to reach the Pottawattamies of Green Bay. Had they aimed at Michilimackinac, they would have found an asylum with La Forest at the fort on the St. Joseph; but unhappily they passed westward of that post, and, by way of Chicago, followed the borders of Lake Michigan northward. The cold was intense; and it was no easy task to grub up wild onions from the frozen ground to save themselves from starving. Tonty fell ill of a fever and a swelling of the limbs, which disabled him from travelling, and hence ensued a long delay. At length they neared Green Bay, where they would have starved, had they not gleaned a few ears of corn and frozen squashes in the fields of an empty Indian town.

FRIENDS IN NEED.

This enabled them to reach the bay, and having patched an old canoe which they had the good luck to find, they embarked in it; whereupon, says Tonty, [Pg 237] "there rose a northwest wind, which lasted five days, with driving snow. We consumed all our food; and not knowing what to do next, we resolved to go back to the deserted town, and die by a warm fire in one of the wigwams. On our way, we saw a smoke; but our joy was short, for when we reached the fire we found nobody there. We spent the night by it; and before morning the bay froze. We tried to break a way for our canoe through the ice, but could not; and therefore we determined to stay there another night, and make moccasins in order to reach the town. We made some out of Father Gabriel's cloak. I was angry with Étienne Renault for not finishing his; but he excused himself on account of illness, because he had a great oppression of the stomach, caused by eating a piece of an Indian shield of raw-hide, which he could not digest. His delay proved our salvation; for the next day, December fourth, as I was urging him to finish the moccasins, and he was still excusing himself on the score of his malady, a party of Kiskakon Ottawas, who were on their way to the Pottawattamies, saw the smoke of our fire, and came to us. We gave them such a welcome as was never seen before. They took us into their canoes, and carried us to an Indian village, only two leagues off. There we found five Frenchmen, who received us kindly, and all the Indians seemed to take pleasure in sending us food; so that, after thirty-four days of starvation, we found our famine turned to abundance."

[Pg 238]

This hospitable village belonged to the Pottawattamies, and was under the sway of the chief who had befriended La Salle the year before, and who was wont to say that he knew but three great captains in the world,—Frontenac, La Salle, and himself.[196]

[Pg 239]

THE ILLINOIS TOWN.

THE SITE OF THE GREAT ILLINOIS TOWN.—This has not till now been determined, though there have been various conjectures concerning it. From a study of the contemporary documents and maps, I became satisfied, first, that the branch of the river Illinois, called the "Big Vermilion," was the *Aramoni* of the French explorers; and, secondly, that the cliff called "Starved Rock" was that known to the French as *Le Rocher*, or the Rock of St. Louis. If I was right in this conclusion, then the position of the Great Village was established; for there is abundant proof that it was on the north side of the river, above the Aramoni, and below Le Rocher. I accordingly went to the village of Utica, which, as I judged by the map, was very near the point in question, and mounted to the top of one of the hills immediately behind it, whence I could see the valley of the Illinois for miles, bounded on the farther side by a range of hills, in some parts rocky and precipitous, and in others covered with forests. Far on the right was a gap in these hills, through which the Big Vermilion flowed to join the Illinois; and somewhat towards the left, at the distance of a mile and a half, was a huge cliff, rising perpendicularly from the opposite margin of the river. This I assumed to be *Le Rocher* of the French, though from where I stood I was unable to discern the distinctive features which I was prepared to find in it. In every other respect, the scene before me was precisely what I had expected to see. There was a meadow on the hither side of the river, on which stood a farmhouse; and this, as it seemed to me, by its relations with surrounding objects, might be supposed to stand in the midst of the space once occupied by the Illinois town.

On the way down from the hill I met Mr. James Clark, the principal inhabitant of Utica, and one of the earliest settlers of this region. I accosted him, told him my objects, and requested [Pg 240] a half hour's conversation with him, at his leisure. He seemed interested in the inquiry, and said he would visit me early in the evening at the inn, where, accordingly, he soon appeared. The conversation took place in the porch, where a number of farmers and others were gathered. I asked Mr. Clark if any Indian remains were found in the neighborhood. "Yes," he replied, "plenty of them." I then inquired if there was any one spot where they were more numerous than elsewhere. "Yes," he answered again, pointing towards the farmhouse on the meadow; "on my farm down yonder by the river, my tenant ploughs up teeth and bones by the peck every spring, besides arrow-heads, beads, stone hatchets, and other things of that sort." I replied that this was precisely what I had expected, as I had been led to believe that the principal town of the Illinois Indians once covered that very spot. "If," I added, "I am right in this belief, the great rock beyond the river is the one which the first explorers occupied as a fort; and I can describe it to you from their accounts of it, though I have never seen it, except from the top of the hill where the trees on and around it prevented me from seeing any part but the front." The men present now gathered around to listen. "The rock," I continued, "is nearly a hundred and fifty feet high, and rises directly from the water. The front and two sides are perpendicular and inaccessible; but there is one place where it is possible for a man to climb up, though with difficulty. The top is large enough and level enough for houses and fortifications." Here several of the men exclaimed: "That's just it." "You've hit it exactly." I then asked if there was any other rock on that side of the river which could answer to the description. They all agreed that there was no such rock on either side, along the whole length of the river. I then said: "If the Indian town was in the place where I suppose it to have been, I can tell you the nature of the country which lies behind the hills on the farther side of the river, though I know nothing about it except what I have learned from writings nearly two centuries old. From the top of the hills, you look out upon a great prairie reaching as far as you can see, except that it is crossed by a belt of woods, following the course of a stream [Pg 241] which enters the main river a few miles below." (See *ante*, p. 221, *note*.) "You are exactly right again," replied Mr. Clark; "we call that belt of timber the 'Vermilion Woods,' and the stream is the Big Vermilion." "Then," I said, "the Big Vermilion is the river which the French called the Aramoni; 'Starved Rock' is the same on which they built a fort called St. Louis, in the year 1682; and your farm is on the site of the great town of the Illinois."

I spent the next day in examining these localities, and was fully confirmed in my conclusions. Mr. Clark's tenant showed me the spot where the human bones were ploughed up. It was no doubt the graveyard violated by the Iroquois. The Illinois returned to the village after their defeat, and long continued to occupy it. The scattered bones were probably collected and restored to their place of burial.

FOOTNOTES:

[179] For the particulars of this desertion, Membré in Le Clerc, ii. 171, *Relation des Découvertes*; Tonty, *Mémoire*, 1684, 1693; *Déclaration faite par devant le Sr Duchesneau, Intendant en Canada, par Moyse Hillaret, charpentier de barque cy-devant au service du Sr de la Salle, Aoust, 1680*.

Moyse Hillaret, the "Maître Moyse" of Hennepin, was a ring-leader of the deserters, and seems to have been one of those captured by La Salle near Fort Frontenac. Twelve days after, Hillaret was examined by La Salle's enemy, the intendant; and this paper is the formal statement made by him. It gives the names of most of the men, and furnishes incidental confirmation of many statements of Hennepin, Tonty, Membré, and the *Relation des Découvertes*. Hillaret, Leblanc, and Le Meilleur, the blacksmith nicknamed La Forge, went off together, and the rest seem to have followed afterwards. Hillaret does not admit that any goods were wantonly destroyed.

There is before me a schedule of the debts of La Salle, made after his death. It includes a claim of this man for wages to the amount of 2,500 livres.

[180] Two of the messengers, Laurent and Messier, arrived safely. The others seem to have deserted.
[181] The Jesuits in North America.
[182] Duchesneau, in *Paris Docs.*, ix. 163.
[183] There had long been a rankling jealousy between the Miamis and the Illinois. According to Membré, La Salle's enemies had intrigued

successfully among the former, as well as among the Iroquois, to induce them to take arms against the Illinois.

[184] The above is from notes made on the spot. The following is La Salle's description of the locality in the *Relation des Découvertes*, written in 1681: "La rive gauche de la rivière, du coté du sud, est occupée par un long rocher, fort étroit et escarpé presque partout, à la réserve d'un endroit de plus d'une lieue de longueur, situé vis-à-vis du village, ou le terrain, tout couvert de beaux chênes, s'étend par une pente douce jusqu'au bord de la rivière. Au delà de cette hauteur est une vaste plaine, qui s'étend bien loin du coté du sud, et qui est traversée par la rivière Aramoni, dont les bords sont couverts d'une lisière de bois peu large."

The Aramoni is laid down on the great manuscript map of Franquelin, 1684, and on the map of Coronelli, 1688. It is, without doubt, the Big Vermilion. *Aramoni* is the Illinois word for "red," or "vermilion." Starved Rock, or the Rock of St. Louis, is the highest and steepest escarpment of the *long rocher* above mentioned.

[185] The Illinois were an aggregation of distinct though kindred tribes,—the Kaskaskias, the Peorias, the Kahokias, the Tamaroas, the Moingona, and others. Their general character and habits were those of other Indian tribes; but they were reputed somewhat cowardly and slothful. In their manners, they were more licentious than many of their neighbors, and addicted to practices which are sometimes supposed to be the result of a perverted civilization. Young men enacting the part of women were frequently to be seen among them. These were held in great contempt. Some of the early travellers, both among the Illinois and among other tribes, where the same practice prevailed, mistook them for hermaphrodites. According to Charlevoix (*Journal Historique*, 303), this abuse was due in part to a superstition. The Miamis and Piankishaws were in close affinities of language and habits with the Illinois. All these tribes belonged to the great Algonquin family. The first impressions which the French received of them, as recorded in the *Relation* of 1671, were singularly favorable; but a closer acquaintance did not confirm them. The Illinois traded with the lake tribes, to whom they carried slaves taken in war, receiving in exchange guns, hatchets, and other French goods. Marquette in *Relation*, 1670, 91.

[186] This is Membré's date. The narratives differ as to the day, though all agree as to the month.

[187] The *Relation des Découvertes* says, five hundred Iroquois and one hundred Shawanoes. Membré says that the allies were Miamis. He is no doubt right, as the Miamis had promised their aid, and the Shawanoes were at peace with the Illinois. Tonty is silent on the point.

[188] Membré says that he went with Tonty: "J'étois aussi à côté du Sieur de Tonty." This is an invention of the friar's vanity. "Les deux pères Récollets étoient alors dans une cabane à une lieue du village, où ils s'étoient retirés pour faire une espèce de retraite, et ils ne furent avertis de l'arrivée des Iroquois que dans le temps du combat."—*Relation des Découvertes.* "Je rencontrai en chemin les pères Gabriel et Zenobe Membré, qui cherchoient de mes nouvelles."—Tonty, *Mémoire*, 1693. This was on his return from the Iroquois. The *Relation* confirms the statement, as far as concerns Membré: "Il rencontra le Père Zenobe [*Membré*], qui venoit pour le secourir, aiant été averti du combat et de sa blessure."

The perverted *Dernières Découvertes*, published without authority, under Tonty's name, says that he was attended by a slave, whom the Illinois sent with him as interpreter. In his narrative of 1684, Tonty speaks of a Sokokis (Saco) Indian who was with the Iroquois and who spoke French enough to serve as interpreter.

[189] Being once in an encampment of Sioux when a quarrel broke out, and the adverse factions raised the war-whoop and began to fire at each other, I had a good, though for the moment a rather dangerous, opportunity of seeing the demeanor of Indians at the beginning of a fight. The fray was quelled before much mischief was done, by the vigorous intervention of the elder warriors, who ran between the combatants.

[190] "Je leur fis connoistre que les Islinois étoient sous la protection du roy de France et du gouverneur du pays, que j'estois surpris qu'ils voulussent rompre avec les François et qu'ils voulussent *attendre* [*sic*] à une paix."—Tonty, *Mémoire*, 1693.

[191] An Indian speech, it will be remembered, is without validity if not confirmed by presents, each of which has its special interpretation. The meaning of the fifth pack of beaver, informing Tonty that the sun was bright,—"que le soleil étoit beau," that is, that the weather was favorable for travelling,—is curiously misconceived by the editor of the *Dernières Découvertes*, who improves upon his original by substituting the words "par le cinquième paquet *ils nous exhortoient à adorer le Soleil.*"

[192] Tonty, *Mémoire*; Membré in Le Clerc, ii. 191. Hennepin, who hated Tonty, unjustly charges him with having abandoned the search too soon, admitting, however, that it would have been useless to continue it. This part of his narrative is a perversion of Membré's account.

[193] "Cependant les Iroquois, aussitôt après le départ du Sr de Tonty, exercèrent leur rage sur les corps morts des Ilinois, qu'ils déterrèrent ou abbattèrent de dessus les échafauds où les Ilinois les laissent longtemps exposés avant que de les mettre en terre. Ils en brûlèrent la plus grande partie, ils en mangèrent même quelques uns, et jettèrent le reste aux chiens. Ils plantèrent les têtes de ces cadavres à demi décharnés sur des pieux," etc.—*Relation des Découvertes*.

[194] *Relation des Découvertes*; Frontenac to the King, *N. Y. Col. Docs.*, ix. 147. A memoir of Duchesneau makes the number twelve hundred.

[195] "Ils [*les Illinois*] trouvèrent dans leur campement des carcasses de leurs enfans que ces anthropophages avoient mangez, ne voulant même d'autre nourriture que la chair de ces infortunez."—*La Potherie*, ii. 145, 146. Compare *note, ante*, p. 211.

[196] Membré in Le Clerc, ii. 199. The other authorities for the foregoing chapter are the letters of La Salle, the *Relation des Découvertes*, in which portions of them are embodied, and the two narratives of Tonty, of 1684 and 1693. They all agree in essential points.

In his letters of this period, La Salle dwells at great length on the devices by which, as he believed, his enemies tried to ruin him and his enterprise. He is particularly severe against the Jesuit Allouez, whom he charges with intriguing "pour commencer la guerre entre les Iroquois et les Illinois par le moyen des Miamis qu'on engageoit dans cette négociation afin ou de me faire massacrer avec mes gens par quelqu'une de ces nations ou de me brouiller avec les Iroquois."—*Lettre (à Thouret?), 22 Août, 1682.* He gives in detail the circumstances on which this suspicion rests, but which are not convincing. He says, further, that the Jesuits gave out that Tonty was dead in order to discourage the men going to his relief, and that Allouez encouraged the deserters, "leur servoit de conseil, bénit mesme leurs balles, et les asseura plusieurs fois que M. de Tonty auroit la teste cassée." He also affirms that great pains were taken to spread the report that he was himself dead. A Kiskakon Indian, he says, was sent to Tonty with a story to this effect; while a Huron named Scortas was sent to him (La Salle) with false news of the death of Tonty. The latter confirms this statement, and adds that the Illinois had been told "que M. de la Salle estoit venu en leur pays pour les donner à manger aux Iroquois."

[Pg 242]

CHAPTER XVII.

1680.

THE ADVENTURES OF HENNEPIN.

HENNEPIN AN IMPOSTOR: HIS PRETENDED DISCOVERY; HIS ACTUAL DISCOVERY; CAPTURED BY THE SIOUX.—THE UPPER MISSISSIPPI.

IT was on the last day of the winter that preceded the invasion of the Iroquois that Father Hennepin, with his two companions, Accau and Du Gay, had set out from Fort Crèvecœur to explore the Illinois to its mouth. It appears from his own later statements, as well as from those of Tonty, that more than this was expected of him, and that La Salle had instructed him to explore, not alone the Illinois, but also the Upper Mississippi. That he actually did so, there is no reasonable doubt; and could he have contented himself with telling the truth, his name would have stood high as a bold and vigorous discoverer. But his vicious attempts to malign his commander and plunder him of his laurels have wrapped his genuine merit in a cloud.

Hennepin's first book was published soon after his return from his travels, and while La Salle was still alive. In it he relates the accomplishment of the [Pg 243] instructions given him, without the smallest intimation that he did more.[197] Fourteen years after, when La Salle was dead, he published another edition of his travels,[198] in which he advanced a new and surprising pretension. Reasons connected with his personal safety, he declares, before compelled him to remain silent; but a time at length had come when the truth must be revealed. And he proceeds to affirm, that, before ascending the Mississippi, he, with his two men, explored its whole course from the Illinois to the sea,—thus anticipating the discovery which forms the crowning laurel of La Salle.

HENNEPIN'S RESOLUTION.

"I am resolved," he says, "to make known here to the whole world the mystery of this discovery, which I have hitherto concealed, that I might not offend the Sieur de la Salle, who wished to keep all the glory and all the knowledge of it to himself. It is for this that he sacrificed many persons whose lives he exposed, to prevent them from making known what they had seen, and thereby crossing his secret plans.... I was certain that if I went down the Mississippi, he would not fail to traduce me to my superiors for not taking the northern route, which I was to have followed in accordance with his desire and the plan we had made together. But I saw myself on the point of dying of hunger, and knew not what to do; because the two men who were with [Pg 244] me threatened openly to leave me in the night, and carry off the canoe and everything in it, if I prevented them from going down the river to the nations below. Finding myself in this dilemma, I thought that I ought not to hesitate, and that I ought to prefer my own safety to the violent passion which possessed the Sieur de la Salle of enjoying alone the glory of this discovery. The two men, seeing that I had made up my mind to follow them, promised me entire fidelity; so, after we had shaken hands together as a mutual pledge, we set out on our voyage."[199]

He then proceeds to recount at length the particulars of his alleged exploration. The story was distrusted from the first.[200] Why had he not told it before? An excess of modesty, a lack of self-assertion, or a too sensitive reluctance to wound the susceptibilities of others, had never been found among his foibles. Yet some, perhaps, might have believed him, had he not in the first edition of his book gratuitously and distinctly declared that he did not make the voyage in question. "We had some designs," he says, "of going down the river Colbert [Mississippi] as far as its mouth; but the tribes that took us prisoners gave us no time to navigate this river both up and down."[201]]

[Pg 245]

HENNEPIN AN IMPOSTOR.

In declaring to the world the achievement which he had so long concealed and so explicitly denied, the worthy missionary found himself in serious embarrassment. In his first book, he had stated that on the twelfth of March he left the mouth of the Illinois on his way northward, and that on the eleventh of April he was captured by the Sioux near the mouth of the Wisconsin, five hundred miles above. This would give him only a month to make his alleged canoe-voyage from the Illinois to the Gulf of Mexico, and again upward to the place of his capture,—a distance of three thousand two hundred and sixty miles. With his means of transportation, three months would have been insufficient.[202] He saw the difficulty; but, on the other hand, he saw that he could not greatly change either date without confusing the parts of his narrative which preceded and which followed. In this perplexity he chose a middle course, which only involved him in additional contradictions. Having, as he affirms, gone down to the Gulf and returned to the mouth of the Illinois, he set out thence to explore the river above; and he assigns the twenty-fourth of April as the date of this departure. This gives him forty-three days for [Pg 246] his voyage to the mouth of the river and back. Looking further, we find that having left the Illinois on the twenty-fourth he paddled his canoe two hundred leagues northward, and was then captured by the Sioux on the twelfth of the same month. In short, he ensnares himself in a hopeless confusion of dates.[203]

Here, one would think, is sufficient reason for rejecting his story; and yet the general truth of the descriptions, and a certain verisimilitude which marks it, might easily deceive a careless reader and perplex a critical one. These, however, are easily explained. Six years before Hennepin published his pretended discovery, his brother friar, Father Chrétien Le Clerc, published an account of the Récollet missions among the Indians, under the title of "Établissement de la Foi." This book, offensive to the Jesuits, is said to have been suppressed by order of government; but a few copies fortunately survive.[204] One of these is now before me. It contains the journal of Father Zenobe Membré, on his descent of the

Mississippi in [Pg 247] 1681, in company with La Salle. The slightest comparison of his narrative with that of Hennepin is sufficient to show that the latter framed his own story out of incidents and descriptions furnished by his brother missionary, often using his very words, and sometimes copying entire pages, with no other alterations than such as were necessary to make himself, instead of La Salle and his companions, the hero of the exploit. The records of literary piracy may be searched in vain for an act of depredation more recklessly impudent.[205]

Such being the case, what faith can we put in the rest of Hennepin's story? Fortunately, there are tests by which the earlier parts of his book can be [Pg 248] tried; and, on the whole, they square exceedingly well with contemporary records of undoubted authenticity. Bating his exaggerations respecting the Falls of Niagara, his local descriptions, and even his estimates of distance, are generally accurate. He constantly, it is true, magnifies his own acts, and thrusts himself forward as one of the chiefs of an enterprise to the costs of which he had contributed nothing, and to which he was merely an appendage; and yet, till he reaches the Mississippi, there can be no doubt that in the main he tells the truth. As for his ascent of that river to the country of the Sioux, the general statement is fully confirmed by La Salle, Tonty, and other contemporary writers.[206] For the details of the journey we must rest on Hennepin alone, whose account of the country and of the peculiar traits of its Indian occupants afford, as far as they go, good evidence of truth. Indeed, this part of his narrative could only have been written by one well versed in the savage life of this northwestern region.[207] Trusting, [Pg 249] then, to his own guidance in the absence of better, let us follow in the wake of his adventurous canoe.

HIS VOYAGE NORTHWARD.

It was laden deeply with goods belonging to La Salle, and meant by him as presents to Indians on the way, though the travellers, it appears, proposed to use them in trading on their own account. The friar was still wrapped in his gray capote and hood, shod with sandals, and decorated with the cord of St. Francis. As for his two companions, Accau[208] and [Pg 250] Du Gay, it is tolerably clear that the former was the real leader of the party, though Hennepin, after his custom, thrusts himself into the foremost place. Both were somewhat above the station of ordinary hired hands; and Du Gay had an uncle who was an ecclesiastic of good credit at Amiens, his native place.

In the forests that overhung the river the buds were feebly swelling with advancing spring. There was game enough. They killed buffalo, deer, beavers, wild turkeys, and now and then a bear swimming in the river. With these, and the fish which they caught in abundance, they fared sumptuously, though it was the season of Lent. They were exemplary, however, at their devotions. Hennepin said prayers at morning and night, and the *angelus* at noon, adding a petition to Saint Anthony of Padua that he would save them from the peril that beset their way. In truth, there was a lion in the path. The ferocious character of the Sioux, or Dacotah, who occupied the region of the Upper Mississippi, was already known to the French; and Hennepin, with excellent reason, prayed that it might be his fortune to meet them, not by night, but by day.

CAPTURED BY THE SIOUX.

On the eleventh or twelfth of April, they stopped in the afternoon to repair their canoe; and Hennepin busied himself in daubing it with pitch, while the others cooked a turkey. Suddenly, a fleet of Sioux canoes swept into sight, bearing a war-party of a hundred and twenty naked savages, who on seeing [Pg 251] the travellers raised a hideous clamor; and, some leaping ashore and others into the water, they surrounded the astonished Frenchmen in an instant.[209] Hennepin held out the peace-pipe; but one of them snatched it from him. Next, he hastened to proffer a gift of Martinique tobacco, which was better received. Some of the old warriors repeated the name *Miamiha*, giving him to understand that they were a war-party, on the way to attack the Miamis; on which, Hennepin, with the help of signs and of marks which he drew on the sand with a stick, explained that the Miamis had gone across the Mississippi, beyond their reach. Hereupon, he says that three or four old men placed their hands on his head, and began a dismal wailing; while he with his handkerchief wiped away their tears, in order to evince sympathy with their affliction, from whatever cause arising. Notwithstanding this demonstration of tenderness, they refused to smoke with him in his peace-pipe, and forced him and his companions to embark and paddle across the river; while they all followed behind, uttering yells and howlings which froze the missionary's blood.

On reaching the farther side, they made their camp-fires, and allowed their prisoners to do the same. Accau and Du Gay slung their kettle; while [Pg 252] Hennepin, to propitiate the Sioux, carried to them two turkeys, of which there were several in the canoe. The warriors had seated themselves in a ring, to debate on the fate of the Frenchmen; and two chiefs presently explained to the friar, by significant signs, that it had been resolved that his head should be split with a war-club. This produced the effect which was no doubt intended. Hennepin ran to the canoe, and quickly returned with one of the men, both loaded with presents, which he threw into the midst of the assembly; and then, bowing his head, offered them at the same time a hatchet with which to kill him, if they wished to do so. His gifts and his submission seemed to appease them. They gave him and his companions a dish of beaver's flesh; but, to his great concern, they returned his peace-pipe,—an act which he interpreted as a sign of danger. That night the Frenchmen slept little, expecting to be murdered before morning. There was, in fact, a great division of opinion among the Sioux. Some were for killing them and taking their goods; while others, eager above all things that French traders should come among them with the knives, hatchets, and guns of which they had heard the value, contended that it would be impolitic to discourage the trade by putting to death its pioneers.

Scarcely had morning dawned on the anxious captives, when a young chief, naked, and painted from head to foot, appeared before them and asked for the pipe, which the friar gladly gave him. He filled it, [Pg 253] smoked it, made the warriors do the same, and, having given this hopeful pledge of amity, told the Frenchmen that, since the Miamis were out of reach, the war-party would return home, and that they must accompany them. To this Hennepin gladly agreed, having, as he declares, his great work of exploration so much at heart that he rejoiced in the prospect of achieving it even in their company.

SUSPECTED OF SORCERY.

He soon, however, had a foretaste of the affliction in store for him; for when he opened his breviary and began to mutter his morning devotion, his new companions gathered about him with faces that betrayed their superstitious terror, and gave him to understand that his book was a bad spirit with which he must hold no more converse. They thought, indeed, that he was muttering a charm for their destruction. Accau and Du Gay, conscious of the danger, begged the friar to dispense with his devotions, lest he and they alike should be tomahawked; but Hennepin says that his sense of duty rose superior to his fears, and that he was resolved to repeat his office at all hazards, though not until he had asked pardon of his two friends for thus imperilling their lives. Fortunately, he presently discovered a device by which his devotion and his prudence were completely reconciled. He ceased the muttering which had alarmed the Indians, and, with the breviary open on his knees, sang the service in loud and cheerful tones. As this had no savor of sorcery, and as they now imagined that the book was teaching its owner [Pg 254] to sing for their amusement, they conceived a favorable opinion of both alike.

These Sioux, it may be observed, were the ancestors of those who committed the horrible but not unprovoked massacres of 1862, in the valley of the St. Peter. Hennepin complains bitterly of their treatment of him, which, however, seems to have been tolerably good. Afraid that he would lag behind, as his canoe was heavy and slow,[210] they placed several warriors in it to aid him and his men in paddling. They kept on their way from morning till night, building huts for their bivouac when it rained, and sleeping on the open ground when the weather was fair,—which, says Hennepin, "gave us a good opportunity to contemplate the moon and stars." The three Frenchmen took the precaution of sleeping at the side of the young chief who had been the first to smoke the peace-pipe, and who seemed inclined to befriend them; but there was another chief, one Aquipaguetin, a crafty old savage, who having lost a son in war with the Miamis, was angry that the party had abandoned their expedition, and thus deprived him of his revenge. He therefore kept up a dismal lament through half the night; while other old men, crouching over Hennepin as he lay trying to sleep, stroked him with their hands, and uttered wailings so lugubrious that he was forced to [Pg 255] the belief that he had been doomed to death, and that they were charitably bemoaning his fate.[211]

THE CAPTIVE FRIAR.

One night, the captives were, for some reason, unable to bivouac near their protector, and were forced to make their fire at the end of the camp. Here they were soon beset by a crowd of Indians, who told them that Aquipaguetin had at length resolved to tomahawk them. The malcontents were gathered in a knot at a little distance, and Hennepin hastened to appease them by another gift of knives and tobacco. This was but one of the devices of the old chief to deprive them of their goods without robbing them outright. He had with him the bones of a deceased relative, which he was carrying home wrapped in skins prepared with smoke after the Indian fashion, and gayly decorated with bands of dyed porcupine quills. He would summon his warriors, and placing these relics in the midst of the assembly, call on all present to smoke in their honor; after which, Hennepin was required to offer a more substantial tribute in the shape of cloth, beads, hatchets, tobacco, and the like, to be laid upon the bundle of bones. The gifts thus acquired were then, in the name of the deceased, distributed among the persons present.

[Pg 256]

On one occasion, Aquipaguetin killed a bear, and invited the chiefs and warriors to feast upon it. They accordingly assembled on a prairie, west of the river, where, after the banquet, they danced a "medicine-dance." They were all painted from head to foot, with their hair oiled, garnished with red and white feathers, and powdered with the down of birds. In this guise they set their arms akimbo, and fell to stamping with such fury that the hard prairie was dented with the prints of their moccasins; while the chief's son, crying at the top of his throat, gave to each in turn the pipe of war. Meanwhile, the chief himself, singing in a loud and rueful voice, placed his hands on the heads of the three Frenchmen, and from time to time interrupted his music to utter a vehement harangue. Hennepin could not understand the words, but his heart sank as the conviction grew strong within him that these ceremonies tended to his destruction. It seems, however, that, after all the chief's efforts, his party was in the minority, the greater part being adverse to either killing or robbing the three strangers.

Every morning, at daybreak, an old warrior shouted the signal of departure; and the recumbent savages leaped up, manned their birchen fleet, and plied their paddles against the current, often without waiting to break their fast. Sometimes they stopped for a buffalo-hunt on the neighboring prairies; and there was no lack of provisions. They passed Lake Pepin, which Hennepin called the Lake of Tears, by reason [Pg 257] of the howlings and lamentations here uttered over him by Aquipaguetin, and nineteen days after his capture landed near the site of St. Paul. The father's sorrows now began in earnest. The Indians broke his canoe to pieces, having first hidden their own among the alder-bushes. As they belonged to different bands and different villages, their mutual jealousy now overcame all their prudence; and each proceeded to claim his share of the captives and the booty. Happily, they made an amicable distribution, or it would have fared ill with the three Frenchmen; and each taking his share, not forgetting the priestly vestments of Hennepin, the splendor of which they could not sufficiently admire, they set out across the country for their villages, which lay towards the north in the neighborhood of Lake Buade, now called Mille Lac.

A HARD JOURNEY.

Being, says Hennepin, exceedingly tall and active, they walked at a prodigious speed, insomuch that no European could long keep pace with them. Though the month of May had begun, there were frosts at night; and the marshes and ponds were glazed with ice, which cut the missionary's legs as he waded through. They swam the larger streams, and Hennepin nearly perished with cold as he emerged from the icy current. His two companions, who were smaller than he, and who could not swim, were carried over on the backs of the Indians. They showed, however, no little endurance; and he declares that he should have dropped by the way, but for their [Pg 258] support. Seeing him disposed to lag, the Indians, to spur him on, set fire to the dry grass behind him, and then, taking him by the hands, ran forward with him to escape the flames. To add to his misery, he was nearly famished, as they gave him only a small piece of smoked meat once a day, though it does not appear that they themselves fared better. On the fifth day, being by this time in extremity, he saw a crowd of squaws and children approaching over the prairie, and presently descried the bark lodges of an Indian town. The goal was reached. He was among the homes of the Sioux.

FOOTNOTES:

[197] *Description de la Louisiane, nouvellement découverte*, Paris, 1683.
[198] *Nouvelle Découverte d'un très grand Pays situé dans l'Amérique*, Utrecht, 1697.
[199] *Nouvelle Découverte*, 248, 250, 251.
[200] See the preface of the Spanish translation by Don Sebastian Fernandez de Medrano, 1699, and also the letter of Gravier, dated 1701, in Shea's *Early Voyages on the Mississippi*. Barcia, Charlevoix, Kalm, and other early writers put a low value on Hennepin's veracity.
[201] *Description de la Louisiane*, 218.

[202] La Salle, in the following year, with a far better equipment, was more than three months and a half in making the journey. A Mississippi trading-boat of the last generation, with sails and oars, ascending against the current, was thought to do remarkably well if it could make twenty miles a day. Hennepin, if we believe his own statements, must have ascended at an average rate of sixty miles, though his canoe was large and heavily laden.

[203] Hennepin here falls into gratuitous inconsistencies. In the edition of 1697, in order to gain a little time, he says that he left the Illinois on his voyage southward on the eighth of March, 1680; and yet in the preceding chapter he repeats the statement of the first edition, that he was detained at the Illinois by floating ice till the twelfth. Again, he says in the first edition that he was captured by the Sioux on the eleventh of April; and in the edition of 1697 he changes this date to the twelfth, without gaining any advantage by doing so.

[204] Le Clerc's book had been made the text of an attack on the Jesuits. See *Reflexions sur un Livre intitulé Premier Établissement de la Foi*. This piece is printed in the *Morale Pratique des Jésuites*.

[205] Hennepin may have copied from the unpublished journal of Membré, which the latter had placed in the hands of his Superior; or he may have compiled from Le Clerc's book, relying on the suppression of the edition to prevent detection. He certainly saw and used it; for he elsewhere borrows the exact words of the editor. He is so careless that he steals from Membré passages which he might easily have written for himself; as, for example, a description of the opossum and another of the cougar,—animals with which he was acquainted. Compare the following pages of the *Nouvelle Découverte* with the corresponding pages of Le Clerc: Hennepin, 252, Le Clerc, ii. 217; H. 253, Le C. ii. 218; H. 257, Le C. ii. 221; H. 259, Le C. ii. 224; H. 262, Le C. ii. 226; H. 265, Le C. ii. 229; H. 267, Le C. ii. 233; H. 270, Le C. ii. 235; H. 280, Le C. ii. 240; H. 295, Le C. ii. 249; H. 296, Le C. ii. 250; H. 297, Le C. ii. 253; H. 299, Le C. ii. 254; H. 301, Le C. ii. 257. Some of these parallel passages will be found in Sparks's *Life of La Salle*, where this remarkable fraud was first fully exposed. In Shea's *Discovery of the Mississippi*, there is an excellent critical examination of Hennepin's works. His plagiarisms from Le Clerc are not confined to the passages cited above; for in his later editions he stole largely from other parts of the suppressed *Établissement de la Foi*.

[206] It is certain that persons having the best means of information believed at the time in Hennepin's story of his journeys on the Upper

Mississippi. The compiler of the *Relation des Découvertes*, who was in close relations with La Salle and those who acted with him, does not intimate a doubt of the truth of the report which Hennepin on his return gave to the Provincial Commissary of his Order, and which is in substance the same which he published two years later. The *Relation*, it is to be observed, was written only a few months after the return of Hennepin, and embodies the pith of his narrative of the Upper Mississippi, no part of which had then been published.

[207] In this connection, it is well to examine the various Sioux words which Hennepin uses incidentally, and which he must have acquired by personal intercourse with the tribe, as no Frenchman then understood the language. These words, as far as my information reaches, are in every instance correct. Thus, he says that the Sioux called his breviary a "bad spirit,"—*Ouackanché*. *Wakanshe*, or *Wakanshecha*, would express the same meaning in modern English spelling. He says elsewhere that they called the guns of his companions *Manzaouackanché*, which he translates, "iron possessed with a bad spirit." The western Sioux to this day call a gun *Manzawakan*, "metal possessed with a spirit." *Chonga (shonka)*, "a dog," *Ouasi (wahsee)*, "a pine-tree," *Chinnen (shinnan)*, "a robe," or "garment," and other words, are given correctly, with their interpretations. The word *Louis*, affirmed by Hennepin to mean "the sun," seems at first sight a wilful inaccuracy, as this is not the word used in general by the Sioux. The Yankton band of this people, however, call the sun *oouee*, which, it is evident, represents the French pronunciation of *Louis*, omitting the initial letter. This Hennepin would be apt enough to supply, thereby conferring a compliment alike on himself, Louis Hennepin, and on the King, Louis XIV., who, to the indignation of his brother monarchs, had chosen the sun as his emblem.

Various trivial incidents touched upon by Hennepin, while recounting his life among the Sioux, seem to me to afford a strong presumption of an actual experience. I speak on this point with the more confidence, as the Indians in whose lodges I was once domesticated for several weeks belonged to a western band of the same people.

[208] Called Ako by Hennepin. In contemporary documents, it is written Accau, Acau, D'Accau, Dacau, Dacan, and D'Accault.

[209] The edition of 1683 says that there were thirty-three canoes; that of 1697 raises the number to fifty. The number of Indians is the same in both. The later narrative is more in detail than the former.

[210] And yet it had, by his account, made a distance of thirteen hundred and eighty miles from the mouth of the Mississippi upward in twenty-four days!

[211] This weeping and wailing over Hennepin once seemed to me an anomaly in his account of Sioux manners, as I am not aware that such practices are to be found among them at present. They are mentioned, however, by other early writers. Le Sueur, who was among them in 1699-1700, was wept over no less than Hennepin. See the abstract of his journal in La Harpe.

[Pg 259]

CHAPTER XVIII.

1680, 1681.

HENNEPIN AMONG THE SIOUX.

SIGNS OF DANGER.—ADOPTION.—HENNEPIN AND HIS INDIAN RELATIVES.—THE HUNTING PARTY.—THE SIOUX CAMP.—FALLS OF ST. ANTHONY.—A VAGABOND FRIAR: HIS ADVENTURES ON THE MISSISSIPPI.—GREYSOLON DU LHUT.—RETURN TO CIVILIZATION.

As Hennepin entered the village, he beheld a sight which caused him to invoke Saint Anthony of Padua. In front of the lodges were certain stakes, to which were attached bundles of straw, intended, as he supposed, for burning him and his friends alive. His concern was redoubled when he saw the condition of the Picard Du Gay, whose hair and face had been painted with divers colors, and whose head was decorated with a tuft of white feathers. In this guise he was entering the village, followed by a crowd of Sioux, who compelled him to sing and keep time to his own music by rattling a dried gourd containing a number of pebbles. The omens, indeed, were exceedingly [Pg 260] threatening; for treatment like this was usually followed by the speedy immolation of the captive. Hennepin ascribes it to the effect of his invocations, that, being led into one of the lodges, among a throng of staring squaws and children, he and his companions were seated on the ground, and presented with large dishes of birch-bark, containing a mess of wild rice boiled with dried whortleberries,—a repast which he declares to have been the best that had fallen to his lot since the day of his captivity.[212]

[Pg 261]

THE SIOUX.

This soothed his fears; but, as he allayed his famished appetite, he listened with anxious interest to the vehement jargon of the chiefs and warriors, who were disputing among themselves to whom the three captives should respectively belong; for it seems that, as far as related to them, the question of distribution had not yet been definitely settled. The debate ended in the assigning of Hennepin to his old enemy Aquipaguetin, who, however, far from persisting in his evil designs, adopted him on the spot as his son. The three companions must now part company. Du Gay, not yet quite reassured of his safety, hastened to confess himself to Hennepin; but Accau proved refractory, and refused the offices of religion, which did not prevent the friar from embracing them both, as he says, with an extreme tenderness. Tired as he was, he was forced to set out with his self-styled father to his village, which was fortunately [Pg 262] not far off. An unpleasant walk of a few miles through woods and marshes brought them to the borders of a sheet of water, apparently Lake Buade, where five of Aquipaguetin's wives received the party in three canoes, and ferried them to an island on which the village stood.

At the entrance of the chief's lodge, Hennepin was met by a decrepit old Indian, withered with age, who offered him the peace-pipe, and placed him on a bear-skin which was spread by the fire. Here, to relieve his fatigue,—for he was well-nigh spent,—a small boy anointed his limbs with the fat of a wild-cat, supposed to be sovereign in these cases by reason of the great agility of that animal. His new father gave him a bark-platter of fish, covered him with a buffalo-robe, and showed him six or seven of his wives, who were thenceforth, he was told, to regard him as a son. The chief's household was numerous; and his allies and relatives formed a considerable clan, of which the missionary found himself an involuntary member. He was scandalized when he saw one of his adopted brothers carrying on his back the bones of a deceased friend, wrapped in the chasuble of brocade which they had taken with other vestments from his box.

HENNEPIN AS A MISSIONARY.

Seeing their new relative so enfeebled that he could scarcely stand, the Indians made for him one of their sweating baths,[213] where they immersed him [Pg 263] in steam three times a week,—a process from which he thinks he derived great benefit. His strength gradually returned, in spite of his meagre fare; for there was a dearth of food, and the squaws were less attentive to his wants than to those of their children. They respected him, however, as a person endowed with occult powers, and stood in no little awe of a pocket compass which he had with him, as well as of a small metal pot with feet moulded after the face of a lion. This last seemed in their eyes a "medicine" of the most formidable nature, and they would not touch it without first wrapping it in a beaver-skin. For the rest, Hennepin made himself useful in various ways. He shaved the heads of the children, as was the custom of the tribe; bled certain asthmatic persons, and dosed others with orvietan, the famous panacea of his time, of which he had brought with him a good supply. With respect to his missionary functions, he seems to have given himself little trouble, unless his attempt to make a Sioux vocabulary is to be regarded as preparatory to a future apostleship. "I could gain nothing over them," he says, "in the way of their salvation, by reason of their natural stupidity." Nevertheless, on one occasion, he baptized a sick child, naming it Antoinette in honor of Saint Anthony of Padua. It seemed to revive after the rite, but soon relapsed and presently [Pg 264] died, "which," he writes, "gave me great joy and satisfaction." In this he was like the Jesuits, who could find nothing but consolation in the death of a newly baptized infant, since it was thus assured of a paradise which, had it lived, it would probably have forfeited by sharing in the superstitions of its parents.

With respect to Hennepin and his Indian father, there seems to have been little love on either side; but Ouasicoudé, the principal chief of the Sioux of this region, was the fast friend of the three white men. He was angry that they had been robbed, which he had been unable to prevent, as the Sioux had no laws, and their chiefs little power; but he spoke his mind freely, and told Aquipaguetin and the rest, in full council, that they were like a dog who steals a piece of meat from a dish and runs away with it. When Hennepin complained of hunger, the Indians had always promised him that early in the summer he should go with them on a buffalo hunt, and have food in abundance. The time at length came, and the inhabitants of all the neighboring villages prepared for departure. To each band was assigned its special hunting-ground, and he was expected to accompany his Indian father. To this he demurred; for he feared lest Aquipaguetin, angry at the words of the great chief, might take this opportunity to revenge the insult put upon him. He therefore gave out that he expected a party of "Spirits"—that is to say, Frenchmen—to meet him [Pg 265] at the mouth of the Wisconsin, bringing a supply of goods for the Indians; and he declares that La Salle had in fact promised to send traders to that place. Be this as it may, the Indians believed him; and, true or false, the assertion, as will be seen, answered the purpose for which it was made.

CAMP OF SAVAGES.

The Indians set out in a body to the number of two hundred and fifty warriors, with their women and children. The three Frenchmen, who though in different villages had occasionally met during the two months of their captivity, were all of the party. They descended Rum River, which forms the outlet of Mille Lac, and which is called the St. Francis by Hennepin. None of the Indians had offered to give him passage; and, fearing lest he should be abandoned, he stood on the bank, hailing the passing canoes and begging to be taken in. Accau and Du Gay presently appeared, paddling a small canoe which the Indians had given them; but they would not listen to the missionary's call, and Accau, who had no love for him, cried out that he had paddled him long enough already. Two Indians, however, took pity on him, and brought him to the place of encampment, where Du Gay tried to excuse himself for his conduct; but Accau was sullen, and kept aloof.

After reaching the Mississippi, the whole party encamped together opposite to the mouth of Rum River, pitching their tents of skin, or building their bark-huts, on the slope of a hill by the side of the water. It was a wild scene, this camp of savages [Pg 266] among whom as yet no traders had come and no handiwork of civilization had found its way,—the tall warriors, some nearly naked, some wrapped in buffalo-robes, and some in shirts of dressed deer-skin fringed with hair and embroidered with dyed porcupine quills, war-clubs of stone in their hands, and quivers at their backs filled with stone-headed arrows; the squaws, cutting smoke-dried meat with knives of flint, and boiling it in rude earthen pots of their own making, driving away, meanwhile, with shrill cries, the troops of lean dogs, which disputed the meal with a crew of hungry children. The whole camp, indeed, was threatened with starvation. The three white men could get no food but unripe berries,—from the effects of which Hennepin thinks they might all have died, but for timely doses of his orvietan.

FALLS OF ST. ANTHONY.

Being tired of the Indians, he became anxious to set out for the Wisconsin to find the party of Frenchmen, real or imaginary, who were to meet him at that place. That he was permitted to do so was due to the influence of the great chief Ouasicoudé, who always befriended him, and who had soundly berated his two companions for refusing him a seat in their canoe. Du Gay wished to go with him; but Accau, who liked the Indian life as much as he disliked Hennepin, preferred to remain with the hunters. A small birch-canoe was given to the two adventurers, together with an earthen pot; and they had also between them a gun, a knife, and a robe of beaver-skin. [Pg 267] Thus equipped, they began their journey, and soon approached the Falls of St. Anthony, so named by Hennepin in honor of the inevitable Saint Anthony of Padua.[214] As they were carrying their canoe by the cataract, they saw five or six Indians, who had gone before, and one of whom had climbed into an oak-tree beside the principal fall, whence in a loud and lamentable voice he was haranguing the spirit of the waters, as a sacrifice to whom he had just hung a robe of beaver-skin among the branches.[215] Their attention was soon engrossed by another object. Looking over the edge of the cliff which overhung the river below the falls, Hennepin saw a snake, [Pg 268] which, as he avers, was six feet long,[216] writhing upward towards the holes of the swallows in the face of the precipice, in order to devour their young. He pointed him out to Du Gay, and they pelted him with stones till he fell into the river, but not before his contortions and the darting of his forked tongue had so affected the Picard's imagination that he was haunted that night with a terrific incubus.

ADVENTURES.

They paddled sixty leagues down the river in the heats of July, and killed no large game but a single deer, the meat of which soon spoiled. Their main resource was the turtles, whose shyness and watchfulness caused them frequent disappointments and many involuntary fasts. They once captured one of more than common size; and, as they were endeavoring to cut off his head, he was near avenging himself by snapping off Hennepin's finger. There was a herd of buffalo in sight on the neighboring prairie; and Du Gay went with his gun in pursuit of them, leaving the turtle in Hennepin's custody. Scarcely was he gone when the friar, raising his eyes, saw that their canoe, which they had left at the edge of the water, had floated out into the current. Hastily turning the turtle on his back, he covered him with his habit of St. Francis, on which, for greater security, he laid a number of stones, and then, being a good swimmer, struck out in pursuit of the canoe, [Pg 269] which he at length overtook. Finding that it would overset if he tried to climb into it, he pushed it before him to the shore, and then paddled towards the place, at some distance above, where he had left the turtle. He had no sooner reached it than he heard a strange sound, and beheld a long file of buffalo—bulls, cows, and calves—entering the water not far off, to cross to the western bank. Having no gun, as became his apostolic vocation, he shouted to Du Gay, who presently appeared, running in all haste, and they both paddled in pursuit of the game. Du Gay aimed at a young cow, and shot her in the head. She fell in shallow water near an island, where some of the herd had landed; and being unable to drag her out, they waded into the water and butchered her where she lay. It was forty-eight hours since they had tasted food. Hennepin made a fire, while Du Gay cut up the meat. They feasted so bountifully that they both fell ill, and were forced to remain two days on the island, taking doses of orvietan, before they were able to resume their journey.

Apparently they were not sufficiently versed in woodcraft to smoke the meat of the cow; and the hot sun soon robbed them of it. They had a few fishhooks, but were not always successful in the use of them. On one occasion, being nearly famished, they set their line, and lay watching it, uttering prayers in turn. Suddenly, there was a great turmoil in the water. Du Gay ran to the line, and, with the help [Pg 270] of Hennepin, drew in two large cat-fish.[217] The eagles, or fish-hawks, now and then dropped a newly caught fish, of which they gladly took possession; and once they found a purveyor in an otter which they saw by the bank, devouring some object of an appearance so wonderful that Du Gay cried out that he had a devil between his paws. They scared him from his prey, which proved to be a spade-fish, or, as Hennepin correctly describes it, a species of sturgeon, with a bony projection from his snout in the shape of a paddle. They broke their fast upon him, undeterred by this eccentric appendage.

THE UPPER MISSISSIPPI.

If Hennepin had had an eye for scenery, he would have found in these his vagabond rovings wherewith to console himself in some measure for his frequent fasts. The young Mississippi, fresh from its northern springs, unstained as yet by unhallowed union with the riotous Missouri, flowed calmly on its way amid strange and unique beauties,—a wilderness, clothed with velvet grass; forest-shadowed valleys; lofty heights, whose smooth slopes seemed levelled with the scythe; domes and pinnacles, ramparts and ruined towers, the work of no human hand. The canoe of the voyagers, borne on the tranquil current, glided in the shade of gray crags festooned with honeysuckles; by trees mantled with wild grape-vines; [Pg 271] dells bright with the flowers of the white euphorbia, the blue gentian, and the purple balm; and matted forests, where the red squirrels leaped and chattered. They passed the great cliff whence the Indian maiden threw herself in her despair;[218] and Lake Pepin lay before them, slumbering in the July sun,—the far-reaching sheets of sparkling water, the woody slopes, the tower-like crags, the grassy heights basking in sunlight or shadowed by the passing cloud; all the fair outline of its graceful scenery, the finished and polished master-work of Nature. And when at evening they made their bivouac fire and drew up their canoe, while dim, sultry clouds veiled the west, and the flashes of the silent heat-lightning gleamed on the leaden water, they could listen, as they smoked their pipes, to the mournful cry of the whippoorwills and the quavering scream of the owls.

Other thoughts than the study of the picturesque occupied the mind of Hennepin when one day he saw his Indian father, Aquipaguetin, whom he had supposed five hundred miles distant, descending the river with ten warriors in canoes. He was eager to be the first to meet the traders, who, as Hennepin had given out, were to come with their goods to the mouth of the Wisconsin. The two travellers trembled [Pg 272] for the consequences of this encounter; but the chief, after a short colloquy, passed on his way. In three days he returned in ill-humor, having found no traders at the appointed spot. The Picard was absent at the time, looking for game; and Hennepin was sitting under the shade of his blanket, which he had stretched on forked sticks to protect him from the sun, when he saw his adopted father approaching with a threatening look, and a war-club in his hand. He attempted no violence, however, but suffered his wrath to exhale in a severe scolding, after which he resumed his course up the river with his warriors.

If Hennepin, as he avers, really expected a party of traders at the Wisconsin, the course he now took is sufficiently explicable. If he did not expect them, his obvious course was to rejoin Tonty on the Illinois, for which he seems to have had no inclination; or to return to Canada by way of the Wisconsin,—an attempt which involved the risk of starvation, as the two travellers had but ten charges of powder left. Assuming, then, his hope of the traders to have been real, he and Du Gay resolved, in the mean time, to join a large body of Sioux hunters, who, as Aquipaguetin had told them, were on a stream which he calls Bull River, now the Chippeway, entering the Mississippi near Lake Pepin. By so doing, they would gain a supply of food, and save themselves from the danger of encountering parties of roving warriors.

[Pg 273]

HE REJOINS THE INDIANS.

They found this band, among whom was their companion Accau, and followed them on a grand hunt along the borders of the Mississippi. Du Gay was separated for a time from Hennepin, who was placed in a canoe with a withered squaw more than eighty years old. In spite of her age, she handled her paddle with great address, and used it vigorously, as occasion required, to repress the gambols of three children, who, to Hennepin's annoyance, occupied the middle of the canoe. The hunt was successful. The Sioux warriors, active as deer, chased the buffalo on foot with their stone-headed arrows, on the plains behind the heights that bordered the river; while the old men stood sentinels at the top, watching for the approach of enemies. One day an alarm was given. The warriors rushed towards the supposed point of danger, but found nothing more formidable than two squaws of their own nation, who brought strange news. A war-party of Sioux, they said, had gone towards Lake Superior, and had met by the way five "Spirits;" that is to say, five Europeans. Hennepin was full of curiosity to learn who the strangers might be; and they, on their part, were said to have shown great anxiety to know the nationality of the three white men who, as they were told, were on the river. The hunt was over; and the hunters, with Hennepin and his companion, were on their way northward to their towns, when they met the five "Spirits" at some distance below the Falls of St. Anthony. They proved to [Pg 274] be Daniel Greysolon du Lhut, with four well-armed Frenchmen.

DE LHUT'S EXPLORATIONS.

This bold and enterprising man, stigmatized by the Intendant Duchesneau as a leader of *coureurs de bois*, was a cousin of Tonty, born at Lyons. He belonged to that caste of the lesser nobles whose name was legion, and whose admirable military qualities shone forth so conspicuously in the wars of Louis XIV. Though his enterprises were independent of those of La Salle, they were at this time carried on in connection with Count Frontenac and certain merchants in his interest, of whom Du Lhut's uncle, Patron, was one; while Louvigny, his brother-in-law, was in alliance with the governor, and was an officer of his guard. Here, then, was a kind of family league, countenanced by Frontenac, and acting conjointly with him, in order, if the angry letters of the intendant are to be believed, to reap a clandestine profit under the shadow of the governor's authority, and in violation of the royal ordinances. The rudest part of the work fell to the share of Du Lhut, who with a persistent hardihood, not surpassed perhaps even by La Salle, was continually in the forest, in the Indian towns, or in remote wilderness outposts planted by himself, exploring, trading, fighting, ruling lawless savages and whites scarcely less ungovernable, and on one or more occasions varying his life by crossing the ocean to gain interviews with the colonial minister Seignelay, amid the splendid vanities of Versailles. Strange to say, this man of hardy enterprise was a [Pg 275] martyr to the gout, which for more than a quarter of a century grievously tormented him; though for a time he thought himself cured by the intercession of the Iroquois saint, Catharine Tegahkouita, to whom he had made a vow to that end. He was, without doubt, an habitual breaker of the royal ordinances regulating the fur-trade; yet his services were great to the colony and to the crown, and his name deserves a place of honor among the pioneers of American civilization.[219]

[Pg 276]

When Hennepin met him, he had been about two years in the wilderness. In September, 1678, he left Quebec for the purpose of exploring the region of the Upper Mississippi, and establishing relations of friendship with the Sioux and their kindred the Assiniboins. In the summer of 1679 he visited three large towns of the eastern division of the Sioux, including those visited by Hennepin in the following year, and planted the King's arms in all of them. Early in the autumn he was at the head of Lake Superior, holding a council with the Assiniboins and the lake tribes, and inducing them to live at peace with the Sioux. In all this, he acted in a public [Pg 277] capacity, under the authority of the governor; but it is not to be supposed that he forgot his own interests or those of his associates. The intendant angrily complains that he aided and abetted the *coureurs de bois* in their lawless courses, and sent down in their canoes great quantities of beaver-skins consigned to the merchants in league with him, under cover of whose names the governor reaped his share of the profits.

In June, 1680, while Hennepin was in the Sioux villages, Du Lhut set out from the head of Lake Superior, with two canoes, four Frenchmen, and an Indian, to continue his explorations.[220] He ascended a river, apparently the Burnt Wood, and reached from thence a branch of the Mississippi, which seems to have been the St. Croix. It was now that, to his surprise, he learned that there were three Europeans on the main river below; and fearing that they might be Englishmen or Spaniards encroaching on the territories of the King, he eagerly pressed forward to solve his doubts. When he saw Hennepin, his mind was set at rest; and the travellers met with mutual cordiality. They followed the Indians to their villages of Mille Lac, where Hennepin had now no reason to complain of their treatment of him. The Sioux gave him and Du Lhut a grand feast of honor, at which were seated a hundred and twenty naked guests; and the great chief Ouasicoudé, with his [Pg 278] own hands, placed before Hennepin a bark dish containing a mess of smoked meat and wild rice.

Autumn had come, and the travellers bethought them of going home. The Sioux, consoled by their promises to return with goods for trade, did not oppose their departure; and they set out together, eight white men in all. As they passed St. Anthony's Falls, two of the men stole two buffalo-robes which were hung on trees as offerings to the spirit of the cataract. When Du Lhut heard of it he was very angry, telling the men that they had endangered the lives of the whole party. Hennepin admitted that in the view of human prudence he was right, but urged that the act was good and praiseworthy, inasmuch as the offerings were made to a false god; while the men, on their part, proved mutinous, declaring that they wanted the robes and meant to keep them. The travellers continued their journey in great ill-humor, but were presently soothed by the excellent hunting which they found on the way. As they approached the Wisconsin, they stopped to dry the meat of the buffalo they had killed, when to their amazement they saw a war-party of Sioux approaching in a fleet of canoes. Hennepin represents himself as showing on this occasion an extraordinary courage, going to meet the Indians with a peace-pipe, and instructing Du Lhut, who knew more of these matters than he, how he ought to behave. The Sioux proved not unfriendly, and said nothing of the theft of the buffalo-robes. They soon went on their [Pg 279] way to attack the Illinois and Missouris, leaving the Frenchmen to ascend the Wisconsin unmolested.

THE RETURN.

After various adventures, they reached the station of the Jesuits at Green Bay; but its existence is wholly ignored by Hennepin, whose zeal for his own Order will not permit him to allude to this establishment of the rival missionaries.[221] He is equally reticent with regard to the Jesuit mission at Michilimackinac, where the party soon after arrived, and where they spent the winter. The only intimation which he gives of its existence consists in the mention of the Jesuit Pierson, who was a Fleming like himself, and who often skated with him on the frozen lake, or kept him company in fishing through a hole in the ice.[222] When the spring opened, Hennepin descended Lake Huron, followed the Detroit to Lake Erie, and proceeded thence to Niagara. Here he spent some time in making a fresh examination of the cataract, and then resumed his voyage on Lake Ontario. He stopped, however, at the great town of the Senecas, near the Genesee, where, with his usual spirit of meddling, he took upon him the functions of the civil and military [Pg 280] authorities, convoked the chiefs to a council, and urged them to set at liberty certain Ottawa prisoners whom they had captured in violation of treaties. Having settled this affair to his satisfaction, he went to Fort Frontenac, where his brother missionary, Buisset, received him with a welcome rendered the warmer by a story which had reached him that the Indians had hanged Hennepin with his own cord of St. Francis.

From Fort Frontenac he went to Montreal; and leaving his two men on a neighboring island, that they might escape the payment of duties on a quantity of furs which they had with them, he paddled alone towards the town. Count Frontenac chanced to be here, and, looking from the window of a house near the river, he saw approaching in a canoe a Récollet father, whose appearance indicated the extremity of hard service; for his face was worn and sunburnt, and his tattered habit of St. Francis was abundantly patched with scraps of buffalo-skin. When at length he recognized the long-lost Hennepin, he received him, as the father writes, "with all the tenderness which a missionary could expect from a person of his rank and quality." He kept him for twelve days in his own house, and listened with interest to such of his adventures as the friar saw fit to divulge.

LA SALLE'S LETTERS.

And here we bid farewell to Father Hennepin. "Providence," he writes, "preserved my life that I might make known my great discoveries to the world." He soon after went to Europe, where the [Pg 281] story of his travels found a host of readers, but where he died at last in a deserved obscurity.[223]

FOOTNOTES:

[212] The Sioux, or Dacotah, as they call themselves, were a numerous people, separated into three great divisions, which were again subdivided into bands. Those among whom Hennepin was a prisoner belonged to the division known as the Issanti, Issanyati, or, as he writes it, *Issati*, of which the principal band was the Meddewakantonwan. The other great divisions, the Yanktons and the Tintonwans, or Tetons, lived west of the Mississippi, extending beyond the Missouri, and ranging as far as the Rocky Mountains. The Issanti cultivated the soil; but the extreme western bands subsisted on the buffalo alone. The former had two kinds of dwelling,— the *teepee*, or skin-lodge, and the bark-lodge. The teepee, which was used by all the Sioux, consists of a covering of dressed buffalo-hide, stretched on a conical stack of poles. The bark-lodge was peculiar to the Eastern Sioux; and examples of it might be seen, until within a few years, among the bands on the St. Peter's. In its general character, it was like the Huron and Iroquois houses, but was inferior in construction. It had a ridge roof, framed of poles, extending from the posts which formed the sides; and the whole was covered with elm-bark. The lodges in the villages to which Hennepin was conducted were probably of this kind.

The name Sioux is an abbreviation of *Nadouessioux*, an Ojibwa word, meaning "enemies." The Ojibwas used it to designate this people, and occasionally also the Iroquois, being at deadly war with both.

Rev. Stephen B. Riggs, for many years a missionary among the Issanti Sioux, says that this division consists of four distinct bands. They ceded all their lands east of the Mississippi to the United States in 1837, and lived on the St. Peter's till driven thence in consequence of the massacres of 1862, 1863. The Yankton Sioux consist of two bands, which are again subdivided. The Assiniboins, or Hohays, are an offshoot from the Yanktons, with whom they are now at war. The Tintonwan, or Teton Sioux, forming the most western division and the largest, comprise seven bands, and are among the bravest and fiercest tenants of the prairie.

The earliest French writers estimate the total number of the Sioux at forty thousand; but this is little better than conjecture. Mr. Riggs, in 1852, placed it at about twenty-five thousand.

[213] These baths consist of a small hut, covered closely with buffalo-skins, into which the patient and his friends enter, carefully closing every aperture. A pile of heated stones is placed in the middle, and water is poured upon them, raising a dense vapor. They are still (1868) in use among the Sioux and some other tribes.

[214] Hennepin's notice of the falls of St. Anthony, though brief, is sufficiently accurate. He says, in his first edition, that they are forty or fifty feet high, but adds ten feet more in the edition of 1697. In 1821, according to Schoolcraft, the perpendicular fall measured forty feet. Great changes, however, have taken place here, and are still in progress. The rock is a very soft, friable sandstone, overlaid by a stratum of limestone; and it is crumbling with such rapidity under the action of the water that the cataract will soon be little more than a rapid. Other changes equally disastrous, in an artistic point of view, are going on even more quickly. Beside the falls stands a city, which, by an ingenious combination of the Greek and Sioux languages, has received the name of Minneapolis, or City of the Waters, and which in 1867 contained ten thousand inhabitants, two national banks, and an opera-house; while its rival city of St. Anthony, immediately opposite, boasted a gigantic water-cure and a State university. In short, the great natural beauty of the place is utterly spoiled.

[215] Oanktayhee, the principal deity of the Sioux, was supposed to live under these falls, though he manifested himself in the form of a buffalo. It was he who created the earth, like the Algonquin Manabozho, from mud brought to him in the paws of a musk-rat. Carver, in 1766, saw an Indian throw everything he had about him into the cataract as an offering to this deity.

[216] In the edition of 1683. In that of 1697 he had grown to seven or eight feet. The bank-swallows still make their nests in these cliffs, boring easily into the soft sandstone.

[217] Hennepin speaks of their size with astonishment, and says that the two together would weigh twenty-five pounds. Cat-fish have been taken in the Mississippi, weighing more than a hundred and fifty pounds.

[218] The "Lover's Leap," or "Maiden's Rock" from which a Sioux girl, Winona, or the "Eldest Born," is said to have thrown herself, in the despair of disappointed affection. The story, which seems founded in truth, will

be found, not without embellishments, in Mrs. Eastman's *Legends of the Sioux*.

[219] The facts concerning Du Lhut have been gleaned from a variety of contemporary documents, chiefly the letters of his enemy Duchesneau, who always puts him in the worst light, especially in his despatch to Seignelay of 10 Nov., 1679, where he charges both him and the governor with carrying on an illicit trade with the English of New York. Du Lhut himself, in a memoir dated 1685 (see Harrisse, *Bibliographie*, 176), strongly denies these charges. Du Lhut built a trading fort on Lake Superior, called Cananistigoyan (La Hontan), or Kamalastigouia (Perrot). It was on the north side, at the mouth of a river entering Thunder Bay, where Fort William now stands. In 1684 he caused two Indians, who had murdered several Frenchmen on Lake Superior, to be shot. He displayed in this affair great courage and coolness, undaunted by the crowd of excited savages who surrounded him and his little band of Frenchmen. The long letter, in which he recounts the capture and execution of the murderers, is before me. Duchesneau makes his conduct on this occasion the ground of a charge of rashness. In 1686 Denonville, then governor of the colony, ordered him to fortify the Detroit; that is, the strait between Lakes Erie and Huron. He went thither with fifty men and built a palisade fort, which he occupied for some time. In 1687 he, together with Tonty and Durantaye, joined Denonville against the Senecas, with a body of Indians from the Upper Lakes. In 1689, during the panic that followed the Iroquois invasion of Montreal, Du Lhut, with twenty-eight Canadians, attacked twenty-two Iroquois in canoes, received their fire without returning it, bore down upon them, killed eighteen of them, and captured three, only one escaping. In 1695 he was in command at Fort Frontenac. In 1697 he succeeded to the command of a company of infantry, but was suffering wretchedly from the gout at Fort Frontenac. In 1710 Vaudreuil, in a despatch to the minister Ponchartrain, announced his death as occurring in the previous winter, and added the brief comment, "c'était un très-honnête homme." Other contemporaries speak to the same effect. "Mr. Dulhut, Gentilhomme Lionnois, qui a beaucoup de mérite et de capacité."—*La Hontan*, i. 103 (1703). "Le Sieur du Lut, homme d'esprit et d'expérience."—*Le Clerc*, ii. 137. Charlevoix calls him "one of the bravest officers the King has ever had in this colony." His name is variously spelled Du Luc, Du Lud, Du Lude, Du Lut, Du Luth, Du Lhut. For an account of the Iroquois virgin, Tegahkouita, whose intercession is said to have cured him of the gout, see Charlevoix, i. 572.

On a contemporary manuscript map by the Jesuit Raffeix, representing the routes of Marquette, La Salle, and Du Lhut, are the following words, referring to the last-named discoverer, and interesting in connection with Hennepin's statements: "M$^{r.}$ du Lude le premier a esté chez les Sioux en 1678, et a esté proche la source du Mississippi, et ensuite vint retirer le P. Louis [*Hennepin*] qui avoit esté fait prisonnier chez les Sioux." Du Lhut here appears as the deliverer of Hennepin. One of his men was named Pepin; hence, no doubt, the name of Lake Pepin.

[220] *Memoir on the French Dominion in Canada, N. Y. Col. Docs.*, ix. 781.

[221] On the other hand, he sets down on his map of 1683 a mission of the Récollets at a point north of the farthest sources of the Mississippi, to which no white man had ever penetrated.

[222] He says that Pierson had come among the Indians to learn their language; that he "retained the frankness and rectitude of our country" and "a disposition always on the side of candor and sincerity. In a word, he seemed to me to be all that a Christian ought to be" (1697), 433.

[223] Since the two preceding chapters were written, the letters of La Salle have been brought to light by the researches of M. Margry. They confirm, in nearly all points, the conclusions given above; though, as before observed (*note*, 186), they show misstatements on the part of Hennepin concerning his position at the outset of the expedition. La Salle writes: "J'ay fait remonter le fleuve Colbert, nommé par les Iroquois Gastacha, par les Outaouais Mississipy par un canot conduit par deux de mes gens, l'un nommé Michel Accault et l'autre Picard, auxquels le R. P. Hennepin se joignit pour ne perdre pas l'occasion de prescher l'Évangile aux peuples qui habitent dessus et qui n'en avoient jamais oui parler." In the same letter he recounts their voyage on the Upper Mississippi, and their capture by the Sioux in accordance with the story of Hennepin himself. Hennepin's assertion, that La Salle had promised to send a number of men to meet him at the mouth of the Wisconsin, turns out to be true. "Estans tous revenus en chasse avec les Nadouessioux [*Sioux*] vers Ouisconsing [*Wisconsin*], le R. P. Louis Hempin [*Hennepin*] et Picard prirent résolution de venir jusqu'à l'embboucheure de la rivière où j'avois promis d'envoyer de mes nouvelles, comme j'avois fait par six hommes que les Jésuistes desbauchèrent en leur disant que le R. P. Louis et ses compagnons de voyage avoient esté tuez."

It is clear that La Salle understood Hennepin; for, after speaking of his journey, he adds: "J'ai cru qu'il estoit à propos de vous faire le narré des aventures de ce canot parce que je ne doute pas qu'on en parle; et si vous souhaitez en conférer avec le P. Louis Hempin, Récollect, qui est repassé en France, il faut un peu le connoistre, car il ne manquera pas d'exagérer toutes choses, c'est son caractère, et à moy mesme il m'a escrit comme s'il eust esté tout près d'estre bruslé, quoiqu'il n'en ait pas esté seulement en danger; mais il croit qu'il luy est honorable de le faire de la sorte, et *il parle plus conformément à ce qu'il veut qu'à ce qu'il scait*."—*Lettre de la Salle, 22 Août, 1682* (1681?), Margry, ii. 259.

On his return to France, Hennepin got hold of the manuscript, *Relation des Découvertes*, compiled for the government from La Salle's letters, and, as already observed, made very free use of it in the first edition of his book, printed in 1683. In 1699 he wished to return to Canada; but, in a letter of that year, Louis XIV. orders the governor [Pg 282] to seize him, should he appear, and send him prisoner to Rochefort. This seems to have been in consequence of his renouncing the service of the French crown, and dedicating his edition of 1697 to William III. of England.

More than twenty editions of Hennepin's travels appeared, in French, English, Dutch, German, Italian, and Spanish. Most of them include the mendacious narrative of the pretended descent of the Mississippi. For a list of them, see *Hist. Mag.*, i. 346; ii. 24.

[Pg 283]

CHAPTER XIX.

1681.

LA SALLE BEGINS ANEW.

His Constancy; his Plans; his Savage Allies; he becomes Snow-blind.— Negotiations.—Grand Council.—La Salle's Oratory.—Meeting with Tonty.—Preparation.—Departure.

In tracing the adventures of Tonty and the rovings of Hennepin, we have lost sight of La Salle, the pivot of the enterprise. Returning from the desolation and horror in the valley of the Illinois, he had spent the winter at Fort Miami, on the St. Joseph, by the borders of Lake Michigan. Here he might have brooded on the redoubled ruin that had befallen him,—the desponding friends, the exulting foes; the wasted energies, the crushing load of debt, the stormy past, the black and lowering future. But his mind was of a different temper. He had no thought but to grapple with adversity, and out of the fragments of his ruin to build up the fabric of success.

He would not recoil; but he modified his plans to meet the new contingency. His white enemies had found, or rather perhaps had made, a savage ally in the Iroquois. Their incursions must be stopped, or [Pg 284] his enterprise would come to nought; and he thought he saw the means by which this new danger could be converted into a source of strength. The tribes of the West, threatened by the common enemy, might be taught to forget their mutual animosities and join in a defensive league, with La Salle at its head. They might be colonized around his fort in the valley of the Illinois, where in the shadow of the French flag, and with the aid of French allies, they could hold the Iroquois in check, and acquire in some measure the arts of a settled life. The Franciscan friars could teach them the Faith; and La Salle and his associates could supply them with goods, in exchange for the vast harvest of furs which their hunters could gather in these boundless wilds. Meanwhile, he would seek out the mouth of the Mississippi; and the furs gathered at his colony in the Illinois would then find a ready passage to the markets of the world. Thus might this ancient slaughter-field of warring savages be redeemed to civilization and Christianity; and a stable settlement, half-feudal, half-commercial, grow up in the heart of the western wilderness. This plan was but a part of the original scheme of his enterprise, adapted to new and unexpected circumstances; and he now set himself to its execution with his usual vigor, joined to an address which, when dealing with Indians, never failed him.

INDIAN FRIENDS.

There were allies close at hand. Near Fort Miami were the huts of twenty-five or thirty savages, exiles [Pg 285] from their homes, and strangers in this western world. Several of the English colonies, from Virginia to Maine, had of late years been harassed by Indian wars; and the Puritans of New England, above all, had been scourged by the deadly outbreak of King Philip's war. Those engaged in it had paid a bitter price for their brief triumphs. A band of refugees, chiefly Abenakis and Mohegans, driven from their native seats, had roamed into these distant wilds, and were wintering in the friendly neighborhood of the French. La Salle soon won them over to his interests. One of their number was the Mohegan hunter, who for two years had faithfully followed his fortunes, and who had been four years in the West. He is described as a prudent and discreet young man, in whom La Salle had great confidence, and who could make himself understood in several western languages, belonging, like his own, to the great Algonquin tongue. This devoted henchman proved an efficient mediator with his countrymen. The New-England Indians, with one voice, promised to follow La Salle, asking no recompense but to call him their chief, and yield to him the love and admiration which he rarely failed to command from this hero-worshipping race.

New allies soon appeared. A Shawanoe chief from the valley of the Ohio, whose following embraced a hundred and fifty warriors, came to ask the protection of the French against the all-destroying

Iroquois. "The Shawanoes are too distant," was La Salle's [Pg 286] reply; "but let them come to me at the Illinois, and they shall be safe." The chief promised to join him in the autumn, at Fort Miami, with all his band. But, more important than all, the consent and co-operation of the Illinois must be gained; and the Miamis, their neighbors and of late their enemies, must be taught the folly of their league with the Iroquois, and the necessity of joining in the new confederation. Of late, they had been made to see the perfidy of their dangerous allies. A band of the Iroquois, returning from the slaughter of the Tamaroa Illinois, had met and murdered a band of Miamis on the Ohio, and had not only refused satisfaction, but had intrenched themselves in three rude forts of trees and brushwood in the heart of the Miami country. The moment was favorable for negotiating; but, first, La Salle wished to open a communication with the Illinois, some of whom had begun to return to the country they had abandoned. With this view, and also, it seems, to procure provisions, he set out on the first of March, with his lieutenant La Forest, and fifteen men.

The country was sheeted in snow, and the party journeyed on snow-shoes; but when they reached the open prairies, the white expanse glared in the sun with so dazzling a brightness that La Salle and several of the men became snow-blind. They stopped and encamped under the edge of a forest; and here La Salle remained in darkness for three days, suffering extreme pain. Meanwhile, he sent forward La [Pg 287] Forest and most of the men, keeping with him his old attendant Hunaut. Going out in quest of pine-leaves,—a decoction of which was supposed to be useful in cases of snow-blindness,— this man discovered the fresh tracks of Indians, followed them, and found a camp of Outagamies, or Foxes, from the neighborhood of Green Bay. From them he heard welcome news. They told him that Tonty was safe among the Pottawattamies, and that Hennepin had passed through their country on his return from among the Sioux.[224]

ILLINOIS ALLIES.

A thaw took place; the snow melted rapidly; the rivers were opened; the blind men began to recover; and launching the canoes which they had dragged after them, the party pursued their way by water. They soon met a band of Illinois. La Salle gave them presents, condoled with them on their losses, and urged them to make peace and alliance with the Miamis. Thus, he said, they could set the Iroquois at defiance; for he himself, with his Frenchmen and his Indian friends, would make his abode among them, supply them with goods, and aid them to defend themselves. They listened, well pleased, promised to carry his message to their countrymen, and furnished him with a large supply of corn.[225] Meanwhile he had rejoined La Forest, whom he now [Pg 288] sent to Michilimackinac to await Tonty, and tell him to remain there till he, La Salle, should arrive.

Having thus accomplished the objects of his journey, he returned to Fort Miami, whence he soon after ascended the St. Joseph to the village of the Miami Indians, on the portage, at the head of the Kankakee. Here he found unwelcome guests. These were three Iroquois warriors, who had been for some time in the place, and who, as he was told, had demeaned themselves with the insolence of conquerors, and spoken of the French with the utmost contempt. He hastened to confront them, rebuked and menaced them, and told them that now, when he was present, they dared not repeat the calumnies which they had uttered in his absence. They stood abashed and confounded, and during the following night secretly left the town and fled. The effect was prodigious on the minds of the Miamis, when they saw that La Salle, backed by ten Frenchmen, could command from their arrogant visitors a respect which they, with their hundreds of warriors, had wholly failed to inspire. Here, at the outset, was an augury full of promise for the approaching negotiations.

There were other strangers in the town,—a band of eastern Indians, more numerous than those who had wintered at the fort. The greater number were from Rhode Island, including, probably, some of King Philip's warriors; others were from New York, and others again from Virginia. La Salle called [Pg 289] them to a council, promised them a new home in the West under the protection of the Great King, with rich lands, an abundance of game, and French traders to supply them with the goods which they had once received from the English. Let them but help him to make peace between the Miamis and the Illinois, and he would insure for them a future of prosperity and safety. They listened with open ears, and promised their aid in the work of peace.

GRAND COUNCIL.

On the next morning, the Miamis were called to a grand council. It was held in the lodge of their chief, from which the mats were removed, that the crowd without might hear what was said. La Salle rose and harangued the concourse. Few men were so skilled in the arts of forest rhetoric and diplomacy. After the Indian mode, he was, to follow his chroniclers, "the greatest orator in North America."[226] He began with a gift of tobacco, to clear the brains of his auditory; next, for he had brought a canoe-load of presents to support his eloquence, he gave them cloth to cover their dead, coats to dress them, hatchets to build a grand scaffold in their honor, and beads, bells, and trinkets of all sorts, to decorate their relatives at a grand funeral feast. All this was mere metaphor. The living, while appropriating the gifts to their own use, were pleased at the compliment offered to their dead; and their delight redoubled as the orator proceeded. One of their [Pg 290] great chiefs had lately been killed; and La Salle, after a eulogy of the departed, declared that he would now raise him to life again; that is, that he would assume his name and give support to his squaws and children. This flattering announcement drew forth an outburst of applause; and when, to confirm his words, his attendants placed before them a huge pile of coats, shirts, and hunting-knives, the whole assembly exploded in yelps of admiration.

Now came the climax of the harangue, introduced by a further present of six guns:—

"He who is my master, and the master of all this country, is a mighty chief, feared by the whole world; but he loves peace, and the words of his lips are for good alone. He is called the King of France, and he is the mightiest among the chiefs beyond the great water. His goodness reaches even to your dead, and his subjects come among you to raise them up to life. But it is his will to preserve the life he has given; it is his will that you should obey his laws, and make no war without the leave of Onontio, who commands in his name at Quebec, and who loves all the nations alike, because such is the will of the Great King. You ought, then, to live at peace with your neighbors, and above all with the Illinois. You have had causes of quarrel with them; but their defeat has avenged you. Though they are still strong, they wish to make peace with you. Be content with the glory of having obliged them to ask for it. You have an interest in preserving them; since, [Pg 291] if the Iroquois destroy them, they will next destroy you. Let us all obey the Great King, and live together in peace, under his protection. Be of my mind, and use these guns that I have given you, not to make war, but only to hunt and to defend yourselves."[227]

THE CHIEFS REPLY.

So saying, he gave two belts of wampum to confirm his words; and the assembly dissolved. On the following day, the chiefs again convoked it, and made their reply in form. It was all that La Salle could have wished. "The Illinois is our brother, because he is the son of our Father, the Great King." "We make you the master of our beaver and our lands, of our minds and our bodies." "We cannot wonder that our brothers from the East wish to live with you. We should have wished so too, if we had known what a blessing it is to be the children of the Great King." The rest of this auspicious day was passed in feasts and dances, in which La Salle and his Frenchmen all bore part. His new scheme was hopefully begun. It remained to achieve the enterprise, twice defeated, of the discovery of the mouth of the Mississippi,—that vital condition of his triumph, without which all other success was meaningless and vain.

To this end he must return to Canada, appease his creditors, and collect his scattered resources. Towards the end of May he set out in canoes from [Pg 292] Fort Miami, and reached Michilimackinac after a prosperous voyage. Here, to his great joy, he found Tonty and Zenobe Membré, who had lately arrived from Green Bay. The meeting was one at which even his stoic nature must have melted. Each had for the other a tale of disaster; but when La Salle recounted the long succession of his reverses, it was with the tranquil tone and cheerful look of one who relates the incidents of an ordinary journey. Membré looked on him with admiration. "Any one else," he says, "would have thrown up his hand and abandoned the enterprise; but, far from this, with a firmness and constancy that never had its equal, I saw him more resolved than ever to continue his work and push forward his discovery."[228]

Without loss of time they embarked together for Fort Frontenac, paddled their canoes a thousand miles, and safely reached their destination. Here, in this third beginning of his enterprise, La Salle found himself beset with embarrassments. Not only was he burdened with the fruitless costs of his two former efforts, but the heavy debts which he had incurred in building and maintaining Fort Frontenac had not been wholly paid. The fort and the seigniory were already deeply mortgaged; yet through the influence of Count Frontenac, the assistance of his [Pg 293] secretary Barrois, a consummate man of business, and the support of a wealthy relative, he found means to appease his creditors and even to gain fresh advances. To this end, however, he was forced to part with a portion of his monopolies. Having first made his will at Montreal, in favor of a cousin who had befriended him,[229] he mustered his men, and once more set forth, resolved to trust no more to agents, but to lead on his followers, in a united body, under his own personal command.[230]

THE TORONTO PORTAGE.

At the beginning of autumn he was at Toronto, where the long and difficult portage to Lake Simcoe detained him a fortnight. He spent a part of it in writing an account of what had lately occurred to a correspondent in France, and he closes his letter thus: "This is all I can tell you this year. I have a hundred things to write, but you could not believe how hard it is to do it among Indians. The canoes and their lading must be got over the portage, and I must speak to them continually and bear all their importunity, or else they will do nothing I want. I hope to write more at leisure next year, and tell you [Pg 294] the end of this business, which I hope will turn out well: for I have M. de Tonty, who is full of zeal; thirty Frenchmen, all good men, without reckoning such as I cannot trust; and more than a hundred Indians, some of them Shawanoes, and others from New England, all of whom know how to use guns."

It was October before he reached Lake Huron. Day after day and week after week the heavy-laden canoes crept on along the lonely wilderness shores, by the monotonous ranks of bristling moss-bearded firs; lake and forest, forest and lake; a dreary scene haunted with yet more dreary memories,—disasters, sorrows, and deferred hopes; time, strength, and wealth spent in vain; a ruinous past and a doubtful future; slander, obloquy, and hate. With unmoved heart, the patient voyager held his course, and drew up his canoes at last on the beach at Fort Miami.

FOOTNOTES:

[224] *Relation des Découvertes.* Compare *Lettre de La Salle* (Margry, ii. 144).

[225] This seems to have been taken from the secret repositories, or *caches*, of the ruined town of the Illinois.

[226] "En ce genre, il étoit le plus grand orateur de l'Amérique Septentrionale."—*Relation des Découvertes.*

[227] Translated from the *Relation*, where these councils are reported at great length.

[228] Membré in Le Clerc, ii. 208. Tonty, in his memoir of 1693, speaks of the joy of La Salle at the meeting. The *Relation*, usually very accurate,

says, erroneously, that Tonty had gone to Fort Frontenac. La Forest had gone thither, not long before La Salle's arrival.

[229] *Copie du Testament du deffunt Sr de la Salle, 11 Août, 1681.* The relative was François Plet, to whom he was deeply in debt.

[230] "On apprendra à la fin de cette année, 1682, le succès de la découverte qu'il étoit résolu d'achever, au plus tard le printemps dernier ou de périr en y travaillant. Tant de traverses et de malheurs toujours arrivés en son absence l'ont fait résoudre à ne se fier plus à personne et à conduire lui-même tout son monde, tout son équipage, et toute son entreprise, de laquelle il espéroit une heureuse conclusion."

The above is a part of the closing paragraph of the *Relation des Découvertes*, so often cited.

[Pg 295]

CHAPTER XX.

1681-1682.

SUCCESS OF LA SALLE.

THE season was far advanced. On the bare limbs of the forest hung a few withered remnants of its gay autumnal livery; and the smoke crept upward through the sullen November air from the squalid wigwams of La Salle's Abenaki and Mohegan allies. These, his new friends, were savages whose midnight yells had startled the border hamlets of New England; who had danced around Puritan scalps, and whom Puritan imaginations painted as incarnate fiends. La Salle chose eighteen of them, whom he added to the twenty-three Frenchmen who remained with him, some of the rest having deserted and others lagged behind. The Indians insisted on taking their squaws with them. These were ten in number, besides three children; and thus the expedition included fifty-four persons, of whom some were useless, and others a burden.

[Pg 296]

On the 21st of December, Tonty and Membré set out from Fort Miami with some of the party in six canoes, and crossed to the little river Chicago.[231] La Salle, with the rest of the men, joined them a few days later. It was the dead of winter, and the streams were frozen. They made sledges, placed on them the canoes, the baggage, and a disabled Frenchman; crossed from the Chicago to the northern branch of the Illinois, and filed in a long procession down its frozen course. They reached the site of the great Illinois village, found it tenantless, and continued their journey, still dragging their canoes, till at length they reached open water below Lake Peoria.

PRUDHOMME.

La Salle had abandoned for a time his original plan of building a vessel for the navigation of the Mississippi. Bitter experience had taught him the difficulty of the attempt, and he resolved to trust to [Pg 297] his canoes alone. They embarked again, floating prosperously down between the leafless forests that flanked the tranquil river; till, on the sixth of February, they issued upon the majestic bosom of the Mississippi. Here, for the time, their progress was stopped; for the river was full of floating ice. La Salle's Indians, too, had lagged behind; but within a week all had arrived, the navigation was once more free, and they resumed their course. Towards evening they saw on their right the mouth of a great river; and the clear current was invaded by the headlong torrent of the Missouri, opaque with mud. They built their camp-fires in the neighboring forest; and at daylight, embarking anew on the dark and mighty stream, drifted swiftly down towards unknown destinies. They passed a deserted town of the Tamaroas; saw, three days after, the mouth of the Ohio;[232] and, gliding by the wastes of bordering swamp, landed on the twenty-fourth of February near the Third Chickasaw Bluffs.[233] They encamped, and the hunters went out for game. All returned, excepting Pierre Prudhomme; and as the others had seen fresh tracks of Indians, La Salle feared that he was killed. While some of his followers built a small stockade fort on a high bluff[234] by the river, others [Pg 298] ranged the woods in pursuit of the missing hunter. After six days of ceaseless and fruitless search, they met two Chickasaw Indians in the forest; and through them La Salle sent presents and peace-messages to that warlike people, whose villages were a few days' journey distant. Several days later Prudhomme was found, and brought into the camp, half-dead. He had lost his way while hunting; and to console him for his woes La Salle christened the newly built fort with his name, and left him, with a few others, in charge of it.

Again they embarked; and with every stage of their adventurous progress the mystery of this vast New World was more and more unveiled. More and more they entered the realms of spring. The hazy sunlight, the warm and drowsy air, the tender foliage, the opening flowers, betokened the reviving life of Nature. For several days more they followed the writhings of the great river on its tortuous course through wastes of swamp and cane-brake, till on the thirteenth of March[235] they found themselves wrapped in a thick fog. Neither shore was visible; but they heard on the right the booming of an Indian drum and the shrill outcries of the war-dance. La Salle at once crossed to the opposite side, where, in less than an hour, his men threw up a rude fort of felled trees. [Pg 299] Meanwhile the fog cleared; and from the farther bank the astonished Indians saw the strange visitors at their work. Some of the French advanced to the edge of the water, and beckoned them to come over. Several of them approached, in a wooden canoe, to within the distance of a gun-shot. La Salle displayed the calumet, and sent a Frenchman to meet them. He was well received; and the friendly mood of the Indians being now apparent, the whole party crossed the river.

THE ARKANSAS.

On landing, they found themselves at a town of the Kappa band of the Arkansas, a people dwelling near the mouth of the river which bears their name. "The whole village," writes Membré to his superior, "came down to the shore to meet us, except the women, who had run off. I cannot tell you the civility and kindness we received from these barbarians, who brought us poles to make huts, supplied us with firewood during the three days we were among them, and took turns in feasting us. But, my Reverend Father, this gives no idea of the good qualities of these savages, who are gay, civil, and free-hearted. The young men, though the most alert and spirited we had seen, are nevertheless so modest that not one of them would take the liberty to enter our hut, but all stood quietly at the door. They are so well formed that we were in admiration at their beauty. We did not lose the value of a pin while we were among them."

Various were the dances and ceremonies with which [Pg 300] they entertained the strangers, who, on their part, responded with a solemnity which their hosts would have liked less if they had understood it better. La Salle and Tonty, at the head of their followers, marched to the open area in the midst of the village. Here, to the admiration of the gazing crowd of warriors, women, and children, a cross was raised bearing the arms of France. Membré, in canonicals, sang a hymn; the men shouted *Vive le Roi*; and La Salle, in the King's name, took formal possession of the country.[236] The friar, not, he flatters himself, without success, labored to expound by signs the mysteries of the Faith; while La Salle, by methods equally satisfactory, drew from the chief an acknowledgement of fealty to Louis XIV.[237]

THE TAENSAS.

After touching at several other towns of this people, the voyagers resumed their course, guided by two of the Arkansas; passed the sites, since become historic, of Vicksburg and Grand Gulf; and, about three hundred miles below the Arkansas, stopped by the edge of a swamp on the western side of the [Pg 301] river.[238] Here, as their two guides told them, was the path to the great town of the Taensas. Tonty and Membré were sent to visit it. They and their men shouldered their birch canoe through the swamp, and launched it on a lake which had once formed a portion of the channel of the river. In two hours, they reached the town; and Tonty gazed at it with astonishment. He had seen nothing like it in America,—large square dwellings, built of sun-baked mud mixed with straw, arched over with a dome-shaped roof of canes, and placed in regular order around an open area. Two of them were larger and better than the rest. One was the lodge of the chief; the other was the temple, or house of the Sun. They entered the former, and found a single room, forty feet square, where, in the dim light,—for there was no opening but the door,—the chief sat awaiting them on a sort of bedstead, three of his wives at his side; while sixty old men, wrapped in white cloaks woven of mulberry-bark, formed his divan. When he spoke, his wives howled to do him honor; and the assembled councillors listened with the reverence due to a potentate for whom, at his death, a hundred victims were to be sacrificed. He received the visitors graciously, and joyfully [Pg 302] accepted the gifts which Tonty laid before him.[239] This interview over, the Frenchmen repaired to the temple, wherein were kept the bones of the departed chiefs. In construction, it was much like the royal dwelling. Over it were rude wooden figures, representing three eagles turned towards the east. A strong mud wall surrounded it, planted with stakes, on which were stuck the skulls of enemies sacrificed to the Sun; while before the door was a block of wood, on which lay a large shell surrounded with the braided hair of the victims. The interior was rude as a barn, dimly lighted from the doorway, and full of smoke. There was a structure in the middle which Membré thinks was a kind of altar; and before it burned a perpetual fire, fed with three logs laid end to end, and watched by two old men devoted to this sacred office. There was a mysterious recess, too, which the strangers were forbidden to explore, but which, as Tonty was told, contained the riches of the nation, consisting of pearls from the Gulf, and trinkets obtained, probably through other tribes, from the Spaniards and other Europeans.

The chief condescended to visit La Salle at his camp,—a favor which he would by no means have granted, had the visitors been Indians. A master of ceremonies and six attendants preceded him, to clear [Pg 303] the path and prepare the place of meeting. When all was ready, he was seen advancing, clothed in a white robe and preceded by two men bearing white fans, while a third displayed a disk of burnished copper,—doubtless to represent the Sun, his ancestor, or, as others will have it, his elder brother. His aspect was marvellously grave, and he and La Salle met with gestures of ceremonious courtesy. The interview was very friendly; and the chief returned well pleased with the gifts which his entertainer bestowed on him, and which, indeed, had been the principal motive of his visit.

THE NATCHEZ.

On the next morning, as they descended the river, they saw a wooden canoe full of Indians; and Tonty gave chase. He had nearly overtaken it, when more than a hundred men appeared suddenly on the shore, with bows bent to defend their countrymen. La Salle called out to Tonty to withdraw. He obeyed; and the whole party encamped on the opposite bank. Tonty offered to cross the river with a peace-pipe, and set out accordingly with a small party of men. When he landed, the Indians made signs of friendship by joining their hands,—a proceeding by which Tonty, having but one hand, was somewhat embarrassed; but he directed his men to respond in his stead. La Salle and Membré now joined him, and went with the Indians to their village, three leagues distant. Here they spent the night. "The Sieur de la Salle," writes Membré, "whose very air, engaging manners, tact, and address attract love and [Pg 304] respect alike, produced such an effect on the hearts of these people that they did not know how to treat us well enough."[240]

The Indians of this village were the Natchez; and their chief was brother of the great chief, or Sun, of the whole nation. His town was several leagues distant, near the site of the city of Natchez; and thither the French repaired to visit him. They saw what they had already seen among the Taensas,—a religious and political despotism, a privileged caste descended from the sun, a temple, and a sacred fire.[241] [Pg 305] La Salle planted a large cross, with the arms of France attached, in the midst of the town; while the inhabitants looked on with a satisfaction which they would hardly have displayed had they understood the meaning of the act.

HOSTILITY.

The French next visited the Coroas, at their village two leagues below; and here they found a reception no less auspicious. On the thirty-first of March, as they approached Red River, they passed in

the fog a town of the Oumas, and three days later discovered a party
of fishermen, in wooden canoes, among the canes along the margin
of the water. They fled at sight of the Frenchmen. La Salle sent men
to reconnoitre, who, as they struggled through the marsh, were
greeted with a shower of arrows; while from the neighboring village
of the Quinipissas,[242] invisible behind the cane-brake, they heard the
sound of an Indian drum and the whoops of the mustering warriors.
La Salle, anxious to keep the peace with all the tribes along the river,
recalled his men, and pursued his voyage. A few leagues below they
saw a cluster of Indian lodges on the left bank, apparently void of
inhabitants. They landed, and found three of them filled with
corpses. It was a village of the Tangibao, sacked by their enemies
only a few days before.[243]

[Pg 306]

And now they neared their journey's end. On the sixth of April the
river divided itself into three broad channels. La Salle followed that
of the west, and Dautray that of the east; while Tonty took the
middle passage. As he drifted down the turbid current, between the
low and marshy shores, the brackish water changed to brine, and the
breeze grew fresh with the salt breath of the sea. Then the broad
bosom of the great Gulf opened on his sight, tossing its restless
billows, limitless, voiceless, lonely as when born of chaos, without
a sail, without a sign of life.

La Salle, in a canoe, coasted the marshy borders of the sea; and then
the reunited parties assembled on a spot of dry ground, a short
distance above the mouth of the river. Here a column was made
ready, bearing the arms of France, and inscribed with the words,
"LOUIS LE GRAND, ROY DE FRANCE ET DE NAVARRE, RÈGNE; LE
NEUVIÈME AVRIL, 1682."

The Frenchmen were mustered under arms; and while the New
England Indians and their squaws looked on in wondering silence,
they chanted the *Te Deum*, the *Exaudiat*, and the *Domine salvum fac
Regem*. Then, amid volleys of musketry and shouts of *Vive le Roi*,

La Salle planted the column in its place, and, standing near it, proclaimed in a loud voice,—

POSSESSION TAKEN.

"In the name of the most high, mighty, invincible, and victorious Prince, Louis the Great, by the grace of God King of France and of Navarre, Fourteenth of that name, I, this ninth day of April, one thousand six hundred and eighty-two, in virtue of the commission [Pg 307] of his Majesty, which I hold in my hand, and which may be seen by all whom it may concern, have taken, and do now take, in the name of his Majesty and of his successors to the crown, possession of this country of Louisiana, the seas, harbors, ports, bays, adjacent straits, and all the nations, peoples, provinces, cities, towns, villages, mines, minerals, fisheries, streams, and rivers, within the extent of the said Louisiana, from the mouth of the great river St. Louis, otherwise called the Ohio, ... as also along the river Colbert, or Mississippi, and the rivers which discharge themselves thereinto, from its source beyond the country of the Nadouessioux ... as far as its mouth at the sea, or Gulf of Mexico, and also to the mouth of the River of Palms, upon the assurance we have had from the natives of these countries that we are the first Europeans who have descended or ascended the said river Colbert; hereby protesting against all who may hereafter undertake to invade any or all of these aforesaid countries, peoples, or lands, to the prejudice of the rights of his Majesty, acquired by the consent of the nations dwelling herein. Of which, and of all else that is needful, I hereby take to witness those who hear me, and demand an act of the notary here present."[244]

[Pg 308]

Shouts of *Vive le Roi* and volleys of musketry responded to his words. Then a cross was planted beside the column, and a leaden plate buried near it, bearing the arms of France, with a Latin inscription, *Ludovicus Magnus regnat.* The weather-beaten voyagers joined their voices in the grand hymn of the *Vexilla Regis:*—

"The   banners   of   Heaven's   King   advance,
The   mystery   of   the   Cross   shines   forth;"

and renewed shouts of *Vive le Roi* closed the ceremony.

On that day, the realm of France received on parchment a stupendous accession. The fertile plains of Texas; the vast basin of the Mississippi, from its frozen northern springs to the sultry borders of the Gulf; from the woody ridges of the Alleghanies to the bare peaks of the Rocky Mountains,—a region of savannas and forests, sun-cracked deserts, and grassy prairies, watered by a thousand rivers, ranged by a thousand warlike tribes, passed beneath the sceptre of the Sultan of Versailles; and all by virtue of a feeble human voice, inaudible at half a mile.

FOOTNOTES:

[231] La Salle, *Relation de la Découverte*, 1682, in Thomassy, *Géologie Pratique de la Louisiane 9; Lettre du Père Zenobe Membré, 3 Juin, 1682; Ibid., 14 Août, 1682*; Membré in Le Clerc, ii. 214; Tonty, 1684, 1693; *Procès Verbal de la Prise de Possession de la Louisiane, Feuilles détachées d'une Lettre de La Salle* (Margry, ii. 164); *Récit de Nicolas de la Salle* (Ibid., i. 547).

The narrative ascribed to Membré and published by Le Clerc is based on the document preserved in the Archives Scientifiques de la Marine, entitled *Relation de la Découverte de l'Embouchure de la Rivière Mississippi faite par le Sieur de la Salle, l'année passée*, 1682. The writer of the narrative has used it very freely, copying the greater part verbatim, with occasional additions of a kind which seem to indicate that he had taken part in the expedition. The *Relation de la Découverte*, though written in the third person, is the official report of the discovery made by La Salle, or perhaps for him by Membré.

[232] Called by Membré the Ouabache (Wabash).

[233] La Salle, *Relation de la Découverte de l'Embouchure, etc.*; Thomassy, 10. Membré gives the same date; but the *Procès Verbal* makes it the twenty-sixth.

[234] Gravier, in his letter of 16 Feb., 1701, says that he encamped near a "great bluff of stone, called Fort Prudhomme, because M. de La Salle, going on his discovery, intrenched himself here with his party, fearing that Prudhomme, who had lost himself in the woods, had been killed by the Indians, and that he himself would be attacked."

[235] La Salle, *Relation*; Thomassy, 11.

[236] *Procès Verbal de la Prise de Possession du Pays des Arkansas, 14 Mars, 1682.*

[237]The nation of the Akanseas, Alkansas, or Arkansas, dwelt on the west bank of the Mississippi, near the mouth of the Arkansas. They were divided into four tribes, living for the most part in separate villages. Those first visited by La Salle were the Kappas, or Quapaws, a remnant of whom still subsists. The others were the Topingas, or Tongengas; the Torimans; and the Osotouoy, or Sauthouis. According to Charlevoix, who saw them in 1721, they were regarded as the tallest and best-formed Indians in America, and were known as *les Beaux Hommes*. Gravier says that they once lived on the Ohio.

[238] In Tensas County, Louisiana. Tonty's estimates of distance are here much too low. They seem to be founded on observations of latitude, without reckoning the windings of the river. It may interest sportsmen to know that the party killed several large alligators, on their way. Membré is much astonished that such monsters should be born of eggs like chickens.

[239] Tonty, 1684, 1693. In the spurious narrative, published in Tonty's name, the account is embellished and exaggerated. Compare Membré in Le Clerc, ii. 227. La Salle's statements in the *Relation* of 1682 (Thomassy, 12) sustain those of Tonty.

[240] Membré in Le Clerc, ii. 232.

[241] The Natchez and the Taensas, whose habits and customs were similar, did not, in their social organization, differ radically from other Indians. The same principle of clanship, or *totemship*, so widely spread, existed in full force among them, combined with their religious ideas, and developed into forms of which no other example, equally distinct, is to be found. (For Indian clanship, see "The Jesuits in North America," *Introduction*.) Among the Natchez and Taensas, the principal clan formed

a ruling caste; and its chiefs had the attributes of demi-gods. As descent was through the female, the chief's son never succeeded him, but the son of one of his sisters; and as she, by the usual totemic law, was forced to marry in another clan,—that is, to marry a common mortal,—her husband, though the destined father of a demi-god, was treated by her as little better than a slave. She might kill him, if he proved unfaithful; but he was forced to submit to her infidelities in silence.

The customs of the Natchez have been described by Du Pratz, Le Petit, Penecaut, and others. Charlevoix visited their temple in 1721, and found it in a somewhat shabby condition. At this time, the Taensas were extinct. In 1729 the Natchez, enraged by the arbitrary conduct of a French commandant, massacred the neighboring settlers, and were in consequence expelled from their country and nearly destroyed. A few still survive, incorporated with the Creeks; but they have lost their peculiar customs.

[242] In St. Charles County, on the left bank, not far above New Orleans.
[243] Hennepin uses this incident, as well as most of those which have preceded it, in making up the story of his pretended voyage to the Gulf.
[244] In the passages omitted above, for the sake of brevity, the Ohio is mentioned as being called also the *Olighin-* (Alleghany) *Sipou*, and *Chukagoua*; and La Salle declares that he takes possession of the country with the consent of the nations dwelling in it, of whom he names the Chaouanons (Shawanoes), Kious, or Nadouessious (Sioux), Chikachas (Chickasaws), Motantees (?), Illinois, Mitchigamias, Arkansas, Natchez, and Koroas. This alleged consent is, of course, mere farce. If there could be any doubt as to the meaning of the words of La Salle, as recorded in the *Procès Verbal de la Prise de Possession de la Louisiane*, it would be set at rest by Le Clerc, who says: "Le Sieur de la Salle prit au nom de sa Majesté possession de ce fleuve, *de toutes les rivières qui y entrent, et de tous les pays qu'elles arrosent*." These words are borrowed from the report of La Salle (see Thomassy, 14). A copy of the original *Procès Verbal* is before me. It bears the name of Jacques de la Metairie, Notary of Fort Frontenac, who was one of the party.

[Pg 309]

CHAPTER XXI.

1682, 1683.

ST. LOUIS OF THE ILLINOIS.

LOUISIANA.—ILLNESS OF LA SALLE: HIS COLONY ON THE ILLINOIS.—FORT ST. LOUIS.—RECALL OF FRONTENAC.—LE FEBVRE DE LA BARRE.—CRITICAL POSITION OF LA SALLE.—HOSTILITY OF THE NEW GOVERNOR.—TRIUMPH OF THE ADVERSE FACTION.—LA SALLE SAILS FOR FRANCE.

LOUISIANA was the name bestowed by La Salle on the new domain of the French crown. The rule of the Bourbons in the West is a memory of the past, but the name of the Great King still survives in a narrow corner of their lost empire. The Louisiana of to-day is but a single State of the American republic. The Louisiana of La Salle stretched from the Alleghanies to the Rocky Mountains; from the Rio Grande and the Gulf to the farthest springs of the Missouri.[245]

[Pg 310]

La Salle had written his name in history; but his hard-earned success was but the prelude of a harder task. Herculean labors lay before him, if he would realize the schemes with which his brain was pregnant. Bent on accomplishing them, he retraced his course, and urged his canoes upward against the muddy current. The party were famished. They had little to subsist on but the flesh of alligators. When they reached the Quinipissas, who had proved hostile on their way down, they resolved to risk an interview with them, in the hope of obtaining food. The treacherous savages dissembled, brought them corn, and on the following night made an attack upon them, but met with a bloody repulse. The party next revisited the Coroas, and found an unfavorable change in their disposition towards them. They feasted them, indeed, but during the repast surrounded them with an overwhelming force of warriors. The French, however, kept so well on their guard, that their entertainers dared not make an attack, and suffered them to depart unmolested.[246]

ILLNESS OF LA SALLE.

And now, in a career of unwonted success and anticipated triumph, La Salle was arrested by a foe against which the boldest heart avails nothing. As he ascended the Mississippi, he was seized by a dangerous illness. Unable to proceed, he sent forward [Pg 311] Tonty to Michilimackinac, whence, after despatching news of their discovery to Canada, he was to return to the Illinois. La Salle himself lay helpless at Fort Prudhomme, the palisade work which his men had built at the Chickasaw Bluffs on their way down. Father Zenobe Membré attended him; and at the end of July he was once more in a condition to advance by slow movements towards Fort Miami, which he reached in about a month.

In September he rejoined Tonty at Michilimackinac, and in the following month wrote to a friend in France: "Though my discovery is made, and I have descended the Mississippi to the Gulf of Mexico, I cannot send you this year either an account of my journey or a map. On the way back I was attacked by a deadly disease, which kept me in danger of my life for forty days, and left me so weak that I could think of nothing for four months after. I have hardly strength enough now to write my letters, and the season is so far advanced that I cannot detain a single day this canoe which I send expressly to carry them. If I had not feared being forced to winter on the way, I should have tried to get to Quebec to meet the new governor, if it is true that we are to have one; but in my present condition this would be an act of suicide, on account of the bad nourishment I should have all winter in case the snow and ice stopped me on the way. Besides, my presence is absolutely necessary in the place to which I am [Pg 312] going. I pray you, my dear sir, to give me once more all the help you can. I have great enemies, who have succeeded in all they have undertaken. I do not pretend to resist them, but only to justify myself, so that I can pursue by sea the plans I have begun here by land."

This was what he had proposed to himself from the first; that is, to abandon the difficult access through Canada, beset with enemies, and open a way to his western domain through the Gulf and the Mississippi. This was the aim of all his toilsome explorations. Could he have accomplished his first intention of building a vessel on the Illinois and descending in her to the Gulf, he would have been able to defray in good measure the costs of the enterprise by means of the furs and buffalo-hides collected on the way and carried in her to France. With a fleet of canoes, this was impossible; and there was nothing to offset the enormous outlay which he and his associates had made. He meant, as we have seen, to found on the banks of the Illinois a colony of French and Indians to answer the double purpose of a bulwark against the Iroquois and a place of storage for the furs of all the western tribes; and he hoped in the following year to secure an outlet for this colony and for all the trade of the valley of the Mississippi, by occupying the mouth of that river with a fort and another colony. This, too, was an essential part of his original design.

But for his illness, he would have gone to France [Pg 313] to provide for its execution. Meanwhile, he ordered Tonty to collect as many men as possible, and begin the projected colony on the banks of the Illinois. A report soon after reached him that those pests of the wilderness the Iroquois were about to renew their attacks on the western tribes. This would be fatal to his plans; and, following Tonty to the Illinois, he rejoined him near the site of the great town.

"STARVED ROCK."

The cliff called "Starved Rock," now pointed out to travellers as the chief natural curiosity of the region, rises, steep on three sides as a castle wall, to the height of a hundred and twenty-five feet above the river. In front, it overhangs the water that washes its base; its western brow looks down on the tops of the forest trees below; and on the east lies a wide gorge or ravine, choked with the mingled foliage of oaks, walnuts, and elms; while in its rocky depths a little brook creeps down to mingle with the river. From the trunk of the stunted cedar that leans forward from the brink, you may drop a plummet into the river below, where the cat-fish and the turtles may plainly be seen gliding over the wrinkled sands of the clear and shallow current. The cliff is accessible only from behind, where a man may climb up, not without difficulty, by a steep and narrow passage. The top is about an acre in extent. Here, in the month of December, La Salle and Tonty began to intrench themselves. They cut away the forest that crowned the rock, built store-houses and dwellings of its remains, [Pg 314]dragged timber up the rugged pathway, and encircled the summit with a palisade.[247]

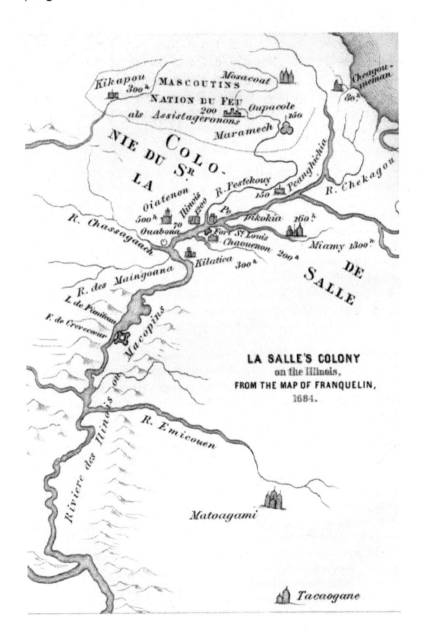

LA SALLE'S COLONY.

Thus the winter passed, and meanwhile the work [Pg 315] of negotiation went prosperously on. The minds of the Indians had been already prepared. In La Salle they saw their champion against the Iroquois, the standing terror of all this region. They gathered round his stronghold like the timorous peasantry of the middle ages around the rock-built castle of their feudal lord. From the wooden ramparts of St. Louis,—for so he named his fort,—high and inaccessible as an eagle's nest, a strange scene lay before his eye. The broad, flat valley of the Illinois was spread beneath him like a map, bounded in the distance by its low wall of woody hills. The river wound at his feet in devious channels among islands bordered with lofty trees; then, far on the left, flowed calmly westward through the vast meadows, till its glimmering blue ribbon was lost in hazy distance.

There had been a time, and that not remote, when these fair meadows were a waste of death and desolation, scathed with fire, and strewn with the ghastly relics of an Iroquois victory. Now all was changed. La Salle looked down from his rock on a concourse of wild human life. Lodges of bark and rushes, or cabins of logs, were clustered on the open plain or along the edges of the bordering forests. Squaws labored, warriors lounged in the sun, naked children whooped and gambolled on the grass. Beyond the river, a mile and a half on the left, the banks were studded once more with the lodges of the Illinois, who, to the number of six thousand, had returned, since their defeat, to this their favorite dwelling-place. [Pg 316] Scattered along the valley, among the adjacent hills, or over the neighboring prairie, were the cantonments of a half-score of other tribes and fragments of tribes, gathered under the protecting ægis of the French,—Shawanoes from the Ohio, Abenakis from Maine, Miamis from the sources of the Kankakee, with others whose barbarous names are hardly worth the record.[248] Nor were these La Salle's only dependants. [Pg 317] By the terms of his patent, he held seigniorial rights over this wild domain; and he now began to grant it out in parcels to his followers. These, however, were as yet but a score,—a lawless band, trained in forest license, and marrying, as their detractors affirm, a new squaw every day in the week. This was after their lord's departure, for his presence imposed a check on these eccentricities.

La Salle, in a memoir addressed to the Minister of the Marine, reports the total number of the Indians around Fort St. Louis at about four thousand warriors, or twenty thousand souls. His diplomacy had [Pg 318] been crowned with a marvellous success,—for which his thanks were due, first to the Iroquois, and the universal terror they inspired; next, to his own address and unwearied energy. His colony had sprung up, as it were, in a night; but might not a night suffice to disperse it?

The conditions of maintaining it were twofold: first, he must give efficient aid to his savage colonists against the Iroquois; secondly, he must supply them with French goods in exchange for their furs. The men, arms, and ammunition for their defence, and the goods for trading with them, must be brought from Canada, until a better and surer avenue of supply could be provided through the entrepôt which he meant to establish at the mouth of the Mississippi. Canada was full of his enemies; but as long as Count Frontenac was in power, he was sure of support. Count Frontenac was in power no longer. He had been recalled to France through the intrigues of the party adverse to La Salle; and Le Febvre de la Barre reigned in his stead.

LA SALLE AND LA BARRE.

La Barre was an old naval officer of rank, advanced to a post for which he proved himself notably unfit. If he was without the arbitrary passions which had been the chief occasion of the recall of his predecessor, he was no less without his energies and his talents. He showed a weakness and an avarice for which his age may have been in some measure answerable. He was no whit less unscrupulous than his predecessor in his secret violation of the royal ordinances [Pg 319] regulating the fur-trade, which it was his duty to enforce. Like Frontenac, he took advantage of his position to carry on an illicit traffic with the Indians; but it was with different associates. The late governor's friends were the new governor's enemies; and La Salle, armed with his monopolies, was the object of his especial jealousy.[249]

Meanwhile, La Salle, buried in the western wilderness, remained for the time ignorant of La Barre's disposition towards him, and made an effort to secure his good-will and countenance. He wrote to him from his rock of St. Louis, early in the spring of 1683, expressing the hope that he should have from him the same support as from Count Frontenac; "although," he says, "my enemies will try to influence you against me." His attachment to Frontenac, he pursues, has been the cause of all the late governor's enemies turning against him. He then recounts his voyage down the Mississippi; says that, with twenty-two Frenchmen, he caused all the tribes along the river to ask for peace; and speaks of his right under the royal patent to build forts anywhere along his route, and grant out lands around them, as at Fort Frontenac.

[Pg 320]

"My losses in my enterprises," he continues, "have exceeded forty thousand crowns. I am now going four hundred leagues south-southwest of this place, to induce the Chickasaws to follow the Shawanoes and other tribes, and settle, like them, at St. Louis. It remained only to settle French colonists here, and this I have already done. I hope you will not detain them as *coureurs de bois*, when they come down to Montreal to make necessary purchases. I am aware that I have no right to trade with the tribes who descend to Montreal, and I shall not permit such trade to my men; nor have I ever issued licenses to that effect, as my enemies say that I have done."[250]

Again, on the fourth of June following, he writes to La Barre, from the Chicago portage, complaining that some of his colonists, going to Montreal for necessary supplies, have been detained by his enemies, and begging that they may be allowed to return, that his enterprise may not be ruined. "The Iroquois," he pursues, "are again invading the country. Last year, the Miamis were so alarmed by them that they abandoned their town and fled; but at my return they came back, and have been induced to settle with the Illinois at my fort of St. Louis. The Iroquois have lately murdered some families of their nation, and they are all in terror again. I am afraid they will take flight, and so prevent the Missouris and [Pg 321] neighboring tribes from coming to settle at St. Louis, as they are about to do.

"Some of the Hurons and French tell the Miamis that I am keeping them here for the Iroquois to destroy. I pray that you will let me hear from you, that I may give these people some assurances of protection before they are destroyed in my sight. Do not suffer my men who have come down to the settlements to be longer prevented from returning. There is great need here of reinforcements. The Iroquois, as I have said, have lately entered the country; and a great terror prevails. I have postponed going to Michilimackinac, because, if the Iroquois strike any blow in my absence, the Miamis will think that I am in league with them; whereas, if I and the French stay among them, they will regard us as protectors. But, Monsieur, it is in vain that we risk our lives here, and that I exhaust my means in order to fulfil the intentions of his Majesty, if all my measures are crossed in the settlements below, and if those who go down to bring munitions, without which we cannot defend ourselves, are detained under pretexts trumped up for the occasion. If I am prevented from bringing up men and supplies, as I am allowed to do by the permit of Count Frontenac, then my patent from the King is useless. It would be very hard for us, after having done what was required, even before the time prescribed, and after suffering severe losses, to have our efforts frustrated by obstacles got up designedly.

[Pg 322]

"I trust that, as it lies with you alone to prevent or to permit the return of the men whom I have sent down, you will not so act as to thwart my plans. A part of the goods which I have sent by them belong not to me, but to the Sieur de Tonty, and are a part of his pay. Others are to buy munitions indispensable for our defence. Do not let my creditors seize them. It is for their advantage that my fort, full as it is of goods, should be held against the enemy. I have only twenty men, with scarcely a hundred pounds of powder; and I cannot long hold the country without more. The Illinois are very capricious and uncertain.... If I had men enough to send out to reconnoitre the enemy, I would have done so before this; but I have not enough. I trust you will put it in my power to obtain more, that this important colony may be saved."[251]

While La Salle was thus writing to La Barre, La Barre was writing to Seignelay, the Marine and Colonial Minister, decrying his correspondent's discoveries, and pretending to doubt their reality. "The Iroquois," he adds, "have sworn his [La Salle's] death. The imprudence of this man is about to involve the colony in war."[252] And again he [Pg 323] writes, in the following spring, to say that La Salle was with a score of vagabonds at Green Bay, where he set himself up as a king, pillaged his countrymen, and put them to ransom, exposed the tribes of the West to the incursions of the Iroquois, and all under pretence of a patent from his Majesty, the provisions of which he grossly abused; but, as his privileges would expire on the twelfth of May ensuing, he would then be forced to come to Quebec, where his creditors, to whom he owed more than thirty thousand crowns, were anxiously awaiting him.[253]

Finally, when La Barre received the two letters from La Salle, of which the substance is given above, he sent copies of them to the Minister Seignelay, with the following comment: "By the copies of the Sieur de la Salle's letters, you will perceive that his head is turned, and that he has been bold enough to give you intelligence of a false discovery, and that, instead of returning to the colony to learn what the King wishes him to do, he does not come near me, but keeps in the backwoods, five hundred leagues off, with the idea of attracting the inhabitants to him, and building up an imaginary kingdom for himself, by debauching all the bankrupts and idlers of this country. If you will look at the two letters I had from him, you can judge the character of this personage better than I can. Affairs with the [Pg 324] Iroquois are in such a state that I cannot allow him to muster all their enemies together and put himself at their head.

All the men who brought me news from him have abandoned him, and say not a word about returning, *but sell the furs they have brought as if they were their own*; so that he cannot hold his ground much longer."[254] Such calumnies had their effect. The enemies of La Salle had already gained the ear of the King; and he had written in August, from Fontainebleau, to his new governor of Canada: "I am convinced, like you, that the discovery of the Sieur de la Salle is very useless, and that such enterprises ought to be prevented in future, as they tend only to debauch the inhabitants by the hope of gain, and to diminish the revenue from beaver-skins."[255]

In order to understand the posture of affairs at this time, it must be remembered that Dutch and English traders of New York were urging on the Iroquois to attack the western tribes, with the object of gaining, through their conquest, the control of the fur-trade of the interior, and diverting it from Montreal to Albany. The scheme was full of danger to Canada, which the loss of the trade would have ruined. La Barre and his associates were greatly alarmed at it. Its complete success would have been fatal to their hopes of profit; but they nevertheless wished it such a measure of success as would ruin their rival, La Salle. Hence, no little satisfaction mingled with [Pg 325] their anxiety when they heard that the Iroquois were again threatening to invade the Miamis and the Illinois; and thus La Barre, whose duty it was strenuously to oppose the intrigue of the English, and use every effort to quiet the ferocious bands whom they were hounding against the Indian allies of the French, was, in fact, but half-hearted in the work. He cut off La Salle from all supplies; detained the men whom he sent for succor; and, at a conference with the Iroquois, told them that they were welcome to plunder and kill him.[256]

A NEW ALARM.

The old governor, and the unscrupulous ring with which he was associated, now took a step to which he was doubtless emboldened by the tone of the King's letter, in condemnation of La Salle's enterprise. He resolved to seize Fort Frontenac, the property of La Salle, under the pretext that the latter had not fulfilled the conditions of the grant, and had not maintained a sufficient garrison.[257] Two of [Pg 326] his associates, La Chesnaye and Le Ber, armed with an order from him, went up and took possession, despite the remonstrances of La Salle's creditors and mortgagees; lived on La Salle's stores, sold for their own profit, and (it is said) that of La Barre, the provisions sent by the King, and turned in the cattle to pasture on the growing crops. La Forest, La Salle's lieutenant, was told that he might retain the command of the fort if he would join the associates; but he refused, and sailed in the autumn for France.[258]

Meanwhile La Salle remained at the Illinois in extreme embarrassment, cut off from supplies, robbed of his men who had gone to seek them, and disabled from fulfilling the pledges he had given to the surrounding Indians. Such was his position, when reports came to Fort St. Louis that the Iroquois were at hand. The Indian hamlets were wild with terror, beseeching him for succor which he had no power to give. Happily, the report proved false. No Iroquois appeared; the threatened attack was postponed, and the summer passed away in peace. But La Salle's position, with the governor his declared enemy, was intolerable and untenable; and there was no resource but in the protection of the court. Early in the autumn, he left Tonty in command of the rock, bade farewell to his savage retainers, and descended to Quebec, intending to sail for France.

On his way, he met the Chevalier de Baugis, an [Pg 327] officer of the King's dragoons, commissioned by La Barre to take possession of Fort St. Louis, and bearing letters from the governor ordering La Salle to come to Quebec,—a superfluous command, as he was then on his way thither. He smothered his wrath, and wrote to Tonty to receive De Baugis well. The chevalier and his party proceeded to the Illinois, and took possession of the fort,—De Baugis commanding for the governor, while Tonty remained as representative of La Salle. The two officers could not live in harmony; but, with the return of spring, each found himself in sore need of aid from the other. Towards the end of March the Iroquois attacked their citadel, and besieged it for six days, but at length withdrew discomfited, carrying with them a number of Indian prisoners, most of whom escaped from their clutches.[259]

Meanwhile, La Salle had sailed for France.

FOOTNOTES:

[245] The boundaries are laid down on the great map of Franquelin, made in 1684, and preserved in the Dépôt des Cartes of the Marine. The line runs along the south shore of Lake Erie, and thence follows the heads of the streams flowing into Lake Michigan. It then turns northwest, and is lost in the vast unknown of the now British Territories. On the south, it is drawn by the heads of the streams flowing into the Gulf, as far west as Mobile, after which it follows the shore of the Gulf to a little south of the Rio Grande; then runs west, northwest, and finally north, along the range of the Rocky Mountains.

[246] Tonty, 1684, 1693.

[247] "Starved Rock" perfectly answers, in every respect, to the indications of the contemporary maps and documents concerning "Le Rocher," the site of La Salle's fort of St. Louis. It is laid down on several contemporary maps, besides the great map of La Salle's discoveries, made in 1684. They all place it on the south side of the river; whereas Buffalo Rock, three miles above, which has been supposed to be the site of the fort, is on the north. The latter is crowned by a plateau of great extent, is but sixty feet high, is accessible at many points, and would require a large force to defend it; whereas La Salle chose "Le Rocher," because a few men could hold it against a multitude. Charlevoix, in 1721, describes both rocks, and says that the top of Buffalo Rock had been occupied by the Miami village, so that it was known as *Le Fort des Miamis*. This is confirmed by Joutel, who found the Miamis here in 1687. Charlevoix then speaks of "Le Rocher," calling it by that name; says that it is about a league below, on the left or south side, forming a sheer cliff, very high, and looking like a fortress on the border of the river. He saw remains of palisades at the top, which, he thinks, were made by the Illinois (*Journal Historique, Let.* xxvii.), though his countrymen had occupied it only three years before. "The French reside on the rock (Le Rocher), which is very lofty and impregnable." (*Memoir on Western Indians*, 1718, *in N. Y. Col. Docs.*, ix. 890.) St. Cosme, passing

this way in 1699, mentions it as "Le Vieux Fort," and says that it is "a rock about a hundred feet high at the edge of the river, where M. de la Salle built a fort, since abandoned." (*Journal de St. Cosme.*) Joutel, who was here in 1687, says, "Fort St. Louis is on a steep rock, about two hundred feet high, with the river running at its base." He adds that its only defences were palisades. The true height, as stated above, is about a hundred and twenty-five feet.

A traditional interest also attaches to this rock. It is said that, in the Indian wars that followed the assassination of Pontiac, a few years after the cession of Canada, a party of Illinois, assailed by the Pottawattamies, here took refuge, defying attack. At length they were all destroyed by starvation, and hence the name of "Starved Rock."

For other proofs concerning this locality, see *ante*, 239.

[248] This singular extemporized colony of La Salle, on the banks of the Illinois, is laid down in detail on the great map of La Salle's discoveries, by Jean Baptiste Franquelin, finished in 1684. There can be no doubt that this part of the work is composed from authentic data. La Salle himself, besides others of his party, came down from the Illinois in the autumn of 1683, and undoubtedly supplied the young engineer with materials. The various Indian villages, or cantonments, are all indicated, with the number of warriors belonging to each, the aggregate corresponding very nearly with that of La Salle's report to the minister. The Illinois, properly so called, are set down at 1,200 warriors; the Miamis, at 1,300; the Shawanoes, at 200; the Ouiatnoens (Weas), at 500; the Peanqhichia (Piankishaw) band, at 150; the Pepikokia, at 160; the Kilatica, at 300; and the Ouabona, at 70,—in all, 3,880 warriors. A few others, probably Abenakis, lived in the fort.

The Fort St. Louis is placed, on the map, at the exact site of Starved Rock, and the Illinois village at the place where, as already mentioned (see 239), Indian remains in great quantities are yearly ploughed up. The Shawanoe camp, or village, is placed on the south side of the river, behind the fort. The country is here hilly, broken, and now, as in La Salle's time, covered with wood, which, however, soon ends in the open prairie. A short time since, the remains of a low, irregular earthwork of considerable extent were discovered at the intersection of two ravines, about twenty-four hundred feet behind, or south of, Starved Rock. The earthwork follows the line of the ravines on two sides. On the east, there is an opening, or gateway, leading to the adjacent prairie. The work is very irregular in form, and shows no trace of the civilized engineer. In the stump of an oak-tree upon it, Dr. Paul counted a hundred and sixty rings of annual growth. The village of the Shawanoes (Chaouenons), on Franquelin's map, corresponds with the position of this earthwork. I am indebted to the kindness of Dr. John Paul and Col. D. F. Hitt, the proprietor of Starved Rock, for a plan of these curious remains and a survey of the neighboring district. I must also express my obligations to Mr. W. E. Bowman, photographer at Ottawa, for views of Starved Rock and other features of the neighboring scenery.

An interesting relic of the early explorers of this region was found a few years ago at Ottawa, six miles above Starved Rock, in the shape of a small iron gun, buried several feet deep in the drift of the river. It consists of a welded tube of iron, about an inch and a half in calibre, strengthened by a series of thick iron rings, cooled on, after the most ancient as well as the most recent method of making cannon. It is about fourteen inches long, the part near the muzzle having been burst off. The construction is very rude. Small field-pieces, on a similar principle, were used in the fourteenth century. Several of them may be seen at the Musée d'Artillerie at Paris. In the time of Louis XIV., the art of casting cannon was carried to a high degree of perfection. The gun in question may have been made by a French blacksmith on the spot. A far less probable supposition is, that it is a relic of some unrecorded visit of the Spaniards; but the pattern of the piece would have been antiquated, even in the time of De Soto.

[249] The royal instructions to La Barre, on his assuming the government, dated at Versailles, 10 May, 1682, require him to give no further permission to make journeys of discovery towards the Sioux and the Mississippi, as his Majesty thinks his subjects better employed in

cultivating the land. The letter adds, however, that La Salle is to be allowed to continue his discoveries, if they appear to be useful. The same instructions are repeated in a letter of the Minister of the Marine to the new intendant of Canada, De Meules.

[250] *Lettre de La Salle à La Barre, Fort St. Louis, 2 Avril, 1683.* The above is condensed from passages in the original.

[251] *Lettre de La Salle à La Barre, Portage de Chicagou, 4 Juin, 1683.* The substance of the letter is given above, in a condensed form. A passage is omitted, in which La Salle expresses his belief that his vessel, the "Griffin," had been destroyed, not by Indians, but by the pilot, who, as he thinks, had been induced to sink her, and then, with some of the crew, attempted to join Du Lhut with their plunder, but were captured by Indians on the Mississippi.

[252] *Lettre de La Barre au Ministre, 14 Nov., 1682.*

[253] *Lettre de La Barre au Ministre, 30 Avril, 1683.* La Salle had spent the winter, not at Green Bay, as this slanderous letter declares, but in the Illinois country.

[254] *Lettre de La Barre au Ministre, 4 Nov., 1683.*

[255] *Lettre du Roy à La Barre, 5 Août, 1683.*

[256] *Mémoire pour rendre compte à Monseigneur le Marquis de Seignelay de l'État où le Sieur de Lasalle a laissé le Fort Frontenac pendant le temps de sa découverte.* On La Barre's conduct, see "Count Frontenac and New France under Louis XIV.," chap. v.

[257] La Salle, when at Mackinaw, on his way to Quebec, in 1682, had been recalled to the Illinois, as we have seen, by a threatened Iroquois invasion. There is before me a copy of a letter which he then wrote to Count Frontenac, begging him to send up more soldiers to the fort, at his (La Salle's) expense. Frontenac, being about to sail for France, gave this letter to his newly arrived successor, La Barre, who, far from complying with the request, withdrew La Salle's soldiers already at the fort, and then made its defenceless state a pretext for seizing it. This statement is made in the memoir addressed to Seignelay, before cited.

[258] These are the statements of the memorial addressed in La Salle's behalf to the minister, Seignelay.

[259] Tonty, 1684, 1693; *Lettre de La Barre au Ministre, 5 Juin, 1684; Ibid., 9 Juillet, 1684.*

[Pg 328]

CHAPTER XXII.

1680-1683.

LA SALLE PAINTED BY HIMSELF.

DIFFICULTY OF KNOWING HIM: HIS DETRACTORS; HIS LETTERS; VEXATIONS OF HIS POSITION; HIS UNFITNESS FOR TRADE; RISKS OF CORRESPONDENCE; HIS REPORTED MARRIAGE; ALLEGED OSTENTATION; MOTIVES OF ACTION; CHARGES OF HARSHNESS; INTRIGUES AGAINST HIM; UNPOPULAR MANNERS; A STRANGE CONFESSION; HIS STRENGTH AND HIS WEAKNESS; CONTRASTS OF HIS CHARACTER.

WE have seen La Salle in his acts. While he crosses the sea, let us look at him in himself. Few men knew him, even of those who saw him most. Reserved and self-contained as he was, with little vivacity or gayety or love of pleasure, he was a sealed book to those about him. His daring energy and endurance were patent to all; but the motive forces that urged him, and the influences that wrought beneath the surface of his character, were hidden where few eyes could pierce. His enemies were free to make their own interpretations, and they did not fail to use the opportunity.

The interests arrayed against him were incessantly at work. His men were persuaded to desert and rob him; the Iroquois were told that he was arming [Pg 329] the western tribes against them; the western tribes were told that he was betraying them to the Iroquois; his proceedings were denounced to the court; and continual efforts were made to alienate his associates. They, on their part, sore as they were from disappointment and loss, were in a mood to listen to the aspersions cast upon him; and they pestered him with letters, asking questions, demanding explanations, and dunning him for money. It is through his answers that we are best able to judge him; and at times, by those touches of nature which make the whole world kin, they teach us to know him and to feel for him.

CHARGES AGAINST LA SALLE.

The main charges against him were that he was a crack-brained schemer, that he was harsh to his men, that he traded where he had no right to trade, and that his discoveries were nothing but a pretence for making money. No accusations appear that touch his integrity or his honor.

It was hard to convince those who were always losing by him. A remittance of good dividends would have been his best answer, and would have made any other answer needless; but, instead of bills of exchange, he had nothing to give but excuses and explanations. In the autumn of 1680, he wrote to an associate who had demanded the long-deferred profits: "I have had many misfortunes in the last two years. In the autumn of '78, I lost a vessel by the fault of the pilot; in the next summer, the deserters I told you about robbed me of eight or ten [Pg 330] thousand livres' worth of goods. In the autumn of '79, I lost a vessel worth more than ten thousand crowns; in the next spring, five or six rascals stole the value of five or six thousand livres in goods and beaver-skins, at the Illinois, when I was absent. Two other men of mine, carrying furs worth four or five thousand livres, were killed or drowned in the St. Lawrence, and the furs were lost. Another robbed me of three thousand livres in beaver-skins stored at Michilimackinac. This last spring, I lost about seventeen hundred livres' worth of goods by the upsetting of a canoe. Last winter, the fort and buildings at Niagara were burned by the fault of the commander; and in the spring the deserters, who passed that way, seized a part of the property that remained, and escaped to New York. All this does not discourage me in the least, and will only defer for a year or two the returns of profit which you ask for this year. These losses are no more my fault than the loss of the ship 'St. Joseph' was yours. I cannot be everywhere, and cannot help making use of the people of the country."

He begs his correspondent to send out an agent of his own. "He need not be very *savant*, but he must be faithful, patient of labor, and fond neither of gambling, women, nor good cheer; for he will find none of these with me. Trusting in what he will write you, you may close your ears to what priests and Jesuits tell you.

"After having put matters in good trim for trade I [Pg 331] mean to withdraw, though I think it will be very profitable; for I am disgusted to find that I must always be making excuses, which is a part I cannot play successfully. I am utterly tired of this business; for I see that it is not enough to put property and life in constant peril, but that it requires more pains to answer envy and detraction than to overcome the difficulties inseparable from my undertaking."

And he makes a variety of proposals, by which he hopes to get rid of a part of his responsibility to his correspondent. He begs him again to send out a confidential agent, saying that for his part he does not want to have any account to render, except that which he owes to the court, of his discoveries. He adds, strangely enough for a man burdened with such liabilities, "I have neither the habit nor the inclination to keep books, nor have I anybody with me who knows how." He says to another correspondent, "I think, like you, that partnerships in business are dangerous, on account of the little practice I have in these matters." It is not surprising that he wanted to leave his associates to manage business for themselves: "You know that this trade is good; and with a trusty agent to conduct it for you, you run no risk. As for me, I will keep the charge of the forts, the command of posts and of men, the management of Indians and Frenchmen, and the establishment of the colony, which will remain my property, leaving your agent and mine to [Pg 332] look after our interests, and drawing my half without having any hand in what belongs to you."

La Salle was a very indifferent trader; and his heart was not in the commercial part of his enterprise. He aimed at achievement, and thirsted after greatness. His ambition was to found another France in the West; and if he meant to govern it also,—as without doubt he did,—it is not a matter of wonder or of blame. His misfortune was, that, in the pursuit of a great design, he was drawn into complications of business with which he was ill fitted to grapple. He had not the instinct of the successful merchant. He dared too much, and often dared unwisely; attempted more than he could grasp, and forgot, in his sanguine anticipations, to reckon with enormous and incalculable risks.

Except in the narrative parts, his letters are rambling and unconnected,—which is natural enough, written, as they were, at odd moments, by camp-fires and among Indians. The style is crude; and being well aware of this, he disliked writing, especially as the risk was extreme that his letters would miss their destination. "There is too little good faith in this country, and too many people on the watch, for me to trust anybody with what I wish to send you. Even sealed letters are not too safe. Not only are they liable to be lost or stopped by the way, but even such as escape the curiosity of spies lie at Montreal, waiting a long time to be forwarded."

HIS LETTERS INTERCEPTED.

Again, he writes: "I cannot pardon myself for the [Pg 333] stoppage of my letters, though I made every effort to make them reach you. I wrote to you in '79 (in August), and sent my letters to M. de la Forest, who gave them in good faith to my brother. I don't know what he has done with them. I wrote you another, by the vessel that was lost last year. I sent two canoes, by two different routes; but the wind and the rain were so furious that they wintered on the way, and I found my letters at the fort on my return. I now send you one of them, which I wrote last year to M. Thouret, in which you will find a full account of what passed, from the time when we left the outlet of Lake Erie down to the sixteenth of August, 1680. What preceded was told at full length in the letters my brother has seen fit to intercept."

This brother was the Sulpitian priest, Jean Cavelier, who had been persuaded that La Salle's enterprise would be ruinous, and therefore set himself sometimes to stop it altogether, and sometimes to manage it in his own way. "His conduct towards me," says La Salle, "has always been so strange, through the small love he bears me, that it was clear gain for me when he went away; since while he stayed he did nothing but cross all my plans, which I was forced to change every moment to suit his caprice."

There was one point on which the interference of his brother and of his correspondents was peculiarly annoying. They thought it for their interest that he [Pg 334] should remain a single man; whereas, it seems that his devotion to his purpose was not so engrossing as to exclude more tender subjects. He writes:—

"I am told that you have been uneasy about my pretended marriage. I had not thought about it at that time; and I shall not make any engagement of the sort till I have given you reason to be satisfied with me. It is a little extraordinary that I must render account of a matter which is free to all the world.

"In fine, Monsieur, it is only as an earnest of something more substantial that I write to you so much at length. I do not doubt that you will hereafter change the ideas about me which some persons wish to give you, and that you will be relieved of the anxiety which all that has happened reasonably causes you. I have written this letter at more than twenty different times; and I am more than a hundred and fifty leagues from where I began it. I have still two hundred more to get over, before reaching the Illinois. I am taking with me twenty-five men to the relief of the six or seven who remain with the Sieur de Tonty."

This was the journey which ended in that scene of horror at the ruined town of the Illinois.

CHARGED WITH OSTENTATION.

To the same correspondent, pressing him for dividends, he says: "You repeat continually that you will not be satisfied unless I make you large returns of profit. Though I have reason to thank you for what you have done for this enterprise, it seems to [Pg 335] me that I have done still more, since I have put everything at stake; and it would be hard to reproach me either with foolish outlays or with the ostentation which is falsely imputed to me. Let my accusers explain what they mean. Since I have been in this country, I have had neither servants nor clothes nor fare which did not savor more of meanness than of ostentation; and the moment I see that there is anything with which either you or the court find fault, I assure you that I will give it up,—for the life I am leading has no other attraction for me than that of honor; and the more danger and difficulty there is in undertakings of this sort, the more worthy of honor I think they are."

His career attests the sincerity of these words. They are a momentary betrayal of the deep enthusiasm of character which may be read in his life, but to which he rarely allowed the faintest expression.

"Above all," he continues, "if you want me to keep on, do not compel me to reply to all the questions and fancies of priests and Jesuits. They have more leisure than I; and I am not subtle enough to anticipate all their empty stories. I could easily give you the information you ask; but I have a right to expect that you will not believe all you hear, nor require me to prove to you that I am not a madman. That is the first point to which you should have attended, before having business with me; and in our long acquaintance, either you must have found me out, or else I must have had long intervals of sanity."

[Pg 336]

To another correspondent he defends himself against the charge of harshness to his men: "The facility I am said to want is out of place with this sort of people, who are libertines for the most part; and to indulge them means to tolerate blasphemy, drunkenness, lewdness, and a license incompatible with any kind of order. It will not be found that I have in any case whatever treated any man harshly, except for blasphemies and other such crimes openly committed. These I cannot tolerate: first, because such compliance would give grounds for another accusation, much more just; secondly, because, if I allowed such disorders to become habitual, it would be hard to keep the men in subordination and obedience, as regards executing the work I am commissioned to do; thirdly, because the debaucheries, too common with this rabble, are the source of endless delays and frequent thieving; and, finally, because I am a Christian, and do not want to bear the burden of their crimes.

INTRIGUES AGAINST HIM.

"What is said about my servants has not even a show of truth; for I use no servants here, and all my men are on the same footing. I grant that as those who have lived with me are steadier and give me no reason to complain of their behavior, I treat them as gently as I should treat the others if they resembled them, and as those who were formerly my servants are the only ones I can trust, I speak more openly to them than to the rest, who are generally spies of my enemies. The twenty-two men who deserted and [Pg 337] robbed me are not to be believed on their word, deserters and thieves as they are. They are ready enough to find some pretext for their crime; and it needs as unjust a judge as the intendant to prompt such rascals to enter complaints against a person to whom he had given a warrant to arrest them. But, to show the falsity of these charges, Martin Chartier, who was one of those who excited the rest to do as they did, was never with me at all; and the rest had made their plot before seeing me." And he proceeds to relate, in great detail, a variety of circumstances to prove that his men had been instigated first to desert, and then to slander him; adding, "Those who remain with me are the first I had, and they have not left me for six years."

"I have a hundred other proofs of the bad counsel given to these deserters, and will produce them when wanted; but as they themselves are the only witnesses of the severity they complain of, while the witnesses of their crimes are unimpeachable, why am I refused the justice I demand, and why is their secret escape connived at?

"I do not know what you mean by having popular manners. There is nothing special in my food, clothing, or lodging, which are all the same for me as for my men. How can it be that I do not talk with them? I have no other company. M. de Tonty has often found fault with me because I stopped too often to talk with them. You do not know the men one must employ here, when you [Pg 338] exhort me to make merry with them. They are incapable of that; for they are never pleased, unless one gives free rein to their drunkenness and other vices. If that is what you call having popular manners, neither honor nor inclination would let me stoop to gain their favor in a way so disreputable: and, besides, the consequences would be dangerous, and they would have the same contempt for me that they have for all who treat them in this fashion.

"You write me that even my friends say that I am not a man of popular manners. I do not know what friends they are. I know of none in this country. To all appearance they are enemies, more subtle and secret than the rest. I make no exceptions; for I know that those who seem to give me support do not do it out of love for me, but because they are in some sort bound in honor, and that in their hearts they think I have dealt ill with them. M. Plct will tell you what he has heard about it himself, and the reasons they have to give.[260] I have seen it for a long time; and these secret stabs they give me show it very plainly. After that, it is not surprising that I open my mind to nobody, and distrust everybody. I have reasons that I cannot write.

"For the rest, Monsieur, pray be well assured that the information you are so good as to give me is [Pg 339] received with a gratitude equal to the genuine friendship from which it proceeds; and, however unjust are the charges made against me, I should be much more unjust myself if I did not feel that I have as much reason to thank you for telling me of them as I have to complain of others for inventing them.

HIS MANNERS.

"As for what you say about my look and manner, I myself confess that you are not far from right. But *naturam expellas*; and if I am wanting in expansiveness and show of feeling towards those with whom I associate, *it is only through a timidity which is natural to me, and which has made me leave various employments, where without it I could have succeeded*. But as I judged myself ill-fitted for them on account of this defect, I have chosen a life more suited to my solitary disposition; which, nevertheless, does not make me harsh to my people, though, joined to a life among savages, it makes me, perhaps, less polished and complaisant than the atmosphere of Paris requires. I well believe that there is self-love in this; and that, knowing how little I am accustomed to a more polite life, the fear of making mistakes makes me more reserved than I like to be. So I rarely expose myself to conversation with those in whose company I am afraid of making blunders, and can hardly help making them. Abbé Renaudot knows with what repugnance I had the honor to appear before Monseigneur de Conti; and sometimes it took me a week to make up my mind to go to the audience,—that is, when I had time to think about [Pg 340] myself, and was not driven by pressing business. It is much the same with letters, which I never write except when pushed to it, and for the same reason. It is a defect of which I shall never rid myself as long as I live, often as it spites me against myself, and often as I quarrel with myself about it."

HIS STRENGTH AND WEAKNESS.

Here is a strange confession for a man like La Salle. Without doubt, the timidity of which he accuses himself had some of its roots in pride; but not the less was his pride vexed and humbled by it. It is surprising that, being what he was, he could have brought himself to such an avowal under any circumstances or any pressure of distress. Shyness; a morbid fear of committing himself; and incapacity to express, and much more to simulate, feeling,—a trait sometimes seen in those with whom feeling is most deep,—are strange ingredients in the character of a man who had grappled so dauntlessly with life on its harshest and rudest side. They were deplorable defects for one in his position. He lacked that sympathetic power, the inestimable gift of the true leader of men, in which lies the difference between a willing and a constrained obedience. This solitary being, hiding his shyness under a cold reserve, could rouse no enthusiasm in his followers. He lived in the purpose which he had made a part of himself, nursed his plans in secret, and seldom asked or accepted advice. He trusted himself, and learned more and more to trust no others. One may fairly infer that distrust was natural to him; but the [Pg 341] inference may possibly be wrong. Bitter experience had schooled him to it; for he lived among snares, pitfalls, and intriguing enemies. He began to doubt even the associates who, under representations he had made them in perfect good faith, had staked their money on his enterprise, and lost it, or were likely to lose it. They pursued him with advice and complaint, and half believed that he was what his maligners called him,—a visionary or a madman. It galled him that they had suffered for their trust in him, and that they had repented their trust. His lonely and shadowed nature needed the mellowing sunshine of success, and his whole life was a fight with adversity.

All that appears to the eye is his intrepid conflict with obstacles without; but this, perhaps, was no more arduous than the invisible and silent strife of a nature at war with itself,—the pride, aspiration, and bold energy that lay at the base of his character battling against the superficial weakness that mortified and angered him. In such a man, the effect of such an infirmity is to concentrate and intensify the force within. In one form or another, discordant natures are common enough; but very rarely is the antagonism so irreconcilable as it was in him. And the greater the antagonism, the greater the pain. There are those in whom the sort of timidity from which he suffered is matched with no quality that strongly revolts against it. These gentle natures may at least have peace, but for him there was no peace.

[Pg 342]

Cavelier de La Salle stands in history like a statue cast in iron; but his own unwilling pen betrays the man, and reveals in the stern, sad figure an object of human interest and pity.[261]

FOOTNOTES:

[260] His cousin, François Plet, was in Canada in 1680, where, with La Salle's approval, he carried on the trade of Fort Frontenac, in order to indemnify himself for money advanced. La Salle always speaks of him with esteem and gratitude.

[261] The following is the character of La Salle, as drawn by his friend, Abbé Bernou, in a memorial to the minister Seignelay: "Il est irréprochable dans ses mœurs, réglé dans sa conduite, et qui veut de l'ordre parmy ses gens. Il est savant, judicieux, politique, vigilant, infatigable, sobre, et intrépide. Il entend suffisament l'architecture civile, militaire, et navale ainsy que l'agriculture; il parle ou entend quatre ou cinq langues des Sauvages, et a beaucoup de facilité pour apprendre les autres. Il sçait toutes leurs manières et obtient d'eux tout ce qu'il veut par son adresse, par son éloquence, et parce qu'il est beaucoup estimé d'eux. Dans ses voyages il ne fait pas meilleure chère que le moindre de ses gens et se donne plus de peine que pas un pour les encourager, et il y a lieu de croire qu'avec la protection de Monseigneur il fondera des colonies plus considérables que toutes celles que les François ont établies jusqu'à présent."—*Mémoire pour Monseigneur le Marquis de Seignelay*, 1682 (Margry, ii. 277).

The extracts given in the foregoing chapter are from La Salle's long letters of 29 Sept., 1680, and 22 Aug., 1682 (1681?). Both are printed in the second volume of the Margry collection, and the originals of both are in the Bibliothèque Nationale. The latter seems to have been written to La Salle's friend, Abbé Bernou; and the former, to a certain M. Thouret.

CHAPTER XXIII.

1684.

A NEW ENTERPRISE.

La Salle at Court: his Proposals.—Occupation of Louisiana.—Invasion of Mexico.—Royal Favor.—Preparation.—A Divided Command.—Beaujeu and La Salle.—Mental Condition of La Salle: his Farewell to his Mother.

When La Salle reached Paris, he went to his old lodgings in Rue de la Truanderie, and, it is likely enough, thought for an instant of the adventures and vicissitudes he had passed since he occupied them before. Another ordeal awaited him. He must confront, not painted savages with tomahawk and knife, but—what he shrank from more—the courtly throngs that still live and move in the pages of Sévigné and Saint-Simon.

The news of his discovery and the rumor of his schemes were the talk of a moment among the courtiers, and then were forgotten. It was not so with their master. La Salle's friends and patrons did not fail him. A student and a recluse in his youth, and a backwoodsman in his manhood, he had what was to him the formidable honor of an interview with royalty itself, and stood with such philosophy [Pg 344] as he could command before the gilded arm-chair, where, majestic and awful, the power of France sat embodied. The King listened to all he said; but the results of the interview were kept so secret that it was rumored in the ante-chambers that his proposals had been rejected.[262]

On the contrary, they had met with more than favor. The moment was opportune for La Salle. The King had long been irritated against the Spaniards, because they not only excluded his subjects from their American ports, but forbade them to enter the Gulf of Mexico. Certain Frenchmen who had sailed on this forbidden sea had been seized and imprisoned; and more recently a small vessel of the royal navy had been captured for the same offence. This had drawn from the King a declaration that every sea should be free to all his subjects; and Count d'Estrées was sent with a squadron to the Gulf, to exact satisfaction of the Spaniards, or fight them if they refused it.[263] This was in time of peace. War had since arisen between the two crowns, and brought with it the opportunity of settling the question forever. In order to do so, the minister Seignelay, like his father Colbert, proposed to establish a French port on the Gulf, as a permanent menace to the Spaniards and a basis of future [Pg 345] conquest. It was in view of this plan that La Salle's past enterprises had been favored; and the proposals he now made were in perfect accord with it.

LA SALLE'S PROPOSALS.

These proposals were set forth in two memorials. The first of them states that the late Monseigneur Colbert deemed it important for the service of his Majesty to discover a port in the Gulf of Mexico; that to this end the memorialist, La Salle, made five journeys of upwards of five thousand leagues, in great part on foot; and traversed more than six hundred leagues of unknown country, among savages and cannibals, at the cost of a hundred and fifty thousand francs. He now proposes to return by way of the Gulf of Mexico and the mouth of the Mississippi to the countries he has discovered, whence great benefits may be expected: first, the cause of God may be advanced by the preaching of the gospel to many Indian tribes; and, secondly, great conquests may be effected for the glory of the King, by the seizure of provinces rich in silver mines, and defended only by a few indolent and effeminate Spaniards. The Sieur de la Salle, pursues the memorial, binds himself to be ready for the accomplishment of this enterprise within one year after his arrival on the spot; and he asks for this purpose only one vessel and two hundred men, with their arms, munitions, pay, and maintenance. When Monseigneur shall direct him, he will give the details of what he proposes. The memorial then describes the boundless extent, the fertility and [Pg 346] resources of the country watered by the river Colbert, or Mississippi; the necessity of guarding it against foreigners, who will be eager to seize it now that La Salle's discovery has made it known; and the ease with which it may be defended by one or two forts at a proper distance above its mouth, which would form the key to an interior region eight hundred leagues in extent. "Should foreigners anticipate us," he adds, "they will complete the ruin of New France, which they already hem in by their establishments of Virginia, Pennsylvania, New England, and Hudson's Bay."[264]

The second memorial is more explicit. The place, it says, which the Sieur de la Salle proposes to fortify, is on the river Colbert, or Mississippi, sixty leagues above its mouth, where the soil is very fertile, the climate very mild, and whence we, the French, may control the continent,—since, the river being narrow, we could defend ourselves by means of fire-ships against a hostile fleet, while the position is excellent both for attacking an enemy or retreating in case of need. The neighboring Indians detest the Spaniards, but love the French, having been won over by the kindness of the Sieur de la Salle. We could form of them an army of more than fifteen thousand savages, who, supported by the French and Abenakis, followers of the Sieur de la Salle, could easily subdue the province of New Biscay (the most northern province of Mexico), where there are but [Pg 347] four hundred Spaniards, more fit to work the mines than to fight. On the north of New Biscay lie vast forests, extending to the river Seignelay[265] (Red River), which is but forty or fifty leagues from the Spanish province. This river affords the means of attacking it to great advantage.

In view of these facts, pursues the memorial, the Sieur de la Salle offers, if the war with Spain continues, to undertake this conquest with two hundred men from France. He will take on his way fifty buccaneers at St. Domingo, and direct the four thousand Indian warriors at Fort St. Louis of the Illinois to descend the river and join him. He will separate his force into three divisions, and attack at the same time the centre and the two extremities of the province. To accomplish this great design, he asks only for a vessel of thirty guns, a few cannon for the forts, and power to raise in France two hundred such men as he shall think fit, to be armed, paid, and maintained six

months at the King's charge. And the Sieur de la Salle binds himself,
if the execution of this plan is prevented for more than three years,
by peace with Spain, to refund to his Majesty all the costs of the
enterprise, on pain of forfeiting the government of the ports he will
have established.[266]

[Pg 348]

LA SALLES'S PLANS.

Such, in brief, was the substance of this singular proposition. And,
first, it is to be observed that it is based on a geographical blunder,
the nature of which is explained by the map of La Salle's discoveries
made in this very year. Here the river Seignelay, or Red River, is
represented as running parallel to the northern border of Mexico,
and at no great distance from it,—the region now called Texas being
almost entirely suppressed. According to the map, New Biscay
might be reached from this river in a few days; and, after crossing
the intervening forests, the coveted mines of Ste. Barbe, or Santa
Barbara, would be within striking distance.[267] That La Salle
believed in the possibility of invading the Spanish province of New
Biscay from Red River there can be no doubt; neither can it
reasonably be doubted that he hoped at some future day to make the
attempt; and yet it is incredible that a man in his sober senses could
have proposed this scheme with the intention of attempting to
execute it at the time and in the manner which he indicates.[268] This
memorial bears [Pg 349] some indications of being drawn up in order
to produce a certain effect on the minds of the King and his minister.
La Salle's immediate necessity was to obtain from them the means
for establishing a fort and a colony within the mouth of the
Mississippi. This was essential to his own plans; nor did he in the
least exaggerate the value of such an establishment to the French
nation, and the importance of anticipating other powers in the
possession of it. But he thought that he needed a more glittering lure
to attract the eyes of Louis and Seignelay; and thus, it may be, he
held before them, in a definite and tangible form, the project of

Spanish conquest which had haunted his imagination from youth,— trusting that the speedy conclusion of peace, which actually took place, would absolve him from the immediate execution of the scheme, and give him time, with the means placed at his disposal, to mature his plans and prepare for eventual action. Such a procedure may be charged with indirectness; but there is a different explanation, which we shall suggest hereafter, and which implies no such reproach.[269]

[Pg 350]

Even with this madcap enterprise lopped off, La Salle's scheme of Mississippi trade and colonization, perfectly sound in itself, was too vast for an individual,—above all, for one crippled and crushed with debt. While he grasped one link of the great chain, another, no less essential, escaped from his hand; while he built up a colony on the Mississippi, it was reasonably certain that evil would befall his distant colony of the Illinois.

LA BARRE REBUKED.

The glittering project which he now unfolded found favor in the eyes of the King and his minister; for both were in the flush of an unparalleled success, and looked in the future, as in the past, for nothing but triumphs. They granted more than the petitioner asked, as indeed they well might, if they expected the accomplishment of all that he proposed [Pg 351] to attempt. La Forest, La Salle's lieutenant, ejected from Fort Frontenac by La Barre, was now at Paris; and he was despatched to Canada, empowered to reoccupy, in La Salle's name, both Fort Frontenac and Fort St. Louis of the Illinois. The King himself wrote to La Barre in a strain that must have sent a cold thrill through the veins of that official. "I hear," he says, "that you have taken possession of Fort Frontenac, the property of the Sieur de la Salle, driven away his men, suffered his land to run to waste, and even told the Iroquois that they might seize him as an enemy of the colony." He adds, that, if this is true, La Barre must make reparation for the wrong, and place all La Salle's property, as well as his men, in the hands of the Sieur de la Forest, "as I am satisfied that Fort Frontenac was not abandoned, as you wrote to me that it had been."[270] Four days later, he wrote to the intendant of Canada, De Meules, to the effect that the bearer, La Forest, is to suffer no impediment, and that La Barre is to surrender to him without reserve all that belongs to La Salle.[271] Armed with this letter, La Forest sailed for Canada.[272]

[Pg 352]

A chief object of his mission, as it was represented to Seignelay, was, not only to save the colony at the Illinois from being broken up by La Barre, but also to collect La Salle's scattered followers, muster the savage warriors around the rock of St. Louis, and lead the whole down the Mississippi, to co-operate in the attack on New Biscay. If La Salle meant that La Forest should seriously attempt to execute such a scheme, then the charges of his enemies that his brain was turned were better founded than he would have us think.[273]

PREPARATION.

He had asked for two vessels,[274] and four were given to him. Agents were sent to Rochelle and Rochefort to gather recruits. A hundred soldiers were enrolled, besides mechanics and laborers; and thirty volunteers, [Pg 353] including gentlemen and burghers of condition, joined the expedition. And, as the plan was one no less of colonization than of war, several families embarked for the new land of promise, as well as a number of girls, lured by the prospect of almost certain matrimony. Nor were missionaries wanting. Among them was La Salle's brother, Cavelier, and two other priests of St. Sulpice. Three Récollets were added,—Zenobe Membré, who was then in France, Anastase Douay, and Maxime Le Clerc. The principal vessel was the "Joly," belonging to the royal navy, and carrying thirty-six guns. Another armed vessel of six guns was added, together with a store-ship and a ketch.

La Salle had asked for sole command of the expedition, with a subaltern officer, and one or two pilots to sail the vessels as he should direct. Instead of complying, Seignelay gave the command of the vessels to Beaujeu, a captain of the royal navy,—whose authority was restricted to their management at sea, while La Salle was to prescribe the route they were to take, and have entire control of the troops and colonists on land.[275] This arrangement displeased both parties. Beaujeu, an old and experienced officer, was galled that a civilian should be set over him,—and he, too, a burgher lately ennobled; nor was La Salle the man to soothe his ruffled spirit. Detesting a divided command, cold, reserved, and [Pg 354] impenetrable, he would have tried the patience of a less excitable colleague. Beaujeu, on his part, though set to a task which he disliked, seems to have meant to do his duty, and to have been willing at the outset to make the relations between himself and his unwelcome associate as agreeable as possible. Unluckily, La Salle discovered that the wife of Beaujeu was devoted to the Jesuits. We have seen the extreme distrust with which he regarded these guides of his youth, and he seems now to have fancied that Beaujeu was their secret ally. Possibly, he suspected that information of his movements would be given to the Spaniards; more probably, he had undefined fears of adverse machinations. Granting that such existed, it was not his interest to stimulate them by needlessly exasperating the naval commander. His deportment, however, was not conciliating; and Beaujeu, prepared to dislike him, presently lost temper. While the vessels still lay at Rochelle; while all was bustle and preparation; while stores, arms, and munitions were embarking; while boys and vagabonds were enlisting as soldiers for the expedition,—Beaujeu was venting his disgust in long letters to the minister.

BEAUJEU AND LA SALLE.

"You have ordered me, Monseigneur, to give all possible aid to this undertaking, and I shall do so to the best of my power; but permit me to take great credit to myself, for I find it very hard to submit to the orders of the Sieur de la Salle, whom I believe to be a man of merit, but who has no experience of [Pg 355] war except with savages, and who has no rank, while I have been captain of a ship thirteen years, and have served thirty by sea and land. Besides, Monseigneur, he has told me that in case of his death you have directed that the Sieur de Tonty shall succeed him. This, indeed, is very hard; for, though I am not acquainted with that country, I should be very dull, if, being on the spot, I did not know at the end of a month as much of it as they do. I beg, Monseigneur, that I may at least share the command with them; and that, as regards war, nothing may be done without my knowledge and concurrence,—for, as to their commerce, I neither intend nor desire to know anything about it."

Seignelay answered by a rebuff, and told him to make no trouble about the command. This increased his irritation, and he wrote: "In my last letter, Monseigneur, I represented to you the hardship of compelling me to obey M. de la Salle, who has no rank, and *never commanded anybody but school-boys*; and I begged you at least to divide the command between us. I now, Monseigneur, take the liberty to say that I will obey without repugnance, if you order me to do so, having reflected that there can be no competition between the said Sieur de la Salle and me.

"Thus far, he has not told me his plan; and he changes his mind every moment. He is a man so suspicious, and so afraid that one will penetrate his secrets, that I dare not ask him anything. He says [Pg 356] that M. de Parassy, commissary's clerk, with whom he has often quarrelled, is paid by his enemies to defeat his undertaking; and many other things with which I will not trouble you....

"He pretends that I am only to command the sailors, and have no authority over the volunteer officers and the hundred soldiers who are to take passage in the 'Joly;' and that they are not to recognize or obey me in any way during the voyage....

"He has covered the decks with boxes and chests of such prodigious size that neither the cannon nor the capstan can be worked."

La Salle drew up a long list of articles, defining the respective rights and functions of himself and Beaujeu, to whom he presented it for signature. Beaujeu demurred at certain military honors demanded by La Salle, saying that if a marshal of France should come on board his ship, he would have none left to offer him. The point was referred to the naval intendant; and the articles of the treaty having been slightly modified, Beaujeu set his name to it. "By this," he says, "you can judge better of the character of M. de la Salle than by all I can say. He is a man who wants smoke [form and ceremony]. I will give him his fill of it, and, perhaps, more than he likes.

"I am bound to an unknown country, to seek what is about as hard to find as the philosopher's stone. It vexes me, Monseigneur, that you should [Pg 357] have been involved in a business the success of which is very uncertain. M. de la Salle begins to doubt it himself."

While Beaujeu wrote thus to the minister, he was also writing to Cabart de Villermont, one of his friends at Paris, with whom La Salle was also on friendly terms. These letters are lively and entertaining, and by no means suggestive of any secret conspiracy. He might, it is true, have been more reserved in his communications; but he betrays no confidence, for none was placed in him. It is the familiar correspondence of an irritable but not ill-natured veteran, who is placed in an annoying position, and thinks he is making the best of it.

La Salle thought that the minister had been too free in communicating the secrets of the expedition to the naval intendant at Rochefort, and through him to Beaujeu. It is hard to see how Beaujeu was to blame for this; but La Salle nevertheless fell into a dispute with him. "He could hardly keep his temper, and used expressions which obliged me to tell him that I cared very little about his affairs, and that the King himself would not speak as he did. He retracted, made excuses, and we parted good friends....

"I do not like his suspiciousness. I think him a good, honest Norman; but Normans are out of fashion. It is one thing to-day, another to-morrow. It seems to me that he is not so sure about his undertaking as he was at Paris. This morning he [Pg 358] came to see me, and told me he had changed his mind, and meant to give a new turn to the business, and go to another coast. He gave very poor reasons, to which I assented, to avoid a quarrel. I thought, by what he said, that he wanted to find a scapegoat to bear the blame, in case his plan does not succeed as he hopes. For the rest, I think him a brave man and a true; and I am persuaded that if this business fails, it will be because he does not know enough, and will not trust us of the profession. As for me, I shall do my best to help him, as I have told you before; and I am delighted to have him keep his secret, so that I shall not have to answer for the result. Pray do not show my letters, for fear of committing me with him. He is too suspicious already; and never was Norman so Norman as he, which is a great hinderance to business."

Beaujeu came from the same province and calls himself jocularly *un bon gros Normand*. His good-nature, however, rapidly gave way as time went on. "Yesterday," he writes, "this Monsieur told me that he meant to go to the Gulf of Mexico. A little while ago, as I said before, he talked about going to Canada. I see nothing certain in it. It is not that I do not believe that all he says is true; but not being of the profession, and not liking to betray his ignorance, he is puzzled what to do.

"I shall go straight forward, without regarding a thousand whims and *bagatelles*. His continual suspicion would drive anybody mad except a Norman [Pg 359] like me; but I shall humor him, as I have always done, even to sailing my ship on dry land, if he likes."

AN OPEN QUARREL.

A few days later, there was an open quarrel. "M. de la Salle came to me, and said, rather haughtily and in a tone of command, that I must put provisions for three months more on board my vessel. I told him it was impossible, as she had more lading already than anybody ever dared to put in her before. He would not hear reason, but got angry and abused me in good French, and found fault with me because the vessel would not hold his three months' provisions. He said I ought to have told him of it before. 'And how would you have me tell you,' said I, 'when you never tell me what you mean to do?' We had still another quarrel. He asked me where his officers should take their meals. I told him that they might take them where he pleased; for I gave myself no trouble in the matter, having no orders. He answered that they should not mess on bacon, while the rest ate fowls and mutton. I said that if he would send fowls and mutton on board, his people should eat them; but, as for bacon, I had often ate it myself. At this, he went off and complained to M. Dugué that I refused to embark his provisions, and told him that he must live on bacon. I excused him as not knowing how to behave himself, having spent his life among school-boy brats and savages. Nevertheless, I offered to him, his brother, and two of his friends, seats at my table and [Pg 360] the same fare as myself. He answered my civility by an impertinence, saying that he distrusted people who offered so much and seemed so obliging. I could not help telling him that I saw he was brought up in the provinces."

This was touching La Salle on a sensitive point. Beaujeu continues: "In fact, you knew him better than I; for I always took him for a gentleman (*honnête homme*). I see now that he is anything but that. Pray set Abbé Renaudot and M. Morel right about this man, and tell them he is not what they take him for. Adieu. It has struck twelve: the postman is just going."

Bad as was the state of things, it soon grew worse. Renaudot wrote to La Salle that Beaujeu was writing to Villermont everything that happened, and that Villermont showed the letters to all his acquaintance. Villermont was a relative of the Jesuit Beschefer; and this was sufficient to suggest some secret machination to the mind of La Salle. Villermont's fault, however, seems to have been simple indiscretion, for which Beaujeu took him sharply to task. "I asked you to burn my letters; and I cannot help saying that I am angry with you, not because you make known my secrets, but because you show letters scrawled in haste, and sent off without being even read over. M. de la Salle not having told me his secret, though M. de Seignelay ordered him to tell me, I am not obliged to keep it, and have as good a right as anybody to make my [Pg 361] conjectures on what I read about it in the *Gazette de Hollande*. Let Abbé Renaudot glorify M. de la Salle as much as he likes, and make him a Cortez, a Pizarro, or an Almagro,—that is nothing to me; but do not let him speak of me as an obstacle in his hero's way. Let him understand that I know how to execute the orders of the court as well as he....

LA SALLE'S INDISCRETION.

"You ask how I get on with M. de la Salle. Don't you know that this man is impenetrable, and that there is no knowing what he thinks of one? He told a person of note whom I will not name that he had suspicions about our correspondence, as well as about Madame de Beaujeu's devotion to the Jesuits. His distrust is incredible. If he sees one of his people speak to the rest, he suspects something, and is gruff with them. He told me himself that he wanted to get rid of M. de Tonty, who is in America."

La Salle's claim to exclusive command of the soldiers on board the "Joly" was a source of endless trouble. Beaujeu declared that he would not set sail till officers, soldiers, and volunteers had all sworn to obey him when at sea; at which La Salle had the indiscretion to say, "If I am not master of my soldiers, how can I make him [Beaujeu] do his duty in case he does not want to do it?"

Beaujeu says that this affair made a great noise among the officers at Rochefort, and adds: "*There are very few people who do not think that his brain is touched. I have spoken to some who have known* [Pg 362] *him twenty years. They all say that he was always rather visionary.*"

It is difficult not to suspect that the current belief at Rochefort had some foundation; and that the deadly strain of extreme hardship, prolonged anxiety, and alternation of disaster and success, joined to the fever which nearly killed him, had unsettled his judgment and given a morbid development to his natural defects. His universal suspicion, which included even the stanch and faithful Henri de Tonty; his needless provocation of persons whose good-will was necessary to him; his doubts whether he should sail for the Gulf or for Canada, when to sail to Canada would have been to renounce, or expose to almost certain defeat, an enterprise long cherished and definitely planned,—all point to one conclusion. It may be thought that his doubts were feigned, in order to hide his destination to the last moment; but if so, he attempted to blind not only his ill wishers, but his mother, whom he also left in uncertainty as to his route.

AN OVERWROUGHT BRAIN.

Unless we assume that his scheme of invading Mexico was thrown out as a bait to the King, it is hard to reconcile it with the supposition of mental soundness. To base so critical an attempt on a geographical conjecture, which rested on the slightest possible information, and was in fact a total error; to postpone the perfectly sound plan of securing the mouth of the Mississippi, to a wild project of leading fifteen thousand savages for an unknown distance [Pg 363] through an unknown country to attack an unknown enemy,—was something more than Quixotic daring. The King and the minister saw nothing impracticable in it, for they did not know the country or its inhabitants. They saw no insuperable difficulty in mustering and keeping together fifteen thousand of the most wayward and unstable savages on earth, split into a score and more of tribes, some hostile to each other and some to the French; nor in the problem of feeding such a mob, on a march of hundreds of miles; nor in the plan of drawing four thousand of them from the Illinois, nearly two thousand miles distant, though some of these intended allies had no canoes or other means of transportation, and though, travelling in such numbers, they would infallibly starve on the way to the rendezvous. It is difficult not to see in all this the chimera of an overwrought brain, no longer able to distinguish between the possible and the impossible.

Preparation dragged slowly on; the season was growing late; the King grew impatient, and found fault with the naval intendant. Meanwhile, the various members of the expedition had all gathered at Rochelle. Joutel, a fellow-townsman of La Salle, returning to his native Rouen, after sixteen years in the army, found all astir with the new project. His father had been gardener to Henri Cavelier, La Salle's uncle; and being of an adventurous spirit he volunteered for the enterprise, of which he was to become the historian. With La Salle's brother the [Pg 364] priest, and two of his nephews, one of whom was a boy of fourteen, Joutel set out for Rochelle, where all were to embark together for their promised land.[276]

A PARTING LETTER

La Salle wrote a parting letter to his mother at Rouen:—

ROCHELLE,   18   July,   1684.
MADAME MY MOST HONORED MOTHER,—

At last, after having waited a long time for a favourable wind, and having had a great many difficulties to overcome, we are setting sail with four vessels, and nearly four hundred men on board. Everybody is well, including little Colin and my nephew. We all have good hope of a happy success. We are not going by way of Canada, but by the Gulf of Mexico. I passionately wish, and so do we all, that the success of this voyage may contribute to your repose and comfort. Assuredly, I shall spare no effort that it may; and I beg you, on your part, to preserve yourself for the love of us.

You need not be troubled by the news from Canada, which are nothing but the continuation of the artifices of my enemies. I hope to be as successful against them as I have been thus far, and to embrace you a year hence with all the pleasure that the most grateful of children can feel with so good a mother as you have always been. Pray let this hope, which shall not disappoint you, support you through whatever trials may happen, and be sure that you will always find me with a heart full of the feelings which are due to you. [Pg 365] Madame my Most Honored Mother, from your most humble and most obedient servant and son, DE LA SALLE.

My brother, my nephews, and all the others greet you, and take their leave of you.

This memorable last farewell has lain for two hundred years among the family papers of the Caveliers.[277]

FOOTNOTES:

[262] *Lettres de l'Abbé Tronson, 8 Avril, 10 Avril, 1684* (Margry, ii. 354).
[263] *Lettres du Roy et du Ministre sur la Navigation du Golfe du Mexique, 1669-1682* (Margry, iii. 3-14).
[264] *Mémoire du Sr de la Salle, pour rendre compte à Monseigneur de Seignelay de la découverte qu'il a faite par l'ordre de sa Majesté.*
[265] This name, also given to the Illinois, is used to designate Red River on the map of Franquelin, where the forests above mentioned are represented.
[266]] *Mémoire du Sr de la Salle sur l'Entreprise qu'il a proposé à Monseigneur le Marquis de Seignelay sur une des provinces de Mexique.*
[267] Both the memorial and the map represent the banks of Red River as inhabited by Indians, called Terliquiquimechi, and known to the Spaniards as *Indios bravos*, or *Indios de guerra*. The Spaniards, it is added, were in great fear of them, as they made frequent inroads into Mexico. La Salle's Mexican geography was in all respects confused and erroneous; nor was Seignelay better informed. Indeed, Spanish jealousy placed correct information beyond their reach.
[268] While the plan, as proposed in the memorial, was clearly impracticable, the subsequent experience of the French in Texas tended to prove that the tribes of that region could be used with advantage in attacking the Spaniards of Mexico, and that an inroad on a comparatively small scale might have been successfully made with their help. In 1689, Tonty actually made the attempt, as we shall see, but failed, from the desertion of his men. In 1697, the Sieur de Louvigny wrote to the Minister

of the Marine, asking to complete La Salle's discoveries, and invade Mexico from Texas. (*Lettre de M. de Louvigny, 14 Oct., 1697.*) In an unpublished memoir of the year 1700, the seizure of the Mexican mines is given as one of the motives of the colonization of Louisiana.

[269] Another scheme, with similar aims, but much more practicable, was at this very time before the court. Count Peñalossa, a Spanish Creole, born in Peru, had been governor of New Mexico, where he fell into a dispute with the Inquisition, which involved him in the loss of property, and for a time of liberty. Failing to obtain redress in Spain, he renounced his allegiance in disgust, and sought refuge in France, where, in 1682, he first proposed to the King the establishment of a colony of French buccaneers at the mouth of Rio Bravo, on the Gulf of Mexico. In January, 1684, after the war had broken out, he proposed to attack the Spanish town of Panuco, with twelve hundred buccaneers from St. Domingo; then march into the interior, seize the mines, conquer Durango, and occupy New Mexico. It was proposed to combine his plan with that of La Salle; but the latter, who had an interview with him, expressed distrust, and showed characteristic reluctance to accept a colleague. It is extremely probable, however, that his knowledge of Peñalossa's original proposal had some influence in stimulating him to lay before the court proposals of his own, equally attractive. Peace was concluded before the plans of the Spanish adventurer could be carried into effect.

[270] *Lettre du Roy à La Barre, Versailles, 10 Avril, 1684.*

[271] *Lettre du Roy à De Meules, Versailles, 14 Avril, 1684.* Seignelay wrote to De Meules to the same effect.

[272] On La Forest's mission,—*Mémoire pour representer à Monseigneur le Marquis de Seignelay la nécessité d'envoyer le Sr de la Forest en diligence à la Nouvelle France; Lettre du Roy à La Barre, 14 Avril, 1684; Ibid., 31 Oct., 1684.*

There is before me a promissory note of La Salle to La Forest, of 5,200 livres, dated at Rochelle, 17 July, 1684. This seems to be pay due to La Forest, who had served as La Salle's officer for nine years. A memorandum is attached, signed by La Salle, to the effect that it is his wish that La Forest reimburse himself, "*par préférence*," out of any property of his (La Salle's) in France or Canada.

[273] The attitude of La Salle, in this matter, is incomprehensible. In July, La Forest was at Rochefort, complaining because La Salle had ordered

him to stay in garrison at Fort Frontenac. *Beaujeu à Villermont, 10 July, 1684.* This means an abandonment of the scheme of leading the warriors at the rock of St. Louis down the Mississippi; but, in the next month, La Salle writes to Seignelay that he is afraid La Barre will use the Iroquois war as a pretext to prevent La Forest from making his journey (to the Illinois), and that in this case he will himself try to go up the Mississippi, and meet the Illinois warriors; so that, in five or six months from the date of the letter, the minister will hear of his departure to attack the Spaniards. (*La Salle à Seignelay, Août, 1684.*) Either this is sheer folly, or else it is meant to delude the minister.

[274] *Mémoire de ce qui aura esté accordé au Sieur de la Salle.*

[275] *Lettre au Roy à La Salle, 12 Avril, 1684; Mémoire pour servir d'Instruction au Sieur de Beaujeu, 14 Avril, 1684.*

[276] Joutel, *Journal Historique*, 12.

[277] The letters of Beaujeu to Seignelay and to Cabart de Villermont, with most of the other papers on which this chapter rests, will be found in Margry, ii. 354-471. This indefatigable investigator has also brought to light a number of letters from a brother officer of Beaujeu, Machaut-Rougemont, written at Rochefort, just after the departure of the expedition from Rochelle, and giving some idea of the views there entertained concerning it. He says: "L'on ne peut pas faire plus d'extravagances que le Sieur de la Salle n'en a fait sur toutes ses prétentions de commandement. Je plains beaucoup le pauvre Beaujeu d'avoir affaire à une humeur si saturnienne.... Je le croy beaucoup visionnaire ... Beaujeu a une sotte commission."

[Pg 366]

CHAPTER XXIV.

1684, 1685.

THE VOYAGE.

THE four ships sailed from Rochelle on the twenty-fourth of July. Four days after, the "Joly" broke her bowsprit, by design as La Salle fancied. They all put back to Rochefort, where the mischief was quickly repaired; and they put to sea again. La Salle, and the chief persons of the expedition, with a crowd of soldiers, artisans, and women, the destined mothers of Louisiana, were all on board the "Joly." Beaujeu wished to touch at Madeira, to replenish his water-casks. La Salle refused, lest by doing so the secret of the enterprise might reach the Spaniards. One Paget, a Huguenot, took up the word in support of Beaujeu. La Salle told him that the affair was none of his; and as Paget persisted with increased warmth and freedom, he demanded of Beaujeu if it was with his consent that a man of no rank spoke to him in that manner. Beaujeu sustained [Pg 367] the Huguenot. "That is enough," returned La Salle, and withdrew into his cabin.[278]

This was not the first misunderstanding; nor was it the last. There was incessant chafing between the two commanders; and the sailors of the "Joly" were soon of one mind with their captain. When the ship crossed the tropic, they made ready a tub on deck to baptize the passengers, after the villanous practice of the time; but La Salle refused to permit it, at which they were highly exasperated, having promised themselves a bountiful ransom, in money or liquor, from their victims. "Assuredly," says Joutel, "they would gladly have killed us all."

ST. DOMINGO.

When, after a wretched voyage of two months the ships reached St. Domingo, a fresh dispute occurred. It had been resolved at a council of officers to stop at Port de Paix; but Beaujeu, on pretext of a fair wind, ran by that place in the night, and cast anchor at Petit Goave, on the other side of the island. La Salle was extremely vexed; for he expected to meet at Port de Paix the Marquis de Saint-Laurent, lieutenant-general of the islands, Bégon the intendant, and De Cussy, governor of La Tortue, who had orders to supply him with provisions and give him all possible aid.

The "Joly" was alone: the other vessels had lagged behind. She had more than fifty sick men on [Pg 368] board, and La Salle was of the number. He sent a messenger to Saint-Laurent, Bégon, and Cussy, begging them to come to him; ordered Joutel to get the sick ashore, suffocating as they were in the hot and crowded ship; and caused the soldiers to be landed on a small island in the harbor. Scarcely had the voyagers sung *Te Deum* for their safe arrival, when two of the lagging vessels appeared, bringing tidings that the third, the ketch "St. François," had been taken by Spanish buccaneers. She was laden with provisions, tools, and other necessaries for the colony; and the loss was irreparable. Beaujeu was answerable for it; for had he anchored at Port de Paix, it would not have occurred. The lieutenant-general, with Bégon and Cussy, who presently arrived, plainly spoke their minds to him.[279]

ILLNESS OF LA SALLE.

La Salle's illness increased. "I was walking with him one day," writes Joutel, "when he was seized of a sudden with such a weakness that he could not stand, and was obliged to lie down on the ground. When he was a little better, I led him to a chamber of a house that the brothers Duhaut had hired. Here we put him to bed, and in the morning he was attacked by a violent fever."[280] "It was so violent that," says another of his shipmates, "his imagination pictured to him things equally terrible and amazing."[281] He lay delirious in the wretched garret, [Pg 369] attended by his brother, and one or two others who stood faithful to him. A goldsmith of the neighborhood, moved at his deplorable condition, offered the use of his house; and Abbé Cavelier had him removed thither. But there was a tavern hard by, and the patient was tormented with daily and nightly riot. At the height of the fever, a party of Beaujeu's sailors spent a night in singing and dancing before the house; and, says Cavelier, "The more we begged them to be quiet, the more noise they made." La Salle lost reason and well-nigh life; but at length his mind resumed its balance, and the violence of the disease abated. A friendly Capucin friar offered him the shelter of his roof; and two of his men supported him thither on foot, giddy with exhaustion and hot with fever. Here he found repose, and was slowly recovering, when some of his attendants rashly told him the loss of the ketch "St. François;" and the consequence was a critical return of the disease.[282]

There was no one to fill his place. Beaujeu would not; Cavelier could not. Joutel, the gardener's son, was apparently the most trusty man of the company; but the expedition was virtually without a head. The men roamed on shore, and plunged into every excess of debauchery, contracting diseases which eventually killed them.

COMPLAINTS OF BEAUJEU.

Beaujeu, in the extremity of ill-humor, resumed [Pg 370] his correspondence with Seignelay. "But for the illness of the Sieur de la Salle," he writes, "I could not venture to report to you the progress of our voyage, as I am charged only with the navigation, and he with the secrets; but as his malady has deprived him of the use of his faculties, both of body and mind, I have thought myself obliged to acquaint you with what is passing, and of the condition in which we are."

He then declares that the ships freighted by La Salle were so slow that the "Joly" had continually been forced to wait for them, thus doubling the length of the voyage; that he had not had water enough for the passengers, as La Salle had not told him that there were to be any such till the day they came on board; that great numbers were sick, and that he had told La Salle there would be trouble if he filled all the space between decks with his goods, and forced the soldiers and sailors to sleep on deck; that he had told him he would get no provisions at St. Domingo, but that he insisted on stopping; that it had always been so,—that whatever he proposed La Salle would refuse, alleging orders from the King; "and now," pursues the ruffled commander, "everybody is ill; and he himself has a violent fever, as dangerous, the surgeon tells me, to the mind as to the body."

The rest of the letter is in the same strain. He says that a day or two after La Salle's illness began, his brother Cavelier came to ask him to take charge [Pg 371] of his affairs; but that he did not wish to meddle with them, especially as nobody knows anything about them, and as La Salle has sold some of the ammunition and provisions; that Cavelier tells him that he thinks his brother keeps no accounts, wishing to hide his affairs from everybody; that he learns from buccaneers that the entrance of the Mississippi is very shallow and difficult, and that this is the worst season for navigating the Gulf; that the Spaniards have in these seas six vessels of from thirty to sixty guns each, besides row-galleys; but that he is not afraid, and will perish, or bring back an account of the Mississippi. "Nevertheless," he adds, "if the Sieur de la Salle dies, I shall pursue a course different from that which he has marked out; for I do not approve his plans."

"If," he continues, "you permit me to speak my mind, M. de la Salle ought to have been satisfied with discovering his river, without undertaking to conduct three vessels with troops two thousand leagues through so many different climates, and across seas entirely unknown to him. I grant that he is a man of knowledge, that he has reading, and even some tincture of navigation; but there is so much difference between theory and practice, that a man who has only the former will always be at fault. There is also a great difference between conducting canoes on lakes and along a river, and navigating ships with troops on distant oceans."[283]

[Pg 372]

While Beaujeu was complaining of La Salle, his followers were deserting him. It was necessary to send them on board ship, and keep them there; for there were French buccaneers at Petit Goave, who painted the promised land in such dismal colors that many of the adventurers completely lost heart. Some, too, were dying. "The air of this place is bad," says Joutel; "so are the fruits; and there are plenty of women worse than either."[284]

It was near the end of November before La Salle could resume the voyage. He was told that Beaujeu had said that he would not wait longer for the store-ship "Aimable," and that she might follow as she could.[285] Moreover, La Salle was on ill terms with Aigron, her captain, who had declared that he would have nothing more to do with him.[286] Fearing, therefore, that some mishap might befall her, he resolved to embark in her himself, with his brother Cavelier, Membré, Douay, and others, the trustiest of his followers. On the twenty-fifth they set sail; the "Joly" and the little frigate "Belle" following. They coasted the shore of Cuba, and landed at the Isle of Pines, where La Salle shot an alligator, which the soldiers ate; and the hunter brought in a wild pig, half of which he sent to Beaujeu. Then they advanced to Cape St. Antoine, where bad weather and contrary winds long detained them. A load of [Pg 373] cares oppressed the mind of La Salle, pale and haggard with recent illness, wrapped within his own thoughts, and seeking sympathy from none.

> A VAIN SEARCH.

At length they entered the Gulf of Mexico, that forbidden sea whence by a Spanish decree, dating from the reign of Philip II., all foreigners were excluded on pain of extermination.[287] Not a man on board knew the secrets of its perilous navigation. Cautiously feeling their way, they held a north-westerly course, till on the twenty-eighth of December a sailor at the mast-head of the "Aimable" saw land. La Salle and all the pilots had been led to form an exaggerated idea of the force of the easterly currents; and they therefore supposed themselves near the Bay of Appalache, when, in fact, they were much farther westward.

On New Year's Day they anchored three leagues from the shore. La Salle, with the engineer Minet, went to explore it, and found nothing but a vast marshy plain, studded with clumps of rushes. Two days after there was a thick fog, and when at length it cleared, the "Joly" was nowhere to be seen. La Salle in the "Aimable," followed closely by the little frigate "Belle," stood westward along the coast. When at the mouth of the Mississippi in 1682, he had taken its latitude, but unhappily could not determine its longitude; and now every eye on board was strained to detect in the monotonous lines [Pg 374] of the low shore some tokens of the great river. In fact, they had already passed it. On the sixth of January, a wide opening was descried between two low points of land; and the adjacent sea was discolored with mud. "La Salle," writes his brother Cavelier, "has always thought that this was the Mississippi." To all appearance, it was the entrance of Galveston Bay.[288] But why did he not examine it? Joutel says that his attempts to do so were frustrated by the objections of the pilot of the "Aimable," to which, with a facility very unusual with him, he suffered himself to yield. Cavelier declares, on the other hand, that he would not enter the opening because he was afraid of missing the "Joly." But he might have entered with one of his two vessels, while the other watched outside for the absent ship. From whatever cause, he lay here five or six days, waiting in vain for Beaujeu;[289] till, at last, thinking that he must have passed westward, he resolved to follow. The "Aimable" and the "Belle" again spread their sails, and coasted the shores of Texas. Joutel, with a boat's crew, tried to land; but the sand-bars and breakers repelled him. A party of Indians swam out through the surf, and were taken on board; but La Salle could learn nothing from them, as their language was unknown to him. [Pg 375] Again Joutel tried to land, and again the breakers repelled him. He approached as near as he dared, and saw vast plains and a dim expanse of forest, buffalo running with their heavy gallop along the shore, and deer grazing on the marshy meadows.

> THE SHORES OF TEXAS.

Soon after, he succeeded in landing at a point somewhere between Matagorda Island and Corpus Christi Bay. The aspect of the country was not cheering, with its barren plains, its reedy marshes, its interminable oyster-beds, and broad flats of mud bare at low tide. Joutel and his men sought in vain for fresh water, and after shooting some geese and ducks returned to the "Aimable." Nothing had been seen of Beaujeu and the "Joly;" the coast was trending southward; and La Salle, convinced that he must have passed the missing ship, turned to retrace his course. He had sailed but a few miles when the wind failed, a fog covered the sea, and he was forced to anchor opposite one of the openings into the lagoons north of Mustang Island. At length, on the nineteenth, there came a faint breeze; the mists rolled away before it, and to his great joy he saw the "Joly" approaching.

"His joy," says Joutel, "was short." Beaujeu's lieutenant, Aire, came on board to charge him with having caused the separation, and La Salle retorted by throwing the blame on Beaujeu. Then came a debate as to their position. The priest Esmanville was present, and reports that La Salle seemed greatly perplexed. He had more cause for perplexity than [Pg 376] he knew; for in his ignorance of the longitude of the Mississippi, he had sailed more than four hundred miles beyond it.

Of this he had not the faintest suspicion. In full sight from his ship lay a reach of those vast lagoons which, separated from the sea by narrow strips of land, line this coast with little interruption from Galveston Bay to the Rio Grande. The idea took possession of him that the Mississippi discharged itself into these lagoons, and thence made its way to the sea through the various openings he had seen along the coast, chief among which was that he had discovered on the sixth, about fifty leagues from the place where he now was.[290]

PERPLEXITY OF LA SALLE.

Yet he was full of doubt as to what he should do. Four days after rejoining Beaujeu, he wrote him the [Pg 377] strange request to land the troops, that he "might fulfil his commission;" that is, that he might set out against the Spaniards.[291] More than a week passed, a gale had set in, and nothing was done. Then La Salle wrote again, intimating some doubt as to whether he was really at one of the mouths of the Mississippi, and saying that, being sure that he had passed the principal mouth, he was determined to go back to look for it.[292] Meanwhile, Beaujeu was in a state of great irritation. The weather was stormy, and the coast was dangerous. Supplies were scanty; and La Salle's soldiers, still crowded in the "Joly," were consuming the provisions of the ship. Beaujeu gave vent to his annoyance, and La Salle retorted in the same strain.

According to Joutel, he urged the naval commander to sail back in search of the river; and Beaujeu refused, unless La Salle should give the soldiers provisions. La Salle, he adds, offered to supply them with rations for fifteen days; and Beaujeu declared this insufficient. There is reason, however, to believe that the request was neither made by the one nor refused by the other so positively as here appears.

FOOTNOTES:

[278] *Lettre (sans nom d'auteur) écrite de St. Domingue, 14 Nov., 1684* (Margry, ii. 492); *Mémoire autographe de l'Abbé Jean Cavelier sur le Voyage de 1684.* Compare Joutel.
[279] *Mémoire de MM. de Saint-Laurens et Bégon* (Margry, ii. 499); Joutel, *Journal Historique,* 28.
[280] *Relation de Henri Joutel* (Margry, iii. 98).
[281] *Lettre (sans nom d'auteur), 14 Nov., 1684* (Margry, ii. 496).

[282] The above particulars are from the memoir of La Salle's brother, Abbé Cavelier, already cited.

[283] *Lettre de Beaujeu au Ministre, 20 Oct., 1684.*

[284] *Relation de Henri Joutel* (Margry, iii. 105).

[285] *Mémoire autographe de l'Abbé Jean Cavelier.*

[286] *Lettre de Beaujeu au Ministre, 20 Oct., 1684.*

[287] *Letter of Don Luis de Onis to the Secretary of State* (American State Papers, xii, 27-31).

[288] "La hauteur nous a fait remarquer ... que ce que nous avions vu le sixième janvier estoit en effet la principale entrée de la rivière que nous cherchions."—*Lettre de La Salle au Ministre, 4 Mars, 1687.*

[289] *Mémoire autographe de l'Abbé Cavelier.*

[290] "Depuis que nous avions quitté cette rivière qu'il croyoit infailliblement estre le fleuve Colbert *[Mississippi]* nous avions fait environ 45 lieues ou 50 au plus." (Cavelier, *Mémoire.*) This, taken in connection with the statement of La Salle that this "principale entrée de la rivière que nous cherchions" was twenty-five or thirty leagues northeast from the entrance of the Bay of St. Louis (Matagorda Bay), shows that it can have been no other than the entrance of Galveston Bay, mistaken by him for the chief outlet of the Mississippi. It is evident that he imagined Galveston Bay to form a part of the chain of lagoons from which it is in fact separated. He speaks of these lagoons as "une espèce de baye fort longue et fort large, *dans laquelle le fleuve Colbert se décharge.*" He adds that on his descent to the mouth of the river in 1682 he had been deceived in supposing that this expanse of salt water, where no shore was in sight, was the open sea. *Lettre de La Salle au Ministre, 4 Mars, 1685.* Galveston Bay and the mouth of the Mississippi differ little in latitude, though separated by about five and a half degrees of longitude.

[291] *Lettre de La Salle à Beaujeu, 23 Jan., 1685* (Margry, ii. 526).

[292] This letter is dated, "De l'emboucheure d'une rivière que *je crois estre* une des descharges du Mississipy" (Margry, ii. 528).

[Pg 378]

CHAPTER XXV.

1685.

LA SALLE IN TEXAS.

A Party of Exploration — Wreck of the "Aimable." — Landing of the Colonists. — A Forlorn Position. — Indian Neighbors. — Friendly Advances of Beaujeu: his Departure. — A Fatal Discovery.

IMPATIENCE to rid himself of his colleague and to command alone no doubt had its influence on the judgment of La Salle. He presently declared that he would land the soldiers, and send them along shore till they came to the principal outlet of the river. On this, the engineer Minet took up the word,—expressed his doubts as to whether the Mississippi discharged itself into the lagoons at all; represented that even if it did, the soldiers would be exposed to great risks; and gave as his opinion that all should reimbark and continue the search in company. The advice was good, but La Salle resented it as coming from one in whom he recognized no right to give it. "He treated me," complains the engineer, "as if I were the meanest of mankind."[293]

[Pg 379]

He persisted in his purpose, and sent Joutel and Moranget with a party of soldiers to explore the coast. They made their way northeastward along the shore of Matagorda Island, till they were stopped on the third day by what Joutel calls a river, but which was in fact the entrance of Matagorda Bay. Here they encamped, and tried to make a raft of drift-wood. "The difficulty was," says Joutel, "our great number of men, and the few of them who were fit for anything except eating. As I said before, they had all been caught by force or surprise, so that our company was like Noah's ark, which contained animals of all sorts." Before their raft was finished, they descried to their great joy the ships which had followed them along the coast.[294]

LANDING OF LA SALLE.

La Salle landed, and announced that here was the western mouth of the Mississippi, and the place to which the King had sent him. He said further that he would land all his men, and bring the "Aimable" and the "Belle" to the safe harborage within. Beaujeu remonstrated, alleging the shallowness of the water and the force of the currents; but his remonstrance was vain.[295]

The Bay of St. Louis, now Matagorda Bay, forms a broad and sheltered harbor, accessible from the sea by a narrow passage, obstructed by sand-bars and by the small island now called Pelican Island. Boats [Pg 380] were sent to sound and buoy out the channel, and this was successfully accomplished on the sixteenth of February. The "Aimable" was ordered to enter; and, on the twentieth, she weighed anchor. La Salle was on shore watching her. A party of men, at a little distance, were cutting down a tree to make a canoe. Suddenly some of them ran towards him with terrified faces, crying out that they had been set upon by a troop of Indians, who had seized their companions and carried them off. La Salle ordered those about him to take their arms, and at once set out in pursuit. He overtook the Indians, and opened a parley with them; but when he wished to reclaim his men, he discovered that they had been led away during the conference to the Indian camp, a league and a half distant. Among them was one of his lieutenants, the young Marquis de la Sablonnière. He was deeply vexed, for the moment was critical; but the men must be recovered, and he led his followers in haste towards the camp. Yet he could not refrain from turning a moment to watch the "Aimable," as she neared the shoals; and he remarked with deep anxiety to Joutel, who was with him, that if she held that course she would soon be aground.

WRECK OF THE "AIMABLE".

They hurried on till they saw the Indian huts. About fifty of them, oven-shaped, and covered with mats and hides, were clustered on a rising ground, with their inmates gathered among and around them. As the French entered the camp, there was the report [Pg 381] of a cannon from the seaward. The startled savages dropped flat with terror. A different fear seized La Salle, for he knew that the shot was a signal of disaster. Looking back, he saw the "Aimable" furling her sails, and his heart sank with the conviction that she had struck upon the reef. Smothering his distress,—she was laden with all the stores of the colony,—he pressed forward among the filthy wigwams, whose astonished inmates swarmed about the band of armed strangers, staring between curiosity and fear. La Salle knew those with whom he was dealing, and, without ceremony, entered the chief's lodge with his followers. The crowd closed around them, naked men and half-naked women, described by Joutel as of singular ugliness. They gave buffalo meat and dried porpoise to the unexpected guests, but La Salle, racked with anxiety, hastened to close the interview; and having without difficulty recovered the kidnapped men, he returned to the beach, leaving with the Indians, as usual, an impression of good-will and respect.

When he reached the shore, he saw his worst fears realized. The "Aimable" lay careened over on the reef, hopelessly aground. Little remained but to endure the calamity with firmness, and to save, as far as might be, the vessel's cargo. This was no easy task. The boat which hung at her stern had been stove in,—it is said, by design. Beaujeu sent a boat from the "Joly," and one or more Indian pirogues were procured. La Salle urged on his men [Pg 382] with stern and patient energy, and a quantity of gunpowder and flour was safely landed. But now the wind blew fresh from the sea; the waves began to rise; a storm came on; the vessel, rocking to and fro on the sand-bar, opened along her side, and the ravenous waves were strewn with her treasures. When the confusion was at its height, a troop of Indians came down to the shore, greedy for plunder. The drum was beat; the men were called to arms; La Salle set his trustiest followers to guard the gunpowder, in fear, not of the Indians alone, but of his own countrymen. On that lamentable night, the sentinels walked their rounds through the dreary bivouac among the casks, bales, and boxes which the sea had yielded up; and here, too, their fate-hunted chief held his drearier vigil, encompassed with treachery, darkness, and the storm.

Not only La Salle, but Joutel and others of his party, believed that the wreck of the "Aimable" was intentional. Aigron, who commanded her, had disobeyed orders and disregarded signals. Though he had been directed to tow the vessel through the channel, he went in under sail; and though little else was saved from the wreck, his personal property, including even some preserved fruits, was all landed safely. He had long been on ill terms with La Salle.[296]

[Pg 383]

All La Salle's company were now encamped on the sands at the left side of the inlet where the "Aimable" was wrecked.[297] "They were all," says the engineer Minet, "sick with nausea and dysentery. Five or six died every day, in consequence of brackish water and bad food. There was no grass, but plenty of rushes and plenty of oysters. There was nothing to make ovens, so that they had to eat flour saved from the wreck, boiled into messes of porridge with this brackish water. Along the shore were quantities of uprooted trees and rotten logs, thrown up by the sea and the lagoon." Of these, and fragments of the wreck, they made a sort of rampart to protect their camp; and here, among tents and hovels, bales, boxes, casks, spars, dismounted cannon, and pens for fowls and swine, were gathered the dejected men and homesick women who were to seize New Biscay, and hold for France a region large as half Europe. The Spaniards, whom they were to conquer, were they [Pg 384] knew not where. They knew not where they were themselves; and for the fifteen thousand Indian allies who were to have joined them, they found two hundred squalid savages, more like enemies than friends.

In fact, it was soon made plain that these their neighbors wished them no good. A few days after the wreck, the prairie was seen on fire. As the smoke and flame rolled towards them before the wind,

La Salle caused all the grass about the camp to be cut and carried away, and especially around the spot where the powder was placed. The danger was averted; but it soon became known that the Indians had stolen a number of blankets and other articles, and carried them to their wigwams. Unwilling to leave his camp, La Salle sent his nephew Moranget and several other volunteers, with a party of men, to reclaim them. They went up the bay in a boat, landed at the Indian camp, and, with more mettle than discretion, marched into it, sword in hand. The Indians ran off, and the rash adventurers seized upon several canoes as an equivalent for the stolen goods. Not knowing how to manage them, they made slow progress on their way back, and were overtaken by night before reaching the French camp. They landed, made a fire, placed a sentinel, and lay down on the dry grass to sleep. The sentinel followed their example, when suddenly they were awakened by the war-whoop and a shower of arrows. Two volunteers, Oris and Desloges, were killed on the spot; a third, named Gayen, was severely [Pg 385] wounded; and young Moranget received an arrow through the arm. He leaped up and fired his gun at the vociferous but invisible foe. Others of the party did the same, and the Indians fled.

BEAUJEU AND LA SALLE.

It was about this time that Beaujeu prepared to return to France. He had accomplished his mission, and landed his passengers at what La Salle assured him to be one of the mouths of the Mississippi. His ship was in danger on this exposed and perilous coast, and he was anxious to find shelter. For some time past, his relations with La Salle had been amicable, and it was agreed between them that Beaujeu should stop at Galveston Bay, the supposed chief mouth of the Mississippi; or, failing to find harborage here, that he should proceed to Mobile Bay, and wait there till April, to hear from his colleague. Two days before the wreck of the "Aimable," he wrote to La Salle: "I wish with all my heart that you would have more confidence in me. For my part, I will always make the first advances; and I will follow your counsel whenever I can do so without risking my ship. I will come back to this place, if you want to know the results of the voyage I am going to make. If you wish, I will go to Martinique for provisions and reinforcements. In fine, there is nothing I am not ready to do: you have only to speak."

La Salle had begged him to send ashore a number of cannon and a quantity of iron, stowed in the "Joly," for the use of the colony; and Beaujeu replies: "I wish very much that I could give you [Pg 386] your iron, but it is impossible except in a harbor; for it is on my ballast, and under your cannon, my spare anchors, and all my stowage. It would take three days to get it out, which cannot be done in this place, where the sea runs like mountains when the slightest wind blows outside. I would rather come back to give it to you, in case you do not send the 'Belle' to Baye du St. Esprit [Mobile Bay] to get it.... I beg you once more to consider the offer I make you to go to Martinique to get provisions for your people. I will ask the intendant for them in your name; and if they are refused, I will take them on my own account."[298]

To this La Salle immediately replied: "I received with singular pleasure the letter you took the trouble to write me; for I found in it extraordinary proofs of kindness in the interest you take in the success of an affair which I have the more at heart, as it involves the glory of the King and the honor of Monseigneur de Seignelay. I have done my part towards a perfect understanding between us, and have never been wanting in confidence; but even if I could be so, the offers you make are so obliging that they would inspire complete trust." He nevertheless declines them,—assuring Beaujeu at the same time that he has reached the place he sought, and is in a fair way of success if he can but have the cannon, cannonballs, and iron stowed on board the "Joly."[299]

[Pg 387]

Directly after he writes again, "I cannot help conjuring you once more to try to give us the iron." Beaujeu replies: "To show you how ardently I wish to contribute to the success of your undertaking, I have ordered your iron to be got out, in spite of my officers and sailors, who tell me that I endanger my ship by moving everything in the depth of the hold on a coast like this, where the seas are like mountains. I hesitated to disturb my stowage, not so much to save trouble as because no ballast is to be got hereabout; and I have therefore had six cannon, from my lower deck battery, let down into the hold to take the place of the iron." And he again urges La Salle to accept his offer to bring provisions to the colonists from Martinique.

DEPARTURE OF BEAUJEU.

On the next day, the "Aimable" was wrecked. Beaujeu remained a fortnight longer on the coast, and then told La Salle that being out of wood, water, and other necessaries, he must go to Mobile Bay to get them. Nevertheless, he lingered a week more, repeated his offer to bring supplies from Martinique, which La Salle again refused, and at last set sail on the twelfth of March, after a leave-taking which was courteous on both sides.[300]

La Salle and his colonists were left alone. Several of them had lost heart, and embarked for home with Beaujeu. Among these was Minet the engineer, who had fallen out with La Salle, and who when he [Pg 388] reached France was imprisoned for deserting him. Even his brother, the priest Jean Cavelier, had a mind to abandon the enterprise, but was persuaded at last to remain, along with his nephew the hot-headed Moranget, and the younger Cavelier, a mere school-boy. The two Récollet friars, Zenobe Membré and Anastase Douay, the trusty Joutel, a man of sense and observation, and the Marquis de la Sablonnière, a debauched noble whose patrimony was his sword, were now the chief persons of the forlorn company. The rest were soldiers, raw and undisciplined, and artisans, most of whom knew nothing of their vocation. Add to these the miserable families and the infatuated young women who had come to tempt fortune in the swamps and cane-brakes of the Mississippi.

La Salle set out to explore the neighborhood. Joutel remained in command of the so-called fort. He was beset with wily enemies, and often at night the Indians would crawl in the grass around his feeble stockade, howling like wolves; but a few shots would put them to flight. A strict guard was kept; and a wooden horse was set in the enclosure, to punish the sentinel who should sleep at his post. They stood in daily fear of a more formidable foe, and once they saw a sail, which they doubted not was Spanish; but she happily passed without discovering them. They hunted on the prairies, and speared fish in the neighboring pools. On Easter Day, the Sieur le Gros, one of the chief men of the [Pg 389] company, went out after the service to shoot snipes; but as he walked barefoot through the marsh, a snake bit him, and he soon after died. Two men deserted, to starve on the prairie, or to become savages among savages. Others tried to escape, but were caught; and one of them was hung. A knot of desperadoes conspired to kill Joutel; but one of them betrayed the secret, and the plot was crushed.

La Salle returned from his exploration, but his return brought no cheer. He had been forced to renounce the illusion to which he had clung so long, and was convinced at last that he was not at the mouth of the Mississippi. The wreck of the "Aimable" itself was not pregnant with consequences so disastrous.

CONDUCT OF BEAUJEU.

NOTE.—The conduct of Beaujeu, hitherto judged chiefly by the printed narrative of Joutel, is set in a new and more favorable light by his correspondence with La Salle. Whatever may have been their mutual irritation, it is clear that the naval commander was anxious to discharge his duty in a manner to satisfy Seignelay, and that he may be wholly acquitted of any sinister design. When he left La Salle on the twelfth of March, he meant to sail in search of the Bay of Mobile (Baye du St. Esprit),—partly because he hoped to find it a safe harbor, where he could get La Salle's cannon out of the hold and find ballast to take their place; and partly to get a supply of wood and water, of which he was in extreme need. He told La Salle that he would wait there till the middle of April, in order that he (La Salle) might send the "Belle" to receive the cannon; but on this point there was no definite agreement between them. Beaujeu was ignorant of the position of the bay, which he thought much nearer than it actually was. After trying two days to reach it, the strong head-winds and the discontent of his crew induced him to bear away for Cuba; and after an encounter with pirates and various adventures, he reached France about the first of July. He was coldly received by Seignelay, who wrote to the [Pg 390] intendant at Rochelle: "His Majesty has seen what you wrote about the idea of the Sieur de Beaujeu, that the Sieur de la Salle is not at the mouth of the Mississippi. He seems to found this belief on such weak conjectures that no great attention need be given to his account, especially as *this man* has been prejudiced from the first against La Salle's enterprise." (*Lettre de Seignelay à Arnoul, 22 Juillet,* 1685. Margry, ii. 604.) The minister at the same time warns Beaujeu to say nothing in disparagement of the enterprise, under pain of the King's displeasure. The narrative of the engineer, Minet, sufficiently explains a curious map, made by him, as he says, not on the spot, but on the voyage homeward, and still preserved in the Archives Scientifiques de la Marine. This map includes two distinct sketches of the mouth of the Mississippi. The first, which corresponds to that made by Franquelin in 1684, is entitled "Embouchure de la Rivière comme M. de la Salle la marque dans sa Carte." The second bears the words, "Costes et Lacs par la Hauteur de sa Rivière, comme nous les avons trouvés." These "Costes et Lacs" are a rude representation of the lagoons of Matagorda Bay and its neighborhood, into which the Mississippi is made to discharge, in accordance with the belief of La Salle. A portion of the coast-line is drawn from actual, though superficial observation. The rest is merely conjectural.

FOOTNOTES:

[293] *Relation de Minet; Lettre de Minet à Seignelay, 6 July, 1685* (Margry, ii. 591, 602).

[294] Joutel, *Journal Historique*, 68; *Relation* (Margry, iii. 143-146) Compare *Journal d'Esmanville* (Margry, ii. 510).

[295] *Relation de Minet* (Margry, ii. 591).

[296] *Procès Verbal du Sieur de la Salle sur le Naufrage de la Flûte l'Aimable*; *Lettre de La Salle à Seignelay, 4 Mars, 1685*; *Lettre de Beaujeu à Seignelay, sans date*. Beaujeu did his best to save the cargo. The loss included nearly all the provisions, 60 barrels of wine, 4 cannon, 1,620

balls, 400 grenades, 4,000 pounds of iron, 5,000 pounds of lead, most of the tools, a forge, a mill, cordage, boxes of arms, nearly all the medicines, and most of the baggage of the soldiers and colonists. Aigron returned to France in the "Joly," and was thrown into prison, "comme il paroist clairement que cet accident est arrivé par sa faute."—*Seignelay au Sieur Arnoul, 22 Juillet, 1685* (Margry, ii. 604).

[297] A map, entitled *Entrée du Lac où on a laisse le Sr de la Salle*, made by the engineer Minet, and preserved in the Archives de la Marine, represents the entrance of Matagorda Bay, the camp of La Salle on the left, Indian camps on the borders of the bay, the "Belle" at anchor within, the "Aimable" stranded at the entrance, and the "Joly" anchored in the open sea.

[298] *Lettre de Beaujeu à La Salle, 18 Fév., 1685* (Margry, ii. 542).

[299] *Lettre de La Salle à Beaujeu, 18 Fév., 1685* (Margry, ii. 546).

[300] The whole of this correspondence between Beaujeu and La Salle will be found in Margry, ii.

[Pg 391]

CHAPTER XXVI.

1685-1687.

ST. LOUIS OF TEXAS.

THE FORT.—MISERY AND DEJECTION.—ENERGY OF LA SALLE: HIS JOURNEY OF
EXPLORATION.—ADVENTURES AND ACCIDENTS.—THE BUFFALO.—DUHAUT.—
INDIAN MASSACRE.—RETURN OF LA SALLE.—A NEW CALAMITY.—A DESPERATE
RESOLUTION.—DEPARTURE FOR CANADA.—WRECK OF THE "BELLE."—
MARRIAGE.—SEDITION.—ADVENTURES OF LA SALLE'S PARTY.—THE CENIS.—THE
CAMANCHES.—THE ONLY HOPE.—THE LAST FAREWELL.

OF what avail to plant a colony by the mouth of a petty Texan river?
The Mississippi was the life of the enterprise, the condition of its
growth and of its existence. Without it, all was futile and
meaningless,—a folly and a ruin. Cost what it might, the Mississippi
must be found.

But the demands of the hour were imperative. The hapless colony,
cast ashore like a wreck on the sands of Matagorda Bay, must gather
up its shattered resources and recruit its exhausted strength, before
it essayed anew its pilgrimage to the "fatal river." La Salle during
his explorations had found a spot which he thought well fitted for a
temporary establishment. It was on the river which he named the [Pg
392] La Vache,[301] now the Lavaca, which enters the head of
Matagorda Bay; and thither he ordered all the women and children,
and most of the men, to remove; while the rest, thirty in number,
remained with Joutel at the fort near the mouth of the bay. Here they
spent their time in hunting, fishing, and squaring the logs of drift-
wood which the sea washed up in abundance, and which La Salle
proposed to use in building his new station on the Lavaca. Thus the
time passed till midsummer, when Joutel received orders to abandon
his post, and rejoin the main body of the colonists. To this end, the
little frigate "Belle" was sent down the bay. She was a gift from the
King to La Salle, who had brought her safely over the bar, and
regarded her as a main-stay of his hopes. She now took on board the

stores and some of the men, while Joutel with the rest followed along shore to the post on the Lavaca. Here he found a state of things that was far from cheering. Crops had been sown, but the drought and the cattle had nearly destroyed them. The colonists were lodged under tents and hovels; and the only solid structure was a small square enclosure of pickets, in which the gunpowder and the brandy were stored. The site was good, a rising ground by the river; but there was no wood within the distance of a league, and no horses or oxen to drag it. Their work must be done by men. Some felled and squared the timber; and others dragged it by main force over the [Pg 393] matted grass of the prairie, under the scorching Texan sun. The gun-carriages served to make the task somewhat easier; yet the strongest men soon gave out under it. Joutel went down to the first fort, made a raft and brought up the timber collected there, which proved a most seasonable and useful supply. Palisades and buildings began to rise. The men labored without spirit, yet strenuously; for they labored under the eye of La Salle. The carpenters brought from Rochelle proved worthless; and he himself made the plans of the work, marked out the tenons and mortises, and directed the whole.[302]

MISERY AND DEJECTION.

Death, meanwhile, made withering havoc among his followers; and under the sheds and hovels that shielded them from the sun lay a score of wretches slowly wasting away with the diseases contracted at St. Domingo. Of the soldiers enlisted for the expedition by La Salle's agents, many are affirmed to have spent their lives in begging at the church doors of Rochefort, and were consequently incapable of discipline. It was impossible to prevent either them or the sailors from devouring persimmons and other wild fruits to a destructive excess. Nearly all fell ill; and before the summer had passed, the graveyard had more than thirty tenants.[303] The bearing of La Salle did not aid to raise the drooping spirits of his [Pg 394] followers. The results of the enterprise had been far different from his hopes; and, after a season of flattering promise, he had entered again on those dark and obstructed paths which seemed his destined way of life. The present was beset with trouble; the future, thick with storms. The consciousness quickened his energies; but it made him stern, harsh, and often unjust to those beneath him.

Joutel was returning to camp one afternoon with the master-carpenter, when they saw game; and the carpenter went after it. He was never seen again. Perhaps he was lost on the prairie, perhaps killed by Indians. He knew little of his trade, but they nevertheless had need of him. Le Gros, a man of character and intelligence, suffered more and more from the bite of the snake received in the marsh on Easter Day. The injured limb was amputated, and he died. La Salle's brother, the priest, lay ill; and several others among the chief persons of the colony were in the same condition.

Meanwhile, the work was urged on. A large building was finished, constructed of timber, roofed with boards and raw hides, and divided into apartments for lodging and other uses. La Salle gave the new establishment his favorite name of Fort St. Louis, and the neighboring bay was also christened after the royal saint.[304] The scene was not without [Pg 395] its charms. Towards the southeast stretched the bay with its bordering meadows; and on the northeast the Lavaca ran along the base of green declivities. Around, far and near, rolled a sea of prairie, with distant forests, dim in the summer haze. At times, it was dotted with the browsing buffalo, not yet scared from their wonted pastures; and the grassy swells were spangled with the flowers for which Texas is renowned, and which now form the gay ornaments of our gardens.

LA SALLE'S EXPLORATIONS.

And now, the needful work accomplished, and the colony in some measure housed and fortified, its indefatigable chief prepared to renew his quest of the "fatal river," as Joutel repeatedly calls it. Before his departure he made some preliminary explorations, in the course of which, according to the report of his brother the priest, he found evidence that the Spaniards had long before had a transient establishment at a spot about fifteen leagues from Fort St. Louis.[305]

[Pg 396]

LIFE AT THE FORT.

It was the last day of October when La Salle set out on his great journey of exploration. His brother Cavelier, who had now recovered, accompanied him with fifty men; and five cannon-shot from the fort saluted them as they departed. They were lightly equipped; but some of them wore corselets made of staves, to ward off arrows. Descending the Lavaca, they pursued their course eastward on foot along the margin of the bay, while Joutel remained in command of the fort. It was two leagues above the mouth of the river; and in it were thirty-four persons, including three Récollet friars, a number of women and girls from Paris, and two young orphan daughters of one Talon, a Canadian, who had lately died. Their live-stock consisted of some hogs and a litter of eight pigs, which, as Joutel does not forget to inform us, passed their time in wallowing in the ditch of the palisade; a cock and hen, with a young family; and a pair of goats, which, in a temporary dearth of fresh meat, were sacrificed to the needs of the invalid Abbé Cavelier. Joutel suffered no man to lie idle. The blacksmith, having no anvil, was supplied with a cannon as a substitute. Lodgings were built for the women and girls, and separate lodgings for the men. A small chapel was afterwards added, and the whole was fenced with a [Pg 397] palisade. At the four corners of the house were mounted eight pieces of cannon, which, in the absence of balls, were loaded with bags of bullets.[306] Between the palisades and the stream lay a narrow strip of marsh, the haunt of countless birds; and at a little distance it deepened into pools full of fish. All the surrounding prairies swarmed with game,—buffalo, deer, hares, turkeys, ducks, geese, swans, plover, snipe, and grouse. The river supplied the colonists with turtles, and the bay with oysters. Of these last, they often found more than they wanted; for when in their excursions they shoved their log canoes into the water, wading shoeless through the deep, tenacious mud, the sharp shells would cut their feet like knives; "and what was worse," says Joutel, "the salt water came into the gashes, and made them smart atrociously."

He sometimes amused himself with shooting alligators. "I never spared them when I met them near the house. One day I killed an extremely large one, which was nearly four feet and a half in girth, and about twenty feet long." He describes with accuracy that curious native of the southwestern plains, the "horned frog," which, deceived by its uninviting appearance, he erroneously supposed to be venomous. "We had some of our animals bitten by snakes; among the others, a bitch that had belonged to the [Pg 398] deceased Sieur le Gros. She was bitten in the jaw when she was with me, as I was fishing by the shore of the bay. I gave her a little theriac [an antidote then in vogue], which cured her, as it did one of our sows, which came home one day with her head so swelled that she could hardly hold it up. Thinking it must be some snake that had bitten her, I gave her a dose of the theriac mixed with meal and water." The patient began to mend at once. "I killed a good many rattle-snakes by means of the aforesaid bitch, for when she saw one she would bark around him, sometimes for a half hour together, till I took my gun and shot him. I often found them in the bushes, making a noise with their tails. When I had killed them, our hogs ate them." He devotes many pages to the plants and animals of the neighborhood, most of which may easily be recognized from his description.

THE BUFFALO.

With the buffalo, which he calls "our daily bread," his experiences were many and strange. Being, like the rest of the party, a novice in the art of shooting them, he met with many disappointments. Once, having mounted to the roof of the large house in the fort, he saw a dark moving object on a swell of the prairie three miles off; and rightly thinking that it was a herd of buffalo, he set out with six or seven men to try to kill some of them. After a while, he discovered two bulls lying in a hollow; and signing to the rest of his party to keep quiet, he made his approach, gun in hand. The bulls presently jumped [Pg 399] up, and stared through their manes at the intruder. Joutel fired. It was a close shot; but the bulls merely shook their shaggy heads, wheeled about, and galloped heavily away. The same luck attended him the next day. "We saw plenty of buffalo. I approached several bands of them, and fired again and again, but could not make one of them fall." He had not yet learned that a buffalo rarely falls at once, unless hit in the spine. He continues: "I was not discouraged; and after approaching several more bands,— which was hard work, because I had to crawl on the ground, so as not to be seen,—I found myself in a herd of five or six thousand, but, to my great vexation, I could not bring one of them down. They all ran off to the right and left. It was near night, and I had killed nothing. Though I was very tired, I tried again, approached another band, and fired a number of shots; but not a buffalo would fall. The skin was off my knees with crawling. At last, as I was going back to rejoin our men, I saw a buffalo lying on the ground. I went towards it, and saw that it was dead. I examined it, and found that the bullet had gone in near the shoulder. Then I found others dead like the first. I beckoned the men to come on, and we set to work to cut up the meat,—a task which was new to us all." It would be impossible to write a more true and characteristic sketch of the experience of a novice in shooting buffalo on foot. A few days after, he went out again, with Father Anastase Douay; approached a [Pg 400] bull, fired, and broke his shoulder. The bull hobbled off on three legs. Douay ran in his cassock to head him back, while Joutel reloaded his gun; upon which the enraged beast butted at the missionary, and knocked him down. He very narrowly escaped with his life. "There was another missionary," pursues Joutel, "named Father Maxime Le Clerc, who was very well fitted for such an undertaking as ours, because he was equal to anything, even to butchering a buffalo; and as I said before that every one of us must lend a hand, because we were too few for anybody to be waited upon, I made the women, girls, and children do their part, as well as him; for as they all wanted to eat, it was fair that they all should work." He had a scaffolding built near the fort, and set them to smoking buffalo meat, against a day of scarcity.[307]

RETURN OF DUHAUT.

Thus the time passed till the middle of January; when late one evening, as all were gathered in the principal building, conversing perhaps, or smoking, or playing at cards, or dozing by the fire in homesick dreams of France, a man on guard came in to report that he had heard a voice from the river. They all went down to the bank, and descried a man in a canoe, who called out, "Dominic!" This was the name of the younger of the two brothers Duhaut, who was one of Joutel's followers. As the canoe [Pg 401] approached, they recognized the elder, who had gone with La Salle on his journey of discovery, and who was perhaps the greatest villain of the company. Joutel was much perplexed. La Salle had ordered him to admit nobody into the fort without a pass and a watchword. Duhaut, when questioned, said that he had none, but told at the same time so plausible a story that Joutel no longer hesitated to receive him. As La Salle and his men were pursuing their march along the prairie, Duhaut, who was in the rear, had stopped to mend his moccasins, and when he tried to overtake the party, had lost his way, mistaking a buffalo-path for the trail of his companions. At night he fired his gun as a signal, but there was no answering shot. Seeing no hope of rejoining them, he turned back for the fort, found one of the canoes which La Salle had hidden at the shore, paddled by night and lay close by day, shot turkeys, deer, and buffalo for food, and, having no knife, cut the meat with a sharp flint, till after a month of excessive hardship he reached his destination. As the inmates of Fort St. Louis gathered about the weather-beaten wanderer, he told them dreary tidings. The pilot of the "Belle," such was his story, had gone with five men to sound along the shore, by order of La Salle, who was then encamped in the neighborhood with his party of explorers. The boat's crew, being overtaken by the night, had rashly bivouacked on the beach without setting a guard; and as they slept, a band of Indians had rushed in [Pg 402] upon them, and butchered them all. La Salle, alarmed by their long absence, had searched along the shore, and at length found their bodies scattered about the sands and half-devoured by wolves.[308] Well would it have been, if Duhaut had shared their fate.

Weeks and months dragged on, when, at the end of March, Joutel, chancing to mount on the roof of one of the buildings, saw seven or eight men approaching over the prairie. He went out to meet them with an equal number, well armed; and as he drew near recognized, with mixed joy and anxiety, La Salle and some of those who had gone with him. His brother Cavelier was at his side, with his cassock so tattered that, says Joutel, "there was hardly a piece left large enough to wrap a farthing's worth of salt. He had an old cap on his head, having lost his hat by the way. The rest were in no better plight, for their shirts were all in rags. Some of them carried loads of meat, because M. de la Salle was afraid that we might not have killed any buffalo. We met with great joy and many embraces. After our greetings were over, M. de la Salle, seeing Duhaut, asked me in an angry tone how it was that [Pg 403] I had received this man who had abandoned him. I told him how it had happened, and repeated Duhaut's story. Duhaut defended himself, and M. de la Salle's anger was soon over. We went into the house, and refreshed ourselves with some bread and brandy, as there was no wine left."[309]

LA SALLE'S ADVENTURES.

La Salle and his companions told their story. They had wandered on through various savage tribes, with whom they had more than one encounter, scattering them like chaff by the terror of their fire-arms. At length they found a more friendly band, and learned much touching the Spaniards, who, they were told, were universally hated by the tribes of that country. It would be easy, said their informants, to gather a host of warriors and lead them over the Rio Grande; but La Salle was in no condition for attempting conquests, and the tribes in whose alliance he had trusted had, a few days before, been at blows with him. The invasion of New Biscay must be postponed to a more propitious day. Still advancing, he came to a large river, which he at first mistook for the Mississippi; and building a fort of palisades, he left here several of his men.[310] The fate of these unfortunates does not appear. He [Pg 404] now retraced his steps towards Fort St. Louis, and, as he approached it, detached some of his men to look for his vessel, the "Belle," for whose safety, since the loss of her pilot, he had become very anxious.

On the next day these men appeared at the fort, with downcast looks. They had not found the "Belle" at the place where she had been ordered to remain, nor were any tidings to be heard of her. From that hour, the conviction that she was lost possessed the mind of La Salle. Surrounded as he was, and had always been, with traitors, the belief now possessed him that her crew had abandoned the colony, and made sail for the West Indies or for France. The loss was incalculable. He had relied on this vessel to transport the colonists to the Mississippi, as soon as its exact position could be ascertained; and thinking her a safer place of deposit than the fort, he had put on board of her all his papers and personal baggage, besides a great quantity of stores, ammunition, and tools.[311] In truth, she was of the last necessity to the unhappy exiles, and their only resource for escape from a position which was fast becoming desperate.

La Salle, as his brother tells us, now fell dangerously ill,—the fatigues of his journey, joined to the effects upon his mind of this last disaster, having overcome his strength, though not his fortitude. "In truth," writes the priest, "after the loss of the [Pg 405] vessel which deprived us of our only means of returning to France, we had no resource but in the firm guidance of my brother, whose death each of us would have regarded as his own."[312]

DEPARTURE FOR CANADA.

La Salle no sooner recovered than he embraced a resolution which could be the offspring only of a desperate necessity. He determined to make his way by the Mississippi and the Illinois to Canada, whence he might bring succor to the colonists, and send a report of their condition to France. The attempt was beset with uncertainties and dangers. The Mississippi was first to be found, then followed through all the perilous monotony of its interminable windings to a goal which was to be but the starting-point of a new and not less arduous journey. Cavelier his brother, Moranget his nephew, the friar Anastase Douay, and others to the number of twenty, were chosen to accompany him. Every corner of the magazine was ransacked for an outfit. Joutel generously gave up the better part of his wardrobe to La Salle and his two relatives. Duhaut, who had saved his baggage from the wreck of the "Aimable," was required to contribute to the necessities of the party; and the scantily-furnished chests of those who had died were used to supply the wants of the living. Each man labored with needle and awl to patch his failing garments, or supply their place with buffalo or deer skins. On the twenty-second of April, after [Pg 406] mass and prayers in the chapel, they issued from the gate, each bearing his pack and his weapons, some with kettles slung at their backs, some with axes, some with gifts for Indians. In this guise, they held their way in silence across the prairie; while anxious eyes followed them from the palisades of St. Louis, whose inmates, not excepting Joutel himself, seem to have been ignorant of the extent and difficulty of the undertaking.[313]

WRECK OF THE "BELLE."

"On May Day," he writes, "at about two in the afternoon, as I was walking near the house, I heard a voice from the river below, crying out several times, *Qui vive?* Knowing that the Sieur Barbier had gone that way with two canoes to hunt buffalo, I thought that it might be one of these canoes coming back with meat, and did not think much of the matter till I heard the same voice again. I answered, *Versailles*, which was the password I had given the Sieur Barbier, in case he should come back in the night. But, as I was going towards the bank, I heard other voices which I had not heard for a long time. I recognized among the rest that of M. Chefdeville, which made me fear that some disaster had happened. I ran down to the bank, and my first greeting was to ask what had become of the 'Belle.' [Pg 407] They answered that she was wrecked on the other side of the bay, and that all on board were drowned except the six who were in the canoe; namely, the Sieur Chefdeville, the Marquis de la Sablonnière, the man named Teissier, a soldier, a girl, and a little boy."[314]

From the young priest Chefdeville, Joutel learned the particulars of the disaster. Water had failed on board the "Belle"; a boat's crew of five men had gone in quest of it; the wind rose, their boat was swamped, and they were all drowned. Those who remained had now no means of going ashore; but if they had no water, they had wine and brandy in abundance, and Teissier, the master of the vessel, was drunk every day. After a while they left their moorings, and tried to reach the fort; but they were few, weak, and unskilful. A violent north wind drove them on a sand-bar. Some of them were drowned in trying to reach land on a raft. Others were more successful; and, after a long delay, they found a stranded canoe, in which they made their way to St. Louis, bringing with them some of La Salle's papers and baggage saved from the wreck.

These multiplied disasters bore hard on the spirits of the colonists; and Joutel, like a good commander as he was, spared no pains to cheer them. "We did what we could to amuse ourselves and drive away care. I encouraged our people to dance and sing in the evenings; for when M. de la Salle was among [Pg 408] us, pleasure was often banished. Now, there is no use in being melancholy on such occasions. It is true that M. de la Salle had no great cause for merry-making, after all his losses and disappointments; but his troubles made others suffer also. Though he had ordered me to allow to each person only a certain quantity of meat at every meal, I observed this rule only when meat was rare. The air here is very keen, and one has a great appetite. One must eat and act, if he wants good health and spirits. I speak from experience; for once, when I had ague chills, and was obliged to keep the house with nothing to do, I was dreary and down-hearted. On the contrary, if I was busy with hunting or anything else, I was not so dull by half. So I tried to keep the people as busy as possible. I set them to making a small cellar to keep meat fresh in hot weather; but when M. de la Salle came back, he said it was too small. As he always wanted to do everything on a grand scale, he prepared to make a large one, and marked out the plan." This plan of the large cellar, like more important undertakings of its unhappy projector, proved too extensive for execution, the colonists being engrossed by the daily care of keeping themselves alive.

MATRIMONY.

A gleam of hilarity shot for an instant out of the clouds. The young Canadian, Barbier, usually conducted the hunting-parties; and some of the women and girls often went out with them, to aid in cutting up the meat. Barbier became enamoured of one of [Pg 409] the girls; and as his devotion to her was the subject of comment, he asked Joutel for leave to marry her. The commandant, after due counsel with the priests and friars, vouchsafed his consent, and the rite was duly solemnized; whereupon, fired by the example, the Marquis de la Sablonnière begged leave to marry another of the girls. Joutel, the gardener's son, concerned that a marquis should so abase himself, and anxious at the same time for the morals of the fort, which La Salle had especially commended to his care, not only flatly refused, but, in the plenitude of his authority, forbade the lovers all further intercourse.

Father Zenobe Membré, superior of the mission, gave unwilling occasion for further merriment. These worthy friars were singularly unhappy in their dealings with the buffalo, one of which, it may be remembered, had already knocked down Father Anastase. Undeterred by his example, Father Zenobe one day went out with the hunters, carrying a gun like the rest. Joutel shot a buffalo, which was making off, badly wounded, when a second shot stopped it, and it presently lay down. The father superior thought it was dead; and, without heeding the warning shout of Joutel, he approached, and pushed it with the butt of his gun. The bull sprang up with an effort of expiring fury, and, in the words of Joutel, "trampled on the father, took the skin off his face in several places, and broke his gun, so that he could hardly manage to get away, and remained [Pg 410] in an almost helpless state for more than three months. Bad as the accident was, he was laughed at nevertheless for his rashness."

The mishaps of the friars did not end here. Father Maxime Le Clerc was set upon by a boar belonging to the colony. "I do not know," says Joutel, "what spite the beast had against him, whether for a beating or some other offence; but, however this may be, I saw the father running and crying for help, and the boar running after him. I went to the rescue, but could not come up in time. The father stooped as he ran, to gather up his cassock from about his legs; and the boar, which ran faster than he, struck him in the arm with his tusks, so that some of the nerves were torn. Thus, all three of our good Récollet fathers were near being the victims of animals."[315]

In spite of his efforts to encourage them, the followers of Joutel were fast losing heart. Father Maxime Le Clerc kept a journal, in which he set down various charges against La Salle. Joutel got possession of the paper, and burned it on the urgent entreaty of the friars, who dreaded what might ensue, should the absent commander become aware of the aspersions cast upon him. The elder Duhaut fomented the rising discontent of the colonists, played the demagogue, told them that La Salle would never return, and tried to make himself their leader. Joutel detected the mischief, and, with a lenity which he afterwards deeply regretted, contented [Pg 411] himself with a rebuke to the offender, and words of reproof and encouragement to the dejected band.

ADVENTURES OF THE TRAVELLERS.

He had caused the grass to be cut near the fort, so as to form a sort of playground; and here, one evening, he and some of the party were trying to amuse themselves, when they heard shouts from beyond the river, and Joutel recognized the voice of La Salle. Hastening to meet him in a wooden canoe, he brought him and his party to the fort. Twenty men had gone out with him, and eight had returned. Of the rest, four had deserted, one had been lost, one had been devoured by an alligator; and the others, giving out on the march, had probably perished in attempting to regain the fort. The travellers told of a rich country, a wild and beautiful landscape,—woods, rivers, groves, and prairies; but all availed nothing, and the acquisition of five horses was but an indifferent return for the loss of twelve men.

After leaving the fort, they had journeyed towards the northeast, over plains green as an emerald with the young verdure of April, till at length they saw, far as the eye could reach, the boundless prairie alive with herds of buffalo. The animals were in one of their tame or stupid moods; and they killed nine or ten of them without the least difficulty, drying the best parts of the meat. They crossed the Colorado on a raft, and reached the banks of another river, where one of the party, named Hiens, a German of [Pg 412] Würtemberg, and an old buccaneer, was mired and nearly suffocated in a mud-hole. Unfortunately, as will soon appear, he managed to crawl out; and, to console him, the river was christened with his name. The party made a bridge of felled trees, on which they crossed in safety. La Salle now changed their course, and journeyed eastward, when the travellers soon found themselves in the midst of a numerous Indian population, where they were feasted and caressed without measure. At another village they were less fortunate. The inhabitants were friendly by day and hostile by night. They came to attack the French in their camp, but withdrew, daunted by the menacing voice of La Salle, who had heard them approaching through the cane-brake.

La Salle's favorite Shawanoe hunter, Nika, who had followed him from Canada to France, and from France to Texas, was bitten by a rattlesnake; and, though he recovered, the accident detained the party for several days. At length they resumed their journey, but were stopped by a river, called by Douay, "La Rivière des Malheurs." La Salle and Cavelier, with a few others, tried to cross on a raft, which, as it reached the channel, was caught by a current of marvellous swiftness. Douay and Moranget, watching the transit from the edge of the cane-brake, beheld their commander swept down the stream, and vanishing, as it were, in an instant. All that day they remained with their companions on the bank, lamenting in despair for the loss of their guardian [Pg 413] angel, for so Douay calls La Salle.[316] It was fast growing dark, when, to their unspeakable relief, they saw him advancing with his party along the opposite bank, having succeeded, after great exertion, in guiding the raft to land. How to rejoin him was now the question. Douay and his companions, who had tasted no food that day, broke their fast on two young eagles which they knocked out of their nest, and then spent the night in rueful consultation as to the means of crossing the river. In the morning they waded into the marsh, the friar with his breviary in his hood to keep it dry, and hacked among the canes till they had gathered enough to make another raft; on which, profiting by La Salle's experience, they safely crossed, and rejoined him.

Next, they became entangled in a cane-brake, where La Salle, as usual with him in such cases, took the lead, a hatchet in each hand, and hewed out a path for his followers. They soon reached the villages of the Cenis Indians, on and near the river Trinity,—a tribe then powerful, but long since extinct. Nothing could surpass the friendliness of their welcome. The chiefs came to meet them, bearing the calumet, and followed by warriors in shirts of embroidered deer-skin. Then the whole village swarmed out like bees, gathering around the [Pg 414] visitors with offerings of food and all that was precious in their eyes. La Salle was lodged with the great chief; but he compelled his men to encamp at a distance, lest the ardor of their gallantry might give occasion of offence. The lodges of the Cenis, forty or fifty feet high, and covered with a thatch of meadow-grass, looked like huge bee-hives. Each held several families, whose fire was in the middle, and their beds around the circumference. The spoil of the Spaniards was to be seen on all sides,—silver lamps and spoons, swords, old muskets, money, clothing, and a bull of the Pope dispensing the Spanish colonists of New Mexico from fasting during summer.[317] These treasures, as well as their numerous horses, were obtained by the Cenis from their neighbors and allies the Camanches, that fierce prairie banditti who then, as now, scourged the Mexican border with their bloody forays. A party of these wild horsemen was in the village. Douay was edified at seeing them make the sign of the cross in imitation of the neophytes of one of the Spanish missions. They enacted, too, the ceremony of the mass; and one of them, in his rude way, drew a sketch of a picture he had seen in some church which he had pillaged, wherein the friar plainly recognized the Virgin weeping at the foot of the cross. They invited the French to join them on a raid into New Mexico; and they spoke with contempt, as their tribesmen will speak to this day, of the Spanish [Pg 415] creoles, saying that it would be easy to conquer a nation of cowards who make people walk before them with fans to cool them in hot weather.[318]

Soon after leaving the Cenis villages, both La Salle and his nephew Moranget were attacked by fever. This caused a delay of more than two months, during which the party seem to have remained encamped on the Neches, or possibly the Sabine. When at length the invalids had recovered sufficient strength to travel, the stock of ammunition was nearly spent, some of the men had deserted, and the condition of the travellers was such that there seemed no alternative but to return to Fort St. Louis. This they accordingly did, greatly aided in their march by the horses bought from the Cenis, and suffering no very serious accident by the way,—excepting the loss of La Salle's servant, Dumesnil, who was seized by an alligator while attempting to cross the Colorado.

DEJECTION.

The temporary excitement caused among the colonists by their return soon gave place to a dejection bordering on despair. "This pleasant land," writes Cavelier, "seemed to us an abode of weariness and a perpetual prison." Flattering themselves with the delusion, common to exiles of every kind, that they were objects of solicitude at home, they watched daily, with straining eyes, for an approaching sail. Ships, indeed, had ranged the coast to seek them, but with no friendly intent. Their thoughts dwelt, [Pg 416] with unspeakable yearning, on the France they had left behind, which, to their longing fancy, was pictured as an unattainable Eden. Well might they despond; for of a hundred and eighty colonists, besides the crew of the "Belle," less than forty-five remained. The weary precincts of Fort St. Louis, with its fence of rigid palisades, its area of trampled earth, its buildings of weather-stained timber, and its well-peopled graveyard without, were hateful to their sight. La Salle had a heavy task to save them from despair. His composure, his unfailing equanimity, his words of encouragement and cheer, were the breath of life to this forlorn company; for though he could not impart to minds of less adamantine temper the audacity of hope with which he still clung to the final accomplishment of his purposes, the contagion of his hardihood touched, nevertheless, the drooping spirits of his followers.[319]

TWELFTH NIGHT.

The journey to Canada was clearly their only hope; and, after a brief rest, La Salle prepared to renew the attempt. He proposed that Joutel should this time be of the party; and should proceed from Quebec to France, with his brother Cavelier, to solicit succors for the colony, while he himself [Pg 417] returned to Texas. A new obstacle was presently interposed. La Salle, whose constitution seems to have suffered from his long course of hardships, was attacked in November with hernia. Joutel offered to conduct the party in his stead; but La Salle replied that his own presence was indispensable at the Illinois. He had the good fortune to recover, within four or five weeks, sufficiently to undertake the journey; and all in the fort busied themselves in preparing an outfit. In such straits were they for clothing, that the sails of the "Belle" were cut up to make coats for the adventurers. Christmas came, and was solemnly observed. There was a midnight mass in the chapel, where Membré, Cavelier, Douay, and their priestly brethren stood before the altar, in vestments strangely contrasting with the rude temple and the ruder garb of the worshippers. And as Membré elevated the consecrated wafer, and the lamps burned dim through the clouds of incense, the kneeling group drew from the daily miracle such consolation as true Catholics alone can know. When Twelfth Night came, all gathered in the hall, and cried, after the jovial old custom, "The King drinks," with hearts, perhaps, as cheerless as their cups, which were filled with cold water.

THE LAST FAREWELL.

On the morrow, the band of adventurers mustered for the fatal journey.[320] The five horses, bought by [Pg 418] La Salle of the Indians, stood in the area of the fort, packed for the march; and here was gathered the wretched remnant of the colony,—those who were to go, and those who were to stay behind. These latter were about twenty in all,—Barbier, who was to command in the place of Joutel; Sablonnière, who, despite his title of marquis, was held in great contempt;[321] the friars, Membré and Le Clerc,[322] and the priest Chefdeville, besides a surgeon, soldiers, laborers, seven women and girls, and several children, doomed, in this deadly exile, to wait the issues of the journey, and the possible arrival of a tardy succor. La Salle had made them a last address, delivered, we are told, with that winning air which, though alien from his usual bearing, seems to have been at times a natural expression of this unhappy man.[323] It was a bitter parting, one of sighs, tears, and embracings,—the farewell of those on whose souls had sunk a heavy boding that they would never [Pg 419] meet again.[324] Equipped and weaponed for the journey, the adventurers filed from the gate, crossed the river, and held their slow march over the prairies beyond, till intervening woods and hills shut Fort St. Louis forever from their sight.

FOOTNOTES:

[301] Called by Joutel, Rivière aux Bœufs.
[302] Joutel, *Journal Historique*, 108; *Relation* (Margry, iii. 174); *Procès Verbal fait au poste de St. Louis, le 18 Avril, 1686*.

[303] Joutel, *Journal Historique*, 109. Le Clerc, who was not present, says a hundred.

[304] The Bay of St. Louis, St. Bernard's Bay, or Matagorda Bay,—for it has borne all these names,—was also called Espiritu Santo Bay by the Spaniards, in common with several other bays in the Gulf of Mexico. An adjoining bay still retains the name.

[305] Cavelier, in his report to the minister, says: "We reached a large village, enclosed with a kind of wall made of clay and sand, and fortified with little towers at intervals, where we found the arms of Spain engraved on a plate of copper, with the date of 1588, attached to a stake. The inhabitants gave us a kind welcome, and showed us some hammers and an anvil, two small pieces of iron cannon, a small brass culverin, some pike-heads, some old sword-blades, and some books of Spanish comedy; and thence they guided us to a little hamlet of fishermen, about two leagues distant, where they showed us a second stake, also with the arms of Spain, and a few old chimneys. All this convinced us that the Spaniards had formerly been here." (Cavelier, *Relation du Voyage que mon frère entreprit pour découvrir l'embouchure du fleuve de Missisipy*.) The above is translated from the original draft of Cavelier, which is in my possession. It was addressed to the colonial minister, after the death of La Salle. The statement concerning the Spaniards needs confirmation.

[306] Compare Joutel with the Spanish account in *Carta en que se da noticia de un viaje hecho á la Bahia de Espíritu Santo y de la poblacion que tenian ahi los Franceses; Coleccion de Varios Documentos*, 25.

[307] For the above incidents of life at Fort St. Louis, see Joutel, *Relation* (Margry, iii. 185-218, *passim*). The printed condensation of the narrative omits most of these particulars.

[308] Joutel, *Relation* (Margry, iii. 206). Compare Le Clerc, ii. 296. Cavelier, always disposed to exaggerate, says that ten men were killed. La Salle had previously had encounters with the Indians, and punished them severely for the trouble they had given his men. Le Clerc says of the principal fight: "Several Indians were wounded, a few were killed, and others made prisoners,—one of whom, a girl of three or four years, was baptized, and died a few days after, as the first-fruit of this mission, and a sure conquest sent to heaven."

[309] Joutel, *Relation* (Margry, iii. 219).

[310] Cavelier says that he actually reached the Mississippi; but, on the one hand, the abbé did not know whether the river in question was the Mississippi or not; and, on the other, he is somewhat inclined to

mendacity. Le Clerc says that La Salle thought he had found the river. According to the *Procès Verbal* of 18 April, 1686, "il y arriva le 13 Février." Joutel says that La Salle told him "qu'il n'avoit point trouvé sa rivière."

[311] *Procès Verbal fait au poste de St. Louis, le 18 Avril, 1686.*

[312] Cavelier, *Relation du Voyage pour découvrir l'Embouchure du Fleuve de Missisipy.*

[313] Joutel, *Journal Historique*, 140; Anastase Douay in Le Clerc, ii. 303; Cavelier, *Relation*. The date is from Douay. It does not appear, from his narrative, that they meant to go farther than the Illinois. Cavelier says that after resting here they were to go to Canada. Joutel supposed that they would go only to the Illinois. La Salle seems to have been even more reticent than usual.

[314] Joutel, *Relation* (Margry, iii. 226).

[315] Joutel, *Relation* (Margry, iii. 244, 246.

[316] "Ce fût une desolation extrême pour nous tous qui desesperions de revoir jamais nostre Ange tutélaire, le Sieur de la Salle.... Tout le jour se passa en pleurs et en larmes."—*Douay in Le Clerc*, ii. 315.

[317] Douay in Le Clerc, ii. 321; Cavelier, *Relation.*

[318] Douay in Le Clerc, ii. 324, 325.

[319] "L'égalité d'humeur du Chef rassuroit tout le monde; et il trouvoit des resources à tout par son esprit qui relevoit les espérances les plus abatues."—Joutel, *Journal Historique*, 152.

"Il seroit difficile de trouver dans l'Histoire un courage plus intrepide et plus invincible que celuy du Sieur de la Salle dans les évenemens contraires; il ne fût jamais abatu, et il espéroit toujours avec le secours du Ciel de venir à bout de son entreprise malgré tous les obstacles qui se présentoient."—*Douay in Le Clerc*, ii. 327.

[320] I follow Douay's date, who makes the day of departure the seventh of January, or the day after Twelfth Night. Joutel thinks it was the twelfth of January, but professes uncertainty as to all his dates at this time, as he lost his notes.

[321] He had to be kept on short allowance, because he was in the habit of bargaining away everything given to him. He had squandered the little that belonged to him at St. Domingo, in amusements "indignes de sa naissance," and in consequence was suffering from diseases which disabled him from walking. (*Procès Verbal, 18 Avril, 1686.*)

[322] Maxime le Clerc was a relative of the author of *L'Établissement de la Foi.*

[323] "Il fit une Harangue pleine d'éloquence et de cet air engageant qui luy estoit si naturel: toute la petite Colonie y estoit presente et en fût touchée jusques aux larmes, persuadée de la nécessité de son voyage et de la droiture de ses intentions."—*Douay in Le Clerc*, ii, 330.

[324] "Nous nous separâmes les uns des autres, d'une manière si tendre et si triste qu'il sembloit que nous avions tous le secret pressentiment que nous ne nous reverrions jamais."—Joutel, *Journal Historique*, 158.

[Pg 420]

CHAPTER XXVII.

1687.

ASSASSINATION OF LA SALLE.

His Followers. — Prairie Travelling — A Hunters' Quarrel — The Murder of Moranget. — The Conspiracy. — Death of La Salle: his Character.

LA SALLE'S FOLLOWERS.

THE travellers were crossing a marshy prairie towards a distant belt of woods that followed the course of a little river. They led with them their five horses, laden with their scanty baggage, and, with what was of no less importance, their stock of presents for Indians. Some wore the remains of the clothing they had worn from France, eked out with deer-skins, dressed in the Indian manner; and some had coats of old sail-cloth. Here was La Salle, in whom one would have known, at a glance, the chief of the party; and the priest, Cavelier, who seems to have shared not one of the high traits of his younger brother. Here, too, were their nephews, Moranget and the boy Cavelier, now about seventeen years old; the trusty soldier Joutel; and the friar Anastase Douay. Duhaut followed, a man of respectable birth and education; and Liotot, the surgeon of the party. [Pg 421] At home, they might perhaps have lived and died with a fair repute; but the wilderness is a rude touchstone, which often reveals traits that would have lain buried and unsuspected in civilized life. The German Hiens, the ex-buccaneer, was also of the number. He had probably sailed with an English crew; for he was sometimes known as *Gemme Anglais*, or "English Jem."[325] The Sieur de Marie; Teissier, a pilot; L'Archevêque, a servant of Duhaut; and others, to the number in all of seventeen,—made up the party; to which is to be added Nika, La Salle's Shawanoe hunter, who, as well as another Indian, had twice crossed the ocean with him, and still followed his fortunes with an admiring though undemonstrative fidelity.

They passed the prairie, and neared the forest. Here they saw buffalo; and the hunters approached, and killed several of them. Then they traversed the woods; found and forded the shallow and rushy stream, and pushed through the forest beyond, till they again reached the open prairie. Heavy clouds gathered over them, and it rained all night; but they sheltered themselves under the fresh hides of the buffalo they had killed.

PRAIRIE TRAVELLING.

It is impossible, as it would be needless, to follow the detail of their daily march.[326] It was such an one, [Pg 422] though with unwonted hardship, as is familiar to the memory of many a prairie traveller of our own time. They suffered greatly from the want of shoes, and found for a while no better substitute than a casing of raw buffalo-hide, which they were forced to keep always wet, as, when dry, it hardened about the foot like iron. At length they bought dressed deer-skin from the Indians, of which they made tolerable moccasins. The rivers, streams, and gullies filled with water were without number; and to cross them they made a boat of bull-hide, like the "bull boat" still used on the Upper Missouri. This did good service, as, with the help of their horses, they could carry it with them. Two or three men could cross in it at once, and the horses swam after them like dogs. Sometimes they traversed the sunny prairie; sometimes dived into the dark recesses of the forest, where the buffalo, descending daily from their pastures in long files to drink at the river, often made a broad and easy path for the travellers. When foul weather arrested them, they built huts of bark and long meadow-grass; and safely sheltered lounged away the day, while their horses, picketed near by, stood steaming in the rain. At night, they usually set a rude stockade about their camp; and here, by [Pg 423] the grassy border of a brook, or at the edge of a grove where a spring bubbled up through the sands, they lay asleep around the embers of their fire, while the man on guard listened to the deep breathing of the slumbering horses, and the howling of the wolves that saluted the rising moon as it flooded the waste of prairie with pale mystic radiance.

They met Indians almost daily,—sometimes a band of hunters, mounted or on foot, chasing buffalo on the plains; sometimes a party of fishermen; sometimes a winter camp, on the slope of a hill or under the sheltering border of a forest. They held intercourse with them in the distance by signs; often they disarmed their distrust, and attracted them into their camp; and often they visited them in their lodges, where, seated on buffalo-robes, they smoked with their entertainers, passing the pipe from hand to hand, after the custom still in use among the prairie tribes. Cavelier says that they once saw a band of a hundred and fifty mounted Indians attacking a herd of buffalo with lances pointed with sharpened bone. The old priest was delighted with the sport, which he pronounces "the most diverting thing in the world." On another occasion, when the party were encamped near the village of a tribe which Cavelier calls Sassory, he saw them catch an alligator about twelve feet long, which they proceeded to torture as if he were a human enemy,—first putting out his eyes, and then leading him to the neighboring prairie, where, having confined him by a [Pg 424] number of stakes, they spent the entire day in tormenting him.[327]

Holding a northerly course, the travellers crossed the Brazos, and reached the waters of the Trinity. The weather was unfavorable, and on one occasion they encamped in the rain during four or five days together. It was not an harmonious company. La Salle's cold and haughty reserve had returned, at least for those of his followers to whom he was not partial. Duhaut and the surgeon Liotot, both of whom were men of some property, had a large pecuniary stake in the enterprise, and were disappointed and incensed at its ruinous result. They had a quarrel with young Moranget, whose hot and hasty temper was as little fitted to conciliate as was the harsh reserve of his uncle. Already at Fort St. Louis, Duhaut had intrigued among the men; and the mild admonition of Joutel had not, it seems, sufficed to divert him from his sinister purposes. Liotot, it is said, had secretly sworn vengeance against La Salle, whom he charged with having caused the death of his brother, or, as some will have it, his nephew. On one of the former journeys this young man's strength had failed; and, La Salle having ordered him to return to the fort, he had been killed by Indians on the way.

MURDER OF MORANGET.

The party moved again as the weather improved, and on the fifteenth of March encamped within a few miles of a spot which La Salle had passed on his [Pg 425] preceding journey, and where he had left a quantity of Indian corn and beans in *cache*; that is to say, hidden in the ground or in a hollow tree. As provisions were falling short, he sent a party from the camp to find it. These men were Duhaut, Liotot,[328] Hiens the buccaneer, Teissier, L'Archevêque, Nika the hunter, and La Salle's servant Saget. They opened the *cache*, and found the contents spoiled; but as they returned from their bootless errand they saw buffalo, and Nika shot two of them. They now encamped on the spot, and sent the servant to inform La Salle, in order that he might send horses to bring in the meat. Accordingly, on the next day, he directed Moranget and De Marle, with the necessary horses, to go with Saget to the hunters' camp. When they arrived, they found that Duhaut and his companions had already cut up the meat, and laid it upon scaffolds for smoking, though it was not yet so dry as, it seems, this process required. Duhaut and the others had also put by, for themselves, the marrow-bones and certain portions of the meat, to which, by woodland custom, they had a perfect right. Moranget, whose rashness and violence had once before caused a fatal catastrophe, fell into a most unreasonable fit of rage, berated and menaced Duhaut and his party, and ended by seizing upon the whole of the meat, including the reserved portions. This added fuel to the fire of Duhaut's old grudge against Moranget and his uncle. There is reason to think [Pg 426] that he had harbored deadly designs, the execution of which was only hastened by the present outbreak. The surgeon also bore hatred against Moranget, whom he had nursed with constant attention when wounded by an Indian arrow, and who had since repaid him with abuse. These two now took counsel apart with Hiens, Teissier, and L'Archevêque; and it was resolved to kill Moranget that night. Nika, La Salle's devoted follower, and Saget, his faithful servant, must die with him. All of the five were of one mind except the pilot Teissier, who neither aided nor opposed the plot.

Night came: the woods grew dark; the evening meal was finished, and the evening pipes were smoked. The order of the guard was arranged; and, doubtless by design, the first hour of the night was assigned to Moranget, the second to Saget, and the third to Nika. Gun in hand, each stood watch in turn over the silent but not sleeping forms around him, till, his time expiring, he called the man who was to relieve him, wrapped himself in his blanket, and was soon buried in a slumber that was to be his last. Now the assassins rose. Duhaut and Hiens stood with their guns cocked, ready to shoot down any one of the destined victims who should resist or fly. The surgeon, with an axe, stole towards the three sleepers, and struck a rapid blow at each in turn. Saget and Nika died with little movement; but Moranget started spasmodically into a sitting posture, gasping and unable to speak; and the murderers [Pg 427] compelled De Marle, who was not in their plot, to compromise himself by despatching him.

The floodgates of murder were open, and the torrent must have its way. Vengeance and safety alike demanded the death of La Salle. Hiens, or "English Jem," alone seems to have hesitated; for he was one of those to whom that stern commander had always been partial. Meanwhile, the intended victim was still at his camp, about six miles distant. It is easy to picture, with sufficient accuracy, the features of the scene,—the sheds of bark and branches, beneath which, among blankets and buffalo-robes, camp-utensils, pack-saddles, rude harness, guns, powder-horns, and bullet-pouches, the men lounged away the hour, sleeping or smoking, or talking among themselves; the blackened kettles that hung from tripods of poles over the fires; the Indians strolling about the place or lying, like dogs in the sun, with eyes half-shut, yet all observant; and, in the neighboring meadow, the horses grazing under the eye of a watchman.

SUSPENSE.

It was the eighteenth of March. Moranget and his companions had
been expected to return the night before; but the whole day passed,
and they did not appear. La Salle became very anxious. He resolved
to go and look for them; but not well knowing the way, he told the
Indians who were about the camp that he would give them a hatchet
if they would guide him. One of them accepted the offer; and La
Salle prepared to set out in the morning, at [Pg 428] the same time
directing Joutel to be ready to go with him. Joutel says: "That
evening, while we were talking about what could have happened to
the absent men, he seemed to have a presentiment of what was to
take place. He asked me if I had heard of any machinations against
them, or if I had noticed any bad design on the part of Duhaut and
the rest. I answered that I had heard nothing, except that they
sometimes complained of being found fault with so often; and that
this was all I knew; besides which, as they were persuaded that I was
in his interest, they would not have told me of any bad design they
might have. We were very uneasy all the rest of the evening."

THE FATAL SHOT.

In the morning, La Salle set out with his Indian guide. He had
changed his mind with regard to Joutel, whom he now directed to
remain in charge of the camp and to keep a careful watch. He told
the friar Anastase Douay to come with him instead of Joutel, whose
gun, which was the best in the party, he borrowed for the occasion,
as well as his pistol. The three proceeded on their way,—La Salle,
the friar, and the Indian. "All the way," writes the friar, "he spoke to
me of nothing but matters of piety, grace, and predestination;
enlarging on the debt he owed to God, who had saved him from so
many perils during more than twenty years of travel in America.
Suddenly, I saw him overwhelmed with a profound sadness, for
which he himself could not account. He was so much moved [Pg 429]
that I scarcely knew him." He soon recovered his usual calmness;

and they walked on till they approached the camp of Duhaut, which was on the farther side of a small river. Looking about him with the eye of a woodsman, La Salle saw two eagles circling in the air nearly over him, as if attracted by carcasses of beasts or men. He fired his gun and his pistol, as a summons to any of his followers who might be within hearing. The shots reached the ears of the conspirators. Rightly conjecturing by whom they were fired, several of them, led by Duhaut, crossed the river at a little distance above, where trees or other intervening objects hid them from sight. Duhaut and the surgeon crouched like Indians in the long, dry, reed-like grass of the last summer's growth, while L'Archevêque stood in sight near the bank. La Salle, continuing to advance, soon saw him, and, calling to him, demanded where was Moranget. The man, without lifting his hat, or any show of respect, replied in an agitated and broken voice, but with a tone of studied insolence, that Moranget was strolling about somewhere. La Salle rebuked and menaced him. He rejoined with increased insolence, drawing back, as he spoke, towards the ambuscade, while the incensed commander advanced to chastise him. At that moment a shot was fired from the grass, instantly followed by another; and, pierced through the brain, La Salle dropped dead.

The friar at his side stood terror-stricken, unable [Pg 430] to advance or to fly; when Duhaut, rising from the ambuscade, called out to him to take courage, for he had nothing to fear. The murderers now came forward, and with wild looks gathered about their victim. "There thou liest, great Bashaw! There thou liest!"[329] exclaimed the surgeon Liotot, in base exultation over the unconscious corpse. With mockery and insult, they stripped it naked, dragged it into the bushes, and left it there, a prey to the buzzards and the wolves.

Thus in the vigor of his manhood, at the age of forty-three, died Robert Cavelier de la Salle, "one of the greatest men," writes Tonty, "of this age;" without question one of the most remarkable explorers whose names live in history. His faithful officer Joutel thus sketches his portrait: "His firmness, his courage, his great knowledge of the arts and sciences, which made him equal to every undertaking, and his untiring energy, which enabled him to surmount every obstacle, would have won at last a glorious success for his grand enterprise, had not all his fine qualities been counterbalanced by a haughtiness of manner which often made him insupportable, and by a harshness towards those under his command which drew upon him an implacable hatred, and was at last the cause of his death."[330]

HIS CHARACTER.

The enthusiasm of the disinterested and chivalrous [Pg 431] Champlain was not the enthusiasm of La Salle; nor had he any part in the self-devoted zeal of the early Jesuit explorers. He belonged not to the age of the knight-errant and the saint, but to the modern world of practical study and practical action. He was the hero not of a principle nor of a faith, but simply of a fixed idea and a determined purpose. As often happens with concentred and energetic natures, his purpose was to him a passion and an inspiration; and he clung to it with a certain fanaticism of devotion. It was the offspring of an ambition vast and comprehensive, yet acting in the interest both of France and of civilization.

Serious in all things, incapable of the lighter pleasures, incapable of repose, finding no joy but in the pursuit of great designs, too shy for society and too reserved for popularity, often unsympathetic and always seeming so, smothering emotions which he could not utter, schooled to universal distrust, stern to his followers and pitiless to himself, bearing the brunt of every hardship and every danger, demanding of others an equal constancy joined to an implicit deference, heeding no counsel but his own, attempting the impossible and grasping at what was too vast to hold,—he contained in his own complex and painful nature the chief springs of his triumphs, his failures, and his death.

It is easy to reckon up his defects, but it is not easy to hide from sight the Roman virtues that redeemed them. Beset by a throng of enemies, he [Pg 432] stands, like the King of Israel, head and shoulders above them all. He was a tower of adamant, against whose impregnable front hardship and danger, the rage of man and of the elements, the southern sun, the northern blast, fatigue, famine, disease, delay, disappointment, and deferred hope emptied their quivers in vain. That very pride which, Coriolanus-like, declared itself most sternly in the thickest press of foes, has in it something to challenge admiration. Never, under the impenetrable mail of paladin or crusader, beat a heart of more intrepid mettle than within the stoic panoply that armed the breast of La Salle. To estimate aright the marvels of his patient fortitude, one must follow on his track through the vast scene of his interminable journeyings,—those thousands of weary miles of forest, marsh, and river, where, again and again, in the bitterness of baffled striving, the untiring pilgrim pushed onward towards the goal which he was never to attain. America owes him an enduring memory; for in this masculine figure she sees the pioneer who guided her to the possession of her richest heritage.[331]

FOOTNOTES:

[325] Tonty also speaks of him as "un flibustier anglois." In another document, he is called "James."

[326] Of the three narratives of this journey, those of Joutel, Cavelier, and Anastase Douay, the first is by far the best. That of Cavelier seems the work of a man of confused brain and indifferent memory. Some of his statements are irreconcilable with those of Joutel and Douay; and known facts of his history justify the suspicion of a wilful inaccuracy. Joutel's account is of a very different character, and seems to be the work of an honest and intelligent man. Douay's account if brief; but it agrees with that of Joutel, in most essential points.

[327] Cavelier, *Relation*.

[328] Called Lanquetot by Tonty.

[329] "Te voilà, grand Bacha, te voilà!"—Joutel, *Journal Historique*, 203.

[330] *Ibid.*

[331] On the assassination of La Salle, the evidence is fourfold: 1. The narrative of Douay, who was with him at the time. 2. That of Joutel, who learned the facts, immediately after they took place, from Douay and

others, and who parted from La Salle an hour or more before his death. 3. A document preserved in the Archives de la Marine, entitled *Relation de la Mort du Sr. de la Salle, suivant le rapport d'un nommé Couture à qui M. Cavelier l'apprit en passant au pays des Akansa, avec toutes les circonstances que le dit Couture a apprises d'un François que M. Cavelier avoit laissé aux dits pays des Akansa, crainte qu'il ne gardât pas le secret.* 4. The authentic [Pg 433]memoir of Tonty, of which a copy from the original is before me, and which has recently been printed by Margry.

The narrative of Cavelier unfortunately fails us several weeks before the death of his brother, the remainder being lost. On a study of these various documents, it is impossible to resist the conclusion that neither Cavelier nor Douay always wrote honestly. Joutel, on the contrary, gives the impression of sense, intelligence, and candor throughout. Charlevoix, who knew him long after, says that he was "un fort honnête homme, et le seul de la troupe de M. de la Salle, sur qui ce célèbre voyageur pût compter." Tonty derived his information from the survivors of La Salle's party. Couture, whose statements are embodied in the *Relation de la Mort de M. de la Salle*, was one of Tonty's men, who, as will be seen hereafter, were left by him at the mouth of the Arkansas, and to whom Cavelier told the story of his brother's death. Couture also repeats the statements of one of La Salle's followers, undoubtedly a Parisian boy, named Barthelemy, who was violently prejudiced against his chief, whom he slanders to the utmost of his skill, saying that he was so enraged at his failures that he did not approach the sacraments for two years; that he nearly starved his brother Cavelier, allowing him only a handful of meal a day; that he killed with his own hand "quantité de personnes," who did not work to his liking; and that he killed the sick in their beds, without mercy, under the pretence that they were counterfeiting sickness in order to escape work. These assertions certainly have no other foundation than the undeniable rigor of La Salle's command. Douay says that he confessed and made his devotions on the morning of his death, while Cavelier always speaks of him as the hope and the staff of the colony.

Douay declares that La Salle lived an hour after the fatal shot; that he gave him absolution, buried his body, and planted a cross on his grave. At the time, he told Joutel a different story; and the latter, with the best means of learning the facts, explicitly denies the friar's printed statement. Couture, on the authority of Cavelier himself, also says that neither he nor Douay was permitted to take any step for burying the body. Tonty says that Cavelier begged leave to do so, but was refused. Douay, unwilling to place upon record facts from which the inference might easily be drawn that he had been terrified from discharging his duty, no doubt invented the story of the burial, as well as that of the edifying behavior of Moranget, after he had been struck in the head with an axe.

[Pg 434]

The locality of La Salle's assassination is sufficiently clear, from a comparison of the several narratives; and it is also indicated on a contemporary manuscript map, made on the return of the survivors of the party to France. The scene of the catastrophe is here placed on a southern branch of the Trinity.

La Salle's debts, at the time of his death, according to a schedule presented in 1701 to Champigny, intendant of Canada, amounted to 106,831 livres, without reckoning interest. This cannot be meant to include all, as items are given which raise the amount much higher. In 1678 and 1679 alone, he contracted debts to the amount of 97,184 livres, of which 46,000 were furnished by Branssac, fiscal attorney of the Seminary of Montreal. This was to be paid in beaver-skins. Frontenac, at the same time, became his surety for 13,623 livres. In 1684, he borrowed 34,825 livres from the Sieur Pen, at Paris. These sums do not include the losses incurred by his family, which, in the memorial presented by them to the King, are set down at 500,000 livres for the expeditions between 1678 and 1683, and 300,000 livres for the fatal Texan expedition of 1684 These last figures are certainly exaggerated.

[Pg 435]

CHAPTER XXVIII.

1687, 1688.

THE INNOCENT AND THE GUILTY.

FATHER ANASTASE DOUAY returned to the camp, and, aghast with grief and terror, rushed into the hut of Cavelier. "My poor brother is dead!" cried the priest, instantly divining the catastrophe from the horror-stricken face of the messenger. Close behind came the murderers, Duhaut at their head. Cavelier, his young nephew, and Douay himself, all fell on their knees, expecting instant death. The priest begged piteously for half an hour to prepare for his end; but terror and submission sufficed, and no more blood was shed. The camp yielded without resistance; and Duhaut was lord of all. In truth, there were none to oppose him; for, except the assassins themselves, the party was now reduced to six [Pg 436] persons,—Joutel, Douay, the elder Cavelier, his young nephew, and two other boys, the orphan Talon and a lad called Barthelemy.

DOUBT AND ANXIETY.

Joutel, for the moment, was absent; and L'Archevêque, who had a kindness for him, went quietly to seek him. He found him on a hillock, making a fire of dried grass in order that the smoke might guide La Salle on his return, and watching the horses grazing in the meadow below. "I was very much surprised," writes Joutel, "when I saw him approaching. When he came up to me he seemed all in confusion, or, rather, out of his wits. He began with saying that there was very bad news. I asked what it was. He answered that the Sieur de la Salle was dead, and also his nephew the Sieur de Moranget, his Indian hunter, and his servant. I was petrified, and did not know what to say; for I saw that they had been murdered. The man added that, at first, the murderers had sworn to kill me too. I easily believed it, for I had always been in the interest of M. de la Salle, and had commanded in his place; and it is hard to please everybody, or prevent some from being dissatisfied. I was greatly perplexed as to what I ought to do, and whether I had not better escape to the woods, whithersoever God should guide me; but, by bad or good luck, I had no gun and only one pistol, without balls or powder except what was in my powder-horn. To whatever side I turned, my life was in great peril. It is true that L'Archevêque assured me that they [Pg 437] had changed their minds, and had agreed to murder nobody else, unless they met with resistance. So, being in no condition, as I just said, to go far, having neither arms nor powder, I abandoned myself to Providence, and went back to the camp, where I found that these wretched murderers had seized everything belonging to M. de la Salle, and even my personal effects. They had also taken possession of all the arms. The first words that Duhaut said to me were, that each should command in turn; to which I made no answer. I saw M. Cavelier praying in a corner, and Father Anastase in another. He did not dare to speak to me, nor did I dare to go towards him till I had seen the designs of the assassins. They were in furious excitement, but, nevertheless, very uneasy and embarrassed. I was some time without speaking, and, as it were, without moving, for fear of giving umbrage to our enemies.

"They had cooked some meat, and when it was supper-time they distributed it as they saw fit, saying that formerly their share had been served out to them, but that it was they who would serve it out in future. They, no doubt, wanted me to say something that would give them a chance to make a noise; but I managed always to keep my mouth closed. When night came and it was time to stand guard, they were in perplexity, as they could not do it alone; therefore they said to M. Cavelier, Father Anastase, me, and the others who were not in the plot with them, that all we had to do was to stand [Pg 438] guard as usual; that there was no use in thinking about what had happened,—that what was done was done; that they had been driven to it by despair, and that they were sorry for it, and meant no more harm to anybody. M. Cavelier took up the word, and told them that when they killed M. de la Salle they killed themselves, for there was nobody but him who could get us out of this country. At last, after a good deal of talk on both sides, they gave us our arms. So we stood guard; during which, M. Cavelier told me how they had come to the camp, entered his hut like so many madmen, and seized everything in it."

Joutel, Douay, and the two Caveliers spent a sleepless night, consulting as to what they should do. They mutually pledged themselves to stand by each other to the last, and to escape as soon as they could from the company of the assassins. In the morning, Duhaut and his accomplices, after much discussion, resolved to go to the Cenis villages; and, accordingly, the whole party broke up their camp, packed their horses, and began their march. They went five leagues, and encamped at the edge of a grove. On the following day they advanced again till noon, when heavy rains began, and they were forced to stop by the banks of a river. "We passed the night and the next day there," says Joutel; "and during that time my mind was possessed with dark thoughts. It was hard to prevent ourselves from being in constant fear among such men, and we could not look at [Pg 439] them without horror. When I thought of the cruel deeds they had committed, and the danger we were in from them, I longed to revenge the evil they had done us. This would have been easy while they were asleep; but M. Cavelier dissuaded us, saying that we ought to leave vengeance to God, and that he himself had more to revenge than we, having lost his brother and his nephew."

JOURNEY TO THE CENIS.

The comic alternated with the tragic. On the twenty-third, they reached the bank of a river too deep to ford. Those who knew how to swim crossed without difficulty, but Joutel, Cavelier, and Douay were not of the number. Accordingly, they launched a log of light, dry wood, embraced it with one arm, and struck out for the other bank with their legs and the arm that was left free. But the friar became frightened. "He only clung fast to the aforesaid log," says Joutel, "and did nothing to help us forward. While I was trying to swim, my body being stretched at full length, I hit him in the belly with my feet; on which he thought it was all over with him, and, I can answer for it, he invoked Saint Francis with might and main. I could not help laughing, though I was myself in danger of drowning." Some Indians who had joined the party swam to the rescue, and pushed the log across.

The path to the Cenis villages was exceedingly faint, and but for the Indians they would have lost the way. They crossed the main stream of the Trinity in a boat of raw hides, and then, being short [Pg 440] of provisions, held a council to determine what they should do. It was resolved that Joutel, with Hiens, Liotot, and Teissier, should go in advance to the villages and buy a supply of corn. Thus, Joutel found himself doomed to the company of three villains, who, he strongly suspected, were contriving an opportunity to kill him; but, as he had no choice, he dissembled his doubts, and set out with his sinister companions, Duhaut having first supplied him with goods for the intended barter.

JOUTEL AND THE CENIS.

They rode over hills and plains till night, encamped, supped on a wild turkey, and continued their journey till the afternoon of the next day, when they saw three men approaching on horseback, one of whom, to Joutel's alarm, was dressed like a Spaniard. He proved, however, to be a Cenis Indian, like the others. The three turned their horses' heads, and accompanied the Frenchmen on their way. At length they neared the Indian town, which, with its large thatched lodges, looked like a cluster of gigantic haystacks. Their approach had been made known, and they were received in solemn state.

Twelve of the elders came to meet them in their dress of ceremony, each with his face daubed red or black, and his head adorned with painted plumes. From their shoulders hung deer-skins wrought with gay colors. Some carried war-clubs; some, bows and arrows; some, the blades of Spanish rapiers, attached to wooden handles decorated with hawk's bells and bunches of feathers. They stopped [Pg 441] before the honored guests, and, raising their hands aloft, uttered howls so extraordinary that Joutel could hardly preserve the gravity which the occasion demanded. Having next embraced the Frenchmen, the elders conducted them into the village, attended by a crowd of warriors and young men; ushered them into their town-hall, a large lodge, devoted to councils, feasts, dances, and other public assemblies; seated them on mats, and squatted in a ring around them. Here they were regaled with sagamite or Indian porridge, corn-cake, beans, bread made of the meal of parched corn, and another kind of bread made of the kernels of nuts and the seed of sunflowers. Then the pipe was lighted, and all smoked together. The four Frenchmen proposed to open a traffic for provisions, and their entertainers grunted assent.

Joutel found a Frenchman in the village. He was a young man from Provence, who had deserted from La Salle on his last journey, and was now, to all appearance, a savage like his adopted countrymen, being naked like them, and affecting to have forgotten his native language. He was very friendly, however, and invited the visitors to a neighboring village, where he lived, and where, as he told them, they would find a better supply of corn. They accordingly set out with him, escorted by a crowd of Indians. They saw lodges and clusters of lodges scattered along their path at intervals, each with its field of corn, beans, and pumpkins, rudely cultivated [Pg 442] with a wooden hoe. Reaching their destination, which was four or five leagues distant, they were greeted with the same honors as at the first village, and, the ceremonial of welcome over, were lodged in the abode of the savage Frenchman. It is not to be supposed, however, that he and his squaws, of whom he had a considerable number, dwelt here alone; for these lodges of the Cenis often contained eight or ten families. They were made by firmly planting in a circle tall, straight young trees, such as grew in the swamps. The tops were then bent inward and lashed together; great numbers of cross-pieces were bound on; and the frame thus constructed was thickly covered with thatch, a hole being left at the top for the escape of the smoke. The inmates were ranged around the circumference of the structure, each family in a kind of stall, open in front, but separated from those adjoining it by partitions of mats. Here they placed their beds of cane, their painted robes of buffalo and deer-skin, their cooking utensils of pottery, and other household goods; and here, too, the head of the family hung his bow, quiver, lance, and shield. There was nothing in common but the fire, which burned in the middle of the lodge, and was never suffered to go out. These dwellings were of great size, and Joutel declares that he has seen some of them sixty feet in diameter.[332]

[Pg 443]

It was in one of the largest that the four travellers were now lodged. A place was assigned them where to bestow their baggage; and they took possession of their quarters amid the silent stares of the whole community. They asked their renegade countryman, the Provençal, if they were safe. He replied that they were; but this did not wholly reassure them, and they spent a somewhat wakeful night. In the morning, they opened their budgets, and began a brisk trade in knives, awls, beads, and other trinkets, which they exchanged for corn and beans. Before evening, they had acquired a considerable stock; and Joutel's three companions declared their intention of returning with it to the camp, leaving him to continue the trade. They went, accordingly, in the morning; and Joutel was left alone. On the one hand, he was glad to be rid of them; on the other, he found his position among the Cenis very irksome, and, as he thought, insecure. Besides the Provençal, who had gone with Liotot and his companions, there were two other French deserters among this tribe, and Joutel was very desirous to see them, hoping that they could tell him the way to the Mississippi; [Pg 444] for he was resolved to escape, at the first opportunity, from the company of Duhaut and his accomplices. He therefore made the present of a knife to a young Indian, whom he sent to find the two Frenchmen and invite them to come to the village. Meanwhile he continued his barter, but under many difficulties; for he could only explain himself by signs, and his customers, though friendly by day, pilfered his goods by night. This, joined to the fears and troubles which burdened his mind, almost deprived him of sleep, and, as he confesses, greatly depressed his spirits. Indeed, he had little cause for cheerfulness as to the past, present, or future. An old Indian, one of the patriarchs of the tribe, observing his dejection and anxious to relieve it, one evening brought him a young wife, saying that he made him a present of her. She seated herself at his side; "but," says Joutel, "as my head was full of other cares and anxieties, I said nothing to the poor girl. She waited for a little time; and then, finding that I did not speak a word, she went away."[333]

WHITE SAVAGES.

Late one night, he lay between sleeping and waking on the buffalo-robe that covered his bed of canes. All around the great lodge, its inmates were buried in sleep; and the fire treasured scalp-locks, the spear and war-club, and shield of whitened bull-hide—that hung by each warrior's resting-place. Such was the weird [Pg 445] scene that lingered on the dreamy eyes of Joutel, as he closed them at last in a troubled sleep. The sound of a footstep soon wakened him; and, turning, he saw at his side the figure of a naked savage, armed with a bow and arrows. Joutel spoke, but received no answer. Not knowing what to think, he reached out his hand for his pistols; on which the intruder withdrew, and seated himself by the fire. Thither Joutel followed; and as the light fell on his features, he looked at him closely. His face was tattooed, after the Cenis fashion, in lines drawn from the top of the forehead and converging to the chin; and his body was decorated with similar embellishments. Suddenly, this supposed Indian rose and threw his arms around Joutel's neck, making himself known, at the same time, as one of the Frenchmen who had deserted from La Salle and taken refuge among the Cenis.

He was a Breton sailor named Ruter. His companion, named Grollet, also a sailor, had been afraid to come to the village lest he should meet La Salle. Ruter expressed surprise and regret when he heard of the death of his late commander. He had deserted him but a few months before. That brief interval had sufficed to transform him into a savage; and both he and his companion found their present reckless and ungoverned way of life greatly to their liking. He could tell nothing of the Mississippi; and on the next day he went home, carrying with him a present of beads for his wives, of which last he had made a large collection.

[Pg 446]

In a few days he reappeared, bringing Grollet with him. Each wore a bunch of turkey-feathers dangling from his head, and each had wrapped his naked body in a blanket. Three men soon after arrived from Duhaut's camp, commissioned to receive the corn which Joutel had purchased. They told him that Duhaut and Liotot, the tyrants of the party, had resolved to return to Fort St. Louis, and build a vessel to escape to the West Indies,—"a visionary scheme," writes Joutel, "for our carpenters were all dead; and even if they had been alive, they were so ignorant that they would not have known how to go about the work; besides, we had no tools for it. Nevertheless, I was obliged to obey, and set out for the camp with the provisions."

On arriving, he found a wretched state of affairs. Douay and the two Caveliers, who had been treated by Duhaut with great harshness and contempt, had been told to make their mess apart; and Joutel now joined them. This separation restored them their freedom of speech, of which they had hitherto been deprived; but it subjected them to incessant hunger, as they were allowed only food enough to keep them from famishing. Douay says that quarrels were rife among the assassins themselves,—the malcontents being headed by Hiens, who was enraged that Duhaut and Liotot should have engrossed all the plunder. Joutel was helpless, for he had none to back him but two priests and a boy.

SCHEMES OF ESCAPE.

He and his companions talked of nothing around [Pg 447] their solitary camp-fire but the means of escaping from the villanous company into which they were thrown. They saw no resource but to find the Mississippi, and thus make their way to Canada,—a prodigious undertaking in their forlorn condition; nor was there any probability that the assassins would permit them to go. These, on their part, were beset with difficulties. They could not return to civilization without manifest peril of a halter; and their only safety was to turn buccaneers or savages. Duhaut, however, still held to his plan of going back to Fort St. Louis; and Joutel and his companions, who with good reason stood in daily fear of him, devised among themselves a simple artifice to escape from his company. The elder Cavelier was to tell him that they were too fatigued for the journey, and wished to stay among the Cenis; and to beg him to allow them a portion of the goods, for which Cavelier was to give his note of hand. The old priest, whom a sacrifice of truth even on less important occasions cost no great effort, accordingly opened the negotiation, and to his own astonishment and that of his companions, gained the assent of Duhaut. Their joy, however, was short; for Ruter, the French savage, to whom Joutel had betrayed his intention, when inquiring the way to the Mississippi, told it to Duhaut, who on this changed front and made the ominous declaration that he and his men would also go to Canada. Joutel and his companions were now filled with alarm; for there was no likelihood that [Pg 448] the assassins would permit them, the witnesses of their crime, to reach the settlements alive. In the midst of their trouble, the sky was cleared as by the crash of a thunderbolt.

THE CRISIS.

Hiens and several others had gone, some time before, to the Cenis villages to purchase horses; and here they had been detained by the charms of the Indian women. During their stay, Hiens heard of

Duhaut's new plan of going to Canada by the Mississippi; and he declared to those with him that he would not consent. On a morning early in May he appeared at Duhaut's camp, with Ruter and Grollet, the French savages, and about twenty Indians. Duhaut and Liotot, it is said, were passing the time by practising with bows and arrows in front of their hut. One of them called to Hiens, "Good-morning;" but the buccaneer returned a sullen answer. He then accosted Duhaut, telling him that he had no mind to go up the Mississippi with him, and demanding a share of the goods. Duhaut replied that the goods were his own, since La Salle had owed him money. "So you will not give them to me?" returned Hiens. "No," was the answer. "You are a wretch!" exclaimed Hiens; "you killed my master."[334] And drawing a pistol from his belt he [Pg 449] fired at Duhaut, who staggered three or four paces and fell dead. Almost at the same instant Ruter fired his gun at Liotot, shot three balls into his body, and stretched him on the ground mortally wounded.

Douay and the two Caveliers stood in extreme terror, thinking that their turn was to come next. Joutel, no less alarmed, snatched his gun to defend himself; but Hiens called to him to fear nothing, declaring that what he had done was only to avenge the death of La Salle,—to which, nevertheless, he had been privy, though not an active sharer in the crime. Liotot lived long enough to make his confession, after which Ruter killed him by exploding a pistol loaded with a blank charge of powder against his head. Duhaut's myrmidon, L'Archevêque, was absent, hunting, and Hiens was for killing him on his return; but the two priests and Joutel succeeded in dissuading him.

The Indian spectators beheld these murders with undisguised amazement, and almost with horror. What manner of men were these who had pierced the secret places of the wilderness to riot in mutual slaughter? Their fiercest warriors might learn a lesson in ferocity from these heralds of civilization. Joutel and his companions, who could not dispense with the aid of the Cenis, were obliged to explain away, as they best might, the atrocity of what they had witnessed.[335]

Hiens, and others of the French, had before [Pg 450] promised to join the Cenis on an expedition against a neighboring tribe with whom they were at war; and the whole party having removed to the Indian village, the warriors and their allies prepared to depart. Six Frenchmen went with Hiens; and the rest, including Joutel, Douay, and the Caveliers, remained behind, in the lodge where Joutel had been domesticated, and where none were now left but women, children, and old men. Here they remained a week or more, watched closely by the Cenis, who would not let them leave the village; when news at length arrived of a great victory, and the warriors soon after returned with forty-eight scalps. It was the French guns that won the battle, but not the less did they glory in their prowess; and several days were spent in ceremonies and feasts of triumph.[336]

When all this hubbub of rejoicing had subsided, Joutel and his companions broke to Hiens their plan of attempting to reach home by way of the Mississippi. As they had expected, he opposed it vehemently, declaring that for his own part he would not run such a risk of losing his head; but at length he consented to their departure, on condition that the elder Cavelier should give him a certificate of his entire innocence of the murder of La Salle, which the priest did not hesitate to do. For the rest, Hiens treated his departing fellow-travellers with the generosity of a successful free-booter; for he gave them a good [Pg 451] share of the plunder he had won by his late crime, supplying them with hatchets, knives, beads, and other articles of trade, besides several horses. Meanwhile, adds Joutel, "we had the mortification and chagrin of seeing this scoundrel walking about the camp in a scarlet coat laced with gold which had belonged to the late Monsieur de la Salle, and which he had seized upon, as also upon all the rest of his property." A well-aimed shot would have avenged the wrong, but Joutel was clearly a mild and moderate person; and the elder Cavelier had constantly opposed all plans of violence. Therefore they stifled their emotions, and armed themselves with patience.

JOUTEL AND HIS PARTY.

Joutel's party consisted, besides himself, of the Caveliers (uncle and nephew), Anastase Douay, De Marle, Teissier, and a young Parisian named Barthelemy. Teissier, an accomplice in the murders of Moranget and La Salle, had obtained a pardon, in form, from the elder Cavelier. They had six horses and three Cenis guides. Hiens embraced them at parting, as did the ruffians who remained with him. Their course was northeast, toward the mouth of the Arkansas,—a distant goal, the way to which was beset with so many dangers that their chance of reaching it seemed small. It was early in June, and the forests and prairies were green with the verdure of opening summer.

They soon reached the Assonis, a tribe near the Sabine, who received them well, and gave them guides to the nations dwelling towards Red River. [Pg 452] On the twenty-third, they approached a village, the inhabitants of which, regarding them as curiosities of the first order, came out in a body to see them; and, eager to do them honor, they required them to mount on their backs, and thus make their entrance in procession. Joutel, being large and heavy, weighed down his bearer, insomuch that two of his countrymen were forced to sustain him, one on each side. On arriving, an old chief washed their faces with warm water from an earthen pan, and then invited them to mount on a scaffold of canes, where they sat in the hot sun listening to four successive speeches of welcome, of which they understood not a word.[337]

At the village of another tribe, farther on their way, they met with a welcome still more oppressive. Cavelier, the unworthy successor of his brother, being represented as the chief of the party, became the principal victim of their attentions. They danced the calumet before him; while an Indian, taking him, with an air of great respect, by the shoulders as he sat, shook him in cadence with the thumping of the drum. They then placed two girls close beside him, as his wives; while, at the same time, an old chief tied a painted feather in his hair. These proceedings so scandalized him that, pretending [Pg 453] to be ill, he broke off the ceremony; but they continued to sing all night, with so much zeal that several of them were reduced to a state of complete exhaustion.

At length, after a journey of about two months, during which they lost one of their number,—De Marle, accidentally drowned while bathing,—the travellers approached the river Arkansas, at a point not far above its junction with the Mississippi. Led by their Indian guides, they traversed a rich district of plains and woods, and stood at length on the borders of the stream. Nestled beneath the forests of the farther shore, they saw the lodges of a large Indian town; and here, as they gazed across the broad current, they presently descried an object which nerved their spent limbs, and thrilled their homesick hearts with joy. It was a tall, wooden cross; and near it was a small house, built evidently by Christian hands. With one accord they fell on their knees, and raised their hands to Heaven in thanksgiving. Two men, in European dress, issued from the door of the house and fired their guns to salute the excited travellers, who on their part replied with a volley. Canoes put out from the farther shore and ferried them to the town, where they were welcomed by Couture and De Launay, two followers of Henri de Tonty.[338]

That brave, loyal, and generous man, always vigilant and always active, beloved and feared alike by [Pg 454] white men and by red,[339] had been ejected, as we have seen, by the agent of the governor, La Barre, from the command of Fort St. Louis of the Illinois. An order from the King had reinstated him; and he no sooner heard the news of La Salle's landing on the shores of the Gulf, and of the disastrous beginnings of his colony,[340] than he prepared, on his own responsibility and at his own cost, to go to his assistance. He collected twenty-five Frenchmen and eleven Indians, and set out from his fortified rock on the thirteenth of February, 1686;[341] descended the Mississippi, and reached its mouth in Holy Week. All was solitude, a voiceless desolation of river, marsh, and sea. He despatched canoes to the east and to the west, searching the coast for some thirty leagues on either side. Finding no trace of his friend, who at that moment was ranging the prairies of Texas in no less fruitless search of his "fatal river," Tonty wrote for him a letter, which he left [Pg 455] in the charge of an Indian chief, who preserved it with reverential care, and gave it, fourteen years after, to Iberville, the founder of Louisiana.[342] Deeply disappointed at his failure, Tonty retraced his course, and ascended the Mississippi to the villages of the Arkansas, where some of his men volunteered to remain. He left six of them; and of this number were Couture and De Launay.[343]

A HOSPITABLE RECEPTION.

Cavelier and his companions, followed by a crowd of Indians, some carrying their baggage, some struggling for a view of the white strangers, entered the log cabin of their two hosts. Rude as it was, they found in it an earnest of peace and safety, and a foretaste of home. Couture and De Launay were moved even to tears by the story of their disasters, and of the catastrophe that crowned them. La Salle's death was carefully concealed from the Indians, many of whom had seen him on his descent of the Mississippi, and who regarded him with prodigious respect. They lavished all their hospitality on his followers; feasted them on corn-bread, dried buffalo meat, and watermelons, and danced the calumet before them, the most august of all their ceremonies. On this occasion, Cavelier's patience [Pg 456] failed him again; and pretending, as before, to be ill, he called on his nephew to take his place. There were solemn dances, too, in which the warriors—some bedaubed with white clay, some with red, and some with both; some wearing feathers, and some the horns of buffalo; some naked, and some in painted shirts of deer-skin, fringed with scalp-locks, insomuch, says Joutel, that they looked like a troop of devils—leaped, stamped, and howled from sunset till dawn. All this was partly to do the travellers honor, and partly to extort presents. They made objections, however, when asked to furnish guides; and it was only by dint of great offers that four were at length procured.

THE MISSISSIPPI.

With these, the travellers resumed their journey in a wooden canoe, about the first of August,[344] descended the Arkansas, and soon reached the dark and inexorable river, so long the object of their search, rolling, like a destiny, through its realms of solitude and shade. They launched their canoe on its turbid bosom, plied their oars against the current, and slowly won their way upward, following the writhings of this watery monster through cane-brake, swamp, and fen. It was a hard and toilsome journey, [Pg 457] under the sweltering sun of August,—now on the water, now knee-deep in mud, dragging their canoe through the unwholesome jungle. On the nineteenth, they passed the mouth of the Ohio; and their Indian guides made it an offering of buffalo meat. On the first of September, they passed the Missouri, and soon after saw Marquette's pictured rock, and the line of craggy heights on the east shore, marked on old French maps as "the Ruined Castles." Then, with a sense of relief, they turned from the great river into the peaceful current of the Illinois. They were eleven days in ascending it, in their large and heavy wooden canoe; when at length, on the afternoon of the fourteenth of September, they saw, towering above the forest and the river, the cliff crowned with the palisades of Fort St. Louis of the Illinois. As they drew near, a troop of Indians, headed by a Frenchman, descended from the rock, and fired their guns to salute them. They landed, and followed the forest path that led towards the fort, when they were met by Boisrondet, Tonty's comrade in the Iroquois war, and two other Frenchmen, who no sooner saw them than they called out, demanding where was La Salle. Cavelier, fearing lest he and his party would lose the advantage they might derive from his character of representative of his brother, was determined to conceal his death; and Joutel, as he himself confesses, took part in the deceit. Substituting equivocation for falsehood, they replied that La Salle had been with them nearly [Pg 458] as far as the Cenis villages, and that, when they parted, he was in good health. This, so far as they were concerned, was, literally speaking, true; but Douay and Teissier, the one a witness and the other a sharer in his death, could not have said so much without a square falsehood, and therefore evaded the inquiry.

Threading the forest path, and circling to the rear of the rock, they climbed the rugged height, and reached the top. Here they saw an area, encircled by the palisades that fenced the brink of the cliff, and by several dwellings, a store-house, and a chapel. There were Indian lodges too; for some of the red allies of the French made their abode with them.[345] Tonty was absent, fighting the Iroquois; but his lieutenant, Bellefontaine, received the travellers, and his little garrison of bush-rangers greeted them with a salute of musketry, mingled with the whooping of the Indians. A *Te Deum* followed at the chapel; "and, with all our hearts," says Joutel, "we gave thanks to God, who had preserved and guided us." At length, the tired travellers were among countrymen and friends. Bellefontaine found a room for the two priests; while Joutel, Teissier, and young Cavelier were lodged in the store-house.

THE JESUIT ALLOUEZ.

The Jesuit Allouez was lying ill at the fort; and [Pg 459] Joutel, Cavelier, and Douay went to visit him. He showed great anxiety when told that La Salle was alive, and on his way to the Illinois; asked many questions, and could not hide his agitation. When, some time after, he had partially recovered, he left St. Louis, as if to shun a meeting with the object of his alarm.[346] Once before, in 1679, Allouez had fled [Pg 460] from the Illinois on hearing of the approach of La Salle.

The season was late, and they were eager to hasten forward that they might reach Quebec in time to return to France in the autumn ships. There was not a day to lose. They bade farewell to Bellefontaine, from whom, as from all others, they had concealed the death of La Salle, and made their way across the country to Chicago. Here they were detained a week by a storm; and when at length they embarked in a canoe furnished by Bellefontaine, the tempest soon forced them to put back. On this, they abandoned their design, and returned to Fort St. Louis, to the astonishment of its inmates.

CONDUCT OF CAVELIER.

It was October when they arrived; and, meanwhile, Tonty had returned from the Iroquois war, where he had borne a conspicuous part in the famous attack on the Senecas by the Marquis de Denonville.[347] He listened with deep interest to the mournful story of his guests. Cavelier knew him well. He knew, so far as he was capable of knowing, his generous and disinterested character, his long and faithful [Pg 461] attachment to La Salle, and the invaluable services he had rendered him. Tonty had every claim on his confidence and affection. Yet he did not hesitate to practise on him the same deceit which he had practised on Bellefontaine. He told him that he had left his brother in good health on the Gulf of Mexico, and drew upon him, in La Salle's name, for an amount stated by Joutel at about four thousand livres, in furs, besides a canoe and a quantity of other goods, all of which were delivered to him by the unsuspecting victim.[348]

This was at the end of the winter, when the old priest and his companions had been living for months on Tonty's hospitality. They set out for Canada on [Pg 462] the twenty-first of March, reached Chicago on the twenty-ninth, and thence proceeded to Michilimackinac. Here Cavelier sold some of Tonty's furs to a merchant, who gave him in payment a draft on Montreal, thus putting him in funds for his voyage home. The party continued their journey in canoes by way of French River and the Ottawa, and safely reached Montreal on the seventeenth of July. Here they procured the clothing of which they were wofully in need, and then descended the river to Quebec, where they took lodging,—some with the Récollet friars, and some with the priests of the Seminary,—in order to escape the questions of the curious. At the end of August they embarked for France, and early in October arrived safely at

Rochelle. None of the party were men of especial energy or force of character; and yet, under the spur of a dire necessity, they had achieved one of the most adventurous journeys on record.

THE COLONISTS ABANDONED.

Now, at length, they disburdened themselves of their gloomy secret; but the sole result seems to have been an order from the King for the arrest of the murderers, should they appear in Canada.[349] [Pg 463] Joutel was disappointed. It had been his hope throughout that the King would send a ship to the relief of the wretched band at Fort St. Louis of Texas. But Louis XIV. hardened his heart, and left them to their fate.

FOOTNOTES:

[332] The lodges of the Florida Indians were somewhat similar. The winter lodges of the now nearly extinct Mandans, though not so high in proportion to their width, and built of more solid materials, as the rigor of a northern climate requires, bear a general resemblance to those of the Cenis.

The Cenis tattooed their faces and some parts of their bodies, by pricking powdered charcoal into the skin. The women tattooed the breasts; and this practice was general among them, notwithstanding the pain of the operation, as it was thought very ornamental. Their dress consisted of a sort of frock, or wrapper of skin, from the waist to the knees. The men, in summer, wore nothing but the waist-cloth.

[333] *Journal Historique*, 237.
[334] "Tu es un misérable. Tu as tué mon maistre."—Tonty, *Mémoire*. Tonty derived his information from some of those present. Douay and Joutel have each left an account of this murder. They agree in essential points; though Douay says that when it took place, Duhaut had moved his camp beyond the Cenis villages, which is contrary to Joutel's statement.
[335] Joutel, *Relation* (Margry, iii. 371).

[336] These are described by Joutel. Like nearly all the early observers of Indian manners, he speaks of the practice of cannibalism.

[337] These Indians were a portion of the Cadodaquis, or Caddoes, then living on Red River. The travellers afterwards visited other villages of the same people. Tonty was here two years afterwards, and mentions the curious custom of washing the faces of guests.

[338] Joutel, *Journal Historique*, 298.

[339] *Journal de St. Cosme*, 1699. This journal has been printed by Mr. Shea, from the copy in my possession. St. Cosme, who knew Tonty well, speaks of him in the warmest terms of praise.

[340] In the autumn of 1685, Tonty made a journey from the Illinois to Michilimackinac, to seek news of La Salle. He there learned, by a letter of the new governor, Denonville, just arrived from France, of the landing of La Salle, and the loss of the "Aimable," as recounted by Beaujeu, on his return. He immediately went back on foot to Fort St. Louis of the Illinois, and prepared to descend the Mississippi, "dans l'espérance de lui donner secours." *Lettre de Tonty au Ministre, 24 Aoust, 1686; Ibid., à Cabart de Villermont, même date*; *Mémoire de Tonty*; *Procès Verbal de Tonty, 13 Avril, 1686.*

[341] The date is from the *Procès Verbal*. In the *Mémoire*, hastily written long after, he falls into errors of date.

[342] Iberville sent it to France, and Charlevoix gives a portion of it. (*Histoire de la Nouvelle France*, ii. 259.) Singularly enough, the date, as printed by him, is erroneous, being 20 April, 1685, instead of 1686. There is no doubt whatever, from its relations with concurrent events, that this journey was in the latter year.

[343] Tonty, *Mémoire; Ibid., Lettre à Monseigneur de Ponchartrain*, 1690. Joutel, *Journal Historique*, 301.

[344] Joutel says that the Parisian boy, Barthelemy, was left behind. It was this youth who afterwards uttered the ridiculous defamation of La Salle mentioned in a preceding note. The account of the death of La Salle, taken from the lips of Couture, was received by him from Cavelier and his companions, during their stay at the Arkansas. Couture was by trade a carpenter, and was a native of Rouen.

[345] The condition of Fort St. Louis, at this time, may be gathered from several passages of Joutel. The houses, he says, were built at the brink of the cliff, forming, with the palisades, the circle of defence. The Indians lived in the area.

[346] Joutel adds that this was occasioned by "une espèce de conspiration qu'on a voulu faire contre les interests de Monsieur de la Salle."—*Journal Historique*, 350.

"Ce Père appréhendoit que le dit sieur ne l'y rencontrast, ... suivant ce que j'en ai pu apprendre, les Pères avoient avancé plusieurs choses pour contrebarrer l'entreprise et avoient voulu détacher plusieurs nations de Sauvages, lesquelles s'estoient données à M. de la Salle. Ils avoient esté mesme jusques à vouloir destruire le fort Saint-Louis, en ayant construit un à Chicago, où ils avoient attiré une partie des Sauvages, ne pouvant en quelque façon s'emparer du dit fort. Pour conclure, le bon Père ayant eu peur d'y estre trouvé, aima mieux se précautionner en prenant le devant.... Quoyque M. Cavelier eust dit au Père qu'il pouvoit rester, il partit quelques sept ou huit jours avant nous."—*Relation* (Margry, iii. 500).

La Salle always saw the influence of the Jesuits in the disasters that befell him. His repeated assertion, that they wished to establish themselves in the valley of the Mississippi, receives confirmation from a document entitled *Mémoire sur la proposition à faire par les R. Pères Jésuites pour la découverte des environs de la rivière du Mississipi et pour voir si elle est navigable jusqu'à la mer*. It is a memorandum of propositions to be made to the minister Seignelay, and was apparently put forward as a feeler, before making the propositions in form. It was written after the return of Beaujeu to France, and before La Salle's death became known. It intimates that the Jesuits were entitled to precedence in the valley of the Mississippi, as having first explored it. It affirms that *La Salle had made a blunder, and landed his colony, not at the mouth of the river, but at another place*; and it asks permission to continue the work in which he has failed. To this end, it petitions for means to build a vessel at St. Louis of the Illinois, together with canoes, arms, tents, tools, provisions, and merchandise for the Indians; and it also asks for La Salle's maps and papers, and for those of Beaujeu. On their part, it pursues, the Jesuits will engage to make a complete survey of the river, and return an exact account of its inhabitants, its plants, and its other productions.

[347] Tonty, Du Lhut, and Durantaye came to the aid of Denonville with a hundred and eighty Frenchmen, chiefly *coureurs de bois*, and four hundred Indians from the upper country. Their services were highly appreciated; and Tonty especially is mentioned in the despatches of Denonville with great praise.

[348] "Monsieur Tonty, croyant M. de la Salle vivant, ne fit pas de difficulté de luy donner pour environ quatre mille liv. de pelleterie, de castors, loutres, un canot, et autres effets."—Joutel, *Journal Historique*, 349.

Tonty himself does not make the amount so great: "Sur ce qu'ils m'assuroient qu'il étoit resté au Golfe de Mexique en bonne santé, je les reçus comme si ç'avoit esté lui mesme et luy prestay [*à Cavelier*] plus de 700 francs."—Tonty, *Mémoire*.

Cavelier must have known that La Salle was insolvent. Tonty had long served without pay. Douay says that he made the stay of the party at the fort very agreeable, and speaks of him, with some apparent compunction, as "ce brave gentilhomme, toujours inséparablement attaché aux intérêts du Sieur de la Salle, dont nous luy avons caché la déplorable destinée."

Couture, from the Arkansas, brought word to Tonty, several months after, of La Salle's death, adding that Cavelier had concealed it, with no other purpose than that of gaining money or supplies from him (Tonty), in his brother's name. Cavelier had a letter from La Salle, desiring Tonty to give him supplies, and pay him 2,652 livres in beaver. If Cavelier is to be believed, this beaver belonged to La Salle.

[349] *Lettre du Roy à Denonville, 1 Mai, 1689.* Joutel must have been a young man at the time of the Mississippi expedition; for Charlevoix saw him at Rouen, thirty-five years after. He speaks of him with emphatic praise; but it must be admitted that his connivance in the deception practised by Cavelier on Tonty leaves a shade on his character, as well as on that of Douay. In other respects, everything that appears concerning him is highly favorable, which is not the case with Douay, who, on one or two occasions, makes wilful misstatements.

Douay says that the elder Cavelier made a report of the expedition to the minister Seignelay. This report remained unknown in an English collection of autographs and old manuscripts, whence I obtained it by purchase, in 1854, both the buyer and seller being at the time ignorant of its exact character. It proved, on examination, to be a portion of the first draft of Cavelier's report to Seignelay. It consists of twenty-six small folio pages, closely written in a clear hand, though in a few places obscured by the fading of the ink, as well as by occasional erasures and interlineations of the writer. It is, as already stated, confused and unsatisfactory in its statements; and all the latter part has been lost. On reaching France, he had the impudence to tell Abbé Tronson, Superior of St. Sulpice, "qu'il avait laissé M. de la Salle dans un très-beau pays avec M. de Chefdeville en bonne santé."—*Lettre de Tronson à Mad. Fauvel-Cavelier, 29 Nov., 1688.*

Cavelier addressed to the King a memorial on the importance of keeping possession of the Illinois. It closes with an earnest petition for money in compensation for his losses, as, according to his own statement, he was completely *épuisé*. It is affirmed in a memorial of the heirs of his cousin, François Plet, that he concealed the death of La Salle some time after his return to France, in order to get possession of property which would otherwise have been seized by the creditors of the deceased. The prudent abbé died rich and very old, at the house of a relative, having inherited a large estate after his return from America. Apparently, this did not satisfy him; for there is before me the copy of a petition, written about 1717, in which he asks, jointly with one of his nephews, to be given possession of the seigniorial property held by La Salle in America. The petition was refused.

Young Cavelier, La Salle's nephew, died some years after, an officer in a regiment. He has been erroneously supposed to be the same with one De la Salle, whose name is appended to a letter giving an account of Louisiana, and dated at Toulon, 3 Sept., 1698. This person was the son of a naval official at Toulon, and was not related to the Caveliers.

[Pg 464]

CHAPTER XXIX.

1688-1689.

FATE OF THE TEXAN COLONY.

TONTY ATTEMPTS TO RESCUE THE COLONISTS: HIS DIFFICULTIES AND HARDSHIPS. — SPANISH HOSTILITY. — EXPEDITION OF ALONZO DE LEON: HE REACHES FORT ST. LOUIS. — A SCENE OF HAVOC. — DESTRUCTION OF THE FRENCH. — THE END.

COURAGE OF TONTY.

HENRI DE TONTY, on his rock of St. Louis, was visited in September by Couture and two Indians from the Arkansas. Then, for the first time, he heard with grief and indignation of the death of La Salle, and the deceit practised by Cavelier. The chief whom he had served so well was beyond his help; but might not the unhappy colonists left on the shores of Texas still be rescued from destruction? Couture had confirmed what Cavelier and his party had already told him, that the tribes south of the Arkansas were eager to join the French in an invasion of northern Mexico; and he soon after received from the governor, Denonville, a letter informing him that war had again been declared against Spain. As bold and enterprising as La Salle himself, Tonty resolved on an effort to learn the condition of the [Pg 465] few Frenchmen left on the borders of the Gulf, relieve their necessities, and, should it prove practicable, make them the nucleus of a war-party to cross the Rio Grande, and add a new province to the domain of France. It was the revival, on a small scale, of La Salle's scheme of Mexican invasion; and there is no doubt that, with a score of French musketeers, he could have gathered a formidable party of savage allies from the tribes of Red River, the Sabine, and the Trinity. This daring adventure and the rescue of his suffering countrymen divided his thoughts, and he prepared at once to execute the double purpose.[350]

TONTY MISREPRESENTED.

He left Fort St. Louis of the Illinois early in December, in a pirogue, or wooden canoe, with five Frenchmen, a Shawanoe warrior, and two Indian slaves; and, after a long and painful journey, he reached the villages of the Caddoes on Red River on the twenty-eighth of March. Here he was told that Hiens and his companions were at a village eighty leagues distant; and thither he was preparing to go in search of them, when all his men, excepting the Shawanoe and one Frenchman, declared themselves disgusted with the journey, and refused to follow him. Persuasion was useless, and there was no means of enforcing obedience. He found himself abandoned; but he still pushed on, with the two who remained faithful. A few days after, they lost nearly all their ammunition in crossing a river. [Pg 466] Undeterred by this accident, Tonty made his way to the village where Hiens and those who had remained with him were said to be; but no trace of them appeared, and the demeanor of the Indians, when he inquired for them, convinced him that they had been put to death. He charged them with having killed the Frenchmen, whereupon the women of the village raised a wail of lamentation; "and I saw," he says, "that what I had said to them was true." They refused to give him guides; and this, with the loss of his ammunition, compelled him to forego his purpose of making his way to the colonists on the Bay of St. Louis. With bitter disappointment, he and his two companions retraced their course, and at length approached Red River. Here they found the whole country flooded. Sometimes they waded to the knees, sometimes to the neck, sometimes pushed their slow way on rafts. Night and day it rained without ceasing. They slept on logs placed side by side to raise them above the mud and water, and fought their way with hatchets through the inundated cane-brakes. They found no game but a bear, which had taken refuge on an island in the flood; and they were forced to eat their dogs. "I never in my life," writes Tonty, "suffered so much." In judging these intrepid exertions, it is to be remembered that he was not, at least in appearance, of a robust constitution, and that he had but one hand.

They reached the Mississippi on the eleventh of July, and the Arkansas villages on the [Pg 467] thirty-first. Here Tonty was detained by an attack of fever. He resumed his journey when it began to abate, and reached his fort of the Illinois in September.[351]

[Pg 468]

A SCENE OF HAVOC.

While the King of France abandoned the exiles of Texas to their fate, a power dark, ruthless, and terrible was hovering around the feeble colony on the Bay of St. Louis, searching with pitiless eye to discover and tear out that dying germ of civilization from the bosom of the wilderness in whose savage immensity it lay hidden. Spain claimed the Gulf of Mexico and all its coasts as her own of unanswerable right, and the viceroys of Mexico were strenuous to enforce her claim. The capture of one of La Salle's four vessels at St. Domingo had made known his designs, and in the course of the three succeeding years no less than four expeditions were sent out from Vera Cruz to find and destroy him. They scoured the whole extent of the coast, and found the wrecks of the "Aimable" and the "Belle;" but the colony of St. Louis,[352] inland and secluded, escaped their search. For a time, the jealousy of the Spaniards was lulled to sleep. They rested in the assurance that the intruders had perished, when fresh advices from the frontier province of New Leon [Pg 469] caused the Viceroy, Galve, to order a strong force, under Alonzo de Leon, to march from Coahuila, and cross the Rio Grande. Guided by a French prisoner, probably one of the deserters from La Salle, they pushed their way across wild and arid plains, rivers, prairies, and forests, till at length they approached the Bay of St. Louis, and descried, far off, the harboring-place of the French.[353] As they drew near, no banner was displayed, no sentry challenged; and the silence of death reigned over the shattered palisades and neglected dwellings. The Spaniards spurred their reluctant horses through the gateway, and a scene of desolation met their sight. No living thing was stirring. Doors were torn from their hinges; broken boxes, staved barrels, and rusty kettles, mingled with a great number of stocks of arquebuses and muskets, were scattered about in confusion. Here, too, trampled in mud and soaked with rain, they saw more than two hundred books, many of which still retained the traces of costly bindings. On the adjacent prairie lay three dead bodies, one of which, from fragments of dress still clinging to the wasted remains, they saw to be that of a woman. It was in vain to question the imperturbable [Pg 470] savages, who, wrapped to the throat in their buffalo-robes, stood gazing on the scene with looks of wooden immobility. Two strangers, however, at length arrived.[354] Their faces were smeared with paint, and they were wrapped in buffalo-robes like the rest; yet these seeming Indians were L'Archevêque, the tool of La Salle's murderer Duhaut, and Grollet, the companion of the white savage Ruter. The Spanish commander, learning that these two men were in the district of the tribe called Texas,[355] had sent to invite them to his camp under a pledge of good treatment; and they had resolved to trust Spanish clemency rather than endure longer a life that had become intolerable. From them the Spaniards learned nearly all that is known of the fate of Barbier, Zenobe Membré, and their companions. Three months before, a large band of Indians had approached the fort, the inmates of which had suffered severely from the ravages of the small-pox. From fear of treachery, they refused to admit their visitors, but received them at a cabin without the palisades. Here the French began a trade with them; when suddenly a band of warriors, yelling [Pg 471] the war-whoop, rushed from an ambuscade under the bank of the river, and butchered the greater number. The children of one Talon, together with an Italian and a young man from Paris named Breman, were saved by the Indian women, who carried them off on their backs. L'Archevêque and Grollet, who with others of their stamp were domesticated in the Indian villages, came to the scene of slaughter, and, as they affirmed, buried fourteen dead bodies.[356]

[Pg 472]

THE SURVIVORS.

L'Archevêque and Grollet were sent to Spain, where, in spite of the pledge given them, they were thrown into prison, with the intention of sending them back to labor in the mines. The Indians, some time after De Leon's expedition, gave up their captives to the Spaniards. The Italian was imprisoned at Vera Cruz. Breman's fate is unknown. Pierre and Jean Baptiste Talon, who were now old enough to bear arms, were enrolled in the Spanish navy, and, being captured in 1696 by a French ship of war, regained their liberty; while their younger brothers and their sister were carried to Spain by the Viceroy.[357] With respect to the ruffian companions of Hiens, the conviction of Tonty that they had been put to death by the Indians may have been well founded; but the buccaneer himself is said to have been killed in a quarrel with his accomplice Ruter, the white savage; and thus in ignominy and darkness died the last embers of the doomed colony of La Salle.

FRUIT OF EXPLORATIONS.

Here ends the wild and mournful story of the explorers of the Mississippi. Of all their toil and [Pg 473] sacrifice, no fruit remained but a great geographical discovery, and a grand type of incarnate energy and will. Where La Salle had ploughed, others were to sow the seed; and on the path which the undespairing Norman had hewn out, the Canadian D'Iberville was to win for France a vast though a transient dominion.

FOOTNOTES:

[350] Tonty, *Mémoire*.

[351] Two causes have contributed to detract, most unjustly, from Tonty's reputation,—the publication, under his name, but without his authority, of a perverted account of the enterprises in which he took part; and the confounding him with his brother, Alphonse de Tonty, who long commanded at Detroit, where charges of peculation were brought against him. There are very few names in French-American history mentioned with such unanimity of praise as that of Henri de Tonty. Hennepin finds

some fault with him; but his censure is commendation. The despatches of the governor, Denonville, speak in strong terms of his services in the Iroquois war, praise his character, and declare that he is fit for any bold enterprise, adding that he deserves reward from the King. The missionary, St. Cosme, who travelled under his escort in 1699, says of him: "He is beloved by all the *voyageurs*.... It was with deep regret that we parted from him: ... he is the man who best knows the country; ... he is loved and feared everywhere.... Your grace will, I doubt not, take pleasure in acknowledging the obligations we owe him."

Tonty held the commission of captain; but, by a memoir which he addressed to Ponchartrain in 1690, it appears that he had never received any pay. Count Frontenac certifies the truth of the statement, and adds a recommendation of the writer. In consequence, probably, of this, the proprietorship of Fort St. Louis of the Illinois was granted in the same year to Tonty, jointly with La Forest, formerly La Salle's lieutenant. Here they carried on a trade in furs. In 1699, a royal declaration was launched against the *coureurs de bois*; but an express provision was added in favor of Tonty and La Forest, who were empowered to send up the country yearly two canoes, with twelve men, for the maintenance of this fort. With such a limitation, this fort and the trade carried on at it must have been very small. In 1702, we find a royal order, to the effect that La Forest is henceforth to reside in Canada, and Tonty on the Mississippi; and that the establishment at the Illinois is to be discontinued. In the same year, Tonty joined D'Iberville in Lower Louisiana, and was sent by that officer from Mobile to secure the Chickasaws in the French interest. His subsequent career and the time of his death do not appear. He seems never to have received the reward which his great merit deserved. Those intimate with the late lamented Dr. Sparks will remember his often-expressed wish that justice should be done to the memory of Tonty.

Fort St. Louis of the Illinois was afterwards reoccupied by the French. In 1718, a number of them, chiefly traders, were living here; but three years later it was again deserted, and Charlevoix, passing the spot, saw only the remains of its palisades.

[352] Fort St. Louis of Texas is not to be confounded with Fort St. Louis of the Illinois.

[353] After crossing the Del Norte, they crossed in turn the Upper Nueces, the Hondo (Rio Frio), the De Leon (San Antonio), and the Guadalupe, and then, turning southward, descended to the Bay of St. Bernard.... Manuscript map of "Route que firent les Espagnols, pour venir enlever les Français restez à la Baye St. Bernard ou St. Louis, après la perte du vaisseau de Mr de la Salle en 1689." (Margry's collection.)

[354] May 1st. The Spaniards reached the fort April 22.

[355] This is the first instance in which the name occurs. In a letter written by a member of De Leon's party, the Texan Indians are mentioned several times. (See *Coleccion de Varios Documentos*, 25.) They are described as an agricultural tribe, and were, to all appearance, identical with the Cenis. The name Tejas, or Texas, was first applied as a local designation to a spot on the river Neches, in the Cenis territory, whence it extended to the whole country. (See Yoakum, *History of Texas*, 52.)

[356] *Derrotero de la Jornada que hizo el General Alonso de Leon para el descubrimiento de la Bahia del Espíritu Santo, y poblacion de Franceses. Ano de 1689.*—This is the official journal of the expedition, signed by Alonzo de Leon. I am indebted to Colonel Thomas Aspinwall for the opportunity of examining it. The name of Espiritu Santo was, as before mentioned, given by the Spaniards to St. Louis, or Matagorda Bay, as well as to two other bays of the Gulf of Mexico.

Carta en que se da noticia de un viaje hecho à la Bahia de Espíritu Santo y de la poblacion que tenian ahi los Franceses. Coleccion de Varios Documentos para la Historia de la Florida, 25.—This is a letter from a person accompanying the expedition of De Leon. It is dated May 18, 1689, and agrees closely with the journal cited above, though evidently by another hand. Compare Barcia, *Ensayo Cronologico*, 294. Barcia's story has been doubted; but these authentic documents prove the correctness of his principal statements, though on minor points he seems to have indulged his fancy.

The Viceroy of New Spain, in a report to the King, 1690, says that, in order to keep the Texas and other Indians of that region in obedience to his Majesty, he has resolved to establish eight missions among them. He adds that he has appointed as governor, or commander, in that province, Don Domingo Teran de los Rios, who will make a thorough exploration of it, carry out what De Leon has begun; prevent the further intrusion of foreigners like La Salle, and go in pursuit of the remnant of the French, who are said still to remain among the tribes of Red River. I owe this document to the kindness of Mr. Buckingham Smith.

[357] *Mémoire sur lequel on a interrogé les deux Canadiens [Pierre et Jean Baptiste Talon] qui sont soldats dans la Compagnie de Feuguerolles. A Brest, 14 Février, 1698.*

Interrogations faites à Pierre et Jean Baptiste Talon à leur arrivée de la Veracrux.—This paper, which differs in some of its details from the preceding, was sent by D'Iberville, the founder of Louisiana, to Abbé Cavelier. Appended to it is a letter from D'Iberville, written in May, 1704, in which he confirms the chief statements of the Talons, by information obtained by him from a Spanish officer at Pensacola.

APPENDIX.

I.

EARLY UNPUBLISHED MAPS OF THE MISSISSIPPI AND THE GREAT LAKES.

MOST of the maps described below are to be found in the Dépôt des Cartes de la Marine et des Colonies, at Paris. Taken together, they exhibit the progress of western discovery, and illustrate the records of the explorers.

1. The map of Galinée, 1670, has a double title,—*Carte du Canada et des Terres découvertes vers le lac Derié, and Carte du Lac Ontario et des habitations qui l'environnent ensemble le pays que Messrs. Dolier et Galinée, missionnaires du seminaire de St. Sulpice, ont parcouru.* It professes to represent only the country actually visited by the two missionaries. Beginning with Montreal, it gives the course of the Upper St. Lawrence and the shores of Lake Ontario, the river Niagara, the north shore of Lake Erie, the Strait of Detroit, and the eastern and northern shores of Lake Huron. Galinée did not know the existence of the peninsula of Michigan, and merges Lakes Huron and Michigan into one, under the name of "Michigané, ou Mer Douce des Hurons." He was also entirely ignorant of the south shore of Lake Erie. He represents the outlet of Lake Superior as far as the Saut Ste. [Pg 476] Marie, and lays down the river Ottawa in great detail, having descended it on his return. The Falls of the Genesee are indicated, as also the Falls of Niagara, with the inscription, "Sault qui tombe au rapport des sauvages de plus de 200 pieds de haut." Had the Jesuits been disposed to aid him, they could have given him much additional information, and corrected his most serious errors; as, for example, the omission of the peninsula of Michigan. The first attempt to map out the Great Lakes was that of Champlain, in 1632. This of Galinée may be called the second.

2. The map of Lake Superior, published in the Jesuit Relation of 1670, 1671, was made at about the same time with Galinée's map. Lake Superior is here styled "Lac Tracy, ou Supérieur." Though not so exact as it has been represented, this map indicates that the Jesuits had explored every part of this fresh-water ocean, and that they had a thorough knowledge of the straits connecting the three Upper Lakes, and of the adjacent bays, inlets, and shores. The peninsula of Michigan, ignored by Galinée, is represented in its proper place.

3. Three years or more after Galinée made the map mentioned above, another, indicating a greatly increased knowledge of the country, was made by some person whose name does not appear. This map, which is somewhat more than four feet long and about two feet and a half wide, has no title. All the Great Lakes, through their entire extent, are laid down on it with considerable accuracy. Lake Ontario is called "Lac Ontario, ou de Frontenac." Fort Frontenac is indicated, as well as the Iroquois colonies of the north shore. Niagara is "Chute haute de 120 toises par où le Lac Erié tombe dans le Lac Frontenac." Lake Erie is "Lac Teiocha-rontiong, dit communément Lac Erié." Lake St. Clair is "Tsiketo, ou Lac de la Chaudière." Lake Huron is "Lac Huron, ou Mer Douce des Hurons." [Pg 477] Lake Superior is "Lac Supérieur." Lake Michigan is "Lac Mitchiganong, ou des Illinois." On Lake Michigan, immediately opposite the site of Chicago, are written the words, of which the following is the literal translation: "The largest vessels can come to this place from the outlet of Lake Erie, where it discharges into Lake Frontenac [Ontario]; and from this marsh into which they can enter there is only a distance of a thousand paces to the River La Divine [Des Plaines], which can lead them to the River Colbert [Mississippi], and thence to the Gulf of Mexico." This map was evidently made after that voyage of La Salle in which he discovered the Illinois, or at least the Des Plaines branch of it. The Ohio is laid down with the inscription, "River Ohio, so called by the Iroquois on account of its beauty, which the Sieur de la Salle descended." (*Ante*, 32, *note*.)

4. We now come to the map of Marquette, which is a rude sketch of a portion of Lakes Superior and Michigan, and of the route pursued by him and Joliet up the Fox River of Green Bay, down the Wisconsin, and thence down the Mississippi as far as the Arkansas. The river Illinois is also laid down, as it was by this course that he returned to Lake Michigan after his memorable voyage. He gives no name to the Wisconsin. The Mississippi is called "Rivière de la Conception;" the Missouri, the Pekitanoui; and the Ohio, the Ouabouskiaou, though La Salle, its discoverer, had previously given it its present name, borrowed from the Iroquois. The Illinois is nameless, like the Wisconsin. At the mouth of a river, perhaps the Des Moines, Marquette places the three villages of the Peoria Indians visited by him. These, with the Kaskaskias, Maroas, and others, on the map, were merely sub-tribes of the aggregation of savages known as the Illinois. On or near the Missouri he places the Ouchage (Osages), the Oumessourit [Pg 478] (Missouris), the Kansa (Kanzas), the Paniassa (Pawnees), the Maha (Omahas), and the Pahoutet (Pah-Utahs?). The names of many other tribes, "esloignées dans les terres," are also given along the course of the Arkansas, a river which is nameless on the map. Most of these tribes are now indistinguishable. This map has recently been engraved and published.

5. Not long after Marquette's return from the Mississippi, another map was made by the Jesuits, with the following title: *Carte de la nouvelle decouverte que les peres Iesuites ont fait en l'année 1672, et continuée par le P. Iacques Marquette de la mesme Compagnie accompagné de quelques françois en l'année 1673, qu'on pourra nommer en françois la Manitoumie.* This title is very elaborately decorated with figures drawn with a pen, and representing Jesuits instructing Indians. The map is the same published by Thevenot, not without considerable variations, in 1681. It represents the Mississippi from a little above the Wisconsin to the Gulf of Mexico, the part below the Arkansas being drawn from conjecture. The river is named "Mitchisipi, ou grande Rivière." The Wisconsin, the Illinois, the Ohio, the Des Moines(?), the Missouri, and the Arkansas

are all represented, but in a very rude manner. Marquette's route, in going and returning, is marked by lines; but the return route is incorrect. The whole map is so crude and careless, and based on information so inexact, that it is of little interest.

6. The Jesuits made also another map, without title, of the four Upper Lakes and the Mississippi to a little below the Arkansas. The Mississippi is called "Riuiere Colbert." The map is remarkable as including the earliest representation of the Upper Mississippi, based, perhaps, on the reports of Indians. The Falls of St. Anthony are indicated by the word "Saut." It is possible that the map [Pg 479] may be of later date than at first appears, and that it may have been drawn in the interval between the return of Hennepin from the Upper Mississippi and that of La Salle from his discovery of the mouth of the river. The various temporary and permanent stations of the Jesuits are marked by crosses.

7. Of far greater interest is the small map of Louis Joliet made and presented to Count Frontenac after the discoverer's return from the Mississippi. It is entitled *Carte de la decouverte du Sr Jolliet ou l'on voit La Communication du fleuve St. Laurens avec les lacs frontenac, Erié, Lac des Hurons et Ilinois.* Then succeeds the following, written in the same antiquated French, as if it were a part of the title: "Lake Frontenac [Ontario] is separated by a fall of half a league from Lake Erié, from which one enters that of the Hurons, and by the same navigation, into that of the Illinois [Michigan], from the head of which one crosses to the Divine River [Rivière Divine; *i. e.*, the Des Plaines branch of the river Ilinois], by a portage of a thousand paces. This river falls into the river Colbert [Mississippi], which discharges itself into the Gulf of Mexico." A part of this map is based on the Jesuit map of Lake Superior, the legends being here for the most part identical, though the shape of the lake is better given by Joliet. The Mississippi, or "Riuiere Colbert," is made to flow from three lakes in latitude 47°; and it ends in latitude 37°, a little below the mouth of the Ohio, the rest being apparently cut off to make room for Joliet's letter to Frontenac (*ante*, 76), which is written on the lower part of the map. The valley of the Mississippi

is called on the map "Colbertie, ou Amerique Occidentale." The Missouri is represented without name, and against it is a legend, of which the following is the literal translation: "By one of these great rivers which come from the west and discharge themselves into the river Colbert, [Pg 480] one will find a way to enter the Vermilion Sea (Gulf of California). I have seen a village which was not more than twenty days' journey by land from a nation which has commerce with those of California. If I had come two days sooner, I should have spoken with those who had come from thence, and had brought four hatchets as a present." The Ohio has no name, but a legend over it states that La Salle had descended it. (See *ante*, 32, *note*).

8. Joliet, at about the same time, made another map, larger than that just mentioned, but not essentially different. The letter to Frontenac is written upon both. There is a third map, of which the following is the title: *Carte generalle de la France septentrionale contenant la descouuerte du pays des Illinois, faite par le S^r. Jolliet.* This map, which is inscribed with a dedication by the Intendant Duchesneau to the minister Colbert, was made some time after the voyage of Joliet and Marquette. It is an elaborate piece of work, but very inaccurate. It represents the continent from Hudson's Strait to Mexico and California, with the whole of the Atlantic and a part of the Pacific coast. An open sea is made to extend from Hudson's Strait westward to the Pacific. The St. Lawrence and all the Great Lakes are laid down with tolerable correctness, as also is the Gulf of Mexico. The Mississippi, called "Messasipi," flows into the Gulf, from which it extends northward nearly to the "Mer du Nord." Along its course, above the Wisconsin, which is called "Miskous," is a long list of Indian tribes, most of which cannot now be recognized, though several are clearly sub-tribes of the Sioux. The Ohio is called "Ouaboustikou." The whole map is decorated with numerous figures of animals, natives of the country, or supposed to be so. Among them are camels, ostriches, and a giraffe, which are placed on the plains west [Pg 481] of the Mississippi. But the most curious figure is that which represents one of the monsters seen by Joliet and Marquette, painted on a rock by the Indians. It corresponds with

Marquette's description (*ante*, 68). This map, which is an early effort of the engineer Franquelin, does more credit to his skill as a designer than to his geographical knowledge, which appears in some respects behind his time.

9. *Carte de l'Amérique Septentrionale depuis l'embouchure de la Rivière St. Laurens jusques au Sein Mexique.* On this curious little map, the Mississippi is called "Riuiere Buade" (the family name of Frontenac); and the neighboring country is "La Frontenacie." The Illinois is "Riuiere de la Diuine ou Loutrelaise," and the Arkansas is "Riuiere Bazire." The Mississippi is made to head in three lakes, and to discharge itself into "B. du S. Esprit" (Mobile Bay). Some of the legends and the orthography of various Indian names are clearly borrowed from Marquette. This map appears to be the work of Raudin, Frontenac's engineer. I owe a tracing of it to the kindness of Henry Harrisse, Esq.

10. *Carte des Parties les plus occidentales du Canada, par le Père Pierre Raffeix*, S. J. This rude map shows the course of Du Lhut from the head of Lake Superior to the Mississippi, and partly confirms the story of Hennepin, who, Raffeix says in a note, was rescued by Du Lhut. The course of Joliet and Marquette is given, with the legend "Voyage et première descouverte du Mississipy faite par le P. Marquette et M^r. Joliet en 1672." The route of La Salle in 1679, 1680, is also laid down.

11. In the Dépôt des Cartes de la Marine is another map of the Upper Mississippi, which seems to have been made by or for Du Lhut. Lac Buade, the "Issatis," the "Tintons," the "Houelbatons," the "Poualacs," and other tribes [Pg 482] of this region appear upon it. This is the map numbered 208 in the *Cartographie* of Harrisse.

12. Another map deserving mention is a large and fine one, entitled *Carte de l'Amérique Septentrionale et partie de la Meridionale ... avec les nouvelles découvertes de la Rivière Missisipi, ou Colbert.* It appears to have been made in 1682 or 1683, before the descent of La Salle to the mouth of the Mississippi was known to the maker,

who seems to have been Franquelin. The lower Mississippi is omitted, but its upper portions are elaborately laid down; and the name *La Louisiane* appears in large gold letters along its west side. The Falls of St. Anthony are shown, and above them is written "Armes du Roy gravées sur cet arbre l'an 1679." This refers to the *acte de prise de possession* of Du Lhut in July of that year, and this part of the map seems made from data supplied by him.

13. We now come to the great map of Franquelin, the most remarkable of all the early maps of the interior of North America, though hitherto completely ignored by both American and Canadian writers. It is entitled *Carte de la Louisiane ou des Voyages du Sr de la Salle et des pays qu'il a découverts depuis la Nouvelle France jusqu'au Golfe Mexique les années 1679, 80, 81, et 82, par Jean Baptiste Louis Franquelin, l'an 1684. Paris.* Franquelin was a young engineer, who held the post of hydrographer to the King, at Quebec, in which Joliet succeeded him. Several of his maps are preserved, including one made in 1681, in which he lays down the course of the Mississippi,—the lower part from conjecture,—making it discharge itself into Mobile Bay. It appears from a letter of the governor, La Barre, that Franquelin was at Quebec in 1683, engaged on a map which was probably that of which the title is given above, though had La Barre known that it was to be called a map of the journeys of [Pg 483] his victim La Salle, he would have been more sparing of his praises. "He" (Franquelin), writes the governor, "is as skilful as any in France, but extremely poor and in need of a little aid from his Majesty as an Engineer; he is at work on a very correct map of the country, which I shall send you next year in his name; meanwhile, I shall support him with some little assistance."— *Colonial Documents of New York*, IX. 205.

The map is very elaborately executed, and is six feet long and four and a half wide. It exhibits the political divisions of the continent, as the French then understood them; that is to say, all the regions drained by streams flowing into the St. Lawrence and the Mississippi are claimed as belonging to France, and this vast domain is separated into two grand divisions, La Nouvelle France and La

Louisiane. The boundary line of the former, New France, is drawn from the Penobscot to the southern extremity of Lake Champlain, and thence to the Mohawk, which it crosses a little above Schenectady, in order to make French subjects of the Mohawk Indians. Thence it passes by the sources of the Susquehanna and the Alleghany, along the southern shore of Lake Erie, across Southern Michigan, and by the head of Lake Michigan, whence it sweeps northwestward to the sources of the Mississippi. Louisiana includes the entire valley of the Mississippi and the Ohio, besides the whole of Texas. The Spanish province of Florida comprises the peninsula and the country east of the Bay of Mobile, drained by streams flowing into the Gulf; while Carolina, Virginia, and the other English provinces, form a narrow strip between the Alleghanies and the Atlantic.

The Mississippi is called "Missisipi, ou Rivière Colbert;" the Missouri, "Grande Rivière des Emissourittes, ou Missourits;" the Illinois, "Rivière des Ilinois, ou Macopins;" the Ohio, which La Salle had before called by its [Pg 484] present name, "Fleuve St. Louis, ou Chucagoa, ou Casquinampogamou;" one of its principal branches is "Ohio, ou Olighin" (Alleghany); the Arkansas, "Rivière des Acansea;" the Red River, "Rivière Seignelay," a name which had once been given to the Illinois. Many smaller streams are designated by names which have been entirely forgotten.

The nomenclature differs materially from that of Coronelli's map, published four years later. Here the whole of the French territory is laid down as "Canada, ou La Nouvelle France," of which "La Louisiane" forms an integral part. The map of Homannus, like that of Franquelin, makes two distinct provinces, of which one is styled "Canada" and the other "La Louisiane," the latter including Michigan and the greater part of New York. Franquelin gives the shape of Hudson's Bay, and of all the Great Lakes, with remarkable accuracy. He makes the Mississippi bend much too far to the West. The peculiar sinuosities of its course are indicated; and some of its bends—as, for example, that at New Orleans—are easily recognized. Its mouths are represented with great minuteness; and it may be inferred from the map that, since La Salle's time, they have advanced considerably into the sea.

Perhaps the most interesting feature in Franquelin's map is his sketch of La Salle's evanescent colony on the Illinois, engraved for this volume. He reproduced the map in 1688, for presentation to the King, with the title *Carte de l'Amérique Septentrionale, depuis le 25 jusq'au 65 degré de latitude et environ 140 et 235 degrés de longitude, etc.* In this map, Franquelin corrects various errors in that which preceded. One of these corrections consists in the removal of a branch of the river Illinois which he had marked on his first map,— as will be seen by referring to the portion of it in this book,—but which does not in fact exist. On this [Pg 485] second map, La Salle's colony appears in much diminished proportions, his Indian settlements having in good measure dispersed.

Two later maps of New France and Louisiana, both bearing Franquelin's name, are preserved in the Dépôt des Cartes de la Marine, as well as a number of smaller maps and sketches, also by him. They all have more or less of the features of the great map of 1684, which surpasses them all in interest and completeness.

The remarkable manuscript map of the Upper Mississippi by Le Sueur belongs to a period later than the close of this narrative.

These various maps, joined to contemporary documents, show that the Valley of the Mississippi received, at an early date, the several names of Manitoumie, Frontenacie, Colbertie, and La Louisiane. This last name, which it long retained, is due to La Salle. The first use of it which I have observed is in a conveyance of the Island of Belleisle made by him to his lieutenant, La Forest, in 1679.

II.

THE ELDORADO OF MATHIEU SÂGEAN.

FATHER HENNEPIN had among his contemporaries two rivals in the fabrication of new discoveries. The first was the noted La Hontan, whose book, like his own, had a wide circulation and proved a great success. La Hontan had seen much, and portions of his story have a substantial value; but his account of his pretended voyage up the "Long River" is a sheer fabrication. His "Long River" [Pg 486] corresponds in position with the St. Peter, but it corresponds in nothing else; and the populous nations whom he found on it—the Eokoros, the Esanapes, and the Gnacsitares, no less than their neighbors the Mozeemlek and the Tahuglauk—are as real as the nations visited by Captain Gulliver. But La Hontan did not, like Hennepin, add slander and plagiarism to mendacity, or seek to appropriate to himself the credit of genuine discoveries made by others.

Mathieu Sâgean is a personage less known than Hennepin or La Hontan; for though he surpassed them both in fertility of invention, he was illiterate, and never made a book. In 1701, being then a soldier in a company of marines at Brest, he revealed a secret which he declared that he had locked within his breast for twenty years, having been unwilling to impart it to the Dutch and English, in whose service he had been during the whole period. His story was written down from his dictation, and sent to the minister Ponchartrain. It is preserved in the Bibliothèque Nationale, and in 1863 it was printed by Mr. Shea.

He was born, he declares, at La Chine in Canada, and engaged in the service of La Salle about twenty years before the revelation of his secret; that is, in 1681. Hence, he would have been, at the utmost, only fourteen years old, as La Chine did not exist before 1667. He was with La Salle at the building of Fort St. Louis of the Illinois, and was left here as one of a hundred men under command of Tonty. Tonty, it is to be observed, had but a small fraction of this number; and Sâgean describes the fort in a manner which shows that he never saw it. Being desirous of making some new discovery, he obtained leave from Tonty, and set out with eleven other Frenchmen and two Mohegan Indians. They ascended the Mississippi a hundred and fifty leagues, carried their canoes by a cataract, went forty leagues farther, and stopped a month to hunt. [Pg 487] While thus employed, they found another river, fourteen leagues distant, flowing south-southwest. They carried their canoes thither, meeting on the way many lions, leopards, and tigers, which did them no harm; then they embarked, paddled a hundred and fifty leagues farther, and found themselves in the midst of the great nation of the Acanibas, dwelling in many fortified towns, and governed by King Hagaren, who claimed descent from Montezuma. The King, like his subjects, was clothed with the skins of men. Nevertheless, he and they were civilized and polished in their manners. They worshipped certain frightful idols of gold in the royal palace. One of them represented the ancestor of their monarch armed with lance, bow, and quiver, and in the act of mounting his horse; while in his mouth he held a jewel as large as a goose's egg, which shone like fire, and which, in the opinion of Sâgean, was a carbuncle. Another of these images was that of a woman mounted on a golden unicorn, with a horn more than a fathom long. After passing, pursues the story, between these idols, which stand on platforms of gold, each thirty feet square, one enters a magnificent vestibule, conducting to the apartment of the King. At the four corners of this vestibule are stationed bands of music, which, to the taste of Sâgean, was of very poor quality. The palace is of vast extent, and the private apartment of the King is twenty-eight or thirty feet square; the walls, to the height of eighteen feet, being of bricks of solid gold, and the pavement of the same. Here the King dwells alone, served only by his wives, of whom he takes a new one every day. The Frenchmen alone had the privilege of entering, and were graciously received.

These people carry on a great trade in gold with a nation, believed by Sâgean to be the Japanese, as the journey to them lasts six months. He saw the departure of one of the [Pg 488] caravans, which consisted of more than three thousand oxen, laden with gold, and an equal number of horsemen, armed with lances, bows, and daggers. They receive iron and steel in exchange for their gold. The King has an army of a hundred thousand men, of whom three fourths are cavalry. They have golden trumpets, with which they make very indifferent music; and also golden drums, which, as well as the drummer, are carried on the backs of oxen. The troops are practised once a week in shooting at a target with arrows; and the King rewards the victor with one of his wives, or with some honorable employment.

These people are of a dark complexion and hideous to look upon, because their faces are made long and narrow by pressing their heads between two boards in infancy. The women, however, are as fair as in Europe; though, in common with the men, their ears are enormously large. All persons of distinction among the Acanibas wear their fingernails very long. They are polygamists, and each man takes as many wives as he wants. They are of a joyous disposition, moderate drinkers, but great smokers. They entertained Sâgean and his followers during five months with the fat of the land; and any woman who refused a Frenchman was ordered to be killed. Six girls were put to death with daggers for this breach of hospitality. The King, being anxious to retain his visitors in his service, offered Sâgean one of his daughters, aged fourteen years, in marriage; and when he saw him resolved to depart, promised to keep her for him till he should return.

The climate is delightful, and summer reigns throughout the year. The plains are full of birds and animals of all kinds, among which are many parrots and monkeys, besides the wild cattle, with humps like camels, which these people use as beasts of burden.

King Hagaren would not let the Frenchmen go till they [Pg 489] had sworn by the sky, which is the customary oath of the Acanibas, that they would return in thirty-six moons, and bring him a supply of beads and other trinkets from Canada. As gold was to be had for the asking, each of the eleven Frenchmen took away with him sixty small bars, weighing about four pounds each. The King ordered two hundred horsemen to escort them, and carry the gold to their canoes; which they did, and then bade them farewell with terrific howlings, meant, doubtless, to do them honor.

After many adventures, wherein nearly all his companions came to a bloody end, Sâgean, and the few others who survived, had the ill luck to be captured by English pirates, at the mouth of the St. Lawrence. He spent many years among them in the East and West Indies, but would not reveal the secret of his Eldorado to these heretical foreigners.

Such was the story, which so far imposed on the credulity of the minister Ponchartrain as to persuade him that the matter was worth serious examination. Accordingly, Sâgean was sent to Louisiana, then in its earliest infancy as a French colony. Here he met various persons who had known him in Canada, who denied that he had ever been on the Mississippi, and contradicted his account of his parentage. Nevertheless, he held fast to his story, and declared that the gold mines of the Acanibas could be reached without difficulty by the river Missouri. But Sauvolle and Bienville, chiefs of the colony, were obstinate in their unbelief; and Sâgean and his King Hagaren lapsed alike into oblivion.

[Pg 493]

INDEX.

-A-

-C-

-E-

-G-

-I-

Iroquois,
Issanti,
Issanyati,
Issati,
Kahokias,
Kanzas,
Kappas,
Kaskaskias,
Kickapoos,
Kilatica,
Kious,
Kiskakon Ottawas,
Knisteneaux,
Koroas,
Malhoumines,
Malouminek,
Mandans,
Maroas,
Mascoutins,
Meddewakantonwan,
Menomonies,
Miamis,
Mitchigamias,
Mohawks,
Mohegans,
Moingona,
Monsonis,
Motantees,
Nadouessioux,
Natchez,
Nation des Folles-Avoines,
Nation of the Prairie,
Neutrals,
Nipissings,

Ojibwas,
Omahas,
Oneidas,
Onondagas,
Osages,
Osotouoy,
Ottawas,
Ouabona,
Ouiatenons,
Oumalouminek,
Oumas,
Outagamies,
Pah-Utahs,
Pawnees,
Peanqhichia,
Peorias,
Pepikokia,
Piankishaws,
Pottawattamies,
Quapaws,
Quinipissas,
Sacs,
Sauteurs,
Sauthouis,
Senecas,
Shawanoes,
Sioux,
Sokokis,
Taensas,
Tamaroas,
Tangibao,
Terliquiquimechi,
Tetons,
Texas,

-J-

-L-

-M-

-O-

-P-

-Q-

-R-

-S-

-Y-

-Z-

ZENOBE (Membré), Father, <u>181</u>.

FRANCIS PARKMAN'S WORKS.

NEW LIBRARY EDITION.

Printed from entirely new plates, in clear and beautiful type, upon a choice laid paper. Illustrated with twenty-six photogravure plates executed by Goupil from historical portraits, and from original drawings and paintings by Howard Pyle, De Cost Smith, Thule de Thulstrup, Frederic Remington, Orson Lowell, Adrien Moreau, and other artists.

Thirteen volumes, medium octavo, cloth, gilt top, price, $26.00; half calf, extra, gilt top, $58.50; half crushed Levant morocco, extra, gilt top, $78.00; half morocco, gilt top, $58.50. Any work separately in cloth, $2.00 per volume.

LIST OF VOLUMES.

PIONEERS OF FRANCE IN THE NEW WORLD	1 vol.
THE JESUITS IN NORTH AMERICA	1 vol.
LA SALLE AND THE DISCOVERY OF THE GREAT WEST	1 vol.
THE OLD RÉGIME IN CANADA	1 vol.
COUNT FRONTENAC AND NEW FRANCE UNDER LOUIS XIV.	1 vol.
A HALF CENTURY OF CONFLICT	2 vols.
MONTCALM AND WOLFE	2 vols.
THE CONSPIRACY OF PONTIAC AND THE INDIAN WAR AFTER THE CONQUEST OF CANADA	2 vols.
THE OREGON TRAIL	1 vol.
LIFE OF PARKMAN. By Charles Haight Farnham	1 vol.

ILLUSTRATIONS

1. PORTRAIT OF FRANCIS PARKMAN.

2. JACQUES CARTIER. From the painting at St. Malo.

3. MADAME DE LA PELTRIE. From the painting in the Convent des Ursulines.

4. FATHER JOGUES HARANGUING THE MOHAWKS. From the picture by Thule de Thulstrup.

5. FATHER HENNEPIN CELEBRATING MASS. From the picture by Howard Pyle.

6. LA SALLE PRESENTING A PETITION TO LOUIS XIV. From the painting by Adrien Moreau.

7. JEAN BAPTISTE COLBERT. From a painting by Claude Lefèvbre at Versailles.

8. JEAN GUYON BEFORE BOUILLÉ. From a picture by Orson Lowell.

9. MADAME DE FRONTENAC. From the painting at Versailles.

10. ENTRY OF SIR WILLIAM PHIPS INTO THE QUEBEC BASIN. From a picture by L. Rossi.

11. THE SACS AND FOXES. From the picture by Charles Bodmer.

12. THE RETURN FROM DEERFIELD. From the painting by Howard Pyle.

13. SIR WILLIAM PEPPERRELL. From the painting by Smibert.

14. MARQUIS DE BEAUHARNOIS, GOVERNOR OF CANADA. From the painting by Tonnières in the Musée de Grenoble.

15. MARQUIS DE MONTCALM. From the original painting in the possession of the present Marquis de Montcalm.

16. MARQUIS DE VAUDREUIL. From the painting in the possession of the Countess de Clermont Tonnerre.

It is hardly necessary to quote here from the innumerable tributes to so famous an American author as Francis Parkman. Among writers who have bestowed the highest praise upon his writings are such names as James Russell Lowell, Dr. John Fisk, President Charles W. Eliot of Harvard University, George William Curtis, Edward Eggleston, W. D. Howells, James Schouler, and Dr. Conan Doyle, as well as many prominent critics in the United States, in Canada, and in England.

In two respects Francis Parkman was exceptionally fortunate. He chose a theme of the closest interest to his countrymen,—the colonization of the American Continent and the wars for its possession,—and he lived through fifty years of toil to complete his great historical series.

The text of the New Library Edition is that of the latest issue of each work prepared for the press by the distinguished author. He carefully revised and added to several of his works, not through change of views, but in the light of new documentary evidence which his patient research and untiring zeal extracted from the hidden archives of the past. Thus he rewrote and enlarged "The Conspiracy of Pontiac"; the new edition of "La Salle and the Discovery of the Great West" (1878), and the 1885 edition of "Pioneers of France" included very important additions; and a short time before his death he added to "The Old Régime" fifty pages, under the title of "The Feudal Chiefs of Acadia." The New Library Edition therefore includes each work in its final state as perfected by the historian. The indexes have been entirely remade.

LITTLE, BROWN, & CO., Publishers,

254 Washington Street. Boston.

CPSIA information can be obtained
at www.ICGtesting.com
Printed in the USA
LVHW051222201218
601201LV00018B/1476/P